PHILIP W. LOWN INSTITUTE
OF ADVANCED JUDAIC STUDIES

BRANDEIS UNIVERSITY

Studies and Texts

EDITED BY
Alexander Altmann

PHILIP W. LOWN INSTITUTE
OF ADVANCED JUDAIC STUDIES
BRANDEIS UNIVERSITY

Studies and Texts: Volume III

BIBLICAL MOTIFS

Origins and Transformations

Edited by

ALEXANDER ALTMANN

HARVARD UNIVERSITY PRESS
Cambridge, Massachusetts
1966

Distributed in Great Britain
by Oxford University Press, London
Library of Congress Catalog Card Number 65–11587
Printed in the United States of America

Preface

The studies contained in the present volume represent, for the most part, the fruits of the Lown Institute research colloquia of the academic year 1962–63. The series of papers read at those sessions was first announced under the over-all title "Image and Symbol: Studies in the Transformations of Biblical Motifs." The reader will find that the emphasis on the symbolic character acquired by Biblical images or motifs is in evidence throughout the volume, although a new title has been given to the book so as to offer greater latitude and scope for the inclusion of further material.

The volume presented here is easily divided into two parts. In the first, a number of important Biblical motifs are treated within the terms of Biblical scholarship; in the second, certain significant post-Biblical developments are traced. A glance at the table of contents will show both the range and the homogeneity of the subjects covered. The editor expresses the hope that this volume will be considered a valuable contribution to the field of Biblical studies, to which, at least in part, an earlier volume (Volume I: *Biblical and Other Studies*) had been dedicated.

All transliterations of cuneiform words and texts are given according to Thureau-Dangin's system, which is generally accepted. Within quotations from ancient texts (both transliterations and translations), square brackets [ ] indicate obliterated passages, half-brackets ⌜ ⌝ indicate dubious readings, angle brackets ⟨ ⟩ indicate material supplied by the editor or translator to fill in omissions in the ancient texts, and parentheses ( ) indicate words added by the translator in order to make the context more intelligible.

The editor expresses sincere thanks to Harvard University Press for helpfulness in all matters concerning the production of this volume. His special thanks are due to Mrs. D. E. Humez for the meticulous care with which she saw it through the press.

Contents

BIBLICAL MOTIFS

Origins and Transformations

Leviathan: Symbol of Evil

By Cyrus H. Gordon

We live in a world where good is mingled with evil. Men have therefore often envisaged the struggle between good and evil as a cosmic battle. Zoroastrianism provides the clearest illustration, whereby Ahuramazda, the god of goodness and light, is pitted against Ahriman, the god of evil and darkness.

In Genesis 1, the Biblical author has sidestepped the embarrassing implication of monotheism, that God is the author of everything, which would make Him the creator of evil as well as good. Instead we read that darkness was in the world before God performed His first creative act: the evoking of light.[1] According to Genesis all of God's creative acts are good; evil is not attributed to Him.

An old myth concerning the triumph of good over evil is reflected in Isaiah, Psalms, and Job; in it evil is symbolized by the dragon, Leviathan. Psalm 74: 13–14 refers to God's victory over the many-headed monster:

אתה פוררת בעזך ים
שברת ראשי תנינים על־המים
אתה רצצת ראשי לויתן
תתננו מאכל לעם לציים

Thou hast broken the Sea with Thy might,
Even smashed the heads of Tannin[im] on the waters;
Thou hast crushed the heads of Leviathan,
Even given him as food for the people . . .[2]

This myth was taken over from ancient Canaan and transformed by the Hebrews, as we now know from Ugaritic literature. Text 67: I: 1–3,

1. The first three and a half verses of Genesis may be rendered: "When God began to order heaven and earth, the earth was chaotic with darkness on the face of the Deep and with the Spirit of God flying over the surface of the waters; and [then] God said: 'Let there be light!' and so there was light. And God saw that the light was good." Note that darkness is associated with תהום, "the Deep," with whom we are to compare the wicked goddess Ti'âmat of the Mesopotamian Creation Epic. The light that God brings into the world is, unlike the pre-existent darkness, "good."

2. This notion gave rise to the belief that Leviathan would be eaten by the righteous in the hereafter (*BT Baba Batra* 75b; cf. *Apocalypse of Baruch* 29:4; see also לויתן in M. Jastrow, *A Dictionary of the Targumim, the Talmud Babli and Yerushalmi* [New York–Berlin, 1926], II, 698).

27–30 [3] confronts us with the following words addressed to Baal, who represents the forces of good:

k tmḫṣ . ltn . bṯn . brḥ
tkly . bṯn . ʿqltn
šlyṭ . d . šbʿt . rašm . . .

When thou smitest Lotan [= Leviathan] the evil dragon,
Even destroyest the crooked dragon,
The mighty one of the seven heads . . .

This passage shows that the Hebrews ascribed to Yahweh the cosmic victory over the same symbol of evil that the Canaanites had ascribed to Baal. The details of the terminology in Isaiah 27: 1 leave no doubt:

ביום ההוא יפקד יהוה
בחרבו הקשה
והגדולה והחזקה
על לויתן נחש ברח
ועל לויתן נחש עקלתון
והרג את־התנין אשר בים

On that day God will visit,
With his sword [that is] mighty
And great and powerful,
Leviathan the evil serpent,
Even Leviathan the crooked serpent,
And slay the monster that is in the sea.

Ugaritic mythology also identified the monster Tannin with Leviathan for in Text ʿnt: III: 38–39 *tnn* is called

bṯn ʿqltn
šlyṭ . d . šbʿt . rašm

The crooked dragon,
The mighty one of the seven heads.

It is interesting to note that Isaiah 27: 1 depicts the victory over Leviathan as taking place eschatologically "on that day" when good will triumph over evil for all time and the world will enjoy eternal perfection. [4]

3. Ugaritic literature is cited here according to the edition of C. H. Gordon, *Ugaritic Textbook* (Rome: Pontifical Biblical Institute, 1965).

4. This is a familiar motif in mythology and religion. The cosmic act (such as the victory over Leviathan) took place when God (or the gods) established order in the world. However, since then things have gone wrong and require that the act be repeated but with enduring efficacy so as to establish the divine order firmly and forever. In other words, the first time God vanquished Leviathan He did not annihilate him; in the end of days He will not only conquer but destroy him so that evil will vanish from the universe.

The Book of Job twice refers to Leviathan. In Job 3:8 (note the context in verses 7–9)[5] Leviathan is associated with the evil that goes with darkness and is opposed to light. In Job 40:25 God taunts Job with the rhetorical question:

תמשך לויתן בחכה
ובחבל תשקיע לשנו

Canst thou pull Leviathan by a hook,
Or depress his tongue with a rope?

This implies that God had put a hook through Leviathan's nose or lip, and tied his tongue, rendering him harmless.

Psalm 104:26 introduces a strictly monotheistic note, in making God the creator of Leviathan; note verses 24–27:

מה־רבו מעשיך יהוה
כלם בחכמה עשית
מלאה הארץ קנינך
זה הים גדול ורחב ידים
שם רמש ואין מספר
חיות קטנות עם־גדלות
שם אניות יהלכון
לויתן זה־יצרת לשחק־בו
כלם אליך ישברון
לתת אכלם בעתו

How manifold are Thy works, Yahweh!
Thou hast made them all with wisdom,
The earth is full of Thy creation.
This is the sea, great and spacious;
Gliding creatures are there without number:
Living things, small and great.
Ships proceed there,
[And] Leviathan whom Thou didst fashion to sport with.
All of them look to Thee
For giving their food in its season.

Here Leviathan is part of nature: a sea monster with whom God plays. God looks after and feeds him along with every other living creature.

5. הנה הלילה ההוא יהי גלמוד
אל־תבא רננה בו
יקבהו ארריֿיום
העתידים ערר לויתן

The Leviathan theme reverberates in the New Testament (Revelation, chapters 12 and 13), although he is not named "Leviathan" there. Note the seven-headed monster (Revelation 12: 3)[6] coming out of the sea (Revelation 13:1)[7] and identified with Satan (Revelation 12: 9),[8] thus symbolizing the forces of evil to be crushed by the forces of good.

The distribution of the Leviathan type of myth is widespread. It is associated with the seven- (or nine-) headed Hydra, slain by Heracles, even as the seven-headed Leviathan is slain by Baal.[9]

The earliest known record of this theme is a Mesopotamian seal cylinder (see Plate I) from Tell Asmar, dating from the Akkad Dynasty (about the twenty-fourth century B.C.E.). It depicts goodly heroes destroying the seven-headed dragon, four of whose heads are already dead, while the other three are still alive and fighting. This seal shows that the myth was current in the Semitic world by the middle of the third millennium, when it was probably already quite old. This sheds light on the history of dualism among the Semites. Long before the rise of Zoroastrianism, dualism is attested to in the art of Mesopotamia and in the texts of Ugarit. Therefore we cannot attribute Jewish, Christian, and Muslim dualistic trends to Iranian influence. Dualism is imbedded in the Semitic world before there is any evidence of it in Iran. Moreover the Judeo-Christian-Muslim terminology (for example, "Satan" as the name of the force opposed to God) is anticipated in Hebrew Scripture (note השטן in Job 2: 1 ff.). The Hebrew terminology shows no trace of Iranism; "Satan" is not Persian, and, as we know from Ugaritic, "Leviathan" was part of the Canaanite heritage that ancient Israel incorporated from the start. However much Zoroastrianism may have favored dualism in the centuries following the establishment of the Achaemenian Empire, the basis for the dualism we find in Rabbinic literature, the Dead Sea Scrolls from Qumran, the New Testament, and the Qoran, is Semitic, as is attested to in the Old Testament and in Ugaritic mythology.

We have at our disposal a corpus of texts that should be better known not only for their bearing on Leviathan, but for many other reasons as well, some of which will appear below. We refer to the corpus of magic bowls

6. *Καὶ ἴδού, δϱάκων μέγας πυῤῥός, ἔχων κεφαλὰς ἑπτὰ καὶ κέϱατα δέκα...*

7. *Καὶ εἶδον ἐκ τῆς Θαλάσσης Θηϱίον ἀναβαῖνον ἔχον κεφαλὰς ἑπτὰ καὶ κέϱατα δέκα...*

8. *Καὶ ἐβλήθη ὁ δϱάκων ὁ μέγας, ὁ ὄφις ὁ ἀϱχαῖος ὁ καλούμενος διάβολος καὶ ὁ σατανᾶς...*

9. A useful compendium for pithy accounts of topics such as "Hydra," "Heracles," "Leviathan," or its Ugaritic form "Lotan" has been written by Joseph Kaster, *Mythological Dictionary* (New York: Putnam, 1963).

Plate I

The "Forces of Good" Slaying the Seven-headed Dragon of Evil
Hydra Seal

from Talmudic Babylonia.[10] Those texts are inscribed spirally in black ink[11] on the interior surface[12] of clay dishes approximating a porridge bowl in size and shape. The scribe sometimes adds a crude drawing (usually in the center), often depicting the demon(s) to be foiled by the incantation. A number of scripts appear on the bowls; Aramaic is used most frequently; next comes Mandaic; a few bowls are lettered in Syriac. Very few are in an unidentified script which some suppose to be Pehlevi.

The Aramaic incantation bowls of Babylonia are anticipated by two Minoan incantation bowls from Knossos. The latter are written in the Linear A script and language, so that they must precede the Mycenaean Age, which was ushered in at Knossos somewhere between 1450 and 1400 B.C.E.[13] This means that the Aramaic bowls which enjoyed their heyday around 500 C.E. follow a tradition recorded on Crete two thousand years earlier. And yet, as we shall see, there is no doubt about the connection between the Minoan and Aramaic bowls. One of the Knossos bowls (text II, 2) begins: *a-ga-nu do-ti . du la-le a-do*,[14] "this bowl is of[15] this demon":[16] that is, this magic bowl is designed to rid the client of nuisance from this particular demon who has been molesting him. The text is supplemented by a drawing of the demon.

The Minoan magic bowls are regularly found inverted;[17] this reversal

10. Data on the bowls found at Nippur have been published with a detailed analysis of the subject by J. A. Montgomery, *Aramaic Incantation Texts from Nippur* (Philadelphia: University Museum, 1913). For the grammar, a chrestomathy of thirty texts, and a glossary, see W. H. Rossell, *A Handbook of Aramaic Magical Texts* (Ringwood, New Jersey: Shelton College Press, 1953). For a general introduction, see C. H. Gordon, *Adventures in the Nearest East* (London: Phoenix House, 1957), chap. xii.

11. The ink has been said to be sepia ink, from cuttlefish. Laboratory tests should be made to determine whether this is so, and whether the ink used on the Minoan bowls from Knossos is the same. This might establish an additional link between the Minoan and Aramaic bowls.

12. Also, rarely, on the exterior.

13. They have been republished in facsimile by W. C. Brice, *Inscriptions in the Minoan Linear Script of Class A* (London: Society of Antiquaries, 1961), texts II, 1, and II, 2, on plates XXII and XXIIa. See p. 15 for the catalogue description, including their provenance in a Middle Minoan III context, which would date those two bowls around the seventeenth century, B.C.E. Cf. the chronological table on p. 17 of R. W. Hutchinson, *Prehistoric Crete* (Baltimore: Penguin, 1962). It is possible, however, that Minoan chronology will have to be reduced somewhat.

14. Both *do* signs are uncertain; they are perhaps to be read as *za* signs. In any case, the words they are in are taken to be cognate with זאת and אז (dialectal Phoenician for זה) respectively. The *d*'s, if correct, might be evidence of the use of Aramaic for inscribing incantations. The *d*'s are favored by *du*, "of."

15. I.e., designed for coping with.

16. The demon is sketched schematically by the scribe, as often on the Aramaic bowls. In the past, the drawing has been mistaken for writing.

17. Many uninscribed magic bowls have been found *in situ* upside-down at Knossos in a context of Late Minoan I (ca. 1550–1450). A large group was found by Hogarth back in 1900; more recently some have been unearthed by Sinclair Hood.

is the same position in which many of the Babylonian bowls have been found.[18] The praxis seems to be the same. There are several theories as to why the bowls were inverted. Spyridon Marinatos[19] believes that food was placed under the bowl to attract the demon, whereupon the inverted bowl was clapped down on him, trapping him under the bowl and placing him under the spell of the incantation. To be sure, the Babylonian bowls do mention the offering of food and drink to the demons,[20] but not for the purpose of trapping them; the texts rather show that the demons have been treated properly so that they may go away contented, and stay away from the client.[21]

Another explanation of the inversion of the bowls is suggested by the spells which frequently tell of overturning the demons, in the sense of turning them back to their original place.[22] There is also a formula calling for the overturning of the earth so as to bring on by sympathetic magic the overturning (that is, the foiling) of the evil forces. For example,

אפיכה אפיכה ארעה אפיכה ארעה רקִיָאוֹס (?) אפיכין כל נידרי[23] ולוטתא ואשלמתא
וחרשי ולוטתא וחרשי ושיקופתא בישתא דישרִין באנשי דנן

18. Not only the Nippur bowls, but also a collection of Mandaic bowls published by Pognon were found inverted (Montgomery, p. 41).

19. *Minos*, 1: 41 (1951). Marinatos not only recognized that the Knossos and Nippur bowls reflected the same schools of magic but ventured the prophetic suggestion that the Minoan incantations would turn out to be spells against evil spirits like those on the Aramaic bowls.

20. Montgomery, Text 36: 7, and Gordon, *Orientalia*, 10: 342–343 (1941).

21. Montgomery, pp. 41–42, makes a case for the bowls as traps for the demons, based on the opening words of his Text 4.

22. E.g., יתהפכון חרשי לעבדיהון "let the black arts be turned on those who have worked them" (Gordon, *Archiv Orientální*, 6: 326 [1934]); ויתהפכון לאחוריהון ויחדרון ויאזלון על עבדניהון ועל משדרניהון "and let them be turned backward so that they return and go to those who have worked them and sent them."

23. This formula is the key to understanding the כל-נדרי prayer recited on the eve of the Day of Atonement. The original function of the prayer was the annulment of curses or oaths (originally *not* in the sense of promises or contractual obligations) that touch off evil forces in the community. We will examine the כל-נידרי according to the Sephardic tradition, recorded in D. A. De Sola Pool and M. Gaster, *The Book of Prayer*, III (London: H. Frowde, 1904), 13: כל-נידרי ואסרי ושבועי וחרמי ונדויי וקונמי וקונחי וקונסי די נדרנא ודי אשתבענא ודי חרמנא ודי נדינא ודי אסרנא על נפשתנא מיום הכפרים שעבר עד יום הכפרים הזה שבא עלינו לשלום. נדרינא לא נדרי ושבועננא לא שבועי וחרמנא לא חרמי ואסרנא לא אסרי. כלהון יהון שביתין ושביקין לא שרירין ולא קימין ונסלח לכל־עדת בני ישראל ולגר הגר בתוכם כי לכל־העם בשגגה.

"As for all the vows and bonds and oaths and execrations . . . which we have sworn and vowed . . . and which we have bound upon ourselves from the last Day of Atonement to this Day of Atonement which has come upon us for peace — our vows are not vows, and our oaths are not oaths, and our execrations are not execrations, and our bonds are not bonds. Let all of them be null and void; not operative and not established, so that all the congregation of the Children of Israel including the proselytes who dwell in their midst will be forgiven; for the entire population has acted unwittingly." The terminology ties in with that of the magic bowls; see Rossell's glossary (*Handbook of*

"Upset, upset is the earth. Upset is the earth - - - . Upset are all the vows and curses and spells and magic and curses and magic and evil blows that may lodge in this man - - -" (C. H. Gordon, *Orientalia*, 10:117 [1941]).

This spell hinges on the concept of "overturning." Even though it ultimately invokes God, [24] He acts in this text through his angel הפכיאיל,[25] whose function is the overturning or foiling of evil. Accordingly the ritual act of inverting the bowl is in harmony with the simultaneous recitation of the spell. Thus the incantation explains the inverted position in which the bowls are so often found.

Though either of the above explanations seems plausible enough, still another must be taken into consideration. The earliest Aramaic spell from Babylonia happens to be on a unique clay tablet written in the cuneiform syllabary (albeit in the Aramaic language) at Uruk during the Seleucid period.[26] While the text is not written on a bowl, it refers to a bowl that is used in the praxis. Interestingly enough the word for "bowl" in the Uruk tablet is *ag-gan-nu* = אגן = *a-ga-nu* of the Knossos bowl. The Uruk passage reads: *ag-gan-nu ma-zi-ga-' mi-ir-ra-' it-ta-ši-da-at a-na-' za-ki-it u-ma-' a-na za-ka-a-a* (that is, אגן מזיגא מרא אתשדת אנה זכית ואנה זכי): "the bowl mixed with poison was spilled [so that] I have won and I am victorious." This would suggest that a fluid (presumably poisonous) was put into the bowl and upon the bowl's being overturned and the liquid spilled, the magician achieves victory, foiling the forces of evil.

The demons in the Aramaic bowls are frequently represented as masculine לילין (sg. לילי) and feminine ליליתא "night spirits," better known as "lilis" (masculine) and "liliths" (feminine). The masculine can be used to cover both genders: לילין דיכרי וניקבתא "lilis male and female" (C. H. Gordon, *Archiv Orientální* 6: 322 [1934]). The Minoan *la-le*, "Night," seems to be the prototype of the lilis but was pronounced simply *layl*

Aramaic Magical Texts, pp. 122–153) for the bowl parallels to נדרי (glossary nos. 469, 470), אסרי (nos. 72, 73), שבעי (nos. 741, 742), חרמי (nos. 301, 302), שביתין (no. 746), שביקין (no. 744), שרירין (no. 807) and קימין (no. 664). The core of כל-נדרי is old, rooted as it is in Talmudic Babylonia. Its purpose is to give the community a fresh start by annulling the evil forces set in motion by destructive (even if unpremeditated) words. Failure to recognize this has brought upon later generations of Jewish leaders endless embarrassment and the needless urge to engage in artificial reinterpretation.

24. The text ends with בשום קדוש קדוש קדוש יהוה צבאות מלא כול הארץ כבודו אמין אמין סלה הללויה לשמך אני עושה "... in the name of Holy, Holy, Holy, Yahweh of Hosts, the whole earth is full of His glory. Amen, amen, selah, halleluiah. For Thy name do I act."

25. בשום הפכיאיל מלאכוא דהפיך לוטתא ואשלמתא וחרשי בישי "... in the name of הפכיאיל, the angel who upsets curses and spells and wicked magic."

26. See Gordon, "The Aramaic Incantation in Cuneiform," *Archiv für Orientforschung*, 12: 105–117 (1938); "The Cuneiform Aramaic Incantation," *Orientalia*, 9: 29–38 (1941); and *The Living Past* (New York: John Day, 1941). (See the plates facing pp. 198–199 for the photograph of both sides of the tablet).

(= Hebrew לַיִל); compare *ya-ne* = *yayn* (that is, יַיִן), "wine."[27] The form *layl* is supported by the appearance of *ll*, "Night," in the Ugaritic ritual texts, for since the diphthong *ay* is regularly reduced to *ê* in Ugaritic, *layl* comes into Ugaritic as *lêl*, which in the consonantal orthography is written *ll*.[28]

The forces of evil appear in the form of Leviathan in two Aramaic bowls. The first is a Nippur incantation published by Montgomery as his Text 2. The part that concerns us is the magician's use of the Leviathan myth, invoked as the cosmic precedent, against the client's tormentors. The sorcerer states: **אזלית ופגעית בהון בסני בישי ובעילדבבי מרירי אמרת להון דאים מידעם חטיתון ביה באבונא בר גריבתא ובאיבא בר זויתאי אשיפנא לכון באישפא דימא ואישפא דלויתן תנינא... מחיתנא עליכון שמתא וגזירתא ואחרמתא דאיתנח על חירמון טורא ועל ליויתן תנינא ועל סדום ועל עמורא.**

I have gone and confronted the evil foes and mighty adversaries [and] said to them: "If ye have in any way sinned against Abuna son of Gribta and against Iba son of Zawitay, I am enchanting you with the spell of the Sea, and the spell of Leviathan the dragon . . . I am bringing down upon you the ban and decree and excommunication which were set upon Mount Hermon and upon Leviathan the dragon and upon Sodom and upon Gomorrah.

The other bowl (Gordon, *Orientalia*, 10: 273 [1941]) contains a variant of this formula: **אזלית פגעית בהון בסוטוני בישי ובעיְלְדבבי מרירי אמרנא להון ואי לכון אם מידעם תעבדון להון... אשפנא עליכון באשפא רבא דימא ובאשפא דליויתן תנינא תוב אם מידעם תאמרון להון... בי קשתא גיבנא לכון וביתירא פשיטנא לכון תוף אם מידעם תעבדון לה[ון...] ... מחיתנא עליכון גזירתא דישמיה ואחרומתא... לליויתן תנינא.**

I have gone [and] confronted the evil satans and mighty foes. I say to them: "Woe unto you if ye do anything to them . . . I am enchanting you with the great spell of the Sea and with the spell of Leviathan the dragon. Again, if ye say anything to them, I am drawing the bow against you and stretching the string against you. Again, if ye do anything to them . . . I am bringing down upon you the decree of the heavens and the excommunication . . . [imposed upon] Leviathan the dragon."

The incantation was probably accompanied by a ritual act such as drawing a bow against the forces of evil. The magical complex thus includes the myth for precedent, the recitation of the spell as written on the bowl, a ritual act, and the depositing of the bowl in the proper place and manner for assuring the client of permanent protection.

27. For *ya-ne* see p. 293 of Gordon, "Toward a Grammar of Minoan," *Orientalia*, 32: 292–297 (1963).

28. M. Astour was the first to recognize that *ll* in Ugaritic texts 22:9 and 23:7 means "Night"; see Gordon, *Ugaritic Textbook*, under **lyl* in the glossary.

We have come a long way. We have traced לילי(י) back to Minoan Crete and Leviathan back from Talmudic Babylonia through the Bible and Ugaritic mythology to Mesopotamia of the mid-third millennium. The לילין were felt to be the particular demons that often torment us mortals. Leviathan, on the other hand, is a monster who sums up cosmic evil and was vanquished by God of old and will be annihilated by God once and for all in the end of days at the inauguration of the Golden Age that will endure forever without evil.

From our modern viewpoint, Leviathan *symbolizes* evil. But did the ancient Semite regard Leviathan as a mere symbol rather than as the actual dragon who was once vanquished and will ultimately be destroyed by the forces of good? I suspect that to the people of Babylonia and Canaan, lilis were quite real and that the world would have been intolerable if they did not believe that God had actually placed Leviathan under an effective ban. Let us not forget that down to fairly modern times most of civilized Europe adhered to the demonic etiology of psychosis and disease. Indeed it still persists in many unsophisticated circles.

As long as men believed in demons, they could be cured of their neuroses by exorcism. The theory of demonic possession did not stigmatize the patient, for it was not his fault that a demon had attached itself to him. In the wake of the Renaissance, Europe began to enter its age of disbelief. Exorcisms are no longer effective because we do not believe in demons. New kinds of psychic therapy have come in. They usually take more time and cost more money. It is doubtful whether any modern school of psychotherapy will survive a tenth as long as the art of exorcism.

God's triumph over Leviathan helped to give men a sense of security for thousands of years. Now that Leviathan has become merely a symbol, we are not better off. It becomes more difficult to remove evil from our lives, once evil becomes, as it has become, a concept which can be symbolized, but not concretized and crushed.

The Divine Warrior in Israel's Early Cult

By Frank Moore Cross, Junior

I

Recent discussion of the history of the early Israelite cultus is voluminous and variegated, but can be schematized for our purposes as follows.

(1) The central or constitutive element in the early cult was the dramatic reenactment, by their recital and by ritual acts, of the events of the Exodus and Conquest. This reenactment of the *magnalia Dei* may be seen as the primary or initial movement in a covenant-renewal ceremony (at either the fall or spring New Year) in which the basis of the community's common life and institutions is restored or renewed.[1] Or it may be placed in the setting of a festival, perhaps Passover, which, it is claimed, is to be distinguished sharply from the festival of law and covenant held in the fall.[2]

(2) The central or constitutive movement in the early cultus was the celebration of the enthronement of Yahweh as king and creator of cosmos by virtue of his victory over his enemy or enemies in a cosmogonic struggle.[3]

1. This view has emerged in the wake of recent studies of ancient Near Eastern covenant forms and their utilization in old Israel. The pioneer work in relating this lore to the Old Testament was that of G. E. Mendenhall, *Law and Covenant in Israel and the Ancient Near East* (Pittsburgh, 1955). It has been followed by a number of important studies, including K. Baltzer, *Das Bundesformular* (Neukirchen, 1960), G. Ernest Wright, "The Lawsuit of God: A Form-critical Study of Deuteronomy 32," *Israel's Prophetic Heritage*, ed. B. W. Anderson and Walter Harrelson (New York, 1962); J. Harvey, "Le 'Rîb-Pattern' réquisitoire prophétique sur la rupture de l'alliance," *Biblica*, 43: 172–196 (1962). Cf. W. Beyerlin, *Herkunft und Geschichte der altesten Sinaitraditionen* (Tübingen, 1961). The writer also has a paper forthcoming on the cult of the league, dealing in particular with the history of the Passover, and some points presumed in this paper are documented in detail in it.

2. This view received classical statement in G. von Rad, *Das formgeschichtliche Problem des Hexateuch* (Stuttgart, 1938), now republished in his *Gesammelte Studien zum Alten Testament* (*Theologische Bücherei*, VIII Munich, 1958), pp. 9–86. It draws heavily on the work of A. Alt, *Die Ursprünge des israelitischen Rechts*, *Kleine Schriften zur Geschichte des Volkes Israel*, I (Munich, 1953), 278–332, and in turn has been extended by H. J. Kraus, *Gottesdienst in Israel*, 2nd ed. (Munich, 1962); cf. Kraus, "Gilgal. Ein Beitrag zur Kultusgeschichte Israels," *Vetus Testamentum*, 1 : 181–199 (1951).

3. This construction had its stimulus in two fundamental works: P. Voltz, *Das Neujahrsfest Jahwes* (Tübingen, 1912), and S. Mowinckel, *Psalmenstudien*, vol. II: *Das Thronbesteigungsfest Jahwäs und der Ursprung der Eschatologie* (1922; reprinted, Amsterdam, 1961); for selected bibliography of more recent works, see R. de Vaux, *Ancient Israel, Its Life and Institutions*, trans. John McHugh (London, 1961), pp. 551f.; and Kraus, *Gottesdienst*, p. 79, n. 92.

The first view has risen out of a preoccupation (on the part of such scholars as Alt, Mendenhall, Baltzer) with the form-critical analysis of early legal and covenantal formulae, and (by men such as Noth and von Rad) of early historical traditions, notably the Israelite epic sources.[4] These investigations led to the reconstruction of the cultic function of cycles of liturgical (apodeictic) law, and of the cultic function of the recitation of the *magnalia Dei*.

The second view stemmed largely from the analysis of the Psalms and the attempt to reconstruct the cultus underlying them. This research was carried out in the new light of lore from neighboring religions, at first (by Volz, Hooke, and especially Mowinckel) primarily from Babylon, and later (by Engnell) from Canaanite sources.[5]

These two "views" are what we may call ideal types, in Weberian language, and neither is found in pure form, perhaps, in current research. Since one deals primarily with the cultus of the league, the other with the ideology of the cult in the era of the kings, they need not be conceived as being in direct opposition to each other, and, in fact, various accommodations of one view to the other have been attempted.

Professor Engnell can argue, for example, that the motifs of Exodus and Conquest, and of covenant renewal of the cultic community, grow out of a progressive historicizing of mythological forms. He would insist, however, that the mythic patterns were typologically primary, since obviously they existed before the foundation of Israelite cultic institutions. This gives a strange picture of the historical development of the cultus: those constitutive "historical" elements discovered in the festival liturgies and hymns of the league are secondary to the cosmogonic and mythological elements derived from analysis of the liturgies and hymns of the monarchy.

Kraus, representing the Alt school, takes the reverse position. The old themes of Exodus and Conquest are in part suppressed in the age of the kings, owing to the inauguration of a royal *Zionfest*.[6] This festival celebrates primarily the election of the house of David and the choice of Zion as the site of Israel's new sanctuary. The rites included a procession of the Ark to Zion's shrine, reenacting the original choice of Zion. This new festival, while preserving some continuities with the traditions of the early sanctuaries

4. In addition to the literature cited in Note 1, see M. Noth, *Überlieferungsgeschichte des Pentateuch* (Stuttgart, 1948). See also Noth's critique of the myth-and-ritual school, "Gott, König, Volk im Alten Testament," *Gesammelte Studien zum Alten Testament* (*Theologische Bücherei*, vol. VI [Munich, 1960]).

5. See especially I. Engnell, *Studies in Divine Kingship in the Ancient Near East* (Uppsala, 1943). Cf. S. Mowinckel, *He That Cometh* , trans. G. W. Anderson (New York, n.d. [1954]), pp. 52–95; and the literature cited by de Vaux, *Ancient Israel*, pp. 526f.

6. H. J. Kraus, *Psalmen*, I (Biblischer Kommentar XV/1, Neukirchen, 1960), 197–206; *Gottesdienst*, pp. 215–220.

of the Ark, also drew deeply, we are told, upon the mythic sources of the old Jebusite cult of 'El 'Elyôn, above all in its incorporation of the motif of the "kingship of God." Kraus thus explains the mythological elements in the royal cultus as lately introduced into Israel with the rise of monarchic forms, and by this means he suggests a mode of dealing with the enthronement hymns. This solution to the problem of historical development is most awkward also: Israel, having had an essentially "historical" cultus in the early time (when Canaanite influence is most expected!), later retrogressed, so to speak, by accepting (in attenuated form, to be sure) mythological lore from the Canaanite cult of Jerusalem. The development thus moved from the era of the league, with its distinctive historical themes, into an era of kingship, when these themes were infused with Canaanite language and mythology—in a word, mythologized.

One can discern certain strengths and weaknesses in these alternative views, one of which we can label as belonging to the "myth and ritual" school, the other of the *Heilsgeschichte* school.

(1) In the position of the myth-and-ritual school there is the tacit assumption that the development of the cult must move from the "natural" to the "historical," a legacy of the tradition of Vatke and Wellhausen. Those of the school merely substitute for Wellhausen's essentially Hegelian concept of natural religion, Canaanite myth and ritual as discerned in current research. For the main part the approach of this school has been phenomenological rather than historical, so that it has not grappled with the problem of "earlier" historical elements, later mythological elements, in the cult. So by and large the school has been content with a simplistic interpretation in terms of a unilinear development: the historicizing of myth. We are never told what was the motive power disintegrating myth into history—in a Hegelian system the movement from the natural to the historical belongs to the very logic of historical process—but while idealistic premises are discarded by the myth-and-ritualists, extraordinarily enough, the framework of the evolution is kept. This posture requires, in our view, the suppression of much of the evidence drawn from the early prose and legal material. Or rather, we should say, this school subordinates early prose and early hymnic tradition to the body of hymns from the royal period. With this subordination come dangers. The royal hymns utilize, in their prosodic style and language, a classical style which had its origin in Bronze Age Canaan. Wholesale borrowings of mythological material were made under the tyranny of this Canaanite aesthetic tradition. In reconstructing the cult underlying the apparent cultic function or *Sitz im Leben* of such hymns, one is never sure whether one arrives at a description of Israel's royal cult or at a picture of an old Canaanite cultus from which the hymnic tradition

stems. Analysis of a borrowed psalm, or of a hymn or liturgy heavily dependent on Canaanite hymnody, is a dangerous and subtle, if not a subjective, process. One must detect not one but a series of *Sitze im Leben.* On the one hand it is obvious that in the reuse of such material, an altered context altered meaning. On the other hand, it is equally important to observe that the transformation of such material cannot have been absolute, that there must have been some continuity between the religious cultures so engaged. There must have been an *Anknüpfungspunkt*, a suitable matrix into which Canaanite lore could be grafted and in which it could remain alive.[7] Control here must come from the corpus of archaic poetry, law, and epic tradition.[8]

(2) The history-of-redemption school has pictured the development along at least two lines: a dominant line bearing the theme of the Exodus–Conquest (*Landnahme*)—that is, the history of redemption—and an alternate theme of revelation (of the Law) at Sinai, preserved in covenant-renewal ceremonies in the central sanctuary of the league at Sukkôt.[9] I think it is not unfair to say that in this analysis, the key to Israel's early cultic history is found in the form-critical distinction between *kērygma* and *didachē*, or rather in the traditional contrast between gospel and law. Such a duplexity in early Israel's cultic development must be repudiated in view of our fresh understanding of the forms of the covenant and covenant renewal.[10] It is now clear that the confession of the *magnalia Dei* or recitation of the epic theme (*das heilsgeschichtliche Credo*), belongs to the covenant formulary as its first element or prologue, to the covenant-renewal ritual as its first movement. The recitation of law and the renewal or actualization of the covenant comes as a consequent step in the ritual drama.[11] In the present shape of epic tradition, the ritual pattern of the covenant-renewal ceremony has been

7. That old Canaanite myth remained alive, however attenuated, in royal psalms or in Prophetic oracles is clear from early apocalyptic. Here myths stemming from old Hebrew sources, especially from hymns and liturgies of the royal cult, break out anew in transformed but vigorous modes of life. Fresh borrowings of myth in apocalyptic composition were exceedingly rare, as becomes clearer with each advance of our knowledge of apocalyptic origins.

8. By "epic" we mean the so-called JE sources and the common poetic tradition that lies behind them.

9. To the fall calendar, Kraus would add a "tent festival" underlying traditions of Sukkôt that preserve traditions of the desert history (*Gottesdienst*, pp. 152–159).

10. See above, Note 1.

11. The parade example of the covenant ritual is Joshua 24: 2–28, in which verses 2–13 recite the history of Yahweh's redemption, 14–28 the subsequent rite of covenant making or renewal. Actually, we must probably see in Deuteronomy disintegrated materials of the old fall festival of Shechem, as is argued by Alt, von Rad, and Baltzer; however, the "disintegrated" cultic materials lying behind the epic material in Exodus 1–24, 32–33, are to be attributed not to the fall festival at Shechem, but to the feast of the old spring New Year (Passover). Probably the celebration of covenant rites in the spring marked the cultus of Gilgal, and later of Shiloh (see below).

displaced. Not only have diverse traditions been introduced to expand the account of the events of the Exodus, the cultic form of traditions also has been dissolved in the interests of the historical or epic form into which our sources recast available tradition. The primary displacement is the intrusion of covenant rites into the middle of the *Heilsgeschichte*, rather than in their proper cultic position, following the historical recital of the call of the Fathers, the deliverance from Egypt, and the gift of the land in the Conquest. That is, the formation of the covenant is placed after the Exodus, before the Conquest, while in the ritual of covenant renewal, the covenant rites proper are placed in the context of the twelve-tribe league, celebrating the gift of the land. But this order of events is based on historical memory, not on the more directly cultic traditions, in which the recitation of the historical acts of God and the recitation of the stipulations of the covenant are two separate acts in a single cultic drama (*pace* von Rad).[12]

Taken in this revised form, the covenant-renewal festival becomes the cultic carrier of Israel's historical traditions, and the early cult can be understood to have a unity comparable to that posited by the myth-and-ritual school. In one, the history of the community's creation is rehearsed or reenacted to reconstitute its life and institutions, since the historical community is conceived as the community of salvation. In the other, the primordial events (the battle of creation, the theophany of Yahweh as king manifest) are recited or reenacted, in order to restore the orders of creation or, to say the same thing, to actualize the "eschatological" kingdom of God.

At least one major problem remains. The history-of-redemption school, while minimizing the impact of borrowings from Canaan, must admit to a considerable invasion of mythological lore in the time of the monarchy. In view of the recrudescence of extraordinarily vivacious motifs of Canaanite origin in Jewish apocalyptic, mediated by Israel's royal ideology, we cannot escape such a conclusion. This sequence in the development of the cult posits a cultus in the early period dominated by historical categories: celebration of the history of Israel's redemption in the Exodus and Conquest, reenactment of the ancient covenant rooted in these gracious acts of Yahweh. The question of how this historical cult rose, out of the mythopoeic religious culture which preceded it is left unanswered, as is the problem of the receptivity of Israel's religion and cult to the increment of mythological symbols and motives in the imperial and monarchic era.

12. This background explains the absence of the "revelation at Sinai" in such archaic materials as those found in Joshua 24, which reflects cultic traditions of the covenant festival at Shechem, and Exodus 15, which reflects traditions of the covenant renewal rites of Gilgal (see below). In this view it was the cultic use of the covenant formulary in the era of the league which displaced the Sinaitic traditions. There can be little doubt, however, that the Sinai traditions ultimately stem from pre-league cult, as well as historical memory, and are "correctly" located in epic tradition.

As a matter of fact, German students of the history of Israel's cultus, notably of the Alt school, appear to be incapable of dealing with the origins of a historical cultus or of tracing the lines of historical continuity between the myth and ritual patterns of pre-Mosaic Canaan and the earliest forms of Israelite religious and cultic practices.[13] The movement from dominantly mythical to dominantly historical patterns is not a natural or inevitable tendency, as is evidenced by the perennial resurgence of mythic forms and language in Biblical religion: in the royal theology, in apocalyptic, in Gnosticism, in Kabbalah. The reason for this failure or inability lies in the refusal of many form-critics or historians of tradition to raise the question of actual historical memory lying behind the cultic pattern: Exodus, Covenant at Sinai, Conquest. The thrust of historical events, recognized as crucial and ultimately meaningful, alone had the power to displace the mythic pattern. Even then we should expect the survival of some mythic forms and the secondary mythologizing of historical experiences to point to their cosmic or transcendent meaning. An obvious example is the description of the victory of Israel and her God over Egypt: the overthrow of the Egyptian in the sea is singled out to symbolize Israel's deliverance, Yahweh's victory. Later, an equation is fully drawn between the "drying up of the sea" and the Creator's defeat of Rahab or Yamm (Isaiah 51 : 9–11); the historical event is thereby given cosmic meaning. As a matter of fact, the earliest sources do not equate the crossing of the sea and the killing of the Dragon by the Divine Warrior,[14] but it is highly likely that the role of the sea in the Exodus story was singled out and stressed precisely because of the ubiquitous motif of the cosmogonic battle between the creator god and Sea in West Semitic mythology.

The tendency of form-critics is to break up patterns into units. This tendency is not inherent in the method, although the philosophical presuppositions which informed the methodology in its early development by Gunkel and Alt led to this tendency, and it persists as a defective inheritance in the modern use of form-critical techniques for historical analysis. Hence some members of the history-of-redemption school actually are driven to

13. Part of the difficulty rests in the persistence of the notion that Israel emerged from the wilderness as a cultural *tabula rasa*. Whether one is inclined to reconstruct the Conquest along lines laid down by G. Ernest Wright in his article, "The Literary and Historical Problem of Joshua 10 and Judges 1," *Journal of Near Eastern Studies*, 5 : 105–114 (1946), or by G. E. Mendenhall in his recent study, "The Hebrew Conquest of Palestine," *Biblical Archaeologist*, 25 : 66–87 (1962), or to take some mediate position, as the writer is inclined to do, it is clear that the elements which were to become Israel shared a sophisticated Canaanite and/or Amorite culture which extended from the northern limits of the Egyptian province of Canaan continuously into the southern reaches of the Wâdī Tumeilat in the Late Bronze Age. On the religion of the Patriarchal Age, see the writer's "Yahweh and the God of the Patriarchs," *Harvard Theological Review*, 55: 225–259 (1962).

14. See the discussion in F. M. Cross and D. N. Freedman, "The Song of Miriam," *Journal of Near Eastern Studies*, 14: 237–250 (1955).

find separate cults or festivals, or separate units of Israel contributing one by one the elements in the historical pattern of Israel's early cult and epic: Exodus traditions stemming from one place, those of the covenant making at Sinai from another, Conquest traditions from a third cult or shrine or tribe. While it is true, obviously, that all elements of later twelve-tribe Israel did not engage in these epic events, but came to share them as historical memories through the "actualizing" of them in the covenantal cultus, it also must be insisted that the pattern—Exodus from Egypt, Covenant at Sinai, Conquest of Canaan—is prior, cultically and historically, to the several elements in the pattern or Gestalt.

We may illustrate these remarks by reference to Gerhard von Rad's important monograph, *Der Heilige Krieg im alten Israel.*[15] Here von Rad describes Israel's sacral warfare as an institution of the era of the Judges, limited to the defensive wars of Israel. Von Rad takes this stand in conscious contradiction of the unanimous witness of Israelite tradition that the wars of Yahweh were par excellence the wars of the Conquest. His view rests on the dogma of the Alt school that only individual tribes entered the land, or infiltrated into it, and that the traditions of the Conquest are a secondary complex composed of unitary traditions of individual tribes. The Conquest so understood is not a historical event, (not even a reinterpreted, schematized set of incidents) nor a historical event covered over with accretions of legend and myth. It is a construct of the *Heilsgeschichte*, but not history. The upshot is that von Rad fails to deal with the crigins of holy war in Israel and in turn with the mythological elements in holy war as practiced by earliest Israel, and indeed as practiced by pre-Yahwistic or non-Israelite peoples.[16] He ignores also the earliest psalmody of Israel, where certain mythic features still cling, and fails to perceive, therefore, the reutilization of some of these mythological elements in the royal cult, in prophecy, and above all in the apocalyptic development of the concept of the Divine Warrior.

We should argue that the development of Israel's cultic themes and institutions was a more complex evolution than is envisaged by either of these schools. In the pre-Yahwistic phase of the religion of patriarchal folk, we can already discern both historical and mythic features. On the one hand, there was the cult of the Divine Kinsman, the tutelary deity who entered into an intimate relationship with a social group, established its justice, directed its battles, guided its destiny. This is Alt's divine type, the "god of

15. *Abhandlungen zur Theologie des Alten und Neuen Testaments*, vol. XX (Zürich, 1951).

16. For an extended treatment of the origins of holy war in Israel as well as for a detailed analysis of cosmic or mythological elements in sacral warfare, see the unpublished dissertation of my student, Patrick D. Miller, Jr. "Holy War and Cosmic War in Early Israel" (Harvard University, 1963).

the Father." On the other hand, there was the cult of Canaanite 'El, the Divine King, "creator of heaven and earth," leader of cosmic armies.[17] How early these types of deity could merge in the cult of one god, we do not know.[18] At all events, these two had coalesced in the figure of Yahweh in the earliest strata of Israelite tradition.

In the era of the league in Canaan the historical impulse become powerful in the Mosaic faith and in the covenant festivals of the central shrine. On the whole, the school of Alt has done great service here in analyzing old prose and legal traditions. Even in the cult of the league, however, themes of mythological origin can be detected, standing in tension with themes of historical memory or enhancing redemptive events by assimilating them to cosmic events. These mythic elements are to be found especially in archaic psalmody, which underwent in transmission less shaping than the prose. It is this subdued mythological element of the old time that breaks out afresh in the cultus and ideology of the monarchy. This movement is counterbalanced by the great prophets, who, while influenced by the royal cult and its liturgical style, recall the more austere themes of the covenant forms of the old time, its legal language, and its relatively minor use of mythological material. As late prophecy and remnants of the royal ideology flow together to create the apocalyptic movement, we may say that the old mythological themes rise to a new crescendo, though even in the apocalyptic the expression of Israel's faith is still firmly controlled by a historical framework. The primordial events of creation and the eschatological events of the new creation are typologically related, but are held apart by the events of human history so that unlike the movement of myth, the primordial event and the eschatological event never merge in a cultic "Now."

In short, Israel's early cultus does visibly emerge from a mythopoeic past; the emergent is new, but in Patriarchal religion there was a *praeparatio*,

17. The regal and military role of 'El is much attenuated in Ugaritic mythology, in which Ba'l chiefly plays the role of Divine Warrior and King. 'El is still vividly portrayed as Divine Warrior, *'ēl gibbôr*, in Philo Byblius, and there is evidence that in southern Canaan this aspect of 'El's mythology persisted into the first millennium. Cf. Eusebius, *Praeparatio evangelica*, I, 10, 17–29; Cross, "Yahweh and the God of the Patriarchs," pp. 253–259; and Miller, "Holy War and Cosmic War in Early Israel."

18. Canaanite 'El in his earliest myths appears best described as the Divine Patriarch: a tent dweller, head of the council of "the sons of 'El," father of the gods, the ancient and wise and compassionate. He rises to power by overthrowing and emasculating his predecessor. He withstands the threat of the young hero by killing him or by consenting to his exercise of authority. 'El is at once Bull, procreator of all, and the old man of waning powers who must be stimulated by magical means to beget children by his wives. The figure of patriarch is illustrated by each of these motifs. This leads one to ask if "the god of the Father," the tutelary deity of Amorite or patriarchal stock, was not easily assimilated to the figure of 'El, the Father. There is little evidence. Such a tendency would explain such appellations as *'ilabrat*, "'El/god of the folk," and perhaps, *'il 'abi* (*sic*), which stands first in the Ugaritic pantheon lists, including a syllabic list. Cf. Cross, "Yahweh and the God of the Patriarchs," pp. 228f., n. 9, and p. 234, n. 35.

and the lines of continuity may be discerned. To this degree we tend to side with the history-of-religion school. In the subsequent history of the cult, in the league, in the days of the kings and prophets, and in the time of the apocalyptic seers, both historical and mythologically derived elements were interwoven, or blended in the cult. But here we must also say that the *Heilsgeschichte* school is correct in emphasizing the transformation of mythic materials when introduced into an Israelite context. In Israel, myth and history always stood in a strong tension, myth serving primarily to give a cosmic dimension and transcendent meaning to the historical, rarely functioning to dissolve history. In this sense the members of the history-of-redemption school are surely right in arguing that the historical modes of religious expression and cultic celebration are the distinctive and the normative in Israel.

II

To illustrate the generalized comments above, I have chosen to discuss some of the transformations of the motif of the Divine Warrior, the Day of Yahweh, and related themes. We may begin with two quotations, each representing one of the schools described above, one from Gerhard von Rad, one from Sigmund Mowinckel. Von Rad writes:

> . . . the Day of Yahweh encompasses a pure event of war, the rise of Yahweh against his enemies, his battle and his victory . . .
>
> There is no support whatsoever in these texts for the supposition that the enthronement of Yahweh, too, belongs to the concept of the Day of Yahweh. . .the entire material for this imagery which surrounds the concept of the Day of Yahweh is of old-Israelite origin. It derives from the tradition of the holy wars of Yahweh, in which Yahweh appeared personally to annihilate his enemies.[19]

Mowinckel writes: . . ."[the] original meaning [of the Day of Yahweh] is really the day of His manifestation or epiphany, the day of His festival, and particularly that festal day which was also the day of His enthronement, his royal day, *the* festival of Yahweh, the day when as king He came and 'wrought salvation for his people.' "[20]

We may begin our comments with a brief exegesis of Psalm 24: 6–10, a tenth century B.C. liturgical piece, which can serve as a testing ground.

19. G. von Rad, "The Origin of the Concept of the Day of Yahweh," *Journal of Semitic Studies*, 4: 103f. (1959).

20. Mowinckel, *He That Cometh*, p. 145.

זה דר דרשי ⟨פניך[21] יהוה⟩[22]
מבקשי פני ⟨אביר⟩[23] יעקב

שאו שערים ראשיכם
⌜ו⌝[24] הנשאו פתחי עולם
ויבא מלך [25]הכבוד

מי זה מלך הכבוד
יהוה עזוז וגבור
יהוה גבור מלחמה

שאו שערים ראשיכם
⌜הנ⌝שאו פתחי עולם
יהוה מלך הכבוד

מי [. . .][26] זה מלך הכבוד
יהוה צבאות
הוא מלך הכבוד

This is the "circle"[27] which seeks thy presence,[28] Yahweh,
Which desires the presence of the Bull of Jacob:[29]

Lift up, O gates, your heads,
Lift yourselves up, ancient doors,
And the king of glory will enter.

Who is this king of glory?
Yahweh mighty and valiant,
Yahweh the warrior.

Lift up, O gates, your heads,
Lift yourselves up, ancient doors,
And the king of glory will enter.

Who is this king of glory?
Yahweh of [Heavenly] Armies,
He is the king of glory.

21. Verse six of the psalm is corrupt, perhaps hopelessly corrupt. However, in the orthography of the tenth century, the proposed reconstruction is possible; at all events, it yields the syllabic symmetry (10/10) expected in this period.

22. Presumably *pnyk yhwh* fell out in an ancient haplography. Some Greek texts read *τον κυριον*, which may be original or may be *ad sensum*.

23. The received reading is impossible. The Septuagint probably read *pnẙ 'bẙr ẙ'qb*, *προσωπον του θεου Ιακωβ*. Cf. Septuagint version of Psalm 132:2 (131:2), which reads *τω θεω Ιακωβ* for *'bẙr ẙ'qb*.

24. Omit the conjunction, for stylistic reasons. Cf. F. M. Cross and D. N. Freedman, "A Royal Song of Thanksgiving: II Samuel 22 = Psalm 18," *Journal of Biblical Literature*, 72 : 19f. (1953).

25. The article may be secondary. It was introduced into prose about the end of the Late Bronze Age and into poetry even later.

26. The *hw'* is a revision in terms of prose, anticipating the last colon.

27. Hebrew *dôr* can mean "circle," "council," or "assembly," as in Canaanite. See F. M. Cross, "The Council of Yahweh in Second Isaiah," *Journal of Near Eastern Studies*, 12: 274, n. 1 (1953), and references. "Generation" is surely unsuitable as the meaning of *dôr* here.

28. Or "epiphany."

29. This archaic title is found elsewhere in the Psalms only in another processional hymn of similar age: Psalm 132 : 2, 5; cf. Genesis 49 : 24.

The psalm is an antiphonal liturgy used in the autumn festival. The portion of the Psalm in verses 6(7)–10, at least, has its origins in the procession of the Ark to the sanctuary at its founding, celebrated annually in the cult of Solomon and perhaps even of David. On this there can be little disagreement. But how are we to understand its archaic phrases? The prosodic form is intriguing: after a verse introducing the strophe, we have a series of so-called tricola, four in number, with elaborate repetitive parallelism. This style is characteristic of the earliest stratum of ancient Yahwistic poetry and is familiar from Ugaritic poetry.[30]

We may see reflected in this liturgy the reenactment of the victory of Yahweh in the primordial battle and his enthronement in the divine council or, better, in his newly built (cosmic) temple.

Such an interpretation assumes a Canaanite myth and ritual pattern standing behind the Israelite rite reflected in the Psalm. This Canaanite "pattern" can be described tersely as follows: Yamm, deified Sea, claimed kingship among the gods. The council of the gods assembled, and, informed of Yamm's intentions to seize the kingship and take Ba'l captive, made no protest. They were cowed and despairing, sitting with heads bowed to their knees. Ba'l rises, rebukes the divine assembly, and goes forth to war. In the (cosmogonic) battle, he is victorious, and he returns to take up kingship.[31] Presumably he returned to the assembled gods and appeared in glory, and the divine council rejoiced. In a later text,[32] Ba'l's temple, symbolic of his new sovereignty,[33] is completed, and the gods sit at banquet celebrating. Ba'l is king. Similarly, in Tablet VI of the Babylonian Creation Epic, Marduk, after battling the primordial ocean, Tiāmat, and creating the universe, receives from the gods a newly constructed temple where the gods sit at banquet celebrating his kingship.[34]

Psalm 24: 6–10 can be fitted into this pattern, provided we assume that it was modified somewhat in the Israelite context. One may observe that the so-called torah liturgy of verses 1–5, the present introduction to the archaic liturgical fragment, begins:

30. Cf. W. F. Albright, "A Catalogue of Early Hebrew Lyric Poems (Psalm 68)," *The Hebrew Union College Annual*, 23: 5f. (1950); Cross and Freedman, "The Song of Miriam," pp. 237–250. *passim.*

31. Texts 137 (III AB B) and 68 (III AB A).

32. Text 51 (II AB). In column VII of this text, there is a repetition of the narrative of Ba'l's going on the warpath (7–14), a return to his temple, theophany (29–35), and proclamation of kingship.

33. See, most recently, A. S. Kapelrud, "Temple Building, a Task for Gods and Kings," *Orientalia*, 32 : 56-62 (1963); cf. Cross and Freedman, "The Song of Miriam," p. 240.

34. The Babylonian account of creation in *Enūma eliš* is not too remote a parallel since there is some evidence that the battle with the dragon Sea is West Semitic in origin. (The evidence is gathered in a paper to be published by my colleague, Thorkild Jacobsen.)

The earth belongs to Yahweh, and its fullness,
The world and those who inhabit it.

He has founded it on Seas,
And on Rivers he has created it.

Moreover, we can have no doubt as to the identity of him who comes. It is the Divine Warrior, "Yahweh mighty and valiant, Yahweh the Warrior, Yahweh Ṣᵉbā'ôt (Yahweh of the cosmic host[35])." The procession of the Ark marks the return of the Divine Warrior from battle:

קומה יהוה לנחתך[36]
אתה וארון עזך

Arise, Yahweh, take thy [royal] seat[37]
Thou and thy Ark of thy might.
(Psalm 132 : 8)

Moreover, the Divine Warrior is recognized as the "glorious king," and the procession of the Warrior-King into his temple may be said to reenact the founding of the Temple (at the fall New Year) and the choice of Zion as the shrine of the Ark.

One may compare the Song of Miriam in Exodus 15: 16–18, a very archaic composition as a whole, probably of the twelfth century.[38]

When thy people pass over, Yahweh,
When thy people pass over whom Thou hast created,
Thou wilt bring them, Thou wilt plant them,
In the mount of thy heritage,
The dais of thy throne,
Which Thou hast made, Yahweh,
Which thy hands established.

Yahweh will reign
Forever and ever.

The reference in verse 17 to Yahweh's building a sanctuary is reminiscent of the building of a new temple by Ba'l, and as Ba'l's temple was an ex-

35. On the epithet, see the writer's remarks and references in "Yahweh and the God of the Patriarchs," pp. 250–256 and n. 133, and W. F. Albright,, *Journal of Biblical Literature*, 67: 377–381 (1948), a review of B. N. Wambacq's study, *L'Epithète divine Jahvé Sᵉba'ôt*.

36. Psalm 132 : 8 reads *lmnwḥtk*, II Chronicles 6 : 41 *lnwḥk*. Read *lnwḥtk*; *mnwḥt* is read in the Psalm by anticipation (cf. v. 14); the shorter reading is better metrically. In Ugaritic, *nḫt* is used precisely of a royal throne:

yaṯibu la-kissi' mulki
la-nḫti la-kaḫṯi darkati

He sits on the throne of kingship,
on the seat, the chair of dominion.

The above is taken from Text 127: 23–24 (a KRT text); cf. 51, I, 34 and 123 : 18; and the Aḥiram Inscription, where *nḥt* is in parallelism with *ḥtr mšpṭh* and *ks' mlkh*.

37. Yahweh goes from his encampment, *miškĕnôt*, to Zion, his permanent "seat." Cf. Psalm 47: 6.

38. On the dating of the hymn, see Cross and Freedman, "The Song of Miriam," pp. 237–250, and below.

pression of his newly-won kingship, so in verse 18, following the description of the sanctuary, we hear the shout, "Yahweh will reign forever and ever." Moreover, the precise wording of the section, the "mount of heritage," "dais of thy throne," echo Canaanite clichés known from Ugarit, used of the cosmic abode of deity or its earthly counterpart.[39]

The strongest evidence for recognizing mythological elements in Psalm 24, to my knowledge, has gone unrecognized. Certain images in Psalm 24 are very strange. The circle of gate towers is commanded to "lift their heads," to receive the returning Warrior, the glorious King. The metaphor seems odd at first look, not to say bizarre. How does a tower lift its head? Where is its head that it may be lifted? I hasten to say that gate types in the ancient Orient did not include the portcullis which moves up and down, only gates which swing sideways on their pivots.

The figure is actually one of full personification of the circle of gate towers, which like a council of elders sat waiting for the return of the army and its Great Warrior gone to battle, and which sat bowed and anxious. Then comes the shout,

שאו שערים ראשיכם

Lift up, O Gates, your heads!

In Ugaritic Text 137: 19–37 [40] we find a picture of the council of the gods assembled in the mountain of 'El. On the approach of emissaries of Ba'l's archfoe, Prince Sea, the gods are cowed and fearful, "dropping their heads onto their knees, down on their princely thrones," sitting in despair. Ba'l, king of the gods, shouts:

š'u 'ilm r'štkm

Lift up, O Gods, your heads!

Ba'l can deal with his foe. The verse addressed to the divine council in this text[41] and the phrase in Psalm 24 are strikingly alike in wording[42] and

39. For references, see Cross and Freedman, "The Song of Miriam," p. 240 and p. 249, n. 59.

40. III AB B : 19–37.

41. In Ugaritic, the colon represents a classical *Gattung*: "the address to the divine assembly." The writer has discussed this literary type in another connection: "The Council of Yahweh in Second Isaiah," pp. 274–277. The address in plural imperatives, especially in repetitive form, is characteristic. This reinforces the conclusion that the Psalm passage is a transformation of the "address to the divine council."

42. The Akkadian idiom *ullū* with *rēšu* can mean "to finish a building or structure to its summit." However, this usage is unrelated to the Hebrew usage. Much closer is the sense "to be proud," or "to show independence." Cf. Judges 8 : 28; Zechariah 2 : 4; Job 10 : 15, and Text 126, III, 12. The latter text has been related to Psalm 24 by Mitchell Dahood, "Ugaritic Studies and the Bible," *Gregorianum*, 43 : 77f. (1962), who renders the idiom "rejoice." The passage is ambiguous: the plowmen may be "looking up" at the coming rain, or may be "taking courage" with the coming of rain, in which case the meaning is much the same as in Text 137.

prosodic form. While the Ugaritic verse is preserved only in a passage anticipating Ba'l's going to do battle with Yamm (Sea), we can claim confidently, in view of the repetitive style of the Ugaritic texts, that the shout was repeated, addressed to the council of gods, when Ba'l returned in victory to receive the kingship.

III

Having given the myth-and-ritual school its due, and more, we wish to approach Psalm 24 by a different path. Central to the early cultus of Israel was the reenactment of the Exodus-Conquest: what we may call the "ritual Conquest." While the motif "creation-kingship" is present in Psalm 24 and is especially popular during the monarchy and in apocalyptic, it was by no means central or formative.[43]

(1) The language of holy war and its symbolism may be said to be the clue to an adequate interpretation of Psalm 24 and its place in the cultic history of Israel. The "Glorious King" is called *gibbôr milḥamâ*, *yahwê ṣĕbā'ôt*. These epithets stem from the old ideology of holy war in the league, from the "Songs of the Wars of Yahweh."

Again, the procession of the Ark, with its immediate background in the Davidic and Solomonic processions to the Jerusalem sanctuary, had a long prehistory in the cult and ritual warfare of old Israel.

In Numbers 10: 35–36, we find the archaic formula:

קומה יהוה [ ] יפצו אויבך
[ ] ינסו משנאיך מפניך
שובה יהוה ⟨ב⟩רבות ⟨קדש⟩[44]
אלפי ישראל

43. Neither was it absent in early Israel. The kingship of the gods was a popular theme in Canaanite religion. The common scholarly position that the concept of Yahweh as reigning or as king is a relatively late development in Israelite thought seems untenable in the light of this, and is directly contradicted by the evidence of the earliest Israelite poems; cf. Numbers 23 : 21; Deuteronomy 33 : 5; Psalm 68 : 25; Exodus 15 : 18. One is astonished by perennial attempts to discover the source of kingship and creation motifs in the Jebusite cult of *'El 'Elyôn* (see, for example, Kraus, *Psalmen*, I, 193–206). In fact, the cult of King 'El (*'ilu milku*), the creator, was widespread in Canaan in the Late Bronze Age. (Cf. Cross, "Yahweh and the God of the Patriarchs," pp. 225-259, and Rémi Lack, "Les Origines de Elyon, le Très-Haut, dans la tradition cultuelle d'Israël," *Catholic Biblical Quarterly*, 24: 44–64 [1962].) Of the many shrines of 'El, Jerusalem was merely one. To be sure, the language of kingship was not used frequently in premonarchic Israel, and with the coming of monarchy and the Canaanite palace-temple, the language of kingship became popular. But this was the resurgence of an old language, not the introduction of a novel, pagan language. The elements making up Israel derived from Canaanite and Amorite stock, spoke a Canaanite dialect, preserved old North Mesopotamian traditions and Canaanite traditions of the second millennium B.C. They did not emerge from the desert as newcomers to culture, speaking a non-Canaanite dialect of the true desert folk.

44. The text is clearly corrupt, and any reconstruction must be speculative. Our reconstruction is patterned on Deuteronomy 33:2–3 and Psalm 68 : 18 (cf. W F. Albright, "A Catalogue of Early Hebrew Lyric Poems," pp. 14, 24f.).

Arise, Yahweh, let thy enemies be scattered,
Let thy adversaries flee before thee.[45]

Return, Yahweh ⟨with⟩ the myriads of ⟨holy ones⟩,
With the thousands of Israel.

Evidently these are liturgical fragments rooting in holy war ideology, used also in the reenactment of the wars of Yahweh.

(2) The "ritual conquest" appears as a basic ingredient of certain cultic traditions in old Israel. And as we examine these traditions, it becomes apparent that the normal locus of holy warfare is discovered in the Exodus-Conquest, not in the primordial battle of creation.

The oldest poetry of Israel, our earliest Biblical sources which survive in unrevised form, is marked by a ubiquitous motif: the march of Yahweh from the southern mountains (or from Egypt) with his heavenly armies. We may mention first Judges 5: 4–5 (compare Psalm 68: 8–9):

יהוה בצאתך משעיר   בצעדך משדה אדם
ארץ רעשה   הרים נזלו
מפני יהוה   זו סיני
מפני יהוה   אלהי ישראל

When Yahweh went forth from Seir
In his stridings from the steppes of Edom,
Earth shook, mountains shuddered:
Before Yahweh, the One of Sinai,
Before Yahweh, God of Israel.[46]

In Deuteronomy 33: 2–3, we read:[47]

Yahweh from Sinai[48] came,
He beamed forth from Seir to us,
He shone from Mount Paran.

45. The couplet appears also, in slightly variant form, in Psalm 68 : 2. Apparently each couplet is the *incipit* of a longer liturgical piece.

46. The reading is based on a reconstruction of the original text lying behind Judges 5: 4–5 and Psalm 68: 8–9. [*'p*] *šmym nṭpw*, "yea, the heavens shake," and *hrym nzlw*, "the mountains shudder," are ancient oral variants. The verbs are to be derived from *ṭpp* and *zll* respectively. Cf. W. F. Albright, "A Catalogue of Early Hebrew Lyric Poems," p. 20; and Isaiah 63 : 19. The colon *gm ᶜbym nṭpw mym*, missing in Psalm 68, is secondary, attracted to *šmym nṭpw*. It is parallel only after reinterpretation of *nṭpw* as "drip," and metrically is impossible.

47. In general the analysis of the text follows the treatment in F. M. Cross and D. N. Freedman, "The Blessing of Moses," *Journal of Biblical Literature*, 67: 191–210 (1948). Changes in readings from that study are noted below. For a new treatment, reviewing recent articles on Deuteronomy 33, see Miller, "Holy War and Cosmic War in Israel," pp. 210–220.

48. Note that here in Judges 5 : 4–5 (*ẓū Sinai*) and in Psalm 68 : 18, Sinai plays a role in the march of Conquest. It is integral to Israel's earliest traditions of Exodus–Conquest.

With him were myriads of holy ones,[49]
At his right had proceeded the divine ones,
Yea, the purified[50] of the peoples.

Psalm 68: 18 reads:

The chariots of Yahweh are two myriads,
Two thousand the bowmen[51] of my Lord,
When he came[52] from Sinai with the Holy ones.

To these may be added the old fragment in the Song of Habakkuk 3: 3–15; Numbers 23: 22–24; 24: 8–9,[53] and, of course, Exodus 15:13:

Thou didst faithfully lead
The people whom thou didst deliver.
Thou didst guide in thy might
To thy holy encampment.[54]

The relation of this motif, the march of Conquest, to the early Israelite cultus has been insufficiently studied. The last-mentioned hymn, Exodus 15, is rooted in the liturgy of the spring festival ("Passover" or Maṣṣôt), and it may be argued that it stems originally from the Gilgal cultus as early as the twelfth century B.C. It rehearses the story of the Exodus in a primitive form,[55] the march of Conquest (13–18), and after the "crossing over,"[56] the arrival at the sanctuary (verses 13, 17).

It will be useful to take the Gilgal cultus, so far as we can reconstruct it, as exemplifying the use of the "ritual Conquest" as a movement in the cultus. It has been recognized that the verses Joshua 3–5 preserve traditions derived from the Gilgal sanctuary and, especially, traditions of its spring ritual, utilized by the Deuteronomic history and probably by an earlier traditionist

49. Reading *qdš* with Milik, Miller, and others instead of *qdš⟨m⟩*. There is now good evidence that here, in Exodus 15 : 11, in Psalm 68 : 18, and elsewhere, *qdš* is to be taken as a collective.

50. *ḥbb*, "to be pure," Akkadian *ebēbu*, was first suggested to me by George Mendenhall, who compared the use of *tēbibtu* at Mari. However, the meaning "military census" is by no means undisputed. See I. J. Gelb et. al., *Assyrian Dictionary* (Chicago, 1956–) IV, 6f., s.v. "*ebēbu*"; G. E. Mendenhall, "The Census Lists of Numbers 1 and 26," *Journal of Biblical Literature*, 77 : 52–66, esp. 56 (1958). Still, the meaning "to be pure," often in a ritual sense, adheres to the root, and may carry such meaning here, whatever the special derived sense of *tēbibtu* at Mari.

51. On the reading, see W. F. Albright, "A Catalogue of Early Hebrew Lyric Poems," pp. 24f. On *ṯann*, "composite bow," see Albright *apud* Cross, *Bulletin of the American Schools of Oriental Research*, 134 : 19, 24, n. 32 (1954).

52. We read בבאו מסיני בקדש, in tenth-century orthography בבא מסיני בקדש.

53. Cf. W. F. Albright, "The Oracles of Balaam," *Journal of Biblical Literature*, 63: 207–233 (1944), for a discussion of the date and interpretation of these texts.

54. The term is *nawê*, which in the early period is used of the tent shrine.

55. On this point, see Cross and Freedman, "The Song of Miriam," pp. 233–240, and notes to the text.

56. The reference must be to the crossing of Jordan, but as in the Gilgal cult, this crossing symbolized the escape at the Red Sea.

to reconstruct the history of Israel's entry into the Promised Land.[57] The festival may be reconstituted from the Joshua materials as follows. (1) The people are required to sanctify themselves, as for holy war, or as in the approach to a sanctuary (Joshua 3: 5). (2) The Ark of the Covenant, palladium of battle, is borne in solemn procession, which at the same time is battle array, to the sanctuary of Gilgal. (3) The Jordan, playing the role of the Red Sea, parts for the passage of the Ark and the people of Israel. The repetition of the Exodus is the transparent symbolism in the processional (Joshua 4: 21–24). At the same time, "from Shittim to Gilgal" (Micah 6: 5) represents the decisive movement of the Conquest, and Gilgal was the battle camp of the Conquest "when they passed over."[58] (4) At the desert sanctuary of Gilgal, twelve stones were set up, memorial to the twelve tribes united in the covenant festival celebrated there; we must understand this festival to be Passover-Maṣṣôt: that is, the festival of the old spring New Year. It is explicitly named Passover, and the tradition of eating parched grain and unleavened bread, as well as the etiological notice of the suspension of manna, lends confirmation (Joshua 5: 10–12). (5) We must note also the circumcision etiology (Joshua 5: 2–8), and finally (6) the appearance of the (angelic) general of the host of Yahweh (Joshua 5: 13–15).

In these fragments of cultic tradition we recognize the use of the ritual procession of the Ark as a means of reenactment of the "history of redemption," of the Exodus–Conquest theme, preparatory to the covenant festival of the spring New Year.[59]

IV

As has become apparent, our thesis is that the two apparently opposed views of the history of Israel's cultus prove to be complementary. The joining of the motif of Conquest and kingship in the royal cult is readily to be explained. The ideology of holy war makes possible the transition from the cultus of the league to the cultus of the kingdom, and ultimately to the ideology of apocalyptic.

57. See H. J. Kraus, "Gilgal. Ein Beitrag zur Kultusgeschichte Israels," *Vetus Testamentum*, 1: 181–199 (1951); cf. Kraus, *Gottesdienst in Israel*, 2nd ed., pp. 179–189 (literature cited on p. 180, n. 87); M. Noth, *Das Buch Josua*, 2nd ed. (Tübingen, 1953), pp. 32–35; Jan Dus, "Die Analyse zweier Ladeerzählungen des Josuabuches (Jos. 3–4 und 6)," *Zeitschrift für die Alttestamentliche Wissenschaft*, 72 : 107–134 (1960).

58. One suspects that Joshua 5 : 1 contains reminiscences of Exodus 15: 13–17. When they crossed over (*'d 'br⌜m⌝*; cf. עד יעבר), the rulers of Transjordan and Canaan (cf. Exodus 15 : 15) heard (cf. Exodus 15:14) and melted with fear (cf. Exodus 15 : 15). Incidentally, there is no hint of the sea drying up, or of a path through the sea, in Exodus 15. These are later accretions, probably arising precisely from the ritual crossing of Jordan.

59. The major spring festival of Gilgal, later at Shiloh, and the major fall festival of Shechem, later Bethel, are thus variant covenant festivals of old sanctuaries which at different times played a role as central sanctuary of the league.

(1) The ideology of holy war in early Israel and in pre-Israelite times was characterized by a number of cosmic elements. This may be seen in the imagery of the heavenly council of Yahweh, which may take on the characteristics of a judicial court or assembly, a royal court, or of a Divine Warrior leading heavenly armies. The "heavenly host" fights in the wars of Yahweh (Judges 5: 20, 23; Joshua 10: 12–13, and so on); these are the wars of *Yahweh Ṣĕbā'ôt*, "Creator of the heavenly armies." The cosmic elements gave mythic depth to the historical events of the Exodus and Conquest. Moreover, we may be sure that the institution of holy war existed in several pre-Yahwistic or non-Yahwistic leagues in southern Palestine: Moab, Edom, Midian.[60] In Numbers 21: 27–30, we actually have a fragment of an old song reflecting holy-war ideology in non-Yahwistic circles. The Mari documents already prefigure certain elements in the holy-war ideology.[61] In these non-Israelite contexts, the mythopoeic motifs of the creator-king and cosmic warrior no doubt were present. At all events the cosmic elements and survivals of myth provided a matrix for the reintroduction of the kingship theme and also especially, of creation motifs of Canaanite or West Semitic lore.

(2) The institution of kingship, and the inauguration of a temple in the Canaanite style in Israel, obviously gave an occasion for the radical mythologizing of the "historical" festivals, especially the "ritual conquest," and the procession of the "Ark of *yahweh ṣĕbā'ôt yôšēb kĕrūbîm*" ("who is enthroned on the cherubim"). In turn the cultic institutions of the league tended to decay; covenant forms and festivals languished or were suppressed in the interests of the royal festivals, in which the eternal decrees of God, the choosing of the house of David and Zion, were celebrated. Nevertheless, the "ritual conquest" persisted, transformed, in the royal cultus.

(3) It is only by such a historical analysis of the cultus that we can understand the "processional way" in Second Isaiah, combining notions of cosmic warfare with the theme of the Second Conquest or Exodus, and with the motif of the processional to Zion.

In Isaiah 40: 3–6, we read:

> A voice [of a herald] cries:
> "Prepare in the desert the way of Yahweh,
> Make straight in the wilderness a highway for our God.
> Every valley shall be exalted, every hill low . . .
> And the glory of Yahweh shall be revealed,
> And all flesh see it together."

In Isaiah 51: 9–11, we read:

> Awake, awake, dress in power, Arm of Yahweh . . .

60. P. W. Miller, Jr., has collected this evidence in his "Holy War and Cosmic War in Early Israel."

61. *Ibid.*

The repetitive imperative, reminiscent of Canaanite style, begins an apostrophe to the arm of the Divine Warrior.

Awake as in ancient times, primeval generations.
Was it not Thou who smote through Rahab,
Who pierced *Tannin* [the dragon]?

The allusion is to the cosmogonic myth, the battle of creation, in which the monster of chaos is slain by the God who thereby establishes kingship.

Was it not Thou who dried up Sea,
The waters of the abysmal Deep?

Suddenly the myth is penetrated by historical memory; the battle with the dragon Sea becomes the redemption from Egypt. Creation and redemption are fused in a poetic identification. Historical and cosmic redemption are one.

Who makes the deep places of the sea a road
For the redeemed to pass over.
The redeemed of Yahweh shall return
And come with shouts of joy to Zion.

Once again time turns fluid, and the Second Conquest, the new redemption, is described in terms of the old. And yet not precisely. As in Isaiah 35: 8–10; 40: 3–5; and so on[62] the old Exodus–Conquest route, the way through the wilderness, becomes at the same time the pilgrimage way to Zion. The march of the Conquest abruptly shifts into the festal, ritual procession to Zion. The procession to Zion and the feast on the holy mountain (compare Isaiah 25: 6–8; 55: 1–5) have recast, so to speak, or redirected the route of the Exodus and Conquest to lead to Zion.

Isaiah 52: 7–12 is another extremely instructive passage. It begins with a picture of the herald of victory and looks forward to the proclamation of God's kingship, and to the return of Yahweh to Zion:

How beautiful on the mountains,
Are the feet of the herald of good tidings,
He who proclaims peace, who brings tidings of good,
Who proclaims victory,
Who says to Zion: "Thy king reigneth."

Thy watchmen lift up [their] voice,
Together they shout with joy;
For they see, eye to eye,
When Yahweh returns to Zion.

It continues (verses 10–12) with a description of the theophany of the Divine Warrior, the proclamation of release to captives, who are to purify themselves to join the procession which bears the holy vessels to Zion. Yahweh marches with Israel.

62. See Bernhard W. Anderson, "Exodus Typology in Second Isaiah," *Israel's Prophetic Heritage*: *Essays in Honor of James Muilenburg*, ed. B. W. Anderson and W. Harrelson (New York, 1962), pp. 177–195.

Yahweh has bared His holy arm
In the eyes of all the nations.
All the ends of the earth see
The victory of our god.

Depart, depart, go out thence,
Touch no unclean thing.
Go out from her midst, cleanse yourselves!
Ye who bear the vessels of Yahweh;
For you go out not in haste,
Nor go in flight:
For Yahweh goes before you,
The God of Israel your rear guard.

In these and other passages,[63] it is necessary to recognize the wedding of two themes: one derived from the ritual Conquest, one from the procession of the Ark to Zion and the manifestation of Yahweh's kingship.

(4) Late Prophetic eschatology was born of this wedding of the kingship and Conquest themes in the cultus. The Day of Yahweh is the day of victory in holy warfare; it is also the Day of Yahweh's festival, when the ritual Conquest was enacted in the procession of the Ark, the procession of the King of Glory to the Temple, when "God went up with the festal blast, Yahweh with the sound of the horn. . . for Yahweh is king of the whole earth."[64]

In apocalyptic, the battle of the sons of light and darkness—the Second Conquest—becomes a central feature of the last days. At the same time it is the time of the manifestation of the kingdom of God, when the dark powers of chaos and evil are subdued, and the new heavens and earth created. Here mythic and historical themes are recombined in a radical tension.

Arise, O Warrior,
Take thy captives, O Glorious One,
And gather thy spoil, Doer of Valor.
Put forth thy hand on the neck of thy enemies,
And thy foot on the heaps of the slain
. . .
O Zion, rejoice exceedingly.
Break forth with joyful song, O Jerusalem,
And exult, all ye cities of Judah.
Open thy gates forever,
That [men] may bring to thee the wealth of nations,
And their kings serve thee.[65]

63. As early as Hosea (2: 16–17), the motif of a second Exodus and Conquest may be detected. In Isaiah 42: 10–16 there is a "new song" of the march of Yahweh: "Yahweh goes forth as a warrior, as a man of war he stirs his wrath. . . ," and in Ezekiel 20: 33–42, there appears the motif of a second Exodus, a covenant in the wilderness, and a return to the land.

64. Psalm 47: 6, 8.

65. *Sérek Milḥāmâ* XII, 9–10, 12–13.

The "Desert Motif" in the Bible and in Qumran Literature

By Shemaryahu Talmon

I

The study of the "desert motif" in the Bible has played an important role in Biblical research since K. Budde introduced it into the discussion. Budde's rather cautious, and fairly balanced, presentation of the "desert" as a formative factor in what he termed "The Nomadic Ideal in the Old Testament,"[1] unloosed a veritable spate of publications which further developed the ideas he had proposed. Budde had taken as his point of departure a presentation of the Rechabites as the proponents of a religious belief which conceived of the God of Israel as a typical god of the desert. Presumably in order to recreate the original experience of this deity, the Rechabites adhered to a mode of life which retained the principles of a desert society,[2] hoping thus to avoid contaminating the pure Yahwistic religion which in Israel had set in with the Conquest of Canaan. Drawing into the discussion the genealogical note in I Chronicles 2:55 which connects the Rechabites with the Kenites,[3] and also the theory that the Israelite religion emanated from a Kenite Yahwism, Budde concluded that the Rechabites not only faithfully adhered to the ancient desert religion, but that they endeavored to serve as its missionaries.[4] According to Budde, the prophets, and especially Hosea, reject this oversimplified concept of Yahweh as a desert god. But Budde nevertheless agrees that the desert plays a decisive role in Hosea's idea of Israel's future purification, and that indirectly the primitive desert ideal made its impression on the prophet's message.

This opening, the hint at an idealization of the desert in Hosea's preaching,

1. K. Budde, *New World*, 4: 726–745 (1895). Republished in German as "Das nomadische Ideal im Alten Testament," *Preussische Jahrbücher* (1896).

2. Jeremiah 35:6–10; II Kings 10:15–16.

3. See the present author's remarks on this passage in *Israel Exploration Journal*, 10:174–180 (1960).

4. Compare also R. deVaux, *Ancient Israel—Its Life and Institutions* (New York, 1961), pp. 14–15. In this work an up-to-date bibliography on the issue under review can be found (pp. 519–520).

was fully exploited by P. Humbert.[5] In Humbert's analysis, the "desert" is for Hosea the ideal period in Israel's history.[6] In the prophet's teaching it also crystallizes into the goal toward which he strives to guide the nation: "Retour aux conditions de la vie de l'époque mosaïque, tel est... le programme d'avenir d'Osée."[7] In Humbert's interpretation this will be a return to the classical setting of Yahwism:[8] "La désert est la patrique classique du yahvisme." Thus the desert was introduced into the basic concepts of Yahwistic religion as a factor of major importance. Now the desert ideal achieved the proportions of a veritable avalanche. It dominated discussions of the history of Israel and of the history of its religion. Under its impact was created the image of Yahweh as a slightly demonic desert deity, an image which originated in the primitivity of pre-Israelite nomads but allegedly was perpetuated as an idea, and as an ideal into the period of the settlement and into prophetic teaching.

Eduard Meyer, the sober historian, advocated an even wider application of the desert concept in the analysis of Hebrew religion and history than K. Budde and P. Humbert had proposed.[9] But the peak of the trend toward the desert ideal was reached with the publication of W. F. Flight's paper, "The Nomadic Idea and Ideal."[10] Not only does Flight subscribe wholeheartedly to the theory that the prophets elevated the "nomadic idea" to a "nomadic ideal," but he further votes for the adoption of this ideal as a beacon for religious orientation in our own times: "The note which needs to be struck in Christianity today is one which corresponds fundamentally to that which the prophets sounded in their day when they advocated a return to the nomadic ideal in the broadest sense. [Mark the definition: "broadest sense." *S. T.*] It is a call back to the essential spiritual simplicity

5. P. Humbert, "Osée, le prophète bedouin," *Revue de l'Histoire et Philosophie de la Religion*, 1:97–118 (1921), and "La logique de la perspective nomade chez Osée et l'unité d'Osée 2, 4–22," *Festschrift für Karl Marti*, ed. K. Budde (Beihefte zur *Zeitschrift für die alttestmentaliche Wissenschaft*, 41:158–166 [Giessen, 1925]).

6. E. Sellin (*Das Zwölfprophetenbuch*, 2nd, 3rd eds. [Leipzig, 1920], I, 236) puts it thus: "Für die vorexilischen Propheten ist die Wüstenzeit die Idealzeit, die 'Normalzeit.' "

7. "La logique de la perspective nomade...," p. 162.

8. *Revue de l'Histoire et Philosophie de la Religion*, 1:106 (1921).

9. E. Meyer, *Die Israeliten und ihre Nachbarstämme*, with supplements by Bernhard Luther (Halle, 1906), pp. 129–141.

10. J. W. Flight, "The Nomadic Idea and Ideal," *Journal of Biblical Literature*, 42: 158–226 (1923). At about the same time, M. Soloweitschik published in Hebrew a discussion of the role played by the "desert" in the history of Israel and in its *Weltanschauung* ("Ha-Midbar be-Toledotaw we-Hashqafat Olamo shel 'Am Jisra'el," *Debir*, 2:16–45 [Berlin, 1923]). Independent of Budde and his followers, whose publications he does not mention, Soloweitschik arrives at conclusions similar to theirs. He presents the desert as the "birthplace of true Yahwism" (*Debir*, 2:30) and as an idealized concept in classical prophecy (pp. 31–40). However, Soloweitschik carefully notes the modulations and the developmental aspects of the desert idea which become apparent in different strata of the Biblical literature.

of faith and life which God has revealed in the life and person of his son Jesus Christ."[11]

One can hardly fail to recognize the somewhat unexpected turn which the desert ideal took in the process of scholarly discussion. What had started out as an analysis of one theme in Old Testament thought and literature ended up by becoming the expression of the quintessence of Biblical religion.

It must be stated in all fairness that scholars sometimes have taken a more balanced view of the role the desert played in Biblical thought. H. P. Smith, hesitantly but correctly, had observed that "the ideal of the Hebrew writers for themselves was agricultural."[12] However, the impact of the desert ideal theory was not really overcome. There results an ambiguity which clearly shows in R. de Vaux's discussion of the issue. He notes that "our oldest Biblical texts show little admiration for nomadic life... that nomadism itself is not the ideal." But he nevertheless agrees that in the prophetic books "we do encounter what has been called the 'nomadic ideal' of the Old Testament... They [the prophets] condemn the comfort and luxury of urban life in their own day (Amos 3:9; 6:8, etc.), and see salvation in a return, at some future date, to the life of the desert, envisaged as a golden age (Hosea 2:16–17; 12:10)."[13] The Rechabites are nevertheless represented, without material evidence, as "the best-known group to organize a return to the desert and to the nomadic ideal." Because of his associations with the Rechabites, Jehu is dubbed "the 'wilderness' king," and Jeremiah is pronounced their "later sympathizer."[14]

The discussion of the reputed desert ideal recently has gained new impetus in the wake of the discovery of the Sectarian literature at Qumran. It is generally maintained that within the spiritual framework of the community that produced these documents we can observe the desert idea not only in the form of a sought-for ideal, but also as a theological concept in operation: that is, as an actuality. R. de Vaux concisely summarizes this approach: "We shall encounter this mystique [*sic!*] of the desert again in the last days of Judaism, among the sectaries of Qumran, when Christian monasticism still lies in the future."[15]

11. Flight, "The Nomadic Idea," p. 224.

12. H. P. Smith, *Religion of Israel* (New York, 1914), p. 12. Flight, "The Nomadic Idea," quotes this statement but does not heed the warning note.

13. *Ancient Israel*, p. 14. See also the *caveat* entered by A. Causse: "...sans doute convient-il de ne pas exagérer, autant que l'on fait Budde et les critiques qui l'ont suivi, le rôle del'idéal nomade dans l'histoire d'Israël et dans le développement du prophétisme" (*Du groupe ethnique à la communauté religieuse* [Paris, 1937], p. 74).

14. G. H. Williams, *Wilderness and Paradise in Christian Thought* (New York, 1962), p. 17. See also Meyer, *Die Israeliten*, p. 136.

15. *Ancient Israel*, p. 14; also W. F. Albright, "Primitivism in Western Asia," in *A Documentary History of Primitivism and Related Ideas*, ed. A. O. Lovejoy, G. Chinard, G. Boas, R. S. Crane (Baltimore, 1935), I, 429–431.

II

I propose to challenge the desert ideal theory on two counts. First, the assumed existence in Biblical society of a reform movement that advocated a "return to the original nomad status," supposedly represented by the Rechabites, and echoed in prophetic teaching, is based on historical premises and on sociological comparisons which cannot be upheld without far-reaching qualifications. In the historical times which are reflected in Biblical literature, Israel never can be defined as a true nomad society. "Nowhere in the Bible are we given a perfect picture of tribal life on the full scale."[16] Nor is there found an indication that in the Biblical period the Israelite tribes proper ever passed through a stage of true nomadism.[17] (Splinter groups like the Midianites, Kenites, Kalebites, and others who attached themselves to Israel may require a separate treatment.) As early as patriarchal times the Israelite society bears the imprint of semisettled life in which only occasional reflections of nomadic life can be discerned. In fact, if we accept the definition recently proposed by Cyrus Gordon, which conceives of the Patriarchs as "merchant-princes,"[18] the often suggested comparison of the patriarchal groups with pre-Islamic Bedouin society becomes altogether misleading. Says Gordon: "It is surprising in retrospect that the Patriarchs could ever have been considered unsophisticated nomadic sheikhs."[19] Quite the contrary, it certainly can be stated that in the Pentateuchal traditions the patriarchal groups are activated by an "agricultural orientation," even though they did not attain the status of a fully sedentary society. The patriarchal stories reflect the very same ideals which in the post-Exodus traditions crystallize in the hope of a permanent settlement in the Promised Land of Canaan. It is immaterial for the issue under review whether these ideals indeed are rooted in an early Israelite socioreligious philosophy, or whether their ascription to the forefathers is a mere anachronism, a retrojection into pre-Exodus days of the concepts of postsettlement authors.[20]

16. DeVaux, *Ancient Israel*, p. 12.

17. If tribal units of the patriarchal era, such as the Benjaminites, could directly be associated with nomadic and seminomadic groups in Mesopotamia of the Mari Age, the picture of early Hebrew society as presented in the Pentateuch could be amplified and possibly further retraced in its development. However, this vexing problem lies beyond the scope of the present paper. For a discussion see J. R. Kupper, *Les Nomades en Mesopotamie aux temps des rois de Mari* (Paris, 1957).

18. C. H. Gordon, "Abraham and the Merchants of Ura," *Journal of Near Eastern Studies*, 17:28–31 (1958); see also W. F. Albright, "Abram the Hebrew: A New Archaeological Interpretation," *Bulletin of the American Schools of Oriental Research*, 163:38–40 (1961); C. H. Gordon, "Abraham of Ur," in *Hebrew and Semitic Studies Presented to G. R. Driver*, ed. D. Winton Thomas and W. D. McHardy (Oxford, 1963), pp. 78–84.

19. C. H. Gordon, "Hebrew Origins in the Light of Recent Discovery," in *Biblical and Other Studies*, ed. A. Altmann (Cambridge, Mass., 1963), p. 10.

20. In any case the question cannot be decided due to the lack of proper evidence, as may be learned from Eduard Meyer's unconvincing attempt to come to a conclusion (*Die Israeliten*, pp. 129–132, 138–141).

Once the patriarchal era is excluded, we are left with the period following upon the Exodus and preceding the Conquest of Canaan as the possible matrix of the image on which was patterned the reputed desert ideal. Historically and sociologically this hypothesis appears to be untenable. Whatever may in reality have been the length of time which the Israelites spent in the desert, the ideological compression of the desert trek into one stereotyped (or schematic) generation, forty years (Deuteronomy 2:14, Psalms 95:10, et cetera), proves that it was considered to have been of minor impact on the sociohistorical development of Israel. Furthermore, even in that comparatively short period, which undoubtedly is portrayed against a desert setting, the tribes of Israel are not presented in the organizational pattern of a typical nomad society. It is interesting to observe that the main characteristics of desert life, and of desert society, as they were abstracted from an analysis of the pre-Islamic Arab tribes, find little expression in the Pentateuchal books which record the desert trek. "Tribal solidarity, desert hospitality and blood vengeance,"[21] insofar as they are reflected in Old Testament literature, are to be found mirrored in the accounts of Israel's sedentary history as recorded in the Former and Latter Prophets, rather than in the Pentateuchal accounts of the desert trek. The few cases of "Bedouin hospitality" which de Vaux adduces to bear out the nomadic character of the patriarchal society[22] in fact prove the opposite. Abraham's reception of the three men at Mamre (Genesis 18:1–8), Lot's welcoming the three angels (Genesis 19:1–8), and the hospitality extended by Laban to Eliezer (Genesis 24:30–32) at best can be viewed as relics of nomadic mores in a predominantly sedentary society. The same may be said of the custom of blood feud which underlies the establishment of Cities of Refuge (Numbers 35:9–15; Deuteronomy 19:1–13). This juridical institution can become operative only in a sedentary society (Joshua chapter 20, *et alibi*) at a stage when blood vengeance, as an acclaimed means of retribution, has lost legal recognition. It is worthy of remark that only one case of executed blood vengeance (II Samuel 3:22–27),[23] and none of a successful retreat to a City of Refuge, actually is recorded in Biblical historical traditions.[24] The sagas of

21. Causse, *Du groupe ethnique*, pp. 15–31; S. Nyström, *Beduinentum und Jahwismus* (Lund, 1946).

22. *Ancient Judaism*, p. 10.

23. Unless the attack of Simeon and Levi on the town of Shechem, in punishment for the rape of their sister Dinah by its prince's son, is also so regarded (Genesis 34:25–29). But this case is atypical.

24. The custom which allowed the accidental killer to seek safety at an altar (Exodus 21:14) must be discussed separately from the institution of "Cities of Refuge." The one man who availed himself of that custom did so at his peril (I Kings 2:28–34; but see I Kings 11:15–16). Adonijah's flight to the altar does not result from a juridicial issue (I Kings 1:50–53). See the recent discussion of "The Biblical Conception of Asylum," by M. Greenberg in *Journal of Biblical Literature*, 78:125–132 (1959).

Cain (Genesis 4:13–16) and of Lamekh (Genesis 4:23–24) are set in hoary antiquity and cannot reflect on patriarchal, or later, concepts. Also, "tribal solidarity" plays an insignificant role in Israelite history. The massacre of the Shechemites by Simeon and Levi may indeed etiologically reflect a feud raid by these tribes on the territory of Shechem (Genesis chapter 34). But their action is met with outright disapproval by the Biblical authors (Genesis 34:30–31, probably also 49:5–7), and cannot be construed as a demonstration of tribal mores. Again, the rallying of the sons of Levi to the help of Moses in the Golden Calf episode (Exodus 32:26) at best reflects guild solidarity, ideologically and etiologically reinterpreted. Korah's rebellion, and the insurrection of Datan and Abiram, in which were involved only parts of the respective ethnic units (Numbers 16:1–35), clearly prove that even in the trek stage the presumed tribal solidarity would not become automatically operative, and that in fact it was in the process of disintegration.

Summing up, we may say that in the Pentateuchal portrayal of the Israelite society in the desert period, the reflection of phenomena which are characteristic of the later sedentary social structure is much more accentuated than is the reverberation of presumed ancient desert ideals in the literature which mirrors Biblical sedentary society. Altogether we note in the Bible a comparative dearth of firsthand information on desert conditions and true nomad life, which, in view of what we have just discussed, is not really surprising. Whenever such information is offered and whenever desert life is reflected in Biblical imagery, they give witness to a deep-seated aversion to and a great fear of such conditions, not a longing for them.

This point will be further considered at a later stage.

Second, little support can be derived from our sources for the attempted presentation of desert life as a social ideal and of the desert period as an ideal period in the conceptual framework of the Biblical writers. The representatives of the Bedouin in Biblical typology are Ishmael and, to a certain degree, Esau. Neither of them, by any stretch of imagination, can be presented as the Biblical writers' ideal type. Wresting a precarious livelihood from the desert as hunters (Genesis 21:20; compare 25:27), being dispersed over vast arid areas (Genesis 25:18), and being in daily combat with others dependent on the same meager resources (Genesis 16:12; compare 27:22) certainly was not the vision of the early Israelite. Nomadism is conceived of as a regression from a higher state of society, not as a desirable goal toward which to progress. Cain, the one-time farmer, the fratricide who undid the cosmic order established by Divine decree (Genesis 9:5–6), is ousted from civilization again to become a roaming Bedouin (Genesis

4:11–12). Nomadism is a punishment, the wilderness the refuge of the outlaw.

Also, the Rechabites cannot be adduced in evidence of the presupposed prophetic "desert ideal." Their nonagricultural mode of life is a reality, not a motif: an occupation (compare I Chronicles 4:38–41; 5:18–22; 7:20–21), not a vocation. They may have resisted the course of cultural development which affected all Israel. But nowhere in the Bible are we told of an effort on their part to propagate their ideals with missionary zeal. Jehu, who for a season joins forces with them (II Kings 10:15–17), is not a "desert king,"[25] nor is Jeremiah a desert prophet. By way of a simile the prophet sets up the Rechabites before the nation as an example of steadfastness. But the *tertium comparationis* lies in their relation to a command, not in the contents of that command. Jeremiah has no admiration for the primitive forms of Rechabite life, nor for the ideas which may underlie it,[26] but he has respect for the tenacity with which they observe man-decreed laws, whereas Israel flagrantly transgresses divinely appointed ordinances.

The desert and the desert period are conceived in the Bible not as intrinsically valuable, but originally and basically as a punishment and a necessary transitory stage in the restoration of Israel to its ideal setting, which is an organized, fully developed society, with a deep appreciation of civilization, settled in the cultivated Land of Israel. The "desert motif" that occurs in the Old Testament expresses the idea of an unavoidable transition period in which Israel recurrently is prepared for the ultimate transfer from social and spiritual chaos to an integrated social and spiritual order. The "trek in the desert" motif represents on the historical and eschatological level what "creatio ex nihilo," the transfer from chaos to cosmos, signifies on the cosmic level.[27]

Whenever the "desert motif" seems to attain the status of a self-contained positive value, this attribution will be shown to result from variational developments of the initial theme, by way of the infusion into it of other, originally unrelated, themes. In essence the process may be described as a "mixing of motifs," which introduces new subsidiary elements into the "desert motif" with a concomitant mutation of its original significance.

III

While we wish to avoid the pitfalls of overemphasis which marred some of the discussions of the "desert theme" in Biblical literature, it can be said

25. Thus Williams, *Wilderness*, p. 17; similarly earlier Meyer, *Die Israeliten*, pp. 137–138.

26. Correctly observed by W. Eichrodt, *Theologie des Alten Testaments*, parts 2/3 (Göttingen, 1961), p. 245.

27. Cf. Jeremiah 31:31–39.

that the analysis of the "desert motif" indeed does give us an insight, sometimes by way of a negative proof, into some fundamental and extremely fruitful religious and social concepts which were operative in Biblical Israel. The analysis also will reveal the exceeding tenacity with which this motif was perpetuated throughout the diverse stages of Biblical literature into post-Biblical Qumran writings and then was infused into Christian imagery, albeit with a fundamentally different significance.[28]

This leads to one more point of interest in the Biblical "desert motif." It appears that this motif is especially well suited for submission to an analysis which will bring out poignant features and characteristics of the "motif" as a literary theme and will illustrate the functions and the developments of a "motif" in a given literary framework. Though we are concerned only with one specific motif in Biblical literature, some typical processes and developments which will emerge in our analysis are transferable to other motifs in Biblical and, *mutatis mutandis*, also in extra-Biblical literature. Therefore it becomes imperative for us to concern ourselves with the definition of the term *motif*, since it is the "desert motif" which is the subject of our inquiry.

The term *motif* seems to have been used in English first in 1848 or 1850 in the field of art. In 1851 *motive* is defined in a handbook for painters as "the principle of action, attitude and composition in a single figure or group..." By 1860, John Ruskin is speaking of "a leading emotional purpose, technically called its motive" in "any great composition." Then *motif* is used in 1887 in the realm of musical theory, to describe "the sort of brief recurring fragment in the operas of Richard Wagner (1813–1893), which Wagner called a Grundthema." Within a year or two, *motif* as a term for a recurrent theme or subject in a work of art was well integrated into the language, and in 1897 the term was used in a literary analysis of the Biblical Book of Ruth.[29]

Since then individual Scriptural motifs often have been investigated. However, little has been done by way of defining the literary phenomenon so described and of mapping out the field in which it can be fruitfully employed in Old Testament research. This lack of proper definition sometimes results in the employment of other literary categories, such as *Gattung*, for the classification of materials which in fact should be subjected to a motif analysis.[30]

28. For this development, which will not be discussed here, see Williams, *Wilderness*...

29. "Motif," "Motive," *A New English Dictionary*, ed. J. A. M. Murray (Oxford, 1908), VI, 695.

30. A case to the point is R. Bach, *Die Aufforderungen zur Flucht und zum Kampf im alttestamentlichen Prophetenspruch*. Wissenschaftliche Monographien zum Alten und Neuen Testament, vol. IX (Neukirchen, 1962).

Decidedly more satisfactory is the situation in the field of New Testament studies, where the Lund School of theology, led by A. Nygrén and G. Aulén, successfully investigated the dominant literary motifs, in order analytically to establish the actual contents of the Christian belief, as crystallized in these motifs.[31] P. L. Berger thus summarizes the role of the "motif" in the Lund method: "The concept of the religious motif, which can be used with advantage in any phenomenological approach to religion, outside as well as inside the Christian tradition, refers to a specific pattern or gestalt of religious experience, that can be traced in a historical development."[32] Elaborating on this definition, we suggest describing "motif," with special application to Old Testament literature, as follows:

> A literary motif is a representative complex theme which recurs within the framework of the Old Testament in variable forms and connections. It is rooted in an actual situation of anthropological or historical nature. In its secondary literary setting, the motif gives expression to ideas and experiences inherent in the original situation, and is employed to reactualize in the audience the reactions of the participants in that original situation. The motif represents the essential meaning of the situation, not the situation itself. It is not a mere reiteration of the sensations involved, but rather a heightened and intensified representation of them.

In view of the composite quality of a motif, its adaptability to new settings, and its compatibility with other themes, its ultimate forms may be far removed from the initial form. Therefore, often a minute analysis will be required to establish their connection and derivation, and to retrace the intermediate stages of development.

Because of its complexity (by definition)[33] a literary "motif" cannot be fully evaluated in isolation. It should be viewed against the background of other, synonymous and antonymous, themes, with which it can be linked in recurring and modifiable patterns. This apposition and opposition will help to clarify the focal meaning of the motif under review and to delineate the limits of its significance within a given body of literature.

IV

We can now proceed to apply the proposed definitions to the investigation of the *midbār* motif. At this stage the Hebrew term *midbār* is to be preferred to the English "desert," since "desert" narrows the more comprehensive *midbār* to the meaning of "parched wilderness." The notion of

31. Anders Nygrén, *Agape and Eros*, trans. P. S. Watson (London, 1953); Gustaf Aulén, *The Faith of the Christian Church*, revised ed., trans. Eric H. Wahlstrom (Philadelphia, 1960).

32. P. L. Berger, "The Sociological Study of Sectarianism," *Social Research*, 21:477 (1954).

33. In this complexity we may perceive one of the fundamental features in which a "motif" differs from a literary "image," which usually is of a simplex nature.

"wilderness" can be expressed in Biblical Hebrew by a number of functionally synonymous terms, such as *šammāh, šemāmāh, ṣiyyāh, yešîmōn*, et cetera, to which allusions will be made but which will not receive a detailed treatment in our discussion.

Our preoccupation with *midbār* as a motif removes from direct scrutiny all those of the 267 occurrences of the term in the Bible which refer to the real physical thing. Our focal interest lies in those passages in which *midbār* is used in a secondary setting as a literary theme. However, before turning to the motif plane, we must determine in rough outline the major aspects of *midbār* in reality, since these aspects serve as the bases of the figurative employment, and therefore will help in establishing its significances.

Midbār can be subdivided into two major classes of connotations, one basic, the other derivative, which again fall into several subgroups: (1) The spatial connotation, in references to geophysical phenomena;[34] (2) The temporal connotation, in the references to a specific historic situation.

Three main subgroups of the spatial-geophysical connotation can be discerned. We shall not present them here in full detail, and we note that the demarcation lines between them are not fixed or static.

1. *Midbār* describes agriculturally unexploited areas, mainly in the foothills of southern Palestine, which serve as the grazing land par excellence for the flocks, and the cattle of the semisedentary and the sedentary-agriculturist population. In this context the term often is paralleled by *'arābāh*, and like it may be translated "steppe." The majority of occurrences of the word *midbār* in the Bible will come under this heading. Here are some illustrations.

Genesis 36:24: "These are the sons of Ṣibe'on: 'Aiah and 'Anah; he is the 'Anah who found the *yēmîm* in the *midbār*, as he pastured the asses of Ṣibe'on his father."

I Samuel 17:28: "And with whom have you left those few sheep in the *midbār*?"

II Chronicles 26:10: "And he built watchtowers in the *midbār*, and hewed out many cisterns, for he had large herds, both in the lowlands and in the plain."

Further reference may be found in I Samuel 25 : 4, 21.[35]

This connotation points to the derivation of the noun *midbār* from a root *dbr*, "to drive out." The root may be connected, by way of metathesis, with

34. A useful summary of Biblical wilderness terminology may be found in A. Schwarzenbach, *Die geographische Terminologie im Hebräischen des Alten Testamentes* (Leiden, 1954), pp. 93–112.

35. In Numbers 14:33 we should read with the Vulgate *tō'îm* instead of the Masoretic *rō'îm*, and translate: "And your children shall wander in the wilderness for forty years." Thus the parallelism with Numbers 32:13 is retained.

rbd and also *rbṣ*, technical terms which describe the grazing of flocks: for example, in Isaiah 13 : 20 : ". . . no Arab [herdsman] will pitch his tent there, no shepherds will tend their flocks there [*yarbîṣū*; RSV = "will make their flocks lie down there"]. But desert animals [*ṣîyyîm*] will graze [*yirbeṣū*] there [RSV = "But wild beasts will lie down there"]."

We shall render this connotation of *midbār* by "drift-land," or, in short, "drift."

The poignant aspects of the drift setting express themselves in (1) the anthropological sphere: descriptions of the fate of man (and his belongings: for example, flocks) vis-à-vis an unaccommodating nature; (2) the sociological sphere: the presentation of the various aspects of shepherd society; (3) the ecological sphere: the description of tent-life phenomena.

2. The geographical setting of the "drift," in the borderland between cultivated land and desert, results in the term *midbār* coming to designate the comparatively thinly inhabited open spaces adjacent to settlements of a temporary (*maḥanēh*), relatively stable (*nāwēh*),[36] or altogether static nature (village or town). These spaces are viewed as an extension of the encampment or the settlement, but are not an integral part of it. The distinction is of an ecological as well as a sociological character.

As an extension of the *maḥanēh*, *midbār* appears, for example, in Exodus 16 : 10: "And as Aaron spoke to the whole congregation of the people of Israel, they looked toward the *midbār*, and, behold, the glory of God appeared in the cloud." (Compare further Numbers 24 : 1.)

The term is applied to the space adjacent to a *nāwēh* in Isaiah 27:10, where Israel in the stage of its destruction appears "like a solitary fortified [*beṣūrah*; better *neṣūrāh* = besieged] city, a forsaken and desolate encampment [*nāwēh*], like a drift [*midbār*] wherein cattle graze."

Very common is the designation of the outskirts of a permanent settlement as its *midbār*. Thus we find the term used with reference to : Be'er Sheba' (Genesis 21 : 14); Bet 'Awen (Joshua 18:12); 'Ein Gedi (I Samuel 24: 1); Teqo'a (II Chronicles 20 : 20); Damascus (I Kings 19: 15), et cetera. It is this connotation which is mirrored in the Qumran term *midbār yerušālayīm*.[37]

3. *Midbār* also is employed to denote the true desert, the arid zones beyond the borders of the cultivated land and the drift (for example, II Samuel 17: 27–29; II Kings 3: 8–9). This meaning is well rendered in English by "wilderness."

36. For a discussion of the diverse aspects of Biblical *nāwēh* and its Akkadian counterpart *nawūm* see J. Bottéro and A. Finet, *Archives Royales de Mari*, XV (Paris, 1954), 237; M. Noth, *Die Ursprünge des alten Israel im Lichte neuer Quellen* (Cologne, 1961), p. 16; D. O. Edzard, "Altbabylonisch *nawūm*," *Zeitschrift für Assyriologie*, N. S., 19: 168–173 (1959).

37. See below, Page 61.

I can be brief in indicating the focal aspects of "wilderness" in Biblical literature.

The "wilderness" is a place of utter desolation: a vast void of parched earth, with no streams or rivers to provide sustenance for plants and wildlife, except for a very few species (Jeremiah 2 : 24). It is a place not fit for human habitation (Jeremiah 9 : 11, 50 : 40, 51 : 43; Job 38 : 26), the few wandering nomads — *'arābîm* — being the only exception (Jeremiah 3 : 2, 9 : 25).

This *midbār* wilderness is the scene of utter cruelty, beast against beast and man against man (Lamentations 5 : 9). It is perilous to enter the vast tracts, which are traversable by only a few paths or byways, often barely recognizable.

However, due to its remoteness from settled land, and due to its terrifying desolation, the "wilderness" becomes the refuge of outlaws and fugitives, who may prefer an off-chance of survival in exceedingly adverse circumstances, to the calamities which are certainly to befall them from the hands of their pursuers. Hagar flees into the desert, to escape the anger and the persecution of Sarah (Genesis 16: 6–14). And there in the wilderness her son Ishmael becomes the prototype of the marauding Bedouin: "He lived in the wilderness and became a bowman" (Genesis 21 : 20). David takes to the Judean desert in his flight before Saul: "And everyone who was in distress and everyone who was in debt, and everyone who was discontented, gathered to him; and he became captain over them" (I Samuel 22 : 2). In repairing to the *midbār*, Elijah tries to save his soul when Jezebel plans to kill him: "He was afraid, and he arose and went [ran] for his life, and came to Be'er Sheba', which belongs to Judah, and left his servant there. But he himself went a day's journey into the wilderness" (I Kings 19: 3–4). This utilization, out of necessity, of the *midbār* as a refuge by one who had been forced out of his society may have been conducive to a new concept, which will be discussed later: the desert as the locus of a seemingly voluntary retreat.

We have already remarked that references to "wilderness reality" are comparatively few in Scripture. This seems to indicate the relatively unimportant role which the "wilderness" or "desert" proper played in the life experience of the Israelites in Biblical times. Those mentions that are made mainly pertain to the arid tracts in the deep south of Palestine and the Sinai peninsula. Thus the word *midbār* becomes a recurrent component of the names of these particular areas, such as *midbar ṣin*, *midbar par'an*, *midbar sinai*, et cetera. The region in its wider extent is also referred to as desert par excellence, with the definite article: *ha-midbār*, or *ha-midbār ha-gadōl*.

The predominant aspects of *midbār* wilderness in the Bible give additional evidence to the unfamiliarity with and the loathing of the "desert" which were typical of the ancient Israelite. It is the attitude of the city-dweller, the farmer, the semisedentary shepherd, even of the ass-nomad, who may traverse the desert on beaten tracks, but who would not voluntarily venture into its depth. This attitude is exceedingly different from that of the true camel-nomad, the Bedouin, to whom the desert is home.

The connotation of *midbār* as a barren, awe-inspiring, howling wilderness is intimately related to yet another category of a rather specific brand of "reality." There are to be found in the Bible some residues of a mythical conception of "wilderness," which is much more fully developed in ancient Semitic mythology[38] and also in post-Biblical midrashic literature. "In Arabic and Accadian folklore, the desert is the natural habitat of noxious demons and jinns."[39] In Ugaritic myth it is Mot, the god of all that lacks life and vitality, whose "natural habitation is the sun-scorched desert, or alternatively, the darkling region of the netherworld."[40] Mot is the eternal destroyer, who periodically succeeds in vanquishing Baal, the god of fertility and life, and in reducing the earth temporarily to waste and chaos. It may be due to this identification in Canaanite myth of desert and darkness with Mot, that any equation of Yahweh with the wilderness is anathema to the Biblical writers. Has he been "a wilderness unto Israel or a land of [thick] darkness" (Jeremiah 2:31), demands Yahweh, so that Israel might have reason to reject him?

These mythical visions of *midbār* wilderness are mirrored in Biblical pronouncements which show the desert to be populated by phantom-like creatures, alongside the scanty animal population. Thus, while looking after asses that were grazing in the *midbār*, Ṣibe'on's son 'Anah found the *yēmîm* (Genesis 36:24), whom the midrash identifies as demonic beings.[41] "There [in the desert] ostriches will dwell, and there satyrs [*śe'îrîm*] will dance" (Isaiah 13:21). The presence of such monsters in fact indicates that a place has been reduced to the primeval state of chaos: "An unknown, foreign and unoccupied territory (which often means 'unoccupied by our people'), still shares in the fluid and larval modality of chaos."[42] Such will be the future fate of Edom: "The hawk and the porcupine shall possess it, the owl and the raven shall dwell in it. He [God] shall stretch the line of confusion [*tōhū*] over it, and the plummet of chaos [*bōhū*] over[43] its nobles"

38. A. Haldar, "The Notion of the Desert in Sumero-Accadian and West-Semitic Religions," *Uppsala Universitets Årsskrift*, 3:1–70 (1950).

39. T. Gaster, *Thespis*, revised ed. (New York, 1961), p. 132, n. 19.

40. *Ibid.*, p. 125.

41. Cf. E. Ben Yehudah, *Thesaurus Totius Hebraitatis*, IV (Jerusalem, n. d.), 2056, n. 2.

42. M. Eliade, *The Sacred and the Profane* (New York, 1961), p. 31.

43. The Masoretic text lacks an equivalent for *over*, and connects the following word, *ḥôrēhā*, with the next verse.

(Isaiah 34:11). "And wild beasts shall meet with hyenas, the satyr [*śā'îr*] shall cry to his fellow; yea there shall the night hag [*lîlît*] alight and find for herself a resting place" (Isaiah 34:14).[44] The *midbār* plays a prominent part in Psalm 29, which brims with mythical creation terminology in a historicized setting: "The voice of the Lord flashes forth flames of fire. The voice of the Lord shakes the wilderness [*midbār*], the Lord shakes the wilderness of Kadesh. The Lord sits down on his throne [*la-mabbūl*],[45] the Lord sits enthroned as king forever."[46]

It is this mythic aspect of *midbār* which is retained in the ritual of driving out a goat (*śā'îr*) into the wilderness (*'ereṣ gezērāh*) to 'Aza'zel as an atonement offering (Leviticus 16:7–10, 22), and which subsequently became permanently associated with the rites of the Day of Atonement (Leviticus 16:29). We shall have occasion to suggest that these mythical undertones of *midbār* possibly influenced some developments of the "desert motif" in the Bible.

V

The above aspects of *midbār* in the geophysical reality (drift wilderness) determine the secondary literary employment of *midbār* language in the Bible.

The "drift wilderness" connotations in the main result in literary imagery which is based predominantly on the figurative employment of one aspect of "typical," not "one-time specific," *midbār* reality. Generally speaking, turning "reality" into an "image" involves a transfer from the original setting onto an altogether different plane. Usually the image serves to achieve a concretization of abstract ideas and relationships.

Again there is no need to go into much detail. Such imagery is the stock-in-trade of Biblical prophets and psalmists. Some examples will suffice.

1. The "leader–led" relationship, between (for example) king and nation or God and nation, is often portrayed as the dependence of the flocks on the shepherd. Says Yahweh: "I will gather the remnant of Israel; I will set them together like sheep in a fold, like a flock in its pasture" (Micah 2:12). A most intricate and abounding employment of the image is found in Ezekiel, chapter 34. Here is one illustration (verses 20–25):

> Therefore, thus says the Lord God to them: Behold, I, I myself will judge between the fat sheep and the lean sheep. Because you push with side and shoulder, and thrust at all the weak with your horns, till you have scattered them abroad, I will save my flock, they shall no longer be a prey; and I will judge between sheep and

44. Cf. further Jeremiah 4:23–27.
45. For this interpretation of *mabbûl* see Y. N. Epstein, *Tarbiz*, 12:82 (1942).
46. Psalm 29:7–10. Cf. further Isaiah 42:11–13, 50:2; Job 38:25–26.

sheep. And I will set up over them one shepherd, my servant David, and he shall feed them; he shall feed them and be their shepherd. . . I will make with them a covenant of peace and banish wild beasts from the land, so that they may dwell securely in the drift [*midbār*—RSV: wilderness] and sleep in the woods." (Compare further Isaiah 40:11; Jeremiah 23:1–6.)

2. The ecological aspects of the "drift" were recaptured especially in tent imagery. Steadfastness and security are likened to a well-anchored tent: "Your eyes will see Jerusalem, a quiet habitation, an immovable tent, whose stakes will never be plucked up, nor will any of its cords be broken" (Isaiah 33:20). Failure and death, on the other hand, are compared to the uprooted tent: "My dwelling is plucked up and removed from me like a shepherd's tent" (Isaiah 38:12, further Jeremiah 10:20). "If their tent-cord is plucked up within them, do they not die..." (Job 4:21). The spreading out of the tent sheets to accommodate an increased population portrays the previously barren woman who was blessed with offspring: "Enlarge the place of your tent, and let the curtains of your habitation be stretched out; hold not back, lengthen your cords and strengthen your stakes" (Isaiah 54:2).

The dusky beauty of a sun-tanned maiden conjures up the image of the pitch-black goat-hair tents of the shepherds: "I am very dark, but comely, O daughters of Jerusalem," says the Shulamite, "like the tents of Kedar, like the curtains of Solomon" (Song of Songs 1:5).

In spite of the reference to Kedar, a typical desert tribe, the last-mentioned image belongs to the "drift" context. Wilderness imagery does not express beauty, success, or security. It crystallizes abject fear, destruction, and desolation, which the Israelite perceived in desert reality (Isaiah 14:17; Zephaniah 2:13).

3. A ruler in his ruin is compared to a vinestock transplanted from fertile ground into the wilderness: "Your mother was like a vine in a vineyard transplanted by the water, fruitful and full of branches... Now it is transplanted in the wilderness, in a dry and thirsty land" (Ezekiel 19:10–13). The fate of such a plant in the desert is certain; it will wither. Like it is the man who puts his trust in human beings and not in God: "He is like a shrub in the desert, and shall not see any good come. He shall dwell in the parched places of the wilderness, in an uninhabited salt land" (Jeremiah 17:6). Man's cruelty at its height is like that of "the ostriches in the wilderness" (Lamentations 4:3), or like that "of wild asses in the desert... seeking prey in the wilderness" (Job 24:5).

Yet, as in reality, the desert also can equal "refuge": "Flee, save yourselves," is the prophet's advice to the Moabites, "Be like a wild ass in the desert" (Jeremiah 48:6). And the Psalmist "would wander afar... would lodge in the wilderness" to find shelter from his enemies, who are likened to "the raging wind and tempest" (Psalms 55:7–8).

This fact gives rise to an incipient positive image which is derived from "wilderness language": namely, the employment of "desert" as a figure for "retreat," as in Jeremiah's famous lament: "O that I had in the desert a wayfarer's lodging place, that I might leave my people and go away from them" (Jeremiah 9:1). This theme was not further developed in Biblical literature. Even in the Jeremiah passage the "positive" aspect is subsidiary. The prophet is not drawn into the desert, as it were, to meditate there and come face to face with his God. He does not seek communion with the Deity, but rather he longs to dissociate himself from his contemporaries.

VI

So far we have dealt with perspectives of *midbār* in its over-all spatial-geophysical connotation. We can now turn to what we termed its "temporal–historical" connotation.

In a rather large number of its occurrences in Biblical literature *midbār* serves as a designation of the clearly circumscribed period which followed upon the Exodus and preceded the Conquest of Canaan. This period roughly falls into two unequal stretches of time. The one, spanning the first two years, includes the events from the Crossing of the Red Sea to the Sinai theophany, and to what immediately follows upon it. The other extends from that point, when Israel is encamped in the Par'an desert to the war against the Midianites, which is the last skirmish against desert people, and after which Israel enters the territories of the Transjordanian states. This period encompasses most of the remaining thirty-eight years. These are the years of the desert trek proper, the wanderings which were imposed upon Israel as a divine punishment for their sins and for their doubting God's power to lead them safely into the Promised Land of Canaan (Deuteronomy 2:14–16). The episodes of this period are surveyed comprehensively in what may be called "The Book of Israel's Failings," which comprises Numbers 11:1–31:20 (or possibly 31:54) to the exclusion of 26:1–30:17, which appear to be a later intrusion. This "book of iniquities" is editorially clearly set apart,[47] and it is the incidents related in this book, and its atmosphere,

47. The preceding part of Numbers ends with the "war song of the ark" (Numbers 10:35–36), which in Rabbinic tradition is considered a separate book and is singled out by a prefixed and an appended inverted letter *nûn*. The composition ends with Numbers 26:1a, which should have been 25:19a. It breaks in the middle of a sentence—*pisqāh be'emṣa' kātûb*, a device employed by the Masoretes to draw attention to a fault in text transmission. The continuation of this passage, and the conclusion of the "book of iniquities" is now found in a worked-over form in Numbers 31:1–19.

which have decisively determined the image of the desert period in subsequent Biblical literature.[48]

We now have to establish the themes and ideas which could be derived from the account of the historical desert trek, and the moods and reactions which this account could be expected to evoke in the audience that was exposed to it. This encounter was achieved either by a direct reminiscent recital of the story, most probably in a cultic setting, or else by employing the trek experience as a literary motif. We may presume that such secondary employment prerequires a historical and sociological disengagement from the historical trek situation and an ontological perspective toward desert conditions. Therefore, it can cause no surprise that figurative desert language is not used at all in the historical portions of the Pentateuch, or in subsequent Biblical historiography. Here, as in legal literature, "desert language" refers to the thing itself, not to its image. Also in Wisdom literature, which is nonhistorical in character, the desert trek does not serve as a source from which literary motifs are drawn. There are, however, some instances of *midbār* imagery which are anchored in the wilderness aspect (for example, Job 1:19, 24:4), or in the creation-myth setting (for example, Job 38:26).

The desert-trek motif makes its first appearance in the Deuteronomistic attempt to recapture the quintessence of the trek experience, and to present it as the typological crystallization of the immanent relation between the nation and God (Deuteronomy 32; compare Psalms 78 and 106). The preponderant employment of the desert motif is found in the books of the pre-Exilic prophets and in the Book of Psalms. Thus it can be stated that the *midbār* theme in fact is concentrated in Biblical literature which originated in the period of the First Temple. With the end of the monarchy, the employment of the desert motif abates, possibly due to the re-experience of actual wilderness-desolation conditions (for example, Malachi 1:3). In post-monarchical literature it is replaced by new themes, which represent similar ideas and notions and which emanate from events and situations which are set in the period of the kingdom.

Two major themes emerge from the traditions pertaining to the desert period in Israel's history. On the one hand, in the first part of this period, it is dominated by the Sinai theophany, in which Yahweh reveals Himself to Israel and establishes a covenant with His people. The second part of the period, on the other hand, is characterized by two mutually complementary strands of significance which run through the account: Yahweh provides Israel with sustenance and guides His people in the chaotic wilderness. In His benevolence He shields them from danger, although the desert

48. Note that out of forty-two occurrences of the term *midbār* in Numbers, twenty-five are found in these twelve chapters, against seventeen in the remaining twenty-two.

period as such had been appointed by Him as a punishment for Israel. But the people, stubborn and without remorse, continue flagrantly to disobey the Lord and to kindle His anger. Worse than the future days of the Judges, the desert period is typified by Israel's wickedness, by an uninterrupted sequence of transgressions. It lacks even the relieving moments of temporary repentance which ameliorate the Biblical verdict on the times of the Judges.

It is our thesis that the theme of "disobedience and punishment" is of much greater impact on the subsequent formulation of the "desert motif" in Biblical literature than is the the concept of the desert as the locale of Divine revelation and of Yahweh's love for Israel. The idealization of the desert, which scholars perceived in the writings of some prophets, derives from an unwarranted isolation of the "revelation in the desert" theme from the preponderant "transgression and punishment" theme, with which it is closely welded in the Pentateuchal account of the desert trek. The widespread opinion that "the pre-exilic prophets for the most part [*sic!*] interpreted the forty years as a period when God was particularly close to Israel, when he loved his chosen people as the bridegroom his bride,"[49] in the last count rests on the slender evidence of two passages, Hosea 2:17 and Jeremiah 2:2, which are discussed out of the wider context of the prophets' message. A closer analysis of this theme, viewed in relation to other concepts and motifs in Biblical, and especially in prophetic, literature, indicates that it is of minor importance. In no way can it be construed to serve as the nucleus of a reputed "desert ideal." The experience of a theophany in the desert is not an intrinsic feature of prophecy as such, but rather a particular instance in the life of *some* prophets. Nor can it be presented as a fundamental aspect of Yahweh, as has been proposed. In fact we now witness attempts to establish a phenomenological relationship between Yahwistic religion and the desert. The conclusion, presented by M. Weber as a result of empirical studies, that a provenance from the borderland between desert and cultivated land (*Grenzgebiete des Kulturlandes im Übergang zur Wüste*) is characteristic of the Biblical prophets,[50] is formulated as a phenomenological axiom in a geography of religion.[51] The desert is tentatively elevated to the position of an especially "geeignete Offenbarungsstätte des wahren Gottes."[52] "Beduinentum und Jahwismus" are conceived of not only as historically related, but as existentially con-

49. Williams, *Wilderness*, pp. 15–16.

50. M. Weber, *Ancient Judaism*, trans. and ed. H. H. Gerth and D. Martindale (Glencoe, Illinois, 1952).

51. G. Lanczkowski, *Altägyptischer Prophetismus. Ägyptologische Abhandlungen*, IV (Wiesbaden, 1960), 52–57.

52. R. Kittel, *Gestalten und Gedanken in Israel* (Leipzig, 1926), p. 42.

sanguineous phenomena, which were most fruitfully mated in the prophetic experience of the desert deity Yahweh in His natural setting.[53] Such a regional determinism cannot be squared with the prevailing prophetic idea of Yahweh as an omnipresent deity who defies any geographical or conceptual circumscription.[54] Therefore, it appears that in revealing Himself in the desert, to the prophet as an individual, or to His people as a group, Yahweh accommodates Himself to the actual habitat of the recipients of this revelation. What the Temple is to Jeremiah and Ezekiel the priests, and to Isaiah the citizen of the metropolis, is the desert—or the drift—to Moses and Amos the herdsmen, and to Elijah who also lived in the *midbār*, the borderland between "Kulturland und Wüste." Not in search of God does Elijah go into the desert, but out of fear of Jezebel. That he experiences a theophany in the wilderness is accidental, not predetermined by Yahweh's desert character. Thus we may assume that initially the theophany in the desert does not reveal the nature of Yahweh, but rather the existential setting of the men who experienced Him there. Being a *historical* deity and not a nature god, and being the exclusive god, invested with geographically and otherwise unrestricted power, Yahweh was not bound to reveal Himself in a specific location, but could permit men to experience Him in their own existential framework. It is for this reason that in the limited historical period of the "trek in the desert," the desert is the exclusive locale of Divine revelation. With the Conquest of Canaan the Israelite concept of Yahweh became charged with new images. It may well be that in the first stage, during the conquest of the central mountain ridge, Yahweh was identified as a "mountain deity." In this identification we may perceive a variation on the Yahweh image of the pre-Conquest times, with its specific attachment to Mount Sinai and Mount Ḥoreb.[55] This concept lingers on into monarchical times among surrounding nations, like the Arameans, who continue to conceive of Yahweh as *'elōhê hārîm* (I Kings 20:23), just as the "desert god" image lingers on in Israel proper. After the establishment of the monarchy, the conception of Yahweh as the royal ruler of an orderly universe overshadows all previous notions. It becomes the dominant motif in Israel's religion, and is carried over into prophetic eschatology, in which neither the "desert god" nor the "mountain god" has a stake.

VII

We now have to consider the "desert motif" in conjunction with other Biblical motifs. This is especially important in view of the twofold signi-

53. Nyström, *Beduinentum und Jahwismus*.

54. This was correctly stressed by K. Budde, *New World*, 4: 734 (1895).

55. Cf. Deuteronomy 4:10; I Kings 8:9; Malachi 3:22, and also Judges 5:5; Psalms 68:9, et cetera.

ficance which we discerned in the account of the desert trek. The figurative employment of the trek traditions mirrors the two diverging phases in the Yahweh–Israel relationship which characterize the period of the desert wanderings. The one or the other, the "Divine grace" or the "Israel's sin and punishment" aspect, can be stressed. The re-enforcement of the one or the other is achieved by infusing into the "trek motif" new images and motifs which are anchored in *midbār* language in the wider sense of the word.

Thus we find in Jeremiah 2:6 a fusion of the historical "trek theme," as an expression of God's benevolence and guidance, with the partly mythical "wilderness–desolation" theme: "They did not say, 'where is the Lord who brought us up from the land of Egypt, who led us in the wilderness,'" and then in a new vein: "...in a land of deserts and pits, in a land of drought and deep darkness, in a land that none passes through, where no man dwells?"

Again in Psalm 78:52 the notion of Divine protection, inherent in the trek motif, is combined with the shepherd image, which has no roots in the historical account, but is derived from the "drift" context: "Then he led forth his people like sheep, and guided them in the wilderness like a flock."

An altogether new element is introduced into the trek motif by Hosea and is further developed by Jeremiah. These modifications deserve special attention, since they were godfathers to the "desert ideal," already referred to.

The predominant motif of the first three chapters of the Book of Hosea portrays Yahweh's steadfast affection for Israel as the unfailing love of a husband for his wayward wife.[56] As punishment for her unfaithfulness the wife will be deprived of her material comforts and will be reduced to abject poverty. It is hoped that this hardship will cause her to repent, to mend her ways, and to prepare herself for a renewed and everlasting fidelity toward her husband. On the plane of the "nation" this process is viewed as a re-enactment of the desert-trek period. That period had served Israel as a transition stage from enslavement in Egypt to a free covenant relationship with Yahweh in Canaan. Accordingly Hosea's "return to the wilderness" motif, like the historical trek through the desert, is not set up as an aim per se, but like it it serves as punishment and as a *rite de passage* toward the true goal—the re-establishment of the wife–Israel in the Land of Canaan.

Now the transition aspect of Hosea's "desert motif" is obviously derived from the account of the historical desert trek. However, the "marital love

56. In this precise form the motif is present only in the first three chapters of the book, as Y. Kaufmann correctly observed. See *Toledot ha-'Emunah ha-Jisr'elit*, vol. III, part 1 (Tel Aviv, 1945), pp. 93–95.

image "has no roots in the desert account,[57] which uses other imagery to conceptualize Yahweh's attachment to Israel: for example, the "parent eagle–fledglings" image (Exodus 19: 4; Deuteronomy 32 : 11). But we have it as an independent motif in the first chapter of the Book of Hosea. Therefore it is feasible that the fusion of these two initially unrelated themes, the "trek motif" and the "love motif" originated with the author of this Book.

Still, the already observed cases of a combination of "trek" images and "drift" images make one look for a traditional "love-*cum-midbār*" motif, with *midbār* standing for "drift" or "wilderness."

Two possible sources come to mind. One is found in the Song of Songs. A major theme of this collection is the romantic attachment of youthful lovers on the "drift." The maiden, in search of her beloved among the shepherds and their flocks, is portrayed "coming up from the drift [*midbār*] like a column of smoke perfumed with myrrh and frankincense" (3:6).[58] Again she is seen "coming up from the drift leaning upon her beloved" (8:5). It may be conjectured that the author of the Book of Hosea infused an independent "love on the drift" theme into the equally independent trek motif, and thus created the quite uncommon motif combination "love in the historical desert period."

The other source which suggests itself is more remote than the first, but has one additional factor in common with the motif employed by Hosea: it deals with Divine love in the *midbār*, in the setting of a Canaanite myth. There is in the "Baal and 'Anat" cycle, a rather outspoken and crude description of Aliyan Baal's mating with a heifer in the *dbr*, the name of a region which presumably was drift—or possibly desert—land:[59]

> Aliyan Baal hearkens
> He loves a heifer in *Dbr*[60]
> A young cow in the fields of *šḥlmmt*
> He lies with her seventy-seven times
> [Yea] eighty-eight times (67: V: 18–22)

Arṣ dbr in the Ugaritic myth is part of the nether world, the domain of Mot, and is inhabited by his helpmates, just as in some Biblical references

57. The Midrash retrojects this theme into the Sinai episode. Moses thus addresses the people on the morning of the theophany: "Arise from your sleep, the bridegroom is at hand, and is waiting to lead his bride under the marriage canopy" (*Pirqê d'Rabbi Eliezer* 41: Midrash *Shir ha-Shirim* 1:12, 5:3; *Debarim Rabbah* 3:12; *Aggadat Bere'shit* 41:126). Cf. L. Ginzberg, *The Legends of the Jews* (New York, 1955), III, 92.

58. The attribution of the metaphor to the maiden may be preferred over its attribution to Solomon's litter (RSV).

59. C. H. Gordon, *Ugaritic Manual*. Analecta Orientalia, vol. XXXV (Rome, 1955), part 2, p. 149; translation by C. H. Gordon, *Ugaritic Literature* (Rome, 1949), p. 42.

60. G. R. Driver, *Ugaritic Myth* (Edinburgh, 1956), p. 107, translates "land of decease." This is hardly acceptable since further on (67:VI:5, 29–30) the "goodness of *ars dbr*" is referred to.

the *midbār* is the abode of demons (Isaiah 13:21–22, 34:11–14). It stands to reason that in the Hosea motif a revised Canaanite mythological theme, "Divine love on the drift" (or better: "in the wilderness") was wedded with the historical wilderness-trek motif.[61] Such an interpretation lends a new dimension to this latter motif. Far from being the "normal" or "ideal" habitat of Yahweh, the wilderness, which is the realm of Mot, the ruler of the nether world, is forced to yield to the supreme power of Yahweh. Where the Canaanite fertility god Baal failed because his power is limited to agricultural areas, Israel's God achieves unimpaired success. "He turns rivers into a desert, springs of water into thirsty ground, a fruitful land into a salty waste." With the very same power, "He turns a desert into pools of water, a parched land into springs of water. And there he lets the hungry dwell" (see Psalm 107: 33–35). He can return his people to the dried-up waste, and from there give them again their vineyards and turn the valley of desolation into the gate of hope (Hosea 2 : 17). Viewed thus, the Hosea passage echoes the covert refutation of the Canaanite fertility-god myth.[62] This same refutation seems to underlie the trek account, and also the desert visions of Deutero-Isaiah.[63]

Whatever its origin and history may be, it should have become clear that the "love in the desert" motif of Hosea does not give expression to a prophetic desert ideal, as has been and is yet asserted by some scholars. At the best it constitutes a fairly isolated and subsidiary theme in the prophet's thought. It is the result of a literary process of motif-mixing, rather than a conscious expression of an explicit theological or existential idea.

However, at this juncture the question must be raised whether or not such a concept can be discerned in the way in which Jeremiah developed this theme. Let us recall that in Hosea's version, the motif depicts God's steadfast love for Israel in spite of the nation's iniquities. This love originally had been revealed in the setting of the "desert trek," where it was coupled with the "expurgatory transition" motif. In the Book of Jeremiah the love

61. The historization of Canaanite myth in Old Testament literature is a well-known phenomenon. A typical example may be found in Isaiah 51:9–11, where the mythical dismemberment of Rahab is welded with the historical tradition of the Crossing of the Red Sea, and is then projected into the vision of the Return from the Exile. See I. L. Seeligmann, *Voraussetzungen der Midraschexegese*. Supplements to *Vetus Testamentum* I, Congress Volume, Copenhagen 1953 (Leiden, 1953), p. 169.

62. E. Jacob finds in the Book of Hosea many more instances of a refutation and a rejection of Canaanite mythical traditions which had found popular acceptance among the prophet's contemporaries. See E. Jacob, "L'Héritage cananéen dans le livre du prophète Osée," *Revue d'Histoire et de Philosophie Religieuses*, 3:250–259 (1963).

63. This technique of covert refutation of Canaanite mythology can be observed in the Biblical creation story and certainly was applied also in other Biblical traditions. See U. Cassuto, *A Commentary on the Book of Genesis*, trans. L. Abrahams (Jerusalem, 1961), pp. 7ff.

theme takes a new turn. It now portrays Israel's affection for God in that remote historical setting. At the same time the transition aspect of the "trek motif" is replaced by the "desolation aspect" of the "wilderness motif": "Thus says Yahweh, I remember for thee [better: "I credit to you"] the kindness of thy youth, the love of thine espousals, how thou wentest after me in the wilderness, in a land that was not sown" (Jeremiah 2 : 2). It must be admitted that this employment of the desert motif by Jeremiah appears to reflect an appreciation of the desert period which deviates considerably from its estimation in the Pentateuchal traditions. If this were to be explained as a deliberate deviation from Pentateuchal historiography, the question would be raised of the prophet's attitude toward, or of his awareness of, this historiography. But in fact no such reinterpretation has to be presupposed. Jeremiah, like Hosea, never develops the historical desert reminiscence into an ideal toward the attainment of which he wants to guide the nation. Also in his view God's love for Israel, evoked by the memory of the nation's fidelity at the time of her youth, ultimately will express itself in a return from the *midbār* into a restituted, renascent land of Israel: "Thus saith Yahweh, the people that were left of the sword [again] found favor in the wilderness, when I went to give rest to Israel." And He turns to His people saying: "I have loved thee with an everlasting love, with lovingkindness I have drawn thee [after me] . . . Again shalt thou plant vineyards upon the mountains of Samaria; the planters shall plant and shall enjoy the fruit thereof" (Jeremiah 31 : 1–4).

Jeremiah's divergence from the Pentateuchal presentation of the desert period therefore should be explained as a literary variation rather than as a case of a deliberate reassessment of history. The apparent contradiction may be resolved by our attempt to explain the "love in the desert" motif as a fusion of two themes which were derived from different aspects of *midbār*. We would describe the process as a combination of the "love in the drift" theme with the "desert trek" motif. Thus Jeremiah's presentation of the desert period does not evidence an unawareness of the Pentateuchal traditions on the part of the prophet, nor does it imply a conscious reworking of these traditions. The variation, which indeed is present, cannot be construed to show that Jeremiah conceived of the desert period as Israel's golden age, for whose return he nostalgically longed.

Summing up, we may say that both in the books of Hosea and Jeremiah, the modification of the appreciation of the trek period results from an unpremeditated process of literary variation and was brought about by the infusion into the desert motif of initially unrelated themes. The underlying factors are less of a conscious historiosophical character than of a literary nature.

The last prophet, and in fact the latest Biblical source, that makes extensive use of the desert motif is Deutero-Isaiah. Under the impression of the striking similarity between Israel's historical situation in the Egyptian Bondage and in the Babylonian Exile, Deutero-Isaiah expresses his hopeful expectation of a new Exodus and a new settlement in Canaan in terms and images which are clearly patterned upon the Pentateuchal trek traditions. "The conception of the new exodus is the most profound and most prominent of the motifs in the tradition which Second Isaiah employs to portray the eschatological finale."[64] But Deutero-Isaiah does not merely borrow a theme from Pentateuchal sources, or from prophets like Hosea and Jeremiah who preceded him. His utilization of the ancient material is selective, and is subject to formative adaptation. He fully retains the established notion of the desert trek as a mere transition stage. However, the original *rite de passage* aspect, for the sake of purification, is completely overshadowed by the "Divine benevolence" theme. The shift of stress is easily explained. It arises out of the fundamentally different theological situation of post-Exilic Israel, compared with that of the Exodus generation. While for the Exodus generation the desert became the locale of purification which perforce must precede the attainment of the *Heils* goal (Canaan), the returning exiles had already successfully passed through the stage of catharsis, which they experienced in the destruction of the Temple, and in the Babylonian Exile. The purging of the Exodus generation from the dross of sinners was effected in the desert, so that only their as yet guiltless sons reached the gates of Canaan. Israel of Deutero-Isaiah's time had been decimated by war, destruction, and dispersion. The returning exiles were the *'aśîrîyāh*, the "holy seed" which Isaiah of Jerusalem had envisaged (Isaiah 6 : 13; compare Ezra 9 : 2). Therefore, the new Exodus fell to the lot of the faithful remnant. Thus the new trek through the desert could be freed from its purgatory qualities and concomitantly be invested with new images of promise and hope. Now the desert motif could be wedded with the theme of the Davidic covenant, and with the vision of the restituted Jerusalem.[65] It is this fusion of the desert motif with the "remnant" idea and with the expectation of a restored Davidic dynasty which, as will be shown, constitutes the basis of the desert theme in Qumran ideology.

In sum we may say that it is altogether futile to speculate on an imaginary prophetic desert ideal, and to present it as the expression of a typical Bedouin zest for freedom which was opposed to the monarchical regime.[66] The prophets

64. J. Muilenburg, "Isaiah," The Interpreter's Bible (Philadelphia, 1956), p. 602.

65. Cf. B. W. Anderson, "Exodus Typology in Second Isaiah," *Israel's Prophetic Heritage: Essays in Honor of J. Muilenburg*, ed. B. W. Anderson and W. Harrelson (New York, 1962), p. 181.

66. "L'atavisme bédouin, l'aversion innée du nomade pour les moeurs et la culture

did not reject the monarchy, but rather accepted it as the form of government which had been divinely decreed for Israel at a specific juncture in its history. The king was conceived of as the pivot of the political order, just as God was in charge of the cosmic order. Disorder and anarchy result in a kingless situation, when the country is thrown back into desert-like chaos (Isaiah 3: 1–12; compare Hosea 3 : 4). Kings indeed did fail in history, and were rebuked and punished for their faults. But nowhere in prophetic literature did the experience of the historical failure of kings result in a request for the abolishment of kingship, and for a return to "free" desert life.

In post-Destruction literature the desert motif occupies an insignificant place. The focal point of history is transferred from preconquest times to the days of the monarchy. It is the House of David which takes the center of the stage, and which becomes a fertile source of literary imagery. Biblical eschatology, the vision of the Messianic golden age, is conceived in terms of a revitalized and purified monarchical regime, based on a "new covenant" between Yahweh and the House of David. This concept is present as early as the books of Amos (9: 11–12) and Hosea (3: 3–5), and it gains momentum the more clearly is perceived the approaching abolition of Israelite sovereignty.

Ezekiel does not portray the future Davidic king in full detail. In essence his politico-eschatological message is not different from that of his precusors: in the ideal age to come, a reunited Israel, governed by one king and purified from idol worship, again will occupy the Land of Canaan (Ezekiel 37: 21–27). When all has been said, Ezekiel and his contemporaries, as well as the prophets of preceding generations, would fully accept the strikingly realistic picture of the golden age which has been painted by Jeremiah: "For if you do this thing indeed [execute justice and righteousness], then there shall enter by the gates of this house kings sitting upon the throne of David, riding in chariots and on horses. . . "(Jeremiah 22:4).

VIII

Bypassing the question of the employment of the desert motif in the Apocrypha, an issue which will be discussed separately, we now turn to the analysis of the desert theme in Qumran literature and ideology. Since today only part of the relevant Qumran material has been published, the conclusions to be presented are, of course, tentative.

In view of the fact that the Qumran Sectaries had established their communal center in the very real Judean desert, the comparative rarity of

modernes, pour toute organisation politique centralisée, sont des tendances encore profondément enracinées chez Osée" (P. Humbert, *Revue de L'Histoire et Philosophie de la Religion*, 1:115 [1921]).

the term *midbār* and its cognates in the Sectarian literature is rather surprising. Only twelve occurrences of *midbār* are listed in the concordances[67] which cover the Qumran material published before 1960.[68] Some of these references occur in tiny fragments which remain unintelligible and therefore will not be considered here.[69]

A classification of the occurrences of *midbār* shows that the term once is used topographically and pertains there to the "great desert," which is located to the south of Palestine.[70] In one other case the cosmic creation aspect of the *midbār* theme is involved.[71] Neither of these bears on the issue at hand.

Only one mention of *midbār* is a direct reminiscence of the desert trek, and it cites, most significantly, the extermination of the unbelieving desert generation (Deuteronomy 9:23): "... and their males were cut off in the desert, and he—God—spoke to them at Kadesh: 'Go ye up and possess (the land,' but they chose the desire of) their own spirit and hearkened not to the voice of their Maker'—the commandments He taught them—'and they murmured in their tents' (Psalm 106:25). And the anger of God was kindled against their congregation."[72] In selecting this Pentateuchal passage when referring to the desert period, the author of the Zadokite Documents aligns himself with the overwhelming majority of Old Testament writers in their depreciative attitude towards this historical period. He further clarifies his view by introducing into his exposition of the Deuteronomy passage the quotation from Psalm 106 which elaborates on the desert generation's recurring acts of rebelliousness against Yahweh. The historiographical review presented in Psalm 106: 13–33 is but a condensed catalogue of the nation's inquities in the desert period, to the exclusion even of the signs of temporary remorse which the Pentateuchal account has preserved. The Sectarian author

67. A. M. Habermann, *The Scrolls From the Judean Desert...* (Tel-Aviv, 1959), p. 38 (Hebrew); K. G. Kuhn, *Konkordanz zu den Qumrantexten* (Göttingen, 1960), p. 115.

68. The following sigla will be used in citing Qumran and other documentary material.

1QM The War Scroll, here cited from *The Scroll of the War of the Sons of Light Against the Sons of Darkness*, ed. with an introduction, emendations, and a commentary by Y. Yadin (Jerusalem, 1955).

1QS The Manual of Discipline, cited from *The Manual of Discipline*, ed. M. Burrows, J. C. Trevor, and W. Brownlee (New Haven, 1951).

1QH The Thanksgiving Psalms, cited from *'Oṣar ha-Megilloth ha-Genuzoth*, ed. E. L. Sukenik and N. Avigad (Jerusalem, 1954).

4QpPs 37 A fragment of a commentary (*pesher*) on Psalm 37.

4QpIs[a] A fragment of a commentary on Isaiah 10:28–11:4.

CD The Cairo Documents of the Damascus Covenanters, cited from *The Zadokite Documents*, ed. with translation and notes by C. Rabin. 2nd revised ed. (Oxford, 1958).

69. D. Barthélemy, O. P., and J. T. Milik, *Discoveries in the Judean Desert*, I. *Qumran Cave I* (Oxford, 1955), p. 130, fragment 29:5–6, and p. 144, fragment 42:6.

70. 1QM 2:12.

71. 1QM 10:12–13; Yadin, *The War...*, pp. 318–320.

72. CD III:6–9; Rabin, *Zadokite Documents*, pp. 10–11.

takes as gloomy a view of the desert trek as does the psalmist, if not more so. It is important to stress that like Psalm 106, which is of the "cultic confession" type, the Zadokite Fragments express the very quintessence of the Sectaries' historiosophy. The arrangement of the book—the combination of historical reports with codices of legal injunctions and with exhortatory orations—suggests that it was viewed by the Covenanters as the "new Law," conceived in the image of the Pentateuch. The Sectaries' intense preoccupation with the materials assembled in the documents is illustrated by the fact that in the central library at Qumran this composition survived in seven manuscripts and also was found in private collections.[73] "The number of appearances is higher than that of Pentateuchal MSS (except Deuteronomy) or of Jeremiah and Ezekiel, for example."[74] Therefore, we safely may conclude that the passage from the Zadokite Documents quoted above authoritatively expresses the Sectaries' criticism of the historical desert generation. In this light their new trek into the desert cannot be viewed as an attempt to identify with values and to realize ideals which supposedly were inherent in the historical desert period. It can only be a re-experience of the transition-and-preparation motif which crystallized in the trek traditions.

That this indeed is the significance of the "desert" in Qumran ideology becomes apparent when the desert motif is evaluated against the background of the Sectaries' vision of the future salvation. In complete parallelism with the Biblical Exodus–Trek–Conquest sequence, the retreat into the desert is for the Sectaries the hiatus between the "historical" exodus from the Jewish society of their days, and the "eschatological" conquest of Jerusalem and of the Land of Israel, which lies ahead of them.

"It was perhaps felt that the present age of Israel's history should fittingly end, as it had begun, with a probationary period."[75] The interim period of the "desert" is but an extension of the obnoxious historical past, and does not reach into the brilliant expanse of the future salvation. The retreat into the desert is the last link with Israel's *Unheilsgeschichte*, which began with the Deluge generation, continued into the days of Jacob's sons, to the exception of the patriarchal era, included the Bondage in Egypt and the desert trek, and lasted throughout the times of the kingdom into the Second

73. M. Baillet, "Fragments du documents de Damas, grotte 6," *Revue Biblique*, 63:513–523 (1956).

74. F. M. Cross, Jr., *The Ancient Library of Qumran and Modern Biblical Studies* (New York, 1958), p. 60, n. 46.

75. F. F. Bruce, *Biblical Exegesis in the Qumran Texts* (Grand Rapids, Michigan, 1957), p. 26. See also N. Wieder, "The 'Law-Interpreter' of the Sect of the Dead Sea Scrolls: The Second Moses," *Journal of Jewish Studies*, 4:172 (1953); Yadin, *The War . . .*, pp. 31ff.; H. Kosmala, *Hebräer-Essener-Christen* (Leiden, 1959), pp. 66, 72–73, 171, n. 19.

Temple period.[76] (Compare Ezekiel chapter 20.) This phase shall end with the onset of the approaching ultimate redemption, of which the historical Conquest of Canaan was a mere deficient foreshadow that came to naught. "At the end [of this new interim period] of the forty years they [the wicked] shall cease to exist [*yittammū*] and no wicked man shall be found on earth. But the meek [*'anāwîm*] shall inherit the earth and delight in peace abounding" (Psalm 37:11).[77] This is an interesting piece of Sectarian hermeneutics. With the aid of the transferred trek terminology, the general motif of "the fall of the wicked," which is depicted in Psalm 37, is invested with the specific Sectarian eschatology. The identification of the Sectaries' adversaries with the evil desert generation is made explicit by the reference to "forty years"[78] —a central trek motif—and is further fortified by the employment in the *pesher* of typical trek–transgression terminology: *ha-mamrîm*[79] *yittammū*,[80] the rebellious will come to an end, whereas, on the other hand, the Sectaries shall inherit—*yîršū*[81]—the Kingdom to Come, in the same manner as the Conquest generation had taken possession of the Land of Canaan.

There are, however, in the Qumran writings references to events which are set in the framework of the desert period, and in which the Covenanters discern prototypes of their own historical experiences. The very image of the "Teacher of Righteousness," and certainly that of the "Law Interpreter," undoubtedly was patterned upon the image of Moses.[82] Their personalities mirror a positive aspect of the *midbār* motif in Qumran literature, just as the life history of Moses reflects, at a certain angle, the Biblical evaluation of the desert period.

The "Teacher's" struggle with the "Wicked Priest" is a re-enactment of the strife of Moses and Aaron against the powers of evil that opposed them in their time: "For in ancient times Moses and Aaron arose by the hand of the Prince of Lights, and Belial raised Jannes and his brother by his evil device, when Israel was delivered for the first time. And in the epoch of the desolation of the land there arose the 'removers of the boundary' 'and they led Israel

76. CD II:5–IV:4. Cf, J. M. Allegro, "A Recently Discovered Fragment of a Commentary on Hosea from Qumran's Fourth Cave," *Journal of Biblical Literature*, 78:142–147 (1959).

77. J. M. Allegro, "A Newly-Discovered Fragment of a Commentary on Psalm XXXVII From Qumrân (4QpPs 37)," *Palestine Exploration Quarterly*, 86:71 (1954). Translation by T. H. Gaster, *The Dead Sea Scriptures in English Translation*, with introduction and notes (New York, 1956), p. 259.

78. Cf. also CD XX:14ff.

79. Cf. Numbers 20:10, 24; 27:14; Deuteronomy 1:26, 43; 9:7, 23, 24; 31:27; Psalms 78:17, 56; 106:7, 33, 43; 107:11, et cetera.

80. Numbers 14:34–45; Deuteronomy 2:14–16.

81. Cf. Numbers 14:24.

82. See N. Wieder, *Journal of Jewish Studies*, 4:158–174 (1953).

astray.' "[83] Moses had been called by Yahweh to bring Israel out of the Egyptian bondage; the "Teacher" was appointed to lead the Sectaries out of their bewilderment and distress. When they had become conscious of their shortcomings and their sins, and for twenty years in vain had craved to be illuminated, then "God 'considered their works', for 'with a perfect heart' did they seek Him; and He raised for them 'a teacher of righteousness' to lead them in 'the way of His heart.' "[84] Moses further had been entrusted with bringing "the Law" to the Children of Israel in the desert, and again the "Teacher" follows the same pattern. Remembering His covenant with the Patriarchs, God "raised from Aaron 'men of understanding' and from Israel 'men of wisdom', 'and He caused them to hear'; and they digged the well: 'the well which princes digged, which the nobles of the people delved with the staff' (Numbers 21:18). The Well is the Law. And those that digged it are 'they that turned (from impiety) of Israel.' "[85] In their characteristic *pesher* technique, the "well" is identified with "the Law." that is, with the Sectaries' law. But the specific wilderness setting in which the "well" episode is embedded in the Pentateuch is not commented upon, nor is it hermeneutically utilized in the Sectarian work. The new significance of the "well" is in no way rooted in wilderness reality. It is again the historical event *in* the desert, not the existential experience *of* the desert which forms the basis of the Covenanters' re-employment of trek traditions.

The combination, in the account of the historical desert period, of a positive stratum with a dominant negative stratum results in an ambivalence of attitudes which makes impossible a full identification of the Sectaries with the Exodus generation. It also may explain the surprisingly weak echo of the Pentateuchal desert in the Sectarian literature. We further have to keep in mind the characteristics of the *pesher* technique, which plays an overwhelming role in the Covenanters' reactualization of Biblical traditions. The *pesher* preponderantly is employed as a means by which to prove that the events which befell the "last generation"—that is to say, the Sectaries—were actually foreshadowed in Biblical prophetic literature, including "prophecies" in the Pentateuch, and to a lesser degree in other Biblical compositions of an essentialy nonhistoriographical character. The *pesher* technique is rarely, if ever, applied to traditions of a definable one-time historical nature. Thus the patriarchal narratives or, for that matter, the historical records incorporated in the Former Prophets are seldom utilized in the *pesher* literature. It is for these reasons that Deutero-Isaiah's desert imagery

83. CD V:17–20; Rabin, *Zadokite Documents*, pp. 20–21.

84. CD I: 10–11; Rabin, *Zadokite Documents*, pp. 2–5.

85. Or "the repentants of Israel"—CD VI:2–5; Rabin, *Zadokite Documents*, pp. 20–23; see also Kosmala, *Hebräer . . .* , p. 73, n. 32.

completely eclipses the actual trek period as a source from which is derived the desert motif in the Sectarian literature.

In Deutero-Isaiah's desert vision, Israel is altogether free from the transgressions of which the trek generation so often is accused. The "sin and punishment" theme being absent, Isaiah's desert motif has become a pure and concentrated expression of the "transition and preparation" idea, which the post-trek generations perceived as the essential meaning of the trek tradition. The reactualization of Deutero-Isaiah's "desert" in the Covenanters' conceptions therefore could be performed without the transformation of contents which would have been a *sine qua non* for such a re-employment of the Pentateuchal traditions.

Thus the famous passage in Isaiah 40: 3, "A voice cries: In the wilderness prepare the way of the Lord, make straight in the desert a highway for our God," was established as a central theme in the Covenanters' ideology.

Two references of great ideological import directly arise out of this Isaiah passage.[86] The day of the Sectaries' secession from Israel "is the time when the way is being prepared in the wilderness."[87] Again, even more explicitly it is stated that the Covenanters "are to be kept apart from any consort with froward men, to the end that they may indeed 'go into the wilderness to prepare the way', i.e., do what Scripture enjoins when it says, 'Prepare in the wilderness the way. . . make straight in the desert a highway for our God.' "[88]

The Sectaries literally accept the prophet's call to go into the desert (Isaiah 40:3), expounding it as a summons to dissociate themselves from their sinful contemporaries (1QS 8: 12–16), and to live in the desert as *šbym ltwrh*—"returners to the Torah" (4QpPs 37 1, 1–2)[89]—according to the laws which had been revealed to them (1QS 9: 19–20). This exodus from society makes them into *šby hamdbr*—"penitents of the desert" (4QpPs 37 2,1), with the stress on "penitents"—who are assured of the future salvation. But no "desert ideal" is involved. "Their retreat. . . is to be understood, not in a framework of nature–spirit dualism of Greek type, but in the ethical or 'spirit–spirit' dualism of apocalypticism. They go into the desert for a season, to be born again as the New Israel, to enter into the Covenant of the last days."[90] One might even go one step further. The intellectualizing interpretation of "going into the desert," as an effort to regain from there God's law, clearly indicates how far removed the Sectaries were from a "nature" ideology expressed in wilderness terms. The wilderness symbolizes the state

86. Also, 1QH 8:4–5 reflects Isaian language. Cf. Isaiah 41:19.
87. 1QS 9:19–20. Translation by Gaster, *The Dead Sea Scriptures*, p. 59.
88. 1QS 8:13–14. Trans. by Gaster, *The Dead Sea Scriptures*, p. 56.
89. Allegro, *Palestine Exploration Quarterly*, 86:71 (1954).
90. Cross, *The Ancient Library of Qumran*, p. 56.

of chaotic lawlessness which is the existential setting of the "man of scoffing who... (preached) to Israel 'waters of falsehood' and caused them to go astray in a wilderness [*tōhū*] without way."[91] The chaos has to be overcome from within so that a way may be paved for the new order, the "New Covenant."[92] This new order, like Israel's settlement in Canaan, will not spring from an even-flowing progress of history, but will be born out of turmoil and upheaval. The establishment of the "New Jerusalem" will be preceded by fierce battles against the powers of darkness. These are the ancient "Wars of Yahweh" (Numbers 21:14) all over again, for which the Covenanters discipline themselves by the rules laid down in the War Scroll. In the description of the last war, we encounter references to the *midbār* which appear to be of decisive importance for the evaluation of the desert motif at Qumran. In this eschatological context the Covenanters significantly present themselves as the "exiles of the desert" (*gōlat ha-midbār*) who return from the "desert of the nations" (*midbār ha-'ammîm*)[93] in order to encamp in the outskirts of Jerusalem (*midbar yerūšālayīm*), on the eve of their onslaught on the holy city.[94]

The last-mentioned reference to *midbar yerūšālayīm* belongs to the ecological connotation aspect of *midbār*, and can be disregarded in our discussion. The other two call for some comment. By designating their pre-eschatological—that is, historical—status as an "exile in the wilderness" the Covenanters emphatically present their desert period as a necessary evil, and certainly not as a "mystic ideal."[95] The theological appellation, "desert of the nations," given to their actual abode in the preredemption era, again proves that they regarded the *midbār* stage as an alien and unwelcome phase in their history. The term is appropriated from Ezekiel, who employs it in an oracle in which he likens God's future judgment of Israel to the judgment He meted out to the Exodus generation in the wilderness: "And I will bring you into the wilderness of the nations, and there will I enter into judgment with you face to face. Like as I entered into judgment with your fathers in the wilderness of the land of Egypt..." (Ezekiel 20:35–36). In all these three manifestations —in the Pentateuch, in the Book of Ezekiel, and in the War Scroll—the *midbār* is a typological crystallization of a predestined "mark time" on Israel's march towards salvation.

91. CD I:14–15; Rabin, *Zadokite Documents*, p. 4–5.

92. Cf. also 1QH 8:4–5 (and Isaiah 41:18).

93. The term recurs, partly in a lacuna, in 4QpIs^a, a fragmentary *pesher* on Isaiah 10:28–11:4 (see J. M. Allegro, "Further Messianic References in Qumran," *Journal of Biblical Literature*, 75:174–187 [1956]), and probably also in a fragmentary Hosea manuscript. See Allegro, *Journal of Biblical Literature*, 78:145 (1959).

94. 1QM 1:2–3.

95. A. Dupont-Sommer, *The Essene Writings from Qumran* (Cleveland and New York, 1962), p. 169, n. 2.

The foregoing analysis showed that Pentateuchal trek imagery is not altogether absent from the Qumran writings. Cross certainly is correct when he defines the Covenanters as "an apocalyptic community, a *Heilsgemeinschaft*, imitating the ancient desert sojourn of Mosaic times in anticipation of the dawning Kingdom of God."[96] However, it is of crucial importance to discern that the Sectaries re-experienced the desert of Mosaic time in reflections mediated by the visions of Ezekiel and Deutero-Isaiah.[97] The camp structure which they adopted was chosen by the Sectaries not because it was best suited to desert conditions, but rather as a typological restitution of the historical pre-Conquest tribal organization. For this reason both "camp" and "tribe" can be divorced from their natural setting, and can be transferred, as imagery, into an altogether different ecological and sociological framework. As was already done by the author of the apocalypse which closes the Book of Ezekiel (chapters 40–48), so also in Qumran literature this "nomadic" imagery was fused with motifs which are rooted in a sedentary state: a static sanctuary, and the renascent Davidic monarchy. Thus the *meḥōqēq* of the Pentateuchal "well" episode (Numbers 21: 17–18), in whom the author of the Zadokite Documents recognizes the "Law Interpreter" (*dōrēš ha-tōrāh*), in the eschatological vision is joined by a scion of the House of David, who is the realization of the *meḥōqēq* projected in Jacob's Blessing (Genesis 49:10):[98] "For the *meḥōqēq* refers to the royal mandate; the families of Israel are the [military] units.[99] *Until* the rightful Messiah *shall come*, the shoot of David, for to him and to his seed has been given the royal mandate over his people for everlasting generations." And again, in a *pesher* on Nathan's prophecy (2 Samuel 7: 11–14): "He is the shoot of David who will arise with the Law-interpreter (*dōrēš ha-tōrāh*), who. . . in Zi[on in the l]ast days; as it is written: And I will raise up the house (*'ōhel*) of David that is fallen" (4QpSam).[100]

In conclusion we may say that true to Biblical tradition, for the Qumran Sectaries the desert initially was a place of refuge from persecution, to which they betook themselves in spite of their innate fear of the wilderness.[101] The

96. Cross, *The Ancient Library of Qumran*, p. 56.

97. Isaiah 35:8–11 may have been another of the Biblical proof texts on which the Sectarian desert-trek idea hinged.

98. Our translation differs somewhat from the one proposed by the editor of the fragment. Cf. Allegro, *Journal of Biblical Literature*, 75:174–175 (1956).

99. Here we follow Y. Yadin's reading: *dglym*. See "Some Notes on Commentaries on Genesis XLIX and Isaiah From Qumran Cave Four," *Israel Exploration Journal*, 7:66 (1957). Allegro (*Journal of Biblical Literature*, 75:174–175) reads *rglym* and translates "feet."

100. Allegro, *Journal of Biblical Literature*, 75:176 (1956).

101. See, e.g., 1QH 8:24, which passage is patterned on the equally fear-inspiring description of the wilderness in Jeremiah 17:5–6; 48:6.

flight into the desert effected their secession from their sinful contemporaries, and thus the "wilderness" developed the dimension of "retreat." Ultimately the "desert" became the locale of a period of purification and preparation for the achievement of a new goal. This goal is the conquest of the Holy Land, culminating in the seizure of Jerusalem, and the re-establishment in it of the supreme sanctuary of Israel, in which the "sons of Zadok," Yahweh's truly appointed priests, will officiate *in aeternum*. The desert is a passage to this goal, not the goal itself.

IX

In another context the present author has endeavored to show that in their basic conceptual framework the Judean Covenanters are true heirs to Biblical Judaism.[102] This dictum holds also for their mode of utilization of the desert motif. Notwithstanding adaptational variations, an unbroken line of interpretation of the desert tradition appears to lead from the Bible to post-Biblical Jewish literature, of which the Covenanters' writings are one manifestation. However, these dissenters from the mainstream of Judaism in the period of the Second Temple are not the sole preservers of this chain of tradition. It can be stated provisionally that also in "normative" rabbinic literature, the desert motif retains the same characteristics, and in essence represents the same ideas, as in Biblical imagery.

The new break-through will occur in Christian literature with a monastic orientation when "retreat from the world" is raised from the status of a temporary disengagement to that of a theological ideal. At the same time, self-imposed poverty, frugality, and simplicity become invested with the glory of self-abnegation, which is expected to clear the way for an unimpeded access to individual salvation set in meta-history. It is in this context that the desert is freed from the Biblical conception of it as a cursed wasteland which has to be traversed and serves rather as a bridge to communal salvation in history. The primitivity of desert life which the Hebrews viewed as a frightening and unwelcome phenomenon is reinterpreted to be joyfully accepted as a prerequisite for the longed-for experience of spiritual bliss. Terrestrial Jerusalem had been envisaged by the Israelites as lying beyond the fringes of the desert. The Christian vision of the celestial Jerusalem sprouts from within the confines of the wilderness.

It would be an intriguing exercise in the history of ideas to pursue the reflections of this early Christian configuration of the desert motif in the reputed desert ideal which modern Old Testament scholars perceived in prophetic literature.

102. S. Talmon, "The Calendar Reckoning of the Sect From the Judean Desert," *Scripta Hierosolymitana*, 4:162ff. (1958).

Political and Cosmic Symbolism in Genesis 14 and in Its Babylonian Sources[1]

Michael C. Astour

1. When and By Whom Was Genesis 14 Written?

Chapter 14 of Genesis, so unlike the other tales of the patriarchal cycle in its style and contents, has attracted more attention from Biblicists than has any other single chapter of the Pentateuch. A. Dupont-Sommer once remarked that the history of the study and interpretation of this chapter would provide material for an interesting doctoral dissertation. This, however, is not the purpose of the present article, and we shall therefore only briefly remind the reader that there have been two main approaches to Genesis 14 during the last seventy years.[2] One school[3] considers Genesis 14 as an authentic historical document describing a real major event in the history of Canaan in the so-called Patriarchal Period; if only the four conqueror kings mentioned in it could be identified and located within the framework of the ancient Eastern chronology, the date of the lifetime of Abraham could be established with sufficient accuracy. The other trend regards it as a "late Jewish midrash," invented for the glorification of Abraham long after the Exile, in the Persian or Greek epoch, and devoid of any historical significance.[4] But even representatives of this critical approach have not

1. All dates given are B.C.; for the second millenium, the so-called "low chronology" is followed. Figures preceded by # refer to the cuneiform sign list in Labat, *Manuel*. Books and articles cited are referred to in the notes by brief designations; an alphabetical listing, by the authors' names and abbreviated titles, of these works follows the article.

2. "There are obvious reasons why this chapter should have come to be regarded in some quarters as a 'shibboleth' between two opposite schools of Old Testament criticism" (Skinner, p. 271).

3. Among others: Hommel (1897); Pinches (1902); Böhl, several articles since 1916; Albright, several articles since 1921; Yeivin (1955); Cornelius (1960). One of Albright's more recent remarks is: "If we could date Gen. XIV, our task in placing Abraham within the framework of Palestinian chronology would be simpler, but though evidence continues to strengthen the case for underlying historicity of this chapter, the four kings cannot yet be identified with historical persons" (1951), p. 6.

4. Nöldeke, in 1869, wrote a chapter on "The unhistoricity of the narrative of Gen. XIV" (pp. 156–172), but dated Genesis 14 before 800; Wellhausen (1889), pp. 311f., considered it a very late artificial composition; as do Gunkel, pp. 254–265, and Lods, pp. 616–622.

always shown complete consistency; they have been puzzled by the apparently genuine aspect of the names of the "Eastern kings," and some of them have agreed that the presumed Jewish midrashist may have borrowed these names from a cuneiform source which perhaps told something about an expedition of an Elamite king to Syria-Palestine.[5] In other words, only the participation of Abraham in the story was introduced by the "midrashist"; the rest could well have contained a historical core. In 1894, Theophilus G. Pinches discovered in a lot of late Babylonian tablets, purchased by the British Museum from a dealer named Spartoli, three tablets mentioning names similar to those of three out of the four kings who, according to Genesis 14, were defeated by Abraham. In 1897, he published the cuneiform texts, with transliteration and an attempt at translation.[6] This was hailed as proof of historicity of Genesis 14. But the real contents and meaning of these "Chedorlaomer texts," as they were promptly dubbed, remained extremely obscure. In 1917, Alfred Jeremias published a new (and not very perfect) transliteration of the three tablets with translation and commentary.[7] He partially uncovered the general character and meaning of these texts and correctly identified one of the four kings mentioned in them, but he was unable to unravel the identity of the other three and the relation of the "Chedorlaomer texts" to Genesis 14. Since then very little has been done to shed light on the persons and events described in the three Spartoli tablets. W. F. Albright's numerous contributions (which will be cited further) were limited to the onomastica of the texts, in which he relied upon Jeremias' transliteration. Eventually, the "Chedorlaomer texts" were completely disregarded. The traditionalist school found understanding them too difficult to be of any help in their efforts to prove the historicity of Genesis 14. The critical school had little interest in restoring the background of what in their eyes was only a "late midrash" (though great work was being done in analyzing such late Jewish works as apocrypha, pseudepigrapha, and Qumran scrolls).

Our task is different. Genesis 14 interests us not from the viewpoint of confirmation or negation of the historical existence of Abraham, but as a literary work of original and controversial character which is still very enigmatic. We shall try to establish its relationship with the principal literary sources within the Pentateuch, the approximate date of its composition, its connections with other contemporary Hebrew works, its allegorical or symbolic significance, if any, and its ideological leanings. Then we shall turn to the

5. Winckler (1900), pp. 33f.; Gunkel, p. 263; Skinner, p. 260 ("An Elamite dominion over Palestine in the earlier part of Hammurabi's reign is perfectly credible"— or so it seemed in 1910); Lods, p. 620.

6. Pinches (1897).

7. Jeremias (1917).

"Chedorlaomer texts," which still are the only extant extra-Biblical parallel to Genesis 14, and shall attempt what has been neglected by Assyriologists since their republication by Jeremias in 1917: to decipher their historical contents and background, as well as the moral and cosmic symbolism of their language. And only in the third place shall we be able to compare the "Chedorlaomer texts" and related Assyrian and Babylonan writings to Genesis 14 and to understand why and in what way its author used them as his sources.

The advocates of the "late midrash" theory contend that Genesis 14 was written and interpolated into the Book of Genesis long after the final composition of the Pentateuch. Lods somewhat vaguely assigned it to the same period as Jonah, Ruth, Achicar, and Tobit;[8] Gunkel compared it to Chronicles, Judith, the Twelve Testaments, Jubilees, Esther, and Daniel,[9] that is, to works of the Hellenistic and Hasmonean periods. But Genesis 14 does not present the internal textual unity that should be expected in so late an interpolation; on the contrary, there is clear evidence of additions, alterations, and editorial work within the chapter in no less degree than within chapters and passages which are attributed to the four main sources (J, E, D, and P). The partisans of the "midrash" school blame the lack of skill of the "late Jewish author" for glaring contradictions in the text which would be considered in any other chapter to be sufficient evidence of a multiplicity of separate sources.[10] To begin with, it is obvious that the episode with the king of Sodom and his contest in generosity with Abraham (verses 17, 21–24) can by no means be harmonized with the rest of the chapter. First, in verse 10, the king of Sodom and the king of Gomorrah fell into bitumen pits while fleeing with their defeated troops; in verse 17 the king of Sodom appears before Abraham safe and sound; this cannot be justified by any contrivances.[11] Second, in verse 23 Abraham proudly declares that, except for what his young men have already eaten, he will not take even "a thread" from the recovered goods of the king of Sodom; he would have no right to speak thus if he had already given away an entire tenth of the recovered goods as tithe to Melchizedek (verse 20). Further, according to the main version (verses 14–15), Abraham won his battle against the four kings with

8. Lods, p. 616.

9. Gunkel, pp. 263f.

10. Skinner, p. 269; Gunkel, pp. 254f.; Lods, p. 620.

11. Cassuto, p. 329, declared, in order to save the unity of the chapter, that the fall of the kings of Sodom and Gomorrah into bitumen pits should be understood as their taking refuge there from their pursuers. However, (1) there was no need for them to seek refuge in so unfitting a place since they had the possibility of fleeing with the rest to the mountains (same verse 10); (2) when elsewhere, II Samuel 17:18, we are told about men hiding in a well, the verb used is "to descend," not "to fall"; (3) a fall into a bitumen pit means a certain and very painful death.

only his 318 servants; in the episode with the king of Sodom he had allies in the victorious campaign—Aner, Eshcol, and Mamre (verse 24); from there they were artificially introduced into verse 13, which originally simply said, "...and he was living in the oaks of Mamre," as it is worded in other chapters of Genesis where this locality is mentioned.[12] The author of the insertion changed the toponym Mamre into a person of this name, and gave him as "brothers" Eshcol, another toponym (*naḫal 'Eškōl* near Hebron),[13] and Aner,[14] probably a name of the same kind. The divine name *Yahwe* in the insertion (verse 22) was then glossed *'Ēl 'Elyôn, maker of heaven and earth,* in order to harmonize it with the preceding verses (belonging to the main version).[15] In verse 2, "the king of Bela, that is, Zoar" is a distortion of "Bela, the king of Zoar."[16] Less important glosses are found in other places.[17]

Genesis 14 is very skillfully included in the patriarchal narrative precisely at the place where it belongs: after the story of the separation of Abraham and Lot and the latter's sojourn in Sodom, and before the story of the destruction of Sodom and Gomorrah and Lot's salvation.[18] The author knows that Abraham lived in the oaks of Mamre and Lot lived in Sodom, that Sodom, Gomorrah and two other cities later disappeared ("the Valley of Siddim, that is, the Salt Sea," verse 3), and that the inhabitants of these cities were wicked men (this is shown by the names he gives their kings). He was, therefore, acquainted with the works of J and E and must have been writing at a later date. But it is not possible that the chapter belongs either to J or to E. Benzinger's attempt to discern in its whole extent two parallel versions, a North Israelite (E) and a Judean (J),[19] completely misses the point. Its style and contents are as remote as possible from J and E. Nor can the chapter be ascribed to P, as Procksch[20] claimed without sufficient reasons. Strangely enough, nobody has ever thought about the Deutero-

12. Genesis 13:18, 18:1; Mamre as a locality: Genesis 23:17, 19; 25:9; 35:27; 49:30; 50:13.

13. Skinner, pp. 265f.

14. Codex Samaritanus: ענרם; Qumran Genesis Apocryphon: ערנם; the place-name ענר (I Chronicles 6:55) is probably corrupted.

15. Meinhold, p. 5.

16. Albright (1921), p. 70: "The words ומלך בלע הוא צער . . . are corrupted from ובלע מלך צער...just as in Jos. 10:3 ודביר מלך עגלון is a mistake for ועגלון מלך דביר..."

17. "The son of Abram's brother," verse 12; "born in his house," verse 14, is probably a gloss on חניכיו.

18. Lods, p. 617.

19. Benzinger, pp. 21–27.

20. Procksch, pp. 500–514. Pfeiffer, p. 160, attributed it to the source S (Southern) which he believed he discerned in Genesis. His reason was that the chapter is devoted to the history of South Palestine and Transjordan. But what about Dan, Damascus, and Hobah in the same chapter, where they play no less a role than the southern places cited?

nomist school, which provided the core of Deuteronomy with introductions and conclusions and then, after the fall of Jerusalem and deportation to Babylonia, began a systematic historiographic codification of the past of Israel and Judah. Apparently, the investigators became so accustomed to the belief that Deuteronomist elements may be found only in Deuteronomy and in the books that follow it in the canon of the Old Testament, that they could not consider as Deuteronomist a chapter included in the first book of the Pentateuch. Yet there is nothing impossible in it per se. Wellhausen had very early recognized a Deuteronomist insertion in Exodus 32:29 and perhaps in Exodus 19:22.[21] According to Pfeiffer, "...the editor who attached D to JE (R^D) is identical with the Deuteronomist of Joshua, Judges, and Samuel, and with the Second Deuteronomist of Kings. He is responsible for the edition of the books from Genesis to Kings (omitting Leviticus and the rest of P) issued about 550 B.C. In the Pentateuch, aside from the addition of D to JE, he made only insignificant changes..."[22] However, Pfeiffer's own list of changes and interpolations introduced by the Deuteronomist editor into Genesis, Exodus, and Numbers[23] shows that the editor's participation was far from insignificant, and that he had ample opportunity to insert an entire chapter into the JE collection he had edited.

If we free ourselves from the bonds of habit, the Deuteronomist character of Genesis 14 becomes evident to us. The concise, recordlike style of Genesis 14, with its lists of names, localities, and tribes, its chronological data and figures, is extremely similar to the style of Dt in his historical work. In particular, in his antiquarian approach and erudition, it is very close to the "first introduction" to Deuteronomy (chapters 1–3), in which we also discern contradictory additions similar to the episode with the king of Sodom in Genesis 14.[24] The names of fabulous or prehistoric peoples in Genesis 14 are essentially the same as in Deuteronomy 2: Rephaim in Bashan, Emim in Moab, Horites in Edom; instead of Zamzummim, Genesis 14 has "Zuzim," which is close enough.[25] The term "Amorites" for the natives of

21. Wellhausen (1883), p. 141.

22. Pfeiffer, pp. 284f.

23. *Ibid.*, p. 285.

24. According to the main version, Deuteronomy 2:1, continued in verse 8, the Israelites went "about Mount Seir," through Elath and Eziongeber, in order to avoid the territory of the Edomites; it is interrupted by the insertion, verses 2–7, which makes them, conversely, pass across the territory of Edom, under the condition of purchasing food and water from the Edomites for money. The words "I will not give you any of their land, no, not so much as for the sole of the foot to tread on" (verse 5) sound somewhat related to "I would not take a thread or a sandal-thong or anything that is yours," in the episode with the king of Sodom, Genesis 14:21; the moral is in both cases the same: we do not need anything that is not ours.

25. The Qumran Genesis Apocryphon has זומזמיא (XXI:29) in its version of Genesis 14, which is very close to the original.

Palestine is also characteristic of D and Dt (who follow E), while J uses the term "Canaanites," and P prefers "Hittites." The concluding episode with Melchizedek, the priest-king of Salem (Jerusalem), expresses the aspirations of the Jerusalem priesthood.

The situation assumed by Genesis 14 reflects the political conditions of the neo-Assyrian and neo-Babylonian epoch, as we know them both from the Deuteronomist history of the last kings of Israel and Judah, and from the Assyrian and Chaldean royal inscriptions. "The *annalistic* official style" of Genesis 14[26] is identical with the style of the Deuteronomist in II Kings. Genesis 14 says about the five kings:

> (4) Twelve years they had served Chedorlaomer, and in the thirteenth year they rebelled. (5) And in the fourteenth year Chedorlaomer and the kings that were with him came and subdued (a list of tribes and cities follows) (11) and they took all goods of Sodom and Gomorrah, and all their provisions, and went away.

From the many analogous passages of the Deuteronomist author in II Kings, we shall quote three:

> (7b) And he (Hezekiah) rebelled against the king of Assyria and would not serve him... (13) And in the fourteenth year of King Hezekiah, Sennacherib king of Assyria came up against all the fortified cities of Judah and took them (II Kings 18).
>
> (1) In his days Nebuchadnezzar king of Babylon came up, and Jehoiakim became his servant three years; then he turned and rebelled against him... (10) At that time the servants of Nebuchadnezzar king of Babylon came up to Jerusalem, and the city was besieged... (12b) The king of Babylon took him prisoner in the eighth year of his reign, (13) and carried off all the treasures of the house of Yahwe, and the treasures of the king's house... (II Kings 24).
>
> (20) And Zedekiah rebelled against the king of Babylon. 25: (1) And in the ninth year of his reign, in the tenth month, on the tenth day of the month, Nebuchadnezzar king of Babylon came with all his army against Jerusalem, and laid siege to it... (II Kings 24).

The similarity is striking and leaves no doubt as to when and by whom Genesis 14 was written. What it describes is a typical situation of the period between the eighth and sixth centuries, many times experienced by Israel and Judah and occurring with distressing monotony in the Assyrian royal inscriptions: a king is forced to recognize Assyrian overlordship, and promises to pay the heavy tribute imposed upon him. A few years later he stops paying tribute, and seeks help from other rebel vassals or outside powers. Then, usually the very next year, an Assyrian punitive expedition, often led by the king, invades the country, devastates it, subdues it again, and carries off to Assyria all movable goods and a large number of people. We shall

26. Skinner, p. 256.

meet a few samples of such official records on subsequent pages.[27] Phrases like "turning" of the conquering army in the course of its campaign (Genesis 14:7) and "the rest fled to the mountain" after defeat(Genesis 14:10) are quite common in Assyrian war descriptions.[28]

This correspondence, both in style and in essence, between Gènesis 14 and the historiographic writings of the Deuteronomist school, which reflect the events of the final period of Israelite and Judean statehood, has passed completely unnoticed. Conversely, in order to emphasize by any means whatever the "late Jewish character" of the chapter, commentators have tried to discover in it allegedly late features of a milieu which "admires military glory all the more because it can conduct no wars itself, and, having no warlike exploits to boast of in the present, revels in the mighty deeds of its ancestors."[29] Lods insisted especially on the very late origin of Genesis 14 because of its ascribing fantastic military successes to Abraham—a total defeat of an army of four mighty kings by only 318 armed servants and a handful of native allies.[30] But this has nothing "late" or "midrashic" in it; Abraham's victory is modeled after a certain pattern of Hebrew heroic sagas, not very early, but indubitably pre-Exilic, in which the extreme disproportion in the sizes of the clashing armed forces constitutes the real point of the story. The 318 armed servants of Abraham[31] exactly correspond to the three hundred warriors of Gideon, with whom he defeated, pursued, and annihilated the army of Midianites, Amalekites, and the sons of the East, who were "like locusts for multitude, and their camels were without number, as the sand which is upon the seashore for multitude" (Judges 7:12); the number of killed enemies is given as a hundred and twenty thousand (Judges 8:10). In this respect, Genesis 14 is much more reserved and less fantastic; it does not mention the strength of the adversary at all. The quoted story of Gideon even insists that Gideon's army originally numbered thirty-two thousand men, but was reduced to a mere three hundred on the direct order of Yahwe: "The people with you are too many for me to give the Midianites in their hand, lest Israel vaunt themselves against me, saying, 'My own hand has delivered me' " (Judges 7:16–19). According to Genesis 14:20, it was God Most High who delivered the enemies into Abraham's hand. The victorious battle is described in the same way in both stories:

27. Pages 85 and 97–98 below.

28. See, e.g., *AR*, II, §§ 237, 244.

29. Gunkel, pp. 263f., quoted with sympathy by Skinner, p. 274, and repeated almost verbatim by Lods, p. 621.

30. Lods, p. 620.

31. Only these 318 men participated in the battle, as is clearly stated in Genesis 14:14–15; the Amorite allies, as we have seen, belong to the interpolated episode with the king of Sodom.

Gideon attacked the Midianite camp by night, having divided his three hundred men into three companies (Judges 7:16–19); Abraham "divided against them by night, he and his servants, and routed them" (Genesis 14:15). Wellhausen considered this variant of the Gideon story a part of "the pre-Deuteronomic narratives,"[32] and Pfeiffer found it to contain "E2 material, i.e., pious denunciations and exhortations in the vein of Deuteronomy, although somewhat earlier (about 650)."[33] Thus, the literary tradition of a handful defeating a numerous host goes back to the direct precursors of the Deuteronomist school, already connected with it by a common ideology.[34] This again agrees with the time and background of Genesis 14, which we established on the ground of other indications.

Another Deuteronomist feature is the merging of Sodom and Gomorrah with Admah and Zeboim. Only Hosea (11:8) knows Admah and Zeboim as a symbol of destruction and annihilation, but he, for his part, does not mention Sodom and Gomorrah. Conversely, the narratives of Genesis, devoted to Lot and the destruction of Sodom and Gomorrah, do not name any other cities that suffered the same fate. The tale about the sinful cities of Sodom and Gomorrah, overthrown by Yahwe, was extremely popular in Judah; it is frequently referred to by Amos, Isaiah, Jeremiah, and Ezekiel (who names only Sodom).[35] Admah should most probably be identified with Adamah or Adam on the left bank of the Jordan, near the mouth of the Jabbok,[36] and Zeboim (צביים, צבים, צבאים) may be equated with the city of *Ṣa-bu-ma*[37] (Amarna 274:6), also located in the middle

32. Wellhausen (1883), pp. 244f.

33. Pfeiffer, p. 329.

34. Incidentally, in the seventh century Judah maintained its own army, which fought against the Assyrians under Hezekiah, then among the Assyrian vassals against the Ethiopians in Egypt under Manasseh, and against the Egyptians under Josiah, besides unavoidable skirmishes with Bedouins along the desert frontier.

35. In the tales of Genesis, Sodom stands on the first place; in Abraham's dialogue with Yahwe, Genesis 18:22–23, only the destruction of Sodom is being envisaged. *Gomorrah* (עמרה) has a fitting etymology: Hebrew התעמר (*hithpael*), "to deal violently, tyrannically," Arabic *ġamara*, "to feel hostility." *Sodom* has no such etymology; as early as in Ugarit there existed an ethnicon *sdmy* and a personal name *Sú-du/dú-mu*. It is possible therefore that Sodom is a genuine ancient name, while Gomorrah was perhaps invented to form a pair with it. In the Aramaic Genesis Apocryphon from Qumran, the name of Gomorrah is written עומרם. "Is it to be compared with the very name of *Qumran*, the initial *q* of which is probably the transcription of an Arabic guttural that should rather be rendered by a *ġ*, and the final *n* of which may have replaced an original *m*, according to a current process?" (Dupont-Sommer, p. 304, n. 3).

36. Glueck, p. 5.

37. Albright (1943), p. 9: "The enigmatic '*Ṣabuma*' of Amarna 274 is to be read *Ṣapuna* = Zaphon, also in the middle Jordan Valley..." However, the signs *ma* and *na* are clearly distinguishable in Amarna 274 (autography in Winckler-Abel, no. 138) and in Amarna 273 (autography in Schröder, no. 155), written by the same princess, as they are in general in the Amarna letters from Syria and Palestine (cf. the script chart in Schröder, II, 77, no. 30, and 87, no. 138).

Jordan valley.[38] One may suppose therefore that the destruction of Admah and Zeboim was the Israelite counterpart of the Judean myth of the destruction of Sodom and Gomorrah.[39] Characteristically, all four cities are for the first time combined in Deuteronomy 29:22, a passage belonging to the so-called "second conclusion" of Deuteronomy, composed during the Captivity (which is mentioned in verse 28 of the same chapter). Thence the names passed into the Table of Nations, Genesis 10:19, as the southern limit of Canaan. No other Biblical writer, except the quoted Deuteronomist passage, mentions the destruction of other cities along with Sodom and Gomorrah.[40]

The strange circular itinerary of the four kings was by no means caused by some strategic motives.[41] As was convincingly shown by Umberto Cassuto,[42] it exactly reproduces, in the opposite direction, the route ascribed by Deuteronomy 1–3 to the Israelites traveling to Transjordan under the leadership of Moses. In the first instance, we have: Ashteroth (in Bashan)—Ham (in Ammon)—Kiriathaim (in Moab)—Seir—El-Paran (that is, certainly Elath) as the southernmost point of the march—thence a sharp turn to the northwest up to En-Mishpat ("which is Kadesh")—Hazazon-Tamar (Tamar, now Kurnub)—the Valley of Siddim (Dead Sea). In the second instance: Arad-Hormah (near the Dead Sea)—Kadesh—Ezion-Geber and Elath—circuit (or crossing) of Seir—Moab and the kingdom of Sihon—past the territory of Ammon—the kingdom of Og the Rephaite, who sat in Ashteroth. Though unnoticed by Cassuto, this is another proof of the close connection of Genesis 14 with the Deuteronomist school and especially with Deuteronomy 1–3.

As to the implications of Genesis 14, Cassuto came to the conclusion already made by Benzinger:[43] the four kings had conquered all regions of Transjordan, Edom, and the Negeb, then they victoriously crossed all Canaan

38. Helck, pp. 189, 191 (map), 622 (map), places "Sapuma" (i.e., *Ṣapuma* or *Ṣabuma*) on the eastern bank of the Jordan, "to the north of the mouth of the Jabbok," quite near Adam-Adamah. The numeration of the Amarna tablets followed here is according to Samuel A. B. Mercer, *The Tell el-Amarna Letters*, 2 vols. (Toronto, 1939).

39. Kraeling, p. 70: "It is possible that they [Admah and Zeboim] are a parallel pair and lay elsewhere, perhaps in the Jordan Valley east of the Benjamite country (Hos. 11:8), where there is a valley of Zeboim (I Sam. 13:8)." Unfortunately, the locality cited in I Samuel 13:8 is spelled צבעים; while Hosea's form צבאים may be regarded as a variant of צביים, there can hardly have been a confusion between ע and א or י.

40. The Revised Standard Version's translation of Jeremiah 49:18 and 50:40, "As when Sodom and Gomorrah and their neighbor cities were overthrown" and "As when God overthrew Sodom and Gomorrah and their neighbor cities," is not exact: the Hebrew text mentions no "cities" and has simply ואת־שכניה "and her [*sic* sing.] inhabitants," rather than "neighbors."

41. As read into the text by Yeivin, p. 119.

42. Cassuto, pp. 328f.

43. Since Abraham liberated Canaan from the conqueror, he has the right to it (Benzinger, p. 22).

from south to north, and Abraham overtook them near Dan (the traditional northern border of Israel), defeated them, and pursued them beyond Damascus: therefore Abraham inherited all fruits of their conquests, and everything from Elath to Dan (even including Damascus and South Syria, claimed by the Israelites as part of "Greater Canaan") legally belongs to Abraham and his descendants.[44] We shall add that the final point of the story is the concluding episode with Melchizedek: the victorious Abraham accepts the blessing of the priestly king of Salem (that is, Jerusalem)[45] and pays him a tithe of his booty; thus the holiness of Jerusalem, the spiritual and secular authority of its priesthood and the latter's right to collect tithe from Israel are all traced back to Abraham. The figure of Melchizedek, as has already been mentioned, personifies the longings of the sixth-century priestly hierarchy of Jerusalem: its rivalry with the secular power of the king and its claims toward directing the entire life of the nation.[46]

Thus Genesis 14 fits completely into the framework of the Deuteronomistic didactic and moralizing historiographic essays, which were never written merely for the sake of writing, but always with a definite attitude and as illustrations of the authors' religious and political principles. The date of circa 550 as the time, and the Babylonian Captivity as the locale, of the composition of Genesis 14 may be accepted as sufficiently proven. Owing to its conciseness and excellently balanced structure, Genesis 14 is one of the most outstanding specimens of politico-ideological symbolism in the Bible. However, its symbolic subtext is not limited to the above.

2. The Personal and Geographical Names in Genesis 14

The names of the kings of the five cities are quite obviously selected in accordance with the reputed sinful and unrighteous character of these cities.[47] This was quite evident to the Midrashists (Bereshit Rabba)[48] and Rashi (*ad* Genesis 14). Four of the five names are immediately transparent: Bera (ברע), "in evil," Birsha (ברשע), "in wickedness," Shemeber (שמאבר), to be read with the Samaritan Recension and Qumran Genesis Apocryphon XXI:25 *Šem-'ābad* (שמאבד), "the name is lost," Bela (בלע), "swal-

44. Cassuto, p. 329.

45. Attempts, such as those of Dhorme (1956), p. 45, to seek Salem near Shechem, or to identify it with Shechem, as does Landersdorfer, pp. 203ff., miss the point. In Psalm 76:3 Salem is identified with Zion, and Psalm 110:2, 4, associates Melchizedek with Zion.

46. It is possible that the second element of the name Melchi-zedek alludes to Zadok, the first priest of the Jerusalem temple. It was precisely in the sixth century that his descendants were described by Ezekiel (44:10–17) and by the Deuteronomist (1 Samuel 2:35) as the sole legitimate priests of Yahwe.

47. Attempts to defend their genuine character as "Amorite names of the second millennium" (Pilter, *passim*) are gratuitous.

48. Ed. Theodor, I, 409f.

lowed or destroyed." The names of these rebellious vassals should be compared to the epithets with which Assyrian kings branded their own unloyal subject kings: for example, "Mutallu of the land of Qummuḫu, a wicked Hittite, who did not fear the name of the gods, a planner of evil, plotter of iniquity, put his trust in Argisti, king of Urartu, an ally who could not save him, and stopped the yearly payment of tribute and tax and withheld his gifts,"[49] or "Marduk-apal-iddina, son of Iakin, king of Chaldea, murderer, exact copy of a wicked demon," et cetera.[50] It is not hard to see that the names of the defeated rebels in Genesis 14 could have been formed after such epithets. As to the fifth name, Shinab (שנאב), it has often been explained[51] as a genuine theophorous name: "Sin (the Babylonian Moon-god) is the father." However, the transcription of the Akkadian divine name *Sin* by ש is singular; the regular Hebrew transcription uses ס (סנחריב, סנבלט); the sibilant in *Sin* could be pronounced "sh" neither in the Assyrian, nor in the Babylonian dialect (the only proof to the contrary, שנאצר, is ambiguous). In the context of the other four names, it is much more plausible to consider this one, too, as pejorative. Rashi probably guessed correctly when he interpreted it שונא אביו שבשמים, "who hated his father in heaven." Indeed, in a fragment of an Assyrian tablet,[52] containing part of a legend about a tyrant who cruelly oppressed the Babylonians by statutory labor, he is characterized not only *lìbba*^{ba}*-šú il-te-im-na* (I:2, 4), "his heart plotted evil," but also *a-bi ka-la ilâni*^{meš} *i-zi-ru* (I:3), "he hated the father of all gods."[53] This method of forming names is quite characteristic of the Deuteronomist: in the only episode of the Book of Judges which was not only edited but completely composed by the Deuteronomist (Judges 3:7–11), the foreign oppressor for whom the Israelites served for eight years until they were delivered by Othniel bears the name Cushan-rishathaim (כושן־רשעתים), "Arab (?)[54] of double-wickedness."

The names of their adversaries—Amraphel king of Shinar, Arioch king of Ellasar, Chedorlaomer king of Elam, and Tidal king of Goim— are of quite a different kind: they are no "speaking names" and have no Hebrew etymologies. Their countries, too, are in quite a different category from Sodom, Gomorrah, et cetera. It is precisely this circumstance that imparts

49. Sargon II's Display Inscription, *AR*, II, § 64.

50. *Ibid.*, § 66.

51. Recently by Koehler-Baumgartner, p. 996.

52. British Museum K. 3657, published by King (1902), I, 220 (transliteration); II, pl. LXXIII (cuneiform text).

53. See also Page 95 below, where we tentatively read *nakru* (KÚR) *a-bi*, "enemy of the father," applied to a godless ruler in one of the "Chedorlaomer texts." For שנא אב ⟩ שנאב, cf. רפא אל ⟩ רפאל.

54. Cf. כושן in parallelism to מדין, Habakkuk 3:7.

to Genesis 14 the external aspect of an authentic historical narrative. But before we can judge it, it is necessary to define the countries referred to.

The name *Shinar* (שנער), whatever its origin, designates Babylonia in all places in the Bible where it is found.[55] It appears in the texts of the second millennium as *Śa-n-ga-ra* (Egyptian),[56] *Ša-an-ḫa-ar* (Amarna letter from Cyprus, 35:49), and *Ša-an-ḫa-ra* (Hittite).[57] There have been suggestions[58] that this name referred not to Babylonia, but to a certain supposed country in northeastern Mesopotamia, where the classical Singara was situated and which still bears the name of Ğebel Sinğar, west of Mossul. However, this region was then an integral part of the kingdom of Mitanni and could not be referred to as a separate great power (as it is in the Cypriot letter). It is true that in the Hittite invocation to the cedar gods the countries of Assur, Babylon, and Šanḫara are mentioned together,[59] but the distinction between Babylon itself and the rest of Babylonia conforms with the official Babylonian royal title under the Cassite dynasty: see, for example, the title of Agum II: *šar Kaš-ši-i ù Ak-ka-di-i šar mât Bâbili^{ki} ra-pa-aš-ti*,[60] "king of Kaššu and Akkad, king of the wide land of Babylon," or of Burnaburiaš: *l u g a l K á. d i n g i r. r a. k i l u g a l K i. e n. g i. k i U r i*,[61] "king of Babylon, king of Sumer and Akkad," still observed by Esarhaddon, who called himself "governor of Babylon, king of Karduniaš."[62] Other Hittite texts clearly show that Šanḫara was a synonym for Babylonia.[63] Amraphel king of Shinar was identified by Pinches with no less a figure on the Babylonian throne than Ḫammurapi;[64] after being abandoned for a

55. See Koehler-Baumgartner, p. 999, where occurrences are listed and Arno Poebel's etymology from *Šingi-Uri*, "Sumer and Akkad," is quoted from *AJSL*, LXVIII (1934).

56. See Gardiner, I, 210*f. for instances.

57. See *ANET*, p. 352, and Note 63 below.

58. Among others, Albright (1921), p. 73, and Böhl (1930), p. 13; they needed the location to make the coalition reported in Genesis 14 less improbable.

59. *ANET*, p. 352.

60. Schrader, III, part 1, p. 136.

61. *Ibid.*, p. 152.

62. *ANET*, p. 290.

63. Schaeffer, pp. 99ff., points to the fact that Tawananna, third wife of the Hittite king Šuppiluliuma, was, according to her own seal, DUMU.SAL LUGAL KUR KÁ. DINGIR.RA, "daughter of the king of the land of Babylon," while in the document KUB XIV:4 it is said that she brought with her certain objects from *Šanḫara*, which is put in apposition to *Ḫattušaš*. The Hittitologist H. G. Güterbock wrote (Schaeffer, p. 103, n. 3): "I also believe that *Šanḫara* is Babylon, in spite of all discussions and arguments to the contrary. My main argument for this is KUB XXVI:74, a story parallel to the passage about the raid on Babylon by Muršili I in the Telipinu text with *Šanḫara* in line 10, where Telipinu says KÁ.DINGIR.RA."

64. The reasoning was as follows: the name *Ḫammurabi*, composed with the West Semitic element *'amm*, could be written also *Am-mu-ra-bi* (this form is actually attested to, although not for the Babylonian lawgiver). Now, if we admit that the last syllable is written *bí* (# 172) instead of *bi* (# 214), the former sign could also be read *ne*, *bil*, and *pil*, whence the possibility of an aberrant reading *Am-mu-ra-pil* (cf. Dhorme [1951], p.

considerable period, this equation was recently revived by Cornelius.[65]

Ellasar (אלסר) used to be identified with Larsa, a city in South Babylonia which had been the capital of an independent kingdom before it was annexed by Ḫammurapi in 1697. This identification was founded less on a similarity of names (which is quite remote) than on a desire to find the prototype of Arioch in its king Warad-Sin.[66] But when it turned out that Warad-Sin had been dead for thirty years when Ḫammurapi mounted the throne of Babylon, the entire construction lost its attractiveness, and the name Ellasar ceased to seem so similar to Larsa.[67] Böhl, having sacrificed the enticing identity Amraphel = Ḫammurapi to another one (Tidal = Tudḫaliaš II), rejected the Larsan equations, instead identifying Ellasar with תלאשר (II Kings 19:12; Isaiah 37:12) in North Mesopotamia, to match the presumed Shinar-Singara.[68] The correspondence is again far from being satisfactory, especially since the real name of Tel-assar was *Til-Bašeri*, as was pointed out by Dhorme.[69] More recently, Yeivin came out with the equation of Elassar with the North Mesopotamian city of *Ilânṣûrâ*, or as he prefers to transliterate it, *Ilânsûrâ*,[70] mentioned in the Mari texts of the eighteenth century; Elassar would have been derived from a presumed form **Ilâssûrâ*, with *n* assimilated to the following *s*.[71] However, it is intrinsically much more probable that a kingdom listed along with such powers as Babylonia and Elam would belong to the same category. Ellasar is easily explained as referring to Assur: either, following Dhorme[72] and Böhl,[73] as transcription of *âl Aššur*, "the

262). However, the form **Am-mu-ra-bí* does not actually occur; and since we know now that the pronunciation of the last syllable was *pí* rather than *bi*, the possibility of its replacement by *bí* appears very improbable.

65. Amraphel = "Ḫammurabi-El, deified toward the end of his life," Cornelius (1960), p. 3. But deification of kings in Babylonia (and, as we know now, in Syria, too) was expressed in writing by putting the divine determinative in front of their names (e.g., ᵈ*Šulgi*), not behind. Names of the type of that suggested by Cornelius did exist, but they were borne by commoners as theophorous names.

66. The reasons were these: if the ideogram forming the first element is read as Sumerian *èri* instead of Akkadian *warad*, "servant," and the divine name *Sin* is replaced by one of its Sumerian equivalents *A-ku* (cf. *ŠL*, IV, 2, no. 13), one gets **Èri-a-ku*, very close to *'Aryôk*.

67. Dhorme, who in 1931 still defended the equation Ellasar = Larsa, tried to replace Warad-Sin by his brother Rîm-Sin, deposed by Ḫammurapi in 1697 (new low chronology), but the supposed series of transformations: "*Rîm-Sin*, *Ri-wa-a-aku*, *Eri-wa-aku*, *Ariok*" (Dhorme [1951], p. 262) is very weak, and he abandoned it later ([1956], I, 42).

68. Böhl (1930), p. 23 (Arioch became, by the same token, an imagined *Aryaka*, "the Aryan"); he changed his opinion later ([1953], p. 46).

69. Dhorme (1951), p. 265.

70. The sign # 6 could, indeed, be read not only *zu*/*ṣu*, but also *sú*.

71. Yeivin, p. 124. He also identified Arioch with *Arriwuk*, "son" (or rather, vassal) of king Zimrilim of Mari (this had been proposed earlier by Böhl [1953], p. 44). However, the king of Ilânṣûrâ at the time of the Mari archives was not Arriwuk but Ḫali-sumu (Kupper, pp. 9, 10 [n. 2], 48, 230 [n. 1], 255). For occurrences of Ilânṣûrâ, see *ARM*, XV, 129.

72. Dhorme (1956), I, 42.

73. Böhl (1953), p. 46.

city of Assur" (compare the Hebrew transcription of *Aššur-aḫḫê-iddina* through אסרחדון), or, even better, as a phonetic reading of the frequent ideogram for the city of Assur: A.LA$_5$.SAR, as suggested by Dossin.[74]

Elam is clear in itself, and, moreover, its king Chedorlaomer (כדרלעמר) bears a name which, though not attested to in the documents, seems perfectly Elamite. Names with the first element *Kudur-* (in Akkadian; *Kutir-* in Elamite) were actually borne by Elamite kings (Kudur-Mabuk, Kudur-Naḫḫundu I and II). The common interpretation of לעמר as the Elamite divine name *Lagamar* is, conversely, not justified (see Pages 91, 93–94 below).

As to the vague term *Gôyîm* ("nations"), the clue is given by the name of its king, Tidal (תדעל). In 1906, Jensen wrote: "Where Tidal did reside, no mortal knows,"[75] but after the discovery of the Boğazköy archives Tidal became the least obscure of the four, since Böhl identified this name with *Tudḫaliya(š)*[76]—a name borne by four kings of Ḫatti: Tudḫaliaš I (*circa* 1635–1620), Tudḫaliaš II (*circa* 1450), Tudḫaliaš III (*circa* 1400–1380), and Tudḫaliaš IV (*circa* 1250–1230). The accuracy of the Hebrew transcription was not doubted even before the archives of Ugarit confirmed it by revealing the alphabetic transcription *Tdġl* or *Ttġl*.[77]

Thus, Genesis 14 puts on the stage four mighty powers of the ancient East: Babylonia, Assyria, Elam, and Ḫatti. Our knowledge of the history of the ancient Near East is now complete enough for us to state with absolute certitude that a coalition of these four powers never took place, even very briefly. Nor is it possible by the trickiest combinations to synchronize any four kings of these countries who could be assumed to have served as prototypes for the four kings of Genesis 14. But at the same time the selection of these four countries is by no means accidental. In the neo-Assyrian and neo-Babylonian time—that is, at the time when Genesis 14 was written — *Ḫatti* became the equivalent of or substitute for the more ancient geographical notion *Amurru*—the territory west of the Euphrates—and Assyria became the synonym or substitute for the older term *Subartu*, which designated Upper Mesopotamia to the north of Babylonia. Now, the Babylonians, followed by the Assyrians, had divided from time immemorial the entire earth (imagined as circular) into four quadrants (*kibrâtum arba'um, kibrât irbitti*),[78] which bore the names of the correspondingly situated countries.

74. Dossin, pp. 118f. The ideogram is usually noted A.USAR, but the reading of USAR is dubious (see Labat, # 579), and it is composed of the signs LA$_5$ (# 482) + SAR (# 152).

75. Jensen, p. 328.

76. Böhl (1916), p. 68; (1924), p. 151; (1930), p. 14.

77. *PRU II*, nos. 39:21; 69:4. The person so named was a simple commoner.

78. *B.u.A.*, II, 375.

The schema (Figure A)[79] played an enormous role in predictions and astrology.

South --- Akkad,
North --- Subartu,
East --- Elam,
West --- Amurru.

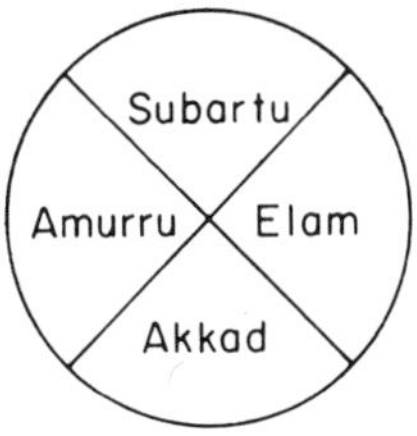

Figure A. The Babylonian Divisions of the World.

Exactly in this order are the four kings listed the first time (Genesis 14:1); the second time (14:9), they are also listed in cross-order, but this time beginning with the East: East–West, South–North.

The equivalence of the notions Subartu and Assyria in the first millennium follows from numerous documents. Thus, in the reports of the astrologers to Esarhaddon, founded on the vast compendium *Anuma Anu, Enlil,*[80] it is said: "If the moon is seen on Nisan 30, the Aḫlamê-Bedouins will devastate the land of Subartu, and a strange tongue will conquer the land of Amurru. We (that is, Assyria) are Subartu."[81] The geographical part of a Sumero-Akkadian dictionary includes the equation: m a. d a S u. b i r. k i | *Subarti* | *mât Aš[šur]*.[82] Nabonidus, in his chronicle, calls Sennacherib "king of Subartu," and the war against Assyria under Nabopalassar is called the war against Subartu.[83]

The quoted dictionary also contains such equations as:

ma.da giš.erin.ki	Cedar Mountains	Land of Ḫatti
má.er.ki	*ditto*	*ditto.*[84]

Now the Cedar Mountains lay in Syria (Amurru), and the city of *Má-er* is Mari, which according to Babylonian notions was located outside of Akkad, and thus within the quadrant of Amurru, here replaced by Ḫatti.

Sargon II writes in his Annals that in 722 he settled Babylonians in the land of Ḫatti;[85] these are evidently the same Babylonians whom, according

79. Cf., e.g., Virolleaud, *Ištar*, in *L'Astrologie chaldéenne*, XXVI, 22–27. The graphic scheme of the four quadrants is taken from Jeremias (1929), p, 112. With distortion of geographical coordinates, one also finds: front—Akkad, rear—Elam, right—Subartu, left—Amurru: *B.u.A.*, II, 375; Jeremias (1929), p. 112.

80. Published by Virolleaud in autography and transliteration as *L'Astrologie chaldéenne*.

81. Thompson, no. 62; *B.u.A.*, II, 376.

82. *B.u.A.*, II, 376.

83. *ANET*, p. 309.

84. *B.u.A.*, II, 376.

85. *AR*, II, §4.

to II Kings 17:24, the king of Assyria settled in the towns of Samaria. He "tore away Mannaeans from their places and settled them in Ḫatti of Amurru" (*sic*).[86] The same king calls the inhabitants of the Philistine Ashdod, Hittites,[87] and Ia'ubidi of Hamath, a Hittite (though from his name he must have been a pure Semite).[88] Sennacherib declares: "In my third campaign I marched against Ḫatti"—but what he describes is the conquest of Phoenician cities, and then he indiscriminately shifts to the term *Amurru* while listing Phoenician and Palestinian kings.[89] Esarhaddon lists kings of Palestine and Phoenicia as "kings of Ḫatti and the other side of the river."[90] In the neo-Babylonian epoch Ḫatti was the commonly used official name of Syria and Palestine. Thus, the neo-Babylonian chronicle published by Wiseman uses exclusively the name "Ḫatti-country" for all of Syria and Palestine, from Carchemish to the border of Egypt, including Hamath, Ashkelon, Judah, and the borders of Arabia—briefly, what the Babylonians of the second millennium called *Amurru*.[91] Only Nabonidus, who liked archaic terms, used the name *Amurru* once.[92] And in the same period the priestly source (P) of Genesis calls the natives of Canaan "Hittites"—clearly under the influence of the official terminology of the time.

It is quite natural that a work composed in the sixth century, even if based on older cosmographical and astrological texts, would have replaced the antiquated terms *Subartu* and *Amurru* by their modern counterparts *Assyria* and *Ḫatti*. If the author of Genesis 14, instead of plain "Babel," "Assur," and "Hittites," used the much rarer "Shinar," the ideographic "Ellasar," and the vague "Goyim,"[93] he was merely following the same style that found its expression in introducing into his work fabulous peoples, and such archaic names as El-Paran, En-Mishpat, Hazazon-Tamar, Salem instead of Jerusalem, or "Valley of Shaweh" for "Valley of the King."

Thus, the symbolism of Genesis 14 is not limited to Palestine. Through the introduction of the kings of the four world quadrants, the author widens his symbolism to universal, even cosmic dimensions. For it must be noted that the Babylonian thought which created the idea of the four quadrants did not limit them to the earth alone. "According to the Babylonian-Assyrian view, heaven and earth are in a certain mutual relation, namely, 'the below,'

86. *Ibid.*, §6.
87. *Ibid.*, §§ 30, 62.
88. *Ibid.*, § 55.
89. *Ibid.*, §§ 233f.
90. *ANET*, p. 291.
91. Wiseman, pp. 68–75 ([mât]*Ḫat-tú* is mentioned eighteen times).
92. Dhorme (1951), p. 163.
93. Nöldeke, p. 154, compared איי הגוים (Genesis 10:5).

the earth, is only a weaker replica of 'the above,' heaven. Macrocosm is essentially equal to microcosm."[94]

> ...The prototypes of all lands, rivers, cities, and temples exist in heaven as certain constellations, while these terrestrial things are only replicas thereof... Accordingly, a comprehensive celestial geography was constructed... Similarly, sun and moon were divided, exactly as the earth, in different countries, so that "the right side of the moon" signified Akkad, "the left side of the moon," Elam, "the upper part of the moon," Amurru, and "the lower part of the moon," Subartu.[95]

We note it here, for we shall meet this cosmic symbolism in our study of the "Chedorlaomer texts."

3. The Characters and Historical References in the "Chedorlaomer Texts"

The above helps us to understand why Genesis 14 presents kings of Babylonia, Assyria, Elam, and Ḫatti, but it leaves open the question of the source whence its author took the names of these four kings, and whether they are arbitrarily picked up or invented, or belong to real historical figures. As already mentioned, the discovery by Pinches of three more or less similar names in the Spartoli tablets earned them the popular name "Chedorlaomer texts" and gave grounds for regarding them as proof of the historicity of Genesis 14. The tablets in question are Sp. III, 2; Sp. 158 + Sp. II, 962; and Sp. II, 987. They belong to a very late period (the Arsacid Age, according to Jeremias; that is, after 142 B.C.), but they certainly are copies or versions of earlier texts; however, for reasons expounded below, their originals could not have been composed earlier than the mid-seventh century. Sp. III, 2, is a summary in prose; the other two tablets are fragments of poetic works presenting the same events in detail, in a very elevated metaphorical language. They contain descriptions of certain disasters that befell the Babylonians, and religious and moralistic interpretations of these events as divine punishment for sins that had been committed. The tablets are partially damaged; moreover, they are full of difficult and intentionally cryptic ideographic writings which are characteristic of Babylonian scholarly works, especially those of later times.[96] In particular, the persons described are disguised under rebuslike spellings or pseudonyms; but knowledge of the

94. *B.u.A.*, II, 107.

95. *Ibid.*, p. 110; cf. also the text VAT 947, quoted in Jeremias (1929), p. 112, in which the division in these same four lands is applied to the star ŠU.PA (= Arcturus, Labat, # 354), identified with the city of Assur.

96. "Strangely enough, the ancient Orientals considered literary products as especially beautiful and venerable if they contained many obscure expressions and unusual writings and were thus more or less unintelligible to ordinary mortals," *B.u.A.*, II, 361.

factual events of Babylonian history makes it perfectly possible to decipher these enigmatic names and to identify their bearers with historical characters.

In Sp. III, 2, the most concise and comprehensive of the three texts, four hostile kings are described. The name of the first is broken off, but the fragmentary lines devoted to him (obverse 1–9a) allow us to identify him with Ibil-Tutu, who appears in Sp. 158 + Sp. II, 962, and whom we shall examine on Pages 94–99 below. The names of the other three are preserved: they were invaders who devastated Babylon and its temple Esagila and were then murdered by their own sons. One of them is a king of Elam whose name begins with *Kudur-* and *may* be read very similarly to Chedorlaomer; he also appears in Sp. II, 987, and is the principal hero of Sp. 158 + Sp. II, 962. The patronymic of the second *may* be read as something very reminiscent of Arioch; he also appears in Sp. II, 987. The name of the third is identical with Tidal. We shall begin our investigation in the order of their appearance in Sp. III, 2.

The name of the first ruler was transliterated by Pinches in the headings of his autography as *Dûr-maḫ-ilâni*, and *Dûr-ṣir-ilâni* ("high wall of the gods," *ṣiru* being one of the values of the ideogram MAḪ) in his transliteration.[97] Jeremias, too, wrote *Dûr*-MAḪ-*ilâni*^{pl}.[98] Actually, the first part of the name is written BÀD.MAḪ (BÀD = *dûr*) only in Sp. III, 2: obverse 9; in Sp. II, 987: 19, the rare combination BÀD.MAḪ is replaced by a more common one, DUR.MAḪ, in which DUR (phonetic *dur*) has the ideographic value of *riksu*, *turru*, "bond."[99] Neither Jeremias, nor Albright, who followed his transliterations, noted this difference in spelling. True, the interchange of homophones does not play any important role here and only indicates that the scribe did not observe a consistent orthography, but this is a valuable precedent for other similar occurrences in our texts. Albright limited himself to rewriting Jeremias' transliteration in the ideograms to which it seemed to point: BÀD.MAḪ.DINGIR.MEŠ,[100] and proceeded from there in his interpretation of the name: "Since BÀD.MAḪ = *tukultu* (Meissner, 2919), and ^{d}MAḪ = *bêlit ilî* or *bêlit ilâni* (Brünnow, 1050 etc.), I have no hesitation in regarding the writing as equivalent to BÀD.MAḪ.MAḪ.DINGIR.MEŠ... *Tukulti-Bêlit-ilî* (*ilâni*) is a perfectly

97. Pinches (1897), pp. 73, 82ff.

98. Jeremias (1917), pp. 80ff.

99. DUR.MAḪ, Akkadianized *durmaḫu*; cf. *Enuma Eliš* VII:95, Marduk's name, no. 38: ^{d}LUGAL. DUR. MAḪ *šar mar-kas ilâni*^{meš} *be-el dur-ma-ḫi*, "^{d} LUGAL. DUR. MAḪ, king of the bond of the gods, lord of Durmaḫu" (King [1902], p. 104). Signification of *durmaḫu*: Speiser in *ANET*, p. 71, n. 139: "Lofty Abode"; Bezold, s.v. "ruler's throne (?)"; *CAD*, s.v.: "a strong rope made of reeds." In the Assyrian commentary to *Enuma Eliš* VII (K. 4406, King [1902], I, 165; II, pl. LIV) we notice an extremely free handling of homophones: DÚR (=*šubtu*, "abode") is translated *mar-ka-su*, as though it were DUR.

100. Albright (1921), p. 71; (1926), p. 236.

regular name, pointing both to the late period because of the use of the element *tukulti*, and to the early period, when *Bêlit-ilî* was one of the most popular Babylonian goddesses."[101]

Now the name *Tukulti-Bêlit-ilî* (*ilâni*), obtained through an unjustified interpolation of another MAḪ, although "perfectly regular," does not occur in cuneiform documents. This is a strange omission for a man who is said to have captured and devastated Babylon and even seized its kingship. Had Albright looked into the cuneiform text of the tablet, he would have found that Jeremias' ambiguous *-ilâni*^{pl} corresponds not to DINGIR.MEŠ, but at best to DINGIR.ME.[102] Now the spelling DINGIR.ME for *ilâni* is utterly improbable in a text where *ilâni* occurs four times (obverse 5; reverse 5, 8, 11) and is always normally written DINGIR.MEŠ. In neo-Babylonian writing, the signs ME (# 532) and MAŠ/BAR (# 74) were written in almost the same way,[103] and in our text they are absolutely identical (see Figure B). The alleged DINGIR (= AN).ME in the name we are now dealing with is absolutely undistinguishable from AN.BAR (= *parzillu*, "iron") in the same tablet, reverse 3. This means that instead of the supposed DINGIR.ME, our name contains the standard ideographic writing DINGIR.MAŠ = ^{d}*Ninurta*.[104] Thus, accepting Albright's felicitous idea that BÀD.MAḪ

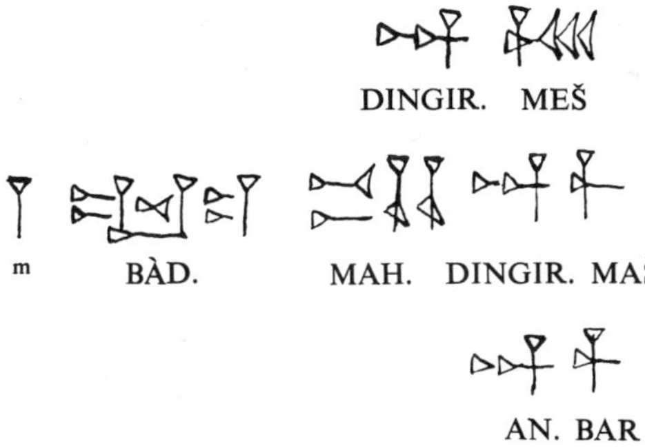

Figure B.

stands for *Tukulti*, we obtain: ^{m}BÀD.MAḪ.DINGIR.MAŠ = ^{m}*Tukulti*-^{d}*Ninurta*. This is also "a perfectly regular name," but it has the following advantages: first, it corresponds to the factual writing of the text; second, a bearer of this name, the Assyrian king Tukulti-Ninurta I (1257–1221,

101. Albright (1921), p. 71, n. 5 = (1926), p. 236, n. 16.

102. Pinches (1897), p. 83, line 9; p. 85, line 19. *CAD*, s.v. *durmaḫu*, quotes the two variants as [^{m}]DUR.MAḪ.DINGIR.ME and ^{m}BÀD.MAḪ.DINGIR.ME.

103. Cf. the signs in Labat, # 74 and # 532.

104. AN.BAR (*parzillu*) and DINGIR.MAŠ (^{d}*Ninurta*) are distinguished conventionally; both are written with the same signs, # 13 and # 74.

according to Cornelius;[105] 1243–1207, according to Moortgat)[106] actually performed what is said in the "Chedorlaomer texts":

(9b) ^{m}*Tukulti-*^{d}*Ninurta aplu* (A) *šá* ^{m}ÌR-^{d}*É-a-ku*

(10) [*Bâbili*^{ki} *âlam ta-*]*na-a-tam*[107] *iš-lul mê* (A^{meš}) *eli Bâbili*^{ki} (E^{ki}) *u É-sag-gíl*

(11) [*ú-šar-da-a*[108] *mâ*]*r-šú ina* ^{iṣ}*kakki qâtâ*^{II}*-šú ki az-lu ú-ṭa-bi-iḫ-šú*

(12) [ ] *ana išâti iq-*⌜*lu*⌝*-ši* ^{amêl}*šîba*^{ba} *u ṣiḫra ina* ^{iṣ}*kakki*

(13a) [*ú-šam-qit*[109] *rab*]*â u ṣiḫra ik-ki-is* (Sp. III, 2: obverse)

"(9b) Tukulti-Ninurta, son of ÌR-Eaku, (10) [Babylon, the city of g]lory, he plundered, water over Babylon and Esagil (11) [he led. His] son, with the weapon of his hands, slaughtered him like a lamb. (12) [ ] in fire he burned her, old and young with weapon (13a) [he overthrew, gr]eat and small he cut down."[110]

In Sp. II, 987, Tukulti-Ninurta is characterized as "king, son of a king" (*šarru mâr šarri*) and "son of a king's daughter" (*mâr mârat šarri*), who "[carried away] the booty" (*šá šal-lat*[...]), "sat on the throne of kingship" (*ina* ^{iṣ}*kussi šarru-tú ú-ši-ib-ma*) and "was called up as lord of Babylon" (*in-nam-bi bêl Bâbili*^{ki}) (lines 17–22). Then in line 27, he is certainly understood as one of those who "carried off the gods among the booty" (*ilâni*^{meš} *ina šal-lat ú-še-iṣ-ṣ*[*u-u*]).

Now here is an excerpt from the Babylonian Chronicle, column IV:1–13:[111]

> The defeat of Kaštiliaš[112] he[113] brought about [............] Before Ninurta he set him [....] Tukulti-Ninurta returned to Babylon and [......] they drew near to Babylon. The wall of Babylon he destroyed, the Babylonians he put to the sword. The treasure of Esagila and Babylon he profanely brought forth and the great god Marduk he removed from his abode and carried him off to Assyria. The rule (*lit.*, way) of his governors he established in Karduniaš.[114] For seven years Tukulti-Ninurta ruled. Thereafter the nobles of Akkad and Karduniaš revolted and they set Adad-šum-uṣur on the throne of his father. As for Tukulti-Ninurta, who had brought evil upon Babylon, Aššur-nâṣir-pal,[115] his

105. Cornelius (1956), p. 309.

106. Moortgat, p. 497.

107. We restore after Sp. II, 987:4: *Bâbili*^{ki} *al ta-na-*[...].

108. Restored according to the context; the verb used to fill the gap is taken from Sennacherib's Bavian inscription, line 12, about leading water into a new canal.

109. Restored according to the context and to obv.:9 of the same text.

110. The lines 12–13a seem to refer to Tukulti-Ninurta rather than to his son.

111. *AR*, I, §141 (Luckenbill's "Tukulti-Urta" is corrected throughout the quotation).

112. Kaštiliaš III (IV), a king of the Cassite Dynasty (1248–1241, with Cornelius; 1237–1229, with Moortgat).

113. = Tukulti-Ninurta.

114. Karduniaš—one of the names of Babylonia under the Cassite Dynasty, and sporadically during the first millennium.

115. Aššur-nâdin-apli of the Assyrian inscriptions.

> son, and the nobles of Assyria revolted and they cast him from his throne; in Kâr-Tukulti-Ninurta they besieged him in his palace and slew him with the sword. For [sixty]-six[116] years, until the time of Tukulti-Aššur,[117] Bêl (Marduk) dwelt in Assyria; in the reign of Tukulti-Aššur, Bêl came (back) to Babylon.[118]

Tukulti-Ninurta I himself boasted many times of his victory and the capture of Kaštiliaš,[119] but was silent about his sack of Babylon and the capture of Marduk's statue. It is interesting that in order to justify his war against Babylonia, he ordered his court poets to compose a lengthy epic in which his action was motivated by the will of gods who were upset by Kaštiliaš' breach of oath.[120]

What is meant, however, by flooding Babylon and Esagila with water? Jeremias understood it as a metaphor, an allegorical image of utter disaster.[121] Indeed, the symbolism of flood dominates both our texts and others which are thematically connected with them. We believe, however, that besides this we are involved with the transference to Tukulti-Ninurta I of the circumstances of Babylon's destruction in a more recent time, also by an Assyrian king who suffered the same fate as Tukulti-Ninurta. We have in mind Sennacherib, who, in 689, completely obliterated Babylon. In his Bavian inscription he boasts of having conquered Babylon, massacred its inhabitants, looted its goods, and smashed its idols; then he continues:[122]

> The city and (its) houses, from its foundation to its top, I destroyed, I devastated, I burned with fire. The wall and outer wall, temples and gods, temple towers of brick and earth, as many as there were, I razed and dumped them into the Araḫtu Canal. Through the midst of that city I dug canals, I flooded its site with water, and the very foundations thereof I destroyed. I made its destruction more complete than that by a flood. That in the days to come the site of that city, and (its) temples and gods, might not be remembered, I completely blotted it out with water and made it like a meadow.

Here the flooding of Babylon is described not in poetic images, but with technical precision. By dumping the rubbish of the demolished buildings into the Araḫtu Canal, Sennacherib caused its water to rise and to submerge the ruined city. The total destruction of the glorious metropolis made a colossal impression upon contemporaries and descendants; we shall hear its echoes in Jewish prophecies of the time of the Captivity.[123] A few years

116. We have completed the figure after *RLA*, I, 334.
117. Ninurta-Tukulti-Aššur of the Assyrian inscriptions.
118. See also the description of the events in Olmstead, p. 53; Saggs, p. 85.
119. *AR*, I, §§ 145, 166, 172.
120. Ebeling (1938); Lambert (1958).
121. Jeremias (1917), p. 81, n. 2.
122. *AR*, II, § 340.
123. See Pages 106–108 below.

later, Sennacherib was slain by his sons (II Kings 19:37). This event is recalled in the chronicle of Nabonidus in these words: "He (Marduk) made his own son murder the king of Subartu, he who upon the wrath of Marduk had brought about the downfall of the country."[124]

However, the investigators of the "Chedorlaomer texts" (Pinches, Hommel, and others) were not at all interested in the name and identity of the person described. What attracted them was his patronymic, which in Sp. III, 2:9 is written ^{m}ÌR.DINGIR.É.A.KU, and in Sp. 987:19, ^{m}ÌR.É.KU.A. If we give the ideogram ÌR ("servant") its Akkadian value, we obtain, respectively, ^{m}*Arad-*^{d}*É-a-ku* and ^{m}*Arad-É-ku-a*; if the Sumerian, ^{m}*Èri-*^{d}*É-a-ku* and ^{m}*Èri-É-ku-a*. In the latter case, it sounds close enough to Arioch (אריוך); in this respect, the older scholars were not wrong, but they were completely misled by their efforts to locate it in Larsa (see Page 77 above). Actually, the pseudo-patronymic *Èri-éaku* is applied to the Assyrian king Tukulti-Ninurta I—and Arioch of Genesis 14, too, is king of Ellasar = A.LA$_5$.SAR = Assyria (see Page 78 above). Of course, the name *Arriwuk* or *Arriyuk* from the Mari texts,[125] which is adduced by Böhl, Albright, Yeivin, and Cornelius,[126] sounds even closer, but there was no such king in Assyria (Ellasar), nor is the existence of a king of this name attested to in Ilânṣûrâ, Alzi, or any other place that may be interpreted as Ellasar. The pseudo-patronymic *Èri-éaku*, on the contrary, appears in one tablet with the prototypes of two other royal names of Genesis 14:1 and 9: Chedorlaomer and Tidal. This enhances the probability of its connection with Arioch not by a simple, but in a geometric progression.

Now, the historical Tukulti-Ninurta I was the son of Shalmaneser I (^{d}*Šulman-ašaridu*), whose name is not in the least related to the quoted patronymic. But since the identity of Tukulti-Ninurta I is established beyond any doubt, it must be admitted that the patronymic ascribed to him in the "Chedorlaomer texts" is instead actually an epithet referring to him, especially since it appears both times in a construction which is grammatically abnormal. Instead of the regular construct state that is always found in Akkadian patronymics (for example, ^{m}*Ia-ú-a mâr Ḫu-um-ri*, ^{m}TAŠ-*da-ma-ni-e mâr* ^{m}*Ša-ba-ku-u*; in our own texts ^{m}*Tu-ud-ḫul-a mâr* ^{m}GAZ.ZA.[...]), we have constructions with the relative pronoun *ša*: ^{m}*Tukulti-*^{d}*Ninurta aplu*

124. *ANET*, p. 309.

125. Mentioned in *ARM*, II, 63:3; 64:3; cf. Kupper, p. 232, n. 1. This name also occurs as *A-ri-ú-uk-ki* at Nuzu: *NPN*, p. 30.

126. Böhl (1953), p. 44 (already proposed in 1945); Albright (1951a), pp. 6f.; Yeivin, p. 124; Cornelius (1960), p. 4 (where he, however, identifies Arioch not with the Arriyuk from the Mari texts, but with a hypothetical namesake whom he locates in Alzi, on the upper Tigris).

(A) *šá* ^{m}*Èri-*^{d}*É-a-ku* (Sp. III, 2:9); ^{m}*Tukulti-*^{d}*Ninurta mâru šá* ^{m}*Èri-É-ku-a* (Sp. II, 987:19).

Both variants of the patronymic contain names of temples beginning with *É* (= *bîtu*), the first element in all (Sumerian) names of Babylonian and Assyrian temples. Personal names so constructed are well known and fairly widespread in occurrence.[127] *É-a-ku* could mean "temple of the Moon god," but there was no shrine of such name;[128] conversely, the existence of the very important shrine *É-ku-a* is well attested to, and we may therefore assume that ^{m}*Èri-*^{d}*É-a-ku* (with the divine determinative in a completely wrong place) is a distortion of ^{m}*Èri-É-ku-a*. Now, *É-ku-a* means "shrine of Marduk";[129] this was the name of the central cella of the great temple Esagila in Babylon, its Holy of Holies containing the statue of Marduk.[130] "*Arad-Ekua* is rather colorless," remarked Albright,[131] but applied to Tukulti-Ninurta I the name reminds us that, according to the quoted Babylonian Chronicle, "The treasure of Esagila and Babylon he profanely brought forth and the great lord Marduk he removed from his abode and carried him off to Assyria" (Page 84 above). In other words, he plundered *É-ku-a*. And taking into account the aforementioned free interchange of homophones, regardless of their ideographic value, in the personal names of our texts (Page 82 above), it is permissible to assume that the sign ÌR ("servant") before *É-ku-a* stands for its homophone IR = *ḫabâtu* or *šalâlu*, "to rob, to plunder,"[132] which also could have the reading *eri*. Thus, the original text, which then underwent an intentional or accidental complication, may be restored: ^{m}*Tukulti-*^{d}*Ninurta šá iḫbat* (= IR) *É-ku-a*, "Tukulti-Ninurta, who sacked Ekua." IR *É-ku-a* was then interpreted as a personal name *ÌR-É-ku-a* or, with the shift of two last signs, ÌR (= *Èri-*)-*É-a-ku*: that is, Arioch.

After the lines about Tukulti-Ninurta I, Sp. III, 2 continues:

(obverse 13b) ^{m}*Tu-ud-ḫul-a mâr* ^{m}GAZ.ZA.[AN ?[133]]

(14) [*Bâbili*^{ki} *âlam ta-na*]-*a-tam iš-lul mê* (A^{meš}) *eli Bâbili*^{ki} (E^{ki}) *u É-sag-gil*
(15) [*ú-šar-da-a*] *mâr-šú ina* ^{is}*kakki qâtâ*^{II}*-šú muḫ-ḫa-šú im-ḫaṣ*
(16) [ ] *be-lu-ú-ti-šú a-na paraṣ* (GARZA) ⸢*bît*⸣ *An-nu-nit* [ ]

"(13b) Tudḫula, son of GAZ.ZA. [AN ?] (14) [Babylon, the city of glo]ry,

127. Clay, p. 148.

128. See the list of Moon temples, Dhorme (1951), pp. 195, 208; list of temples beginning with *É-* in *ŠL*, II, 3, no. 324.

129. *Ku-a* = *Marduk*: Brünnow, no. 10661; Labat, # 122.

130. *B.u.A.*, II, 304f.; *RLA*, I, 354f.

131. Albright (1926), p. 237.

132. Brünnow, nos. 5377, 5384, 5388; Labat, # 232.

133. Traces of the vertical wedge of sign # 13 are visible in Pinches' autography.

he plundered, water over Babylon and Esagil (15) [he led.] His son, with the weapon of his hands, smashed his skull, (16) [... seized (?)] his dominion according to the decree of the ⌈temple⌉ of Anunit."[134]

As in the first case, we are not told of what country Tudḫula was king. But his name speaks for itself; it is Hittite. There was only one case in history when a Hittite took and plundered Babylon. This was Muršiliš I, who captured and devastated Babylon in 1530, putting an end to its First (Amorite) Dynasty. The Babylonian Chronicle records briefly: "The Hittites marched against Samsuditana (the last king of the First Dynasty) and against the land of Akkad."[135] Like Tukulti-Ninurta I (and the rest of the conquerors mentioned in our texts) he carried off from Babylon the statues of Marduk and his spouse Ṣarpanit, which were not returned until twenty-four years later by the Cassite king Agum II.[136] Immediately after his return to Ḫatti he was murdered. Here is how this is told in the historical survey by the Hittite king Telepinuš (*circa* 1460):[137]

> And he (Muršiliš) went to Ḫalpa (Aleppo) and destroyed Ḫalpa and brought prisoners from Ḫalpa and their goods to Ḫattušaš. Then he went to Babylon and destroyed Babylon, he also attacked the Hurrians (?), (and) brought prisoners (and) goods from Babylon to Ḫattušaš. And Ḫantiliš was butler and he had Muršiliš's sister (?)[138] Ḫa[rapši]liš as (his) wife. And Zidantaš led (???) Ḫantiliš, and they [committed] an evil deed and slew Muršiliš and perpetrated a blood (-crime).

There can be no doubt that Sp. III, 2, has Muršiliš in mind. Even if his murderer was not his son, as our text supposes (by analogy with the fate that met Tukulti-Ninurta I), Ḫantiliš was related to him by marriage, anyway, and his accomplice Zidantaš could have been an even closer relative. A good guess would be to consider him a son of Labarnaš the Younger, whom his father, King Ḫattušiliš I, removed from the succession in favor of Muršiliš, his sister's son.[139] It is remarkable enough that Babylonian authors of the Chaldean period remembered the murder of the Hittite conqueror that had occurred a thousand years earlier and a thousand miles from Babylon.

Why does our text use the pseudonym Tudḫula for Muršiliš? (We may

134. Anunit (Annunit) is the protective goddess of the cities of Akkad and Sippar, Ištar in her warrior hypostasis. It is interesting that in the "Tukulti-Ninurta Epic" the conquest of Babylon by this king is associated with Anunit: BM. 98731:C:17–20, Lambert, pp. 48f.

135. King (1907), II, 22, rev.: 10.

136. II R 38; V R 33; transliteration in Schrader, III, part 1, pp. 138, 140, col. I:44–II:21.

137. Friedrich, pp. 6ff., §§ 9–11, lines 28–34.

138. Thus translated by Forrer and generally followed in literature; but according to Cornelius (1956), p. 302, the sign really reads "wife," and Ḫantiliš was the seducer of Muršiliš's wife during the king's absence.

139. See Hattušiliš I's political testament, translation in Gurney, pp. 171f.

note that the Babylonian Chronicle does not mention at all the name of the king who led the Hittites against Samsuditana and the land of Akkad.) The use of ciphered names is generally characteristic of the style of our texts. As Jeremias remarked about another of them, "The name that was execrable for the Babylonians was perhaps intentionally written in a cryptic way."[140] The pseudonym is close enough: the founder of the dynasty to which Muršiliš I belonged was Tudḫaliaš I. Since the Hittite kings assumed new names after their accession to the throne, but often continued to use the old ones too,[141] the possibility that Tudḫaliaš was Muršiliš's other name cannot be ruled out. Then in the thirteenth century Hattušiliš III, who regularly corresponded with the Babylonian kings Kadašman-Turgu and his son Kadašman-Enlil II,[142] was succeeded by Tudḫaliaš IV, who exchanged letters with the Assyrian kings Shalmaneser I and his son Tukulti-Ninurta I.[143] There could be confusion with the much earlier successor of another Ḫattušiliš (I). But even more important is the circumstance already noticed by Pinches: "In Accadian [that is, as we say now, in Sumerian] *Tudḫula* apparently means 'The Evil Offspring.'"[144] This is shown by the unusual syncopated orthography *-ḫul-a*.[145] Such a splendid pun with an authentic Hittite name must have caused particular delight to the learned scribe who conceived it.[146]

The name ᵐGAZ.ZA.[ ], given as Tudḫula's patronymic, must be understood in the same way. There were no such names in the Hittite royal house. This is a symbolic name which must be explained ideographically. The sign GAZ means "to kill," and more precisely, according to its oldest pictographic form, "to bend the skull inward with a pestle or an ax,"[147] and GAZ.ZA = *hašâlu*, "to break, to fracture, to trample, to crush."[148] And it is explicitly said that Tudḫula, "son" of GAZ.ZA.[ ], perished by having his skull

140. Jeremias (1917), p. 82, n. *a*.

141. Thus, Hattušiliš I's original name was Labarnaš, and he occasionally used it after having taken the new one (Gurney, p. 23; p. 171, n. 1); the king Urḫi-Teššub's throne name was was Muršiliš (III).

142. *B.u.A.*, I, 62f., with references to Hittite documents.

143. Weidner, pp. 64ff. (Hittite letters published by H. Otten).

144. Pinches (1897), p. 74. Indeed, TU/TUD = *alâdu* (*tu-ud-da*), "to beget" (Brünnow, no. 1070) or *banû*, "to beget" (*ibid.* no. 1071); ḪUL = *lemênu*, "to be evil," *lemnu*, "evil" (adj.), *lemuttu*, "evil" (abstract) (# 456); ḪUL.A = *lemuttu*, "evil" (Delitzsch [1914], p. 216).

145. Cf. the normal orthography ᵐ*Tu-ud-ḫa-li-ia*, Weidner, p. 65.

146. There may have been an even more refined play of ideographic meanings. If the name *Muršiliš* (Akkadian transcription *Mur-si-li*, Clay, p. 109) were written **Mur-sil*, its first element would mean in Akkadian "child" (*mûru*), and the second, SIL, would be understood as the ideogram for several verbs with the meanings "to destroy," "to crush," "to smash," "to cut off," and so on (*ŠL*, II, 1, no. 12). Now ḪUL, besides *lemênu*, "to be evil," also has the value of *lapâtu*, "to crush, to destroy" (# 456), so that *Tu-ud-ḫul-a* was, for a Babylonian scribe, exactly equivalent to **Mur-sil*!

147. *ŠL*, II, 2, no. 192.

148. *Ibid.*, no. 192:6.

smashed. The narrative of Telepinuš does not specify by what weapon Muršiliš was slain, but if we follow Cornelius' idea that the murder of Muršiliš was transferred by Greek poets to Agamemnon,[149] we may note that according to *Odyssey* IV:535 Aegisthus "slew him, as one slayeth an ox at the stall," and we know from *Odyssey* III:440–454 that horned cattle used to be killed by a blow of the ax. Did the circumstances of the great Hittite conqueror's murder survive in the memories of alien peoples, far to the east and to the west of Hatti?

But at the same time we are probably entitled to regard GAZ.ZA.[AN?] as a cryptogram hiding the real name of Muršiliš's foster-father. If one writes his name thus: **Ḫat-uš-ìli* (signs ḪAD.UŠ.AN),[150] its first sign has also the value SÌG = *maḫâṣu*, "to smite, to kill," and its second sign is the ideogram for UŠ = *rêdu*, "soldier," or NITAḪ = *zikaru*, "male." Now by replacing these signs by their synonyms: ḪAD/SÌG (= *maḫâṣu*, "to kill") by GAZ (= *dâku*, "to slay"), and UŠ/NITAḪ (= *zikaru*, "male") by ZA (= *amêlu*, "man"), we obtain instead of **Ḫat-uš-ìli* its equivalent GAZ.ZA.AN.[151]

Thus *Tu-ud-ḫul-a* (who passed into Genesis 14 in the very correct transliteration תדעל)—or, to call him by his real name, Muršiliš I—did to Babylon as Tukulti-Ninurta I did three centuries later, and he, too, fell victim of what the Babylonians considered divine retribution.

Tudḫula is followed in Sp. III, 2, by a person definitely called "king of Elam," [*šar*] *E-lam-mat*,[152] whose name is ideographically written ^{m}KU.KU.KU.MAL in Sp. III, 2, and ^{m}KU.KU.KU.KU.MAL in the other two tablets. To him is ascribed the devastation of not only the city of Babylon but of all of Babylonia:

(1) [^{m}KU.KU.KU.MAL *šar*] *E-lam-mat âl Aḫ*-[*ḫi*?]-*e ikmi*[153] *mâtum rab-ba-a-tum iš-lul*

(2) [ ]-*ku a-bu-ba-niš iš-kun má-ḫa-zu* ^{mât}*Akkadi*^{ki} *gab-bi parakkê-ši*-[*na*]

149. Cornelius (1956), p. 302.

150. For non-gemination of *t*, cf. ^{âl} *Ḫatuš* in Cappadocian tablets, *Ḫa-ti* in three Amarna letters, ^{mât}*Ḫa-ta* and *Ḫa-at-at*^{ki} in one Amarna letter each, and ^{m}*Ḫa-tu-ši-li* in two tablets from Ugarit. [In the recently discovered Boğazköy text: KBo XII 41:3; the name Ḫattušiliš is written $^{m\ GIŠ}$ḪAD . AN^{LIM}: that is, *Ḫat-ìlim*. Cf. H. Otten in *Mitteilungen der Deutschen Orientalischen Gesellschaft*, 94:7 (1963).]

151. This presumed ideographic play may seem exaggerated; but cf. Meissner's characteristic of Babylonian learned works, quoted in Note 96 above.

152. *Šar* restored after Sp. II, 987:6: ^{m}KU.KU.KU.KU.MAL *šar* ^{mât}*E-la-mat*. In Sp. 158 + Sp. II, 962:rev.:36 *E-lam-mat* is written without the determinative *mât*.

153. The sign which Jeremias did not find possible to transliterate is certainly # 481: LAL = *kamû*, "to bind, to capture," which supplies the predicate to the sentence; cf. *ka-mu-tu*, "capture," a few lines below, line 5 of the same text. The word following the sign *âl*, "city," is too damaged to be restored; its first sign may be read *aḫ*/*eḫ*/*iḫ*/*uḫ*; should we suppose here a phonetic spelling of A.ḪA, ideographic for *Tu-ba*, part of the city of Babylon (*RLA*, I, 34)?

(3) [*ana išat*]*i iq-lu* ^{m}KU.KU.KU.MAL *mâr-šú ina paṭri parzilli qabli-šú lìbba^{ba}-šú it-ta*[ ] (Sp. III, 2: reverse)

"(1) [KU.KU.KU.MAL, king of] Elam, captured the [...] city, he plundered the great land, (2) [ ] he made all the cities of Akkad similar to the deluge, their shrines (3) [in fire] he burned. (As for) KU.KU.KU.MAL, his son [pierced] his heart with the iron dagger of his waist."

It was already clear to Pinches that the ideographic spelling KU.KU.KU.(KU.)MAL disguises an Elamite name with the first element *Kudur-*, for the sign KU was read not only *ku*, but *dúr* as well. This is how Assurbanipal spelled the name of an Elamite king: ^{m}*Ku-dúr-na-an-ḫu-un-di.*[154] This king wrote his name, in Elamite, ^{m}*Ku-tir-*^{d}*Naḫ-ḫu-un-te,*[155] but the Babylonians rendered it ^{m}*Kudur*(NÍG.DU)-^{d}*Na-ḫu-un-du* and the cognate name of a more ancient Elamite ruler as ^{m}*Ku-du-ur-ma-bu-uk.*[156] Pinches tried to read the last two (or, in the alternative spelling, three) signs *laḫ-mal* or *laḫ-ga-mal,* in order to obtain a name corresponding to Chedorlaomer,[157] but his process was wrong. We shall see that Albright found a more plausible way of proceeding in this direction. Meanwhile, following our method, we shall try to define what Elamite king with a name beginning with *Kudur* inscribed himself in Babylonian history by devastating all the cities and temples of the country. This same Elamite *Kudur*-KU.KU.MAL is the principal hero of another of our texts (Sp. 158 + Sp. II, 962), in which his villainies and sacrileges are described in poetic language and with ample details; he is said to have plundered the temples of Nippur, Babylon, Uruk, and Borsippa; also, "princes [ ] he killed with weapon, of all the temples he [carried off] the booty, their goods he took and brought them to Elam" (reverse: 34–36). According to Sp. II, 987:8, the gods ordered him to "exercise kingship in Babylon, the city of Karduniaš."

It follows from all this that our texts refer to Kutir-Naḫḫunte (Kudur-Naḫḫundu)[158] III. Many centuries later, Assurbanipal still recalled him as the one who had carried off the goddess Innin (Ištar) from her temple in Uruk—allegedly 1535 or 1635 years before the Assyrian king returned her from the captured Elamite capital ("in reality... a thousand years should be deducted!")[159]—and who "brought his hand against the sanctuaries of

154. Cf. the cuneiform writing in King (1898), I, lv. The syllable *an* stands in an incorrect place; it should have stood as a determinative ^{d}, before *Na-ḫu-un-di*, name of an Elamite goddess.

155. King (1898), I, lv. The sign *naḫ* is actually *laḫ* (# 321), which had such a reading in Elamite and neo-Babylonian.

156. Cf. also the name of an Elamite king, a contemporary of the First Dynasty of Babylon, spelled LA.AN.KU.KU (reading unknown) (König, pp. 27, 36).

157. Pinches (1898), p. 68; (1902), pp. 222f.

158. To avoid confusion, we shall henceforth use this variant of the name.

159. Olmstead, p. 486.

Akkad and ruined the land of Akkad."[160] We learn from older Babylonian and Elamite documents that in 1174 the Elamite king Šutruk-Naḫḫunte I, accompanied by his elder son Kudur-Naḫḫundu, invaded Babylonia, killed its king Zababa-šum-iddina, carried off divine statues, steles, and *kudurru* stones from Ešnunna, Sippar, and Kiš, and terribly laid waste to the major part of the country. According to his own inscription, he captured eight hundred towns. Kudur-Naḫḫundu was appointed king of Babylonia and imposed upon the Babylonians tribute and taxes. In 1170, he completely routed Enlil-nâdin-aḫḫê, the legal pretender to the Babylonian throne, and put an end to the centuries-old Cassite dynasty. In the same year he succeeded his father on the throne of Elam and carried off to Susa the statues of Marduk from Babylon and of Innin from Uruk.[161] The series of Elamite invasions of the years 1174–1169 was the worst disaster of all that Babylonia had suffered hitherto, and left a colossal impression. Nebuchadnezzar I (king from 1147 on), who succeeded in repelling the Elamites after a long and exhausting war, wrote in his hymn[162] how [Šutruk-Naḫḫunte] deposed king Zababa-šum-iddina, broke his kingship, [put in his place] Kudur-Naḫ-ḫundu his first-born, who perpetrated more crimes and sins than all his ancestors had, defeated king Enlil-nâdin-aḫḫê, and "overthrew the people of all the land of Akkad like the deluge" (*nîšê* ^{mât}*Akkadi kul-lat-si-na a-bu-biš is-pu-nu*, line 7). Further, in an astrological text of the Arsacid period, to which we shall return, the Elamite invasion is compared with the universal deluge.

True, our text claims that *Kudur*-KU.MAL, like the two invaders who precede him there, was slain by his own son. With respect to Kudur-Naḫḫundu III we have no data confirming his violent death—but, on the other hand, we have no data that would contradict it. It is known, however, that he died after only four years of reign in Susa (*circa* 1166).[163] His death in the prime of life, so soon after the destruction and sacrileges he had committed in Babylonia, must have been perceived by the Babylonians as divine punishment. It may also be that our text blended to a degree Kudur-Naḫḫundu III with Kudur-Naḫḫundu IV (693–692), a contemporary of Sennacherib who intervened in Babylonian affairs and supported Chaldeans against Assyrians. Defeated by Sennacherib, he was deposed after only ten months of rule and, apparently, murdered, as we gather from the Annals of Sennacherib: "At that time, at the command of Assur, my lord, Kudur-Naḫundi, the king of Elam, did not fill three months, but died suddenly, on a day not of his fate."[164] We

160. *AR*, II, § 923.

161. Olmstead, p. 58; Moortgat, p. 391; Cameron, pp. 109–113.

162. III R 38, 2, published in transliteration and translation by Winckler (1894), pp. 535ff.

163. Cameron, p. 111.

164. *AR*, II, 251.

have seen that the flooding of Babylon by Sennacherib found its reflection in Sp. III, 2; we shall see presently that another contemporary of Sennacherib is actually presented by our texts as the fourth of the criminal kings; there is, therefore, nothing impossible in a merger of this kind.

All these historical facts agree in the best way with what the three Spartoli tablets tell about *Kudur*-KU.(KU.)MAL.[165] Probably because of this historical correspondence, Jeremias read KU.KU.KU.MAL as *Ku-dur-nâḫu-te*, and KU.KU.KU.KU.MAL as *Ku-dúr-nâḫ-ḫun-te*. He proceeded from the fact that the sign KU also has the values *nâḫu*, "to rest" (Brünnow, number 10540) and *ḫun* (Brünnow, number 10503). To make the decipherment complete, it only remained for him to assume for MAL the hypothetical reading **te*, nowhere attested to so far.[166] Albright, who in 1942 accepted Jeremias' readings, tried to circumvent this difficulty by reading not only KU, but the group KU.MAL (= ḪUN.GÁ) as a form of the root *nâḫu* (Brünnow, number 10607): for example, as a presumed abstract **nâḫûtu*, which would permit for KU.KU.KU.MAL the reading *Ku-dúr-nâḫûti*.[167] In addition to the form **nâḫûtu* not appearing in the Akkadian vocabulary, Albright's interpretation does not agree with the presence of an extra KU in the alternative writing of the name (it would give *Ku-dúr-naḫ-nâḫûtu/i*). We therefore retain the decipherment by Jeremias, which we would tentatively complete by a reference to the equation ᵈMAL = *al-ba* = *ᵈŠa*[*maš*], that is, ᵈUTU;[168] now the sign # 379, besides UTU, has also, among others, the values *tú* and *ḫúd*, which would provide for the first spelling the possibility of reading *Ku-dúr-nâḫu-tú* or *Ku-dúr-nâḫ-ḫúd*, and for the second, *Ku-dúr-nâḫ-ḫun-tú*. We shall show that this strange and unparalleled orthography is bound to the symbolic significance of the group KU.MAL.

But only with this orthography could the name Kudur-Naḫḫundu be reinterpreted as "Chedorlaomer." The latter name, though its first element is Elamite, is not attested to. Jeremias correctly surmised that here "a confusion with Kutur-Naḫḫunte" could have taken place.[169] Albright, who still hoped in 1926 that an Elamite king **Kudur-Lagamar* had existed in one

165. Albright (1942), pp. 33f., having accepted the reading Kudur-Naḫḫundu, identified the bearer of this name in the "Chedorlaomer texts" with an earlier ruler of Elam, the *sukkal-maḫ* ("Great Regent") Kuter-Naḫḫunte I, whom he placed *circa* 1625–1610, on the basis of Cameron, pp. 78, 81, 82. According to the most recent research by Hinz, his accession to supreme power in Elam occurred about 1664, computed to "low chronology" (Hinz, pp. 4f., 10, 12). However, no Elamite invasion of Babylon took place in the Old Babylonian period. The "Chedorlaomer texts" clearly have the twelfth-century conqueror in mind, and Cameron himself (p. 111) identified precisely this Elamite king with the one mentioned in the "Chedorlaomer texts."

166. Jeremias (1917), p. 82, n. *a*.

167. Albright (1942), p. 34.

168. *ŠL*, IV, 1, no. 458.

169. Jeremias (1917), p. 96.

of the "Dark Ages" (which by now have shrunk very considerably on the timetable of the ancient East), recognized in 1942 that "we now know the names of some 40 kings of Elam who flourished between 2100 and 1100 B.C., and there is no Kudur-Lagamar among them."[170] He even reconstructed the transition from "Kudur-Naḫḫundi" to "Chedorlaomer": *Kudur-Naḡḡundi* > **Kudur-Laḡḡundi* > **K^{e}dor-laḡomed* (with dissimilation *nd* > *md*) > *K^{e}dor-laḡomer* (because of the confusion of ד and ר).[171] However, he recently abandoned this rather complicated hypothesis.[172] His earlier (1921–1926) decipherment of KU.KU.KU.KU.MAL is much simpler, and we may accept it as its alternative, aberrant reading, brought about by the abnormal MAL at its end. Albright applied to the second pair KU.KU its value *laḫâmu*,[173] which gives *Ku-dúr-laḫam-mal*.[174] Of course, *laḫam-mal* has no relation to the Elamite divine name *Lagamar*,[175] which in its turn derives from the Akkadian *Lagamal*:[176] this is a purely Semitic name (*lâ gamal* = "merciless"), and its *g* could not be replaced either by the cuneiform *ḫ* or by the Hebrew ע.[177] Conversely, the Jewish author, having met in a cuneiform document a spelling that could be wrongly read *laḫam-mal*, rendered its *ḫ* by his own ע because it was common practice (as in the case of *Tudḫula* > תדעל). The passage *l* > ר is of the same order as the transition *Aššur-bân-apal* > *אסרבנפל > אסנפר (*'Osnappar*, Ezra 4:10).

Now we return to the first of the four kings who in Sp. III, 2, precedes Tukulti-Ninurta. Unfortunately, the beginning of the tablet is badly damaged and the king's name is lost. We give what remains, with our conjectural readings and restorations:

(3) [*i*]*p-še-tu-šú la* [*ṭa-a-ba-ti*]
(4) [*pa-ri*(?)]*-ṣu ḫa-am-mu-*[*ú*[178]]
(5) [ ]*îmuru ilâni*^{meš} *nab-nit* A[.AB.BA (?)]

170. Albright (1942), p. 33.

171. *Ibid.*, p. 34.

172. Acccording to Cornelius (1960), p. 1, n. 2, referring to Albright's letter to him.

173. Meissner, no. 8121 = Delitzsch (1896), p. 375; *ŠL*, II, 4, no. 536:275:e.

174. Albright (1921), p. 71, n. 4 = (1926), p. 233, n. 8.

175. Assurbanipal, in the list of Elamite gods carried off from Susa, writes it ^{d}*La-ga-ma-ru*; Kudur-Naḫḫundu I, ^{d}*La-ga-ma-ri* (King [1898], I, lv).

176. Son of Ninurta, also known as a goddess (*B.u.A.*, II, 30).

177. Albright's attempt to presume an original *ḡ* (i.e., *ġ*) in the Elamite name *Lagamar* ([1926], p. 233, n. 8; [1942], p. 34) is not justified: both in Akkadian and in Elamite, it is always written by the sign *ga* (# 319), which in Elamite had the reading *kà*, and not once by *ḫa*, which would correspond to the pronunciation **ġa*. *Laḫam-mal* reflects not the supposed Elamite pronunciation, but merely a play on ideograms.

178. Pinches presumed here *Ḫa-am-mu-*[*ra-bi*]! Besides the absence of a personal name determinative, the context is such that any possibility of an allusion to the great and revered monarch is absolutely excluded. *Ḫammû*, "usurper, rebel," fits here excellently; therefore we have tentatively completed the previous word [*pa-ri*]-*ṣu*, "liar, deceiver, impostor."

(6) [ ]BU *ûmu*^{mu} [ ] ^{d}*Šamaš mu-nam-mir* [ ]
(7) [ ]*bêl bêlê* ^{d}*Marduk ina kun-nu lìbbi*^{bi}*-šú*
(8) [ ] ⌈*ina tar-ṣu palî XIII nakru a-bi*⌉[179] *ma-al-ku la za-nin*

(9a) [*É-sag-gil* (?)[180]]*ina* ^{iṣ}*kakki*[181] *ú-šam-qit* (Sp. III, 2: obverse)

"(3) [ ] his b[ad][182] deeds [ ]
(4) [the impost]or (?), the usurpe[r]
(5) [ ] the gods saw the offspring of the s[ea (?)[183]]
(6) [ ] ... day [ ] Šamaš the illuminator [ ]
(7) [ ] lord of lords, Marduk, in the truthfulness of his heart
(8) [ ] ⌈in the time of the thirteenth year of reign, the father-hater,⌉ the prince who did not take care
(9a) [of Esagila (?)], he overthrew with weapons."

We see that here the accusations are of a different order from those in the cases of the other three kings. We are dealing with an usurper who was negligent of the maintenance of temples and was overthrown by the will of Marduk in the thirteenth year of his reign. In the tablet Sp. 158 + Sp. 962, reverse, one of the similarly composed paragraphs[184] is devoted to this fourth king, to whom earlier students of the texts paid little attention, because his name did not recall to them anything of Genesis 14:

(24) *i-nu-um šá É-zi-da* [ ]*-ta-šú*
(25) *u* ^{d}*Nabû pa-qid kiš-šat ur-ri-*[*id*[185] ... *ištu* ^{iṣ}*kussi*(?)]*-šú*
(26) *šap-liš ana Ti-amat*^{ki} *iš-ku-*[*nu pa-ni-šú*[186]]

179. The entire first half of line 8 is rendered in Pinches' autography by signs in outline, which in his system means that the signs in the original are badly mutilated and dubious. The signs he believed to have observed give no consistent sense; one of them cannot be equated with any known cuneiform sign. Jeremias remarked: "Is the text correct?" and could not not achieve much in translating it. Our starting point was the fourth sign in Pinches' autography, in which we recognized the neo-Babylonian form of the figure XIII; it has no other sense. Then we tried to substitute signs with similar outlines for the first (which must be divided in two), second, third, and fifth signs of line 8.

180. Completed after Sp. II, 987:15 [*a*]*-a-ú šar* ^{mât}*E-lam-mat šá iz-nun-nu É-sag-gíl*, "which is the king of Elam that should take care of Esagila?" and Nebuchadnezzar II's building narrative (Schrader, III, part 2, p. 10, I:19): *za-nin É-sag-il ù É-zi-da*.

181. Two signs of Pinches' autography corrected according to King's excerpt from this tablet, King (1898), p. li.

182. We complete *la* [*ṭa-a-ba-ti*], literally "no-good," cf. Sp. II, 987:7 *šá eli-šú lâ ṭa-a-bi* [. . .], "what is not good to them. . ."

183. Tentative restoration A[.AB.BA], the reasons for which will become clear from our identification of the ruler described here.

184. All of them begin by *i-nu-um*, "when"; cf. translation of the first two (out of five, of which the one transliterated here is the fifth) paragraphs on Page 101 below.

185. Completed after the preceding paragraphs, rev.:3, 7, 12.

186. Completed by Jeremias after rev. 31 of the same tablet: *šap-liš ana* BÀD.SI.AB.BA (Borsippa) *iš-ku-nu pa-ni-šú*.

(27) *^{m}I-bil-^{d}Tu-tu*[187] *šá qí-rib Ti-amat iḫ-mut ^{d}Šamaš*[188]
(28) *i-bir-ma Ti-amat^{ki} ir-ma-a la šu-bat-su*
(29) *šá É-zi-da bîti ki-nim šu-ḫar-ru-ur šak-ki-e-šú*

"(24) When of Ezida[189] [ ] ...
(25) and Nabû, the overseer of the totality <of heaven and earth>[190] descen[ded ... from] his [throne (?)],
(26) down toward the Sea Country he tur[ned his face]
(27) Ibil-Tutu, whom the Sun-god hastened[191] into the midst of the Sea,
(28) sailed across the Sea Country, set up his pseudoresidence,[192]
(29) (while) the statutes of Ezida, the legitimate temple, came to an end."[193]

Since the previously mentioned three kings were real persons, the fourth one, his pseudonym notwithstanding, is certainly a historical figure. From what is said of Ibil-Tutu it clearly follows that we are dealing with the well-known Marduk-apal-iddina II (Merodach-Baladan of the Bible), contemporary of Sargon II and Sennacherib, chief of the Chaldean tribe of Bit-Iakin, which lived in the lagoons of *Nâr-Marrati* ("Bitter River," the northern extension of the Persian Gulf), who several times seized Babylon and proclaimed himself king of Babylonia. There is small wonder that the author

187. The second sign of this name (# 172) has the principal readings *ne*, *ṭe*, *bil*, *pil*, *kúm*, and several secondary ones, including *bí*. Pinches transliterated it *^{m}I-ne-^{d}Tu-tu* or *Ide-Tutu*; Jeremias opted for the value *bí* and wrote *^{m}I-bi-^{d}Tu-tu* (without differentiating *bí* by a diacritical mark), in which he was followed by Albright, who normalized the name *Ibî-Tutu* = "Tutu (Marduk) has given a name (= *ibbî* from *nabû*)" ([1926], p. 236 and n. 15). However, names of this type were spelled *I-bi-*; in our case, one must rather read *^{m}I-bil-^{d}Tu-tu*, as Clay, p. 83, read *I-bil-^{d}Ea*, *I-bil-^{d}Papsukal*. We shall see the advantages of this reading.

188. Written: ^{d}UTU.GÀL, a nonstandard writing which may be interpreted in two ways: (1) either by substituting GAL for GÀL, which would give U_4.GAL = (a) *me-ḫu-ú*, "raging storm, south hurricane," (b) *ûgallu*, "storm demon" (*ŠL*, II, 3, no. 381:353); (2) or by completing it to ^{d}UTU.GÀL. LU = *^{d}Ninurta*; *^{d}Šamaš* (*ŠL*, II, 3, no. 381:146; Deimel, no. 1105), which is more probable in view of the determinative ^{d}; Šamaš is mentioned in connection with the same ruler in the opening lines of Sp. III, 2, and according to the epilogue to the Code of Ḫammurapi, it is Šamaš who overthrows sinful kings and brings about their defeat (rev.: XXVII: 11–40, *ANET*, p. 179).

189. The temple of Nabû in Borsippa, Babylon's twin city; Ezida was the twin sanctuary of Esagila.

190. Nabû's standard title was *pâqid kâl šamê irṣitim*, "overseer of all of heaven and earth," *RLA*, I, 416; our text skipped the words *šamê irṣitim*, though the preceding *kiš-šat* remained in the construct state.

191. Thus translated by Pinches; Jeremias preferred the other verb *ḫamâṭu*, "to burn": "whom the Southern Sun (?) burned within the sea." This could signify death from fever, and the man we identify with Ibil-Tutu actually died on a swampy island of the Persian Gulf (see Page 98 below). But because of the sequence of events in our text we prefer to understand these words in the sense that Ibil-Tutu, by the curse of Šamaš, was compelled to flee to a sea island, which really happened with his historical prototype.

192. The felicitous rendering of *lâ šubatsu* (*lit.*, "his non-residence") by "his pseudo-residence" belongs to Pinches (1897), p. 65.

193. Another possible translation would be: "The incantations of Ezida, the legitimate temple, became silent."

of the "Chedorlaomer texts" included him among the sinful kings, along with foreign plunderers. From the point of view of the old Babylonian cities, and especially of their clergy, Marduk-apal-iddina was not a "Babylonian patriot" (as he was very incorrectly styled by Meissner),[194] but a foreign invader no better than—or even worse than—the Assyrians.[195] He arrested and deported members of the Babylonian nobility, and the climax of his abuses was the twice-repeated evacuation of Babylonian gods to his residences in the Sea Country (in 710 and 700). This alone was enough to put him, in the eyes of the priests and of all pious Babylonians, on an equal level with Muršiliš, Tukulti-Ninurta, and Kudur-Naḫḫundu, each of whom also robbed Babylon of its gods. An analogous step of the last Babylonian king Nabonidus—concentration of all the gods of Babylonia in the capital city—provoked such indignation that Cyrus was hailed as liberator. The following excerpts from Assyrian records, devoted to Marduk-apal-iddina, will demonstrate the striking correspondence of the data of our texts with historical facts.

> *From the records of Sargon II*: (a) In my twelfth year of reign, Marduk-apal-iddina, son of Iakini, king of Kaldu (Chaldea), whose settlements are situated in the secluded sea of the east, put his trust in the Bitter Sea and (its) mighty waves, and violated the oath and curse of the great gods, and withheld his tribute. Ḫumbanigaš, the Elamite, came to his aid. The (tribes of) Ru'a, Ḫindaru, Iatburu, Puqudu, all of the Sutû, desert folk, he alienated from me. He prepared for battle and descended upon the land of Sumer and Akkad. For twelve years, against the heart of the gods, he held sway over Babylon, the city of the lord of lords, and ruled it.[196] Marduk, the great god, saw the evil works of the (people of) Kaldu, which he hated, and decreed that his royal scepter and throne should be taken away (from him). Me, Sargon, the humble king, he singled out from among all princes and raised my head. That I might turn back the feet of the hostile and evil Kaldu folk from the land of Sumer and Akkad, he made mighty my weapons.[197]
>
> (b) And when that Marduk-apal-iddina heard of the approach of my expedition, he was seized with anxiety for his own (safety) and fled from Babylon to the city of Iqbi-Bêl, like a *sudinnu*-bird, at night. The inhabitants of his cities and the gods who dwelt therein he gathered together

194. *B.u.A.*, I, 31.

195. Saggs, p. 111, summarizes the situation under Marduk-apal-iddina: "During this time, the economy of the great cities of Babylonia suffered severe damage, the tribesmen interfering with the free flow of trade and practicing various extortions upon the towns; Chaldaean control was highly unpopular with the great cities of Babylonia and down to within a few years of the final extinction of Assyria itself the cities were constantly appealing to the Assyrian kings for assistance against the havoc wrought by Chaldaean tribesmen."

196. Note Sp. III, 2: obv.: 8 (Page 95 above): the impious ruler was overthrown in his thirteenth year of reign!

197. *AR*, II, § 31 (Annals).

> into one (body) and brought them into Dûr-Iakin, whose defenses he strengthened.[198]
>
> (c) (After I took Dûr-Iakin) the people of Sippar, Nippur, Babylon, Borsippa,who were imprisoned therein through no fault of theirs,—I broke their bonds and caused them to behold the light. Their fields which since the days of old, during the anarchy in the land, the Sutû had seized, I returned to them... The freedom of Ur, Uruk, Eridu, Larsa, Kisik and Nimid-Laguda, I (re-)established, and brought back their captured gods to their cities. Their (the gods') revenues, which had stopped, I restored.[199]
>
> *From the Annals of Sennacherib*: That same Marduk-apal-iddina... . gathered together the gods of his whole land in their shrines, and loaded them into ships and fled like a bird to the city of Nagite the swampy, which is in the midst of the sea.[200]

This was Marduk-apal-iddina's last defeat: we learn from Sennacherib's Nebî Yunus Slab Inscription that he died in Nagitu.[201] Everything agrees here to the smallest details; Sp. III, 2:3–9a, tells about Marduk-apal-iddina's first expulsion by Sargon II, in 710, after twelve years of reign in Babylon; Sp. 158 + Sp. II, 962: reverse: 24–29 refers to his final flight to the island city of Nagitu. Even the religiously stylized phraseology of Sargon's Annals and the Spartoli texts, ascribing the overthrow of the impious usurper to the will of Marduk, is the same in both cases and must have originated in the pro-Assyrian circles of Babylonian clergy.

The custom of calling hostile kings by modified and abridged names is attested to for the very epoch of Marduk-apal-iddina. Thus, Sennacherib calls the Chaldeans Nergal-ušezib and Mušezib-Marduk exclusively by the hypocorism *Šûzubu*. This apparently had a pejorative implication. The pseudonym given by the "Chedorlaomer texts" to Marduk-apal-iddina becomes quite transparent upon closer examination. The normal ideographic spelling of his name is $^{m\,d}$AMAR.UTU.IBILA.SUM^{na}. *I-bil* is the phonetic rendering of IBILA (*apal*), and ^{d}*Tu-tu* is one of the most common names of Marduk.[202] It was perhaps chosen to replace *Marduk* either because it was reminiscent of the deluge,[203] or because of association with *Bît-Tutu*, where the army of Marduk-apal-iddina, commanded by Nergal-ušezib, was totally defeated in 700.

We have seen that the first three invader kings had not only inscribed themselves in Babylonian chronicles as guilty of the worst debacles ever

198. *Ibid.*, § 66 (Display Inscription).

199. *Ibid.*, § 40 (Annals).

200. *Ibid.*, § 242 (final edition of the Annals).

201. *Ibid.*, § 345.

202. *Enuma Eliš* VII:9–34 (names nos. 13–17), *ANET*, p. 70; Böhl (1953), p. 293; *RLA*, I, 419.

203. TU = ÚRU = *abûbu* (# 58); A.MA.RU, another of Marduk's names, also signifies "deluge."

inflicted on Babylon, but that they also represented Assyria, Ḫatti, and Elam: that is, three of the four world quadrants—North, West, and East. This selection is, of course, not accidental. One of our texts, Sp. II, 987:3, says about Babylon: [*Bâbi*]*li*[ki] *mar-kas šamê*[e] *šá ana ir-bit šârê munnadû*,[204] "Babylon, the bond (= hub) of heaven <and earth>,[205] which is founded toward the four winds." It is therefore subject to blows from all four cardinal points. Ibil-Tutu—that is, Marduk-apal-iddina—completes this scheme: he is king of Babylonia (Akkad)—that is, of the southern world quadrant—and his proper domain, the Sea Country, is situated to the south of Babylon. We have completed the correspondence with Genesis 14, where one of the four kings, along with the Assyrian, the Elamite, and the Hittite, is king of Shinar: that is, Babylonia.

Böhl and Albright, having rejected the popular and persistent identification of Amraphel, king of Shinar, with the great Ḫammurapi, sought some other Akkadian prototype for his name, and invented such names as *Amur*(*ru*)-*âpil* or *Amur*(*ru*)-*âpili*, "The god Amurru is my rewarder,"[206] or *Amurru-ippal*, *Immer-apla*-(*iddin*), "or the like."[207] But no kings with such names ever existed in Babylonia (or elsewhere), while the "Chedorlaomer texts" clearly point to Marduk-apal-iddina as the prototype of Amraphel. One of the numerous ideograms for the name of Marduk was written (and pronounced) ^{d}A.MA.RU,[208] which signifies "deluge"; and even the regular ideogram for it, ^{d}AMAR.UTU, could also be read ^{d}AMAR.U_4—that is, again *amaru*. A normal hypocorism of ^{d}AMAR.U_4-(or ^{d}A.MA.RU-) *apal-iddina*[209] would be *Amar*(*u*)-*apal* = *'Amrāphel*, or rather, with the Septuagint, *Amarphal*.

To summarize: what is told in the "Chedorlaomer texts" about the four hostile kings, as well as their very names, identifies them with four absolutely historical kings of Assyria, Ḫatti, Elam, and Babylonia. These are the same four countries as those in Genesis 14. The names, too, of the four conqueror kings of Genesis 14 coincide with the names or surnames of the four kings

204. The ideogram RU (# 68), not transliterated by Jeremias, has the significations *nadû*, "to throw upon the earth, to place, to found," *šuršudu*, "to found," and synonyms. Cf. the bilingual cosmogonic text in King (1902), I, 130–139, with such correspondences as obv.:6: E n . l í l . k i n u r u É . k u r . r a n u d i m: *Ni-ip-pu-ru ul e-pu-uš É-kur ul ba-ni*, "Nippur had not been made, Ekur (its temple) had not been built."

205. The text skipped (*û*) *irṣiti*(*m*); cf. [âl]*Bâb-ilâni*[meš] *mar-kas šamê*[e] *ù irṣiti*[ti], Balawat Gate Inscription, V:44ff.

206. Böhl (1930), p. 13.

207. Albright (1921), p. 71 = (1926), p. 233.

208. Brünnow, no. 11566; Deimel, no. 79; *ŠL*, IV, 1, no. 949:101. Entered in Akkadian as *amarakku*, "hurricane, deluge."

209. In personal names, both *nadânu*, "to give" (and its verbal forms), and *aplu*, "son," could be written by the signs AŠ (# 1) and MU (# 61). Such spellings for *-apal-iddina* as -AŠ.AŠ or -MU.MU facilitated haplographies.

of the "Chedorlaomer texts," either directly, or through alternative readings of some of their ideographic components. True, these four kings were by no means contemporary with each other: one of them invaded Babylonia in 1530, the second in 1240 (or 1229), the third in 1174–1170; the fourth was active there between 721 and 700. But the "Chedorlaomer texts" do not even pretend that they assaulted Babylonia at one and the same time; on the contrary, they quite clearly describe events that happened at different times. The "Chedorlaomer texts" is not a historiographic work, but a religious edifying one, which develops a consistent historico-philosophical moral idea and has chosen as illustrations four prominent examples from the ages-long Babylonian history, united by the following common particularities: the cosmic scheme of the four world quadrants, sacrilegious sacking of Babylonian temples and carrying off their gods,[210] and tragic ends for the invaders after they have served as tools of divine wrath to punish the Babylonians for their sins.

Strangely enough, the authors who turned to the "Chedorlaomer texts" for confirmation of the historicity of Genesis 14 did not notice the most important and conspicuous circumstance: that the four kings described there are not synchronized, and that their activity takes place in Babylonia, where it belongs, and not in Palestine.

4. Religious Philosophy of History and Cosmic Symbolism

The source from which the Deuteronomist author of Genesis 14 borrowed the names of his four conqueror kings may thus be definitely established as those religious didactic Babylonian works of the late seventh or early sixth century that reached us in late Babylonian copies as the "Chedorlaomer texts," which fully deserve this designation. While these texts render quite correctly the historical facts described, and only present them in a tendentious moralistic light, the Deuteronomist author made contemporaries out of the four kings whose lifetimes were divided by hundreds of years. He transformed their four distinct invasions into a single joint expedition and transferred the arena of their action from Babylonia to Palestine. We shall try to elucidate later what suggested this idea to him. But this borrowing was not a mechanical one, as was supposed by some advocates of the "midrash" theory, who alleged that the author of Genesis 14 needed impressive names and took the first ones he met. The truth is that the Deuteronomist author found in the "Chedorlaomer texts" a religious philosophy of history that was extraordinary close to his own.

The conclusion of Sp.III, 2, presents the previously described tragic fates

210. See Sp. II, 987:27:[*il*]*âni*^{meš} *ina šal-lat ú-še-iṣ-ṣ*[*u-ú*], "they carried off gods within their booty."

of the four kings as due to the direct intervention of Marduk, and the god is then implored "to restore Babylon and Esagila, the shining" (line 9) and promised that "there will be no sinners" any more (line 12: *bêl ḫi-ṭu la i-*[*ši* ...]). The tablet II, 987, begins by a description of the Assembly of gods; one of them (perhaps Marduk) pronounces a sentence upon Babylon:

(3) [ ] *Bâbili*^{ki} (E^{ki}) *mar-kas šamê*^{e} *šá ana ir-bit šârê munnadû* [ ]
(4) [*i-*]*šim-šu-nu-tum šer*$_{9}$*-tam šá ina Bâbili*^{ki} (TIN.TIR^{ki}) *âli ta-na-*[*a-tim*]
(5) *i-šim-šu-nu-tum ším-mat šu-ut Bâbili*^{ki} (E^{ki}) *ṣa-ḫar u ra-*[*bu-ú*]
(6) *ina mil-ki-šú-nu ki-nim ana* ^{m}*Ku-dúr-nâḫ-ḫun-tú šar* ^{mât}*E-lam-mat*
(7) *ú-kan-nu-ú ri-di gà-na šá eli-šú lâ* (NU) *ṭa-a-bi* [ ]
(8) *ina Bâbili*^{ki} (E^{ki}) *âl Kar-*^{d}*Dun-iá-àš šarru-tam ip-pu-uš* [ ]

"(3) [ ] Babylon, the bond of heaven <and earth>, which is founded toward the four winds [ ] (4) [he] determined before them the punishment which is in Babylon, the city of glo[ry], (5) he determined the destiny concerning Babylon, small and gr[eat.] (6) In their just counsel, to Kudur-Naḫḫuntu, king of Elam, (7) they ordained: 'Descend! Go, what is bad to him, [do!...] (8) In Babylon, the city of Karduniaš, exercise kingship! [ ]'"

In Sp. 158 + Sp. II, 962: reverse, the idea of divine punishment is expounded in symmetrically constructed paragraphs, of which we quote the first two (in translation only):

(2) When a governor[211] spe[aks] peace, [(but)....]
(3) the *šedu* (protective genius) of Ešarra,[212] the temple of [the totality of gods,] descends,[213]
(4) the hostile Elamite hastens evil,
(5) and Bêl (Marduk) incites evil plans against Babylon.

* * *

(6) When he does not pronounce justice, (but) stands upon iniquity,
(7) from Ešarra, the temple of the totality of gods, the *šedu* descends,
(8) the hostile Elamite takes away his possession,
(9) and Enlil, who is enthroned above him, burns with anger.

* * *

In a late Babylonian astrological text, known from a tablet of the Arsacid period,[214] the idea of divine retribution through sending an Elamite invasion

211. *Ra-bi-ṣu*, here, as pointed out by Jeremias, is obviously "governor" or "viceroy," not "demon."

212. *É-šár-ra* was the name of several temples (among others, that of the god Aššur in the city of the same name). Jeremias understood it here as a symbolic designation of heaven. But the context hardly allows such an interpretation. Here, it is rather Anu's temple in Uruk (*RLA*, II, 476).

213. The descent of the protective genius from the temple meant that the temple became defenseless and open to the enemy.

214. BM. 55.466 + 55.486 + 55.627; King (1902): cuneiform text, II, pl. LXVII-LXXII; transliteration, I, 209–214; translation by Jeremias (1929), pp. 121f., mainly based on that by B. Landsberger, *Archiv für Keilschriftforschung*, vol. I, no. 2, pp. 69f.

is expounded even more consistently: Marduk, angered by the sins of the Babylonians, thinks about sending a deluge upon them; they are accused especially of lying, treachery, false speeches, and dishonest plans. But after the inhabitants performed atonement incantations, he, instead of sending the flood, "ordered the Elamites to overthrow the country." In Sp. 987, 24, we also have *sa-pi-in-nu mâti ka*[*lâmi*], "overthrow of the entire country," proceded by the ideogram ŠU.RA,[215] which we understand as ŠU, Sumerian particle of intensification, plus RA = *maḫâṣu, dâku, nêru, nêrtu*, "to kill, smite, murder; a murder," and also *raḫâṣu*, "to wash, submerge, flood," and *riḫṣu*, "flood"; thus ŠU.RA = "tremendous flood." We have seen already that Nebuchadnezzar I, a witness to the Elamite invasions of the twelfth century, says that Kudur-Naḫḫundu *nišê* ^{mât}*Akkadi kul-lat-si-na a-bu-biš is-pu-nu*,[216] "overthrew all people of the land of Akkad like a deluge." The allegorical image of flood is present in all of the "Chedorlaomer texts"; the comparison is made according to a double association: the heavy ordeals are equated to the flood both because of their terrible impact and because of the motif of divine retribution for sins which is inherent in the myth of the Deluge. This also explains why three out of the four hostile kings are said to have "led water upon" Babylon and Esagila: actually, the first to have done it was Sennacherib in 689, but the idea harmonized so well with the immemorially ancient symbolism of the Deluge that it was retrojected into the past. Esarhaddon, in his apologetic version of Babylon's destruction by his father, bypasses him completely and uses instead the same religious symbolism and justification:[217]

> Before my time, in the reign of an earlier king, there befell evil omens in Sumer and Akkad. The people who dwelt in Šuanna[218] answered each other "nay,"[219] ⌜plotting rebellion⌝ the while, ⌜*forsaking their gods,*⌝ *abandoning* [*the worship*] *of the goddesses of their cult, and going away to other* (*lands*). They stretched their hands into Esagila, the temple of the gods, *an inviolable shrine*, and squandered gold, silver, and precious stones in Elam in payment (for aid). Anger seized the lord of the gods, Marduk. For the overthrow of the land and the destruction of its people he devised evil plans. The Araḫtu Canal, ⌜a river of abundance,⌝ *a mighty river, a raging torrent*, whose floods were high, ⌜like unto⌝ the deluge, ⌜was brought up and poured⌝ [its waters] into the city of his abode and his sanctuary, and made it like unto a ruin heap. The gods (and) the goddesses, who dwelt therein, went up to heaven. The people

215. Not KU (?) RA, as in Jeremias (1917), p. 94; cf. autography, Pinches (1897), p. 85.

216. See Page 92 above.

217. We quote the Black Stone Inscription (*AR*, II, § 642), with words appearing only in the version of BM. Prism 78.273 (§ 649), printed in italics.

218. Part of Babylon, by extension = Babylon.

219. I.e., "split into factions" (Luckenbill's comment).

living in its midst, having been apportioned to the yoke and the fetter, went into slavery.

We see an extraordinary similarity between Esarhaddon's narrative and the spirit, attitude, images, and phraseology of the "Chedorlaomer texts." It is quite clear that it was composed for Esarhaddon by the Babylonian priests of Marduk; we know that he broke with the radically secular and anti-Babylonian policy of his father Sennacherib and returned to the policy of his grandfather Sargon, who was favorable to the Babylonian clergy and nobility and sought their support.

Now the idea according to which elemental calamities and, especially, the destructive invasions of foreign conquerors are to be considered divine punishment for the sins of the people, was strongly propagated by the prophets of Israel and Judah, from Amos and Hosea to Jeremiah and Ezekiel. Jeremias has remarked that "the Israelite prophetic writings show, in their way, the same attitude" as the "Chedorlaomer texts" and related Babylonian texts.[220] The Deuteronomist school made of it the cornerstone of its historiographic construction. Of course, this idea is common to most religions, and it naturally finds its expression in periods of heavy national calamities and catastrophes. But it is more than probable that such a coincidence of basic attitudes must have raised the interest of the Deuteronomist and attracted him toward Babylonian works of this character. He must also have been struck by the similarity between the symbolism of flood as punishment of a sinful city, and his own people's myth about the destruction of Sodom and Gomorrah by Yahwe. The latter myth may plausibly be viewed as an original Palestinian variant of the ancient Sumerian deluge myth, which came very early to the West Semitic environment and evolved there along a distinct line.[221] Although, according to Genesis 19:24–25, Sodom and Gomorrah were destroyed by a fiery rain (a motif inspired by the scorched condition and sterility of the Dead Sea valley), this story was doubtless blended with the international motif of flooding with water (as implied in Genesis 13:10 and underlined in Genesis 14:3). In all the passages of the Bible which mention the destruction of Sodom and Gomorrah, the term used is the verb הפך, "to overturn, to overthrow"; but in Akkadian, too, the verb *sapânu*, "to overthrow," is used to describe the effect of the deluge (*abûbu*).

220. Jeremias (1917), p. 70. "The nature of the composition was first explained clearly by Alfred Jeremias... who pointed out the striking similarity of the viewpoint to the so-called Deuteronomic attitude of the historical books of the Old Testament" (Albright [1926], p. 237). Actually, Jeremias only indirectly hinted at one passage of Deuteronomy; the credit for disclosing the similarity with the Deuteronomist school belongs to Albright.

221. It has already been pointed out that the history of Lot and his daughters after the destruction of Sodom gives the impression that in the original version they were the only people who survived the catastrophe; see Gunkel, pp. 197f.

Besides the wide use of the deluge symbolism, the "Chedorlaomer texts" have recourse to yet another kind of cosmic symbolism: identification of things celestial and terrestrial. We have seen already that according to the Babylonians the earth and all earthly countries, rivers, and cities are but reflections of their heavenly counterparts, represented by constellations.[222] The celestial Babylon was seen in the constellation *Ikû* (AŠ.GÁN), "acre" (surface unit of ploughed field), which combined our Cetus and Aries; the latter was personified as the "farmhand," *amêlagru* (lúKU.MAL or simply KU.MAL), who tills the "acre";[223] at the same time, it also represented the great temple Esagila within the celestial Babylon.[224] The constellation *Enzu* (UZA), "goat," our Lyra, was the celestial Ezida, the temple of Nabû in Borsippa.[225] Now the "Chedorlaomer texts" often have recourse to astronomic symbols for terrestrial cities and shrines. Describing Kudur-Naḫ̮ḫ̮undu's invasion of Babylon, Sp. 158 + Sp. II, 962: obverse: 15 says: *a-na* AŠ.GÁN *šu-*[ ]... *is-ni-qa*, "against AŠ.GÁN (= the constellation *Ikû*) ... he advanced." In Sp. 987:24, UZA (*Enzu*) is mentioned after the text relates how Kuḏur-Naḫ̮ḫ̮undu and Tukulti-Ninurta seized power in Babylon; this should be understood as symbolic designation of Ezida, which is so often cited in Sp. 158 + Sp. 2, 962. In Sp. III, 2: reverse 9, Esagila bears the epithet *ni-bu*, "luminous," the astronomical term for the brightest star of a constellation.[226] In a related text cited above,[227] a lengthy astrological commentary explains, among other details, that Mars and the Moon are "the lords of the secret (*niṣirtu*) of Elam," Jupiter and the Sun are "the lords of the secret of Akkad," and "the place of the secret of the Sun is (the constellation) lúKU.MAL."[228] Since KU.MAL (Aries) was symbolically identical with Esagila, we are now able to grasp the reason for the name *Kudur-Naḫ̮ḫ̮undu* being cryptically written KU.KU.KU.MAL: the author, faithful to his method, expressed by this spelling the idea that the Elamite invader "overthrew" (KU.KU = *sakâpu*, "to knock down, to overthrow")[229] Esagila (KU.MAL)!

222. See Pages 80–81 above.

223. *B.u.A.*, II, 107, 410; Jeremias (1929), pp. 208, 210, 214f.; *ŠL*, II, 1, no. 1:71; IV, 2, nos. 189, 190, 244.

224. *B.u.A.*, II, 107; Jeremias (1929), pp. 108ff., 214ff., 286; *RLA*, I, 353. Moreover one of the most common ideograms for the city of Babylon was E*ki*, but E was also the ideogram for *i-ku* (*ikû*); see *CAD*, VII, 67f.

225. In the text mentioned in Note 214 above, rev.: 6–7, it is stated: "Therefore the Goat-star (UZA) which is visible together with Scorpio, equals Ezida"; cf. *ŠL*, IV, 2, no. 145.

226. Jeremias (1917), p. 82, n. *b*.

227. King (1902), I, 209–214.

228. Rev. : 24–33.

229. *ŠL*, II, 4, no. 536:275:h.

Traces of cosmic symbolism are also perceptible in Genesis 14. It could not be by hazard that the number of Chedorlaomer's adversaries is equal to twelve—the traditional number of months and signs of the zodiac, symbolizing the annual cycle.[230] The invaders, on their circular route, prevail over eleven armies, but are defeated by the twelfth; the time of troubles is over, a new year is inaugurated by Abraham's victory, as it was in Babylonia by the *akîtu* festival which celebrated Marduk's victory over Tiamat.[231] And it is noteworthy that in the astrological text about the Elamite invasion of Babylon, this is symbolically preceded by the story of Marduk's victorious fight with Tiamat, and the very invasion is motivated by the conjunction of heavenly bodies personifying Marduk and Tiamat.[232] The strange number of armed servants of Abraham, 318, was explained by H. Winckler as another astral figure: allegedly the number of nights in a lunar year when the moon is visible.[233] This hypothesis has both advantages and shortcomings. It has in its favor its agreement with the year-cycle pattern which may be detected in Genesis 14; the very term by which these 318 men are introduced, *ḥanikîm*, derives from the same root *ḥānak*, "to dedicate, to inaugurate," as *Ḥanôk* (Enoch), to whom was ascribed a lifetime of 365 years (Genesis 5:23), corresponding to the number of days in a solar year, and the later feast of *Ḥanukkā* (Hanukka), which originally was a feast of lights in honor of the inauguration of a new solar cycle after the winter solstice.[234] This number is also actually found at least once, and as early as the Amarna Age—not directly, it is true, but as 1 + 317.[235] On the other hand, proof that 318 was

230. A systematic list of the twelve signs of the Zodiac appears for the first time in a Babylonian text from the fifth year of Darius II (i.e., 419/8), but the names of the zodiacal constellations are extremely old, and so is the number twelve (twelve months in a year, twelve double hours in a day), especially with the Hebrews, who had a predilection for arrangements by twelve.

231. The same is true for the original meaning of the New Year Festival with the Hebrews; see the essays by Oesterley and Widengren.

232. King (1902), I, 211, lines 1–7; p. 211, lines 8–23.

233. Winckler (1900), p. 27. The calculation is as follows: the lunar years consists of 354 nights; the moon is invisible for three nights each month, i.e., $12 \times 3 = 36$ nights in a year; $354 - 36 = 318$.

234. See, e.g., *JE*, VI, 224, with further references. The term *ḥanikîm* seems to appear as early as the fifteenth century, in the Akkadian-written Taanach letter 6:8 (*ḫa-na-ku-u-ka*), with the probable meaning of "warriors" or something similar, as was first pointed out by Ernst Sellin (quoted by Skinner, p. 266). This equation was frequently adduced by Albright: (1931), p. 221; (1939), p. 96; (1944), p. 24; (1951), p. 6 (as to the relationship of this term to the Egyptian *ḥnkw*, Albright's opinions varied from article to article). The occurrence of this apparently ancient word in Genesis 14 cannot serve as indication of the chapter's equally ancient origin, since the root חנך continued to exist in Hebrew.

235. Scarabs issued by the Pharaoh Amenophis III in honor of the arrival of his bride, the Mitannian princess Giluḫipa, state that she came accompanied by 317 maidservants; see Breasted, II, §§ 806f.; compared to Genesis 14 by Jeremias (1930), p. 289. Gordon, p. 87, n. 1, noted: "The number 318 is conventional, to judge from the fact that princess Giluhepa of Mitanni, with her 317 maids, was in a party of 318."

actually considered a specific figure in the ancient East is still lacking. The old Talmudic explanation of it as a gematria of *Eliezer*, the only slave of Abraham mentioned by name,[236] may be simpler.[237] However, in view of the astral accessories of the "Chedorlaomer texts," some allegoric meaning for this figure seems quite possible.

But one element in Genesis 14 is certainly of astral origin and was directly borrowed from the "Chedorlaomer texts." This is the Valley of Siddim—a name not found elsewhere in the Bible. The only convincing etymology of it was given by Koehler,[238] who derived it from **שׂדד**, "to drive bordering furrows," and supported it with parallels from other Semitic languages: Ugaritic *šd* II, "acre,"[239] Akkadian *šiddu*, "area unit (of a field)," Syriac *sedā'*, "spatium sulcis." This etymology is fully confirmed by the Aramaic Genesis Apocryphon from Qumran, where **עמק השׂדים** is translated by **עמקא די סדיא** (XXI:25). Thus *Śiddîm* is an exact translation of Akkadian *ikû*, "acre," the name of the constellation *mulIkû*, the celestial counterpart of Babylon, transferred according to the principle **מלכותא דארעא כמלכותא דרקיע** to the terrestrial Babylon as well. We have seen that in the "Chedorlaomer texts" AŠ.GÁN (= *mulIkû*) was used as a synonym for Babylon, to indicate the goal of Kudur-Naḫḫundu's invasion. The author of Genesis 14 transferred the astral symbolic name of Babylon to the region of Sodom and Gomorrah, just as he did with the expeditions of the four kings from the same "Chedorlaomer texts."

This shows that the author of Genesis 14 consciously associated Babylon with Sodom and Gomorrah. He was similar, in this respect, to other Jewish writers of the latter part of the Babylonian captivity, who with burning hatred predicted the imminent destruction of their captor's capital by the Medes and Persians, and borrowed their images both from memories of the flooding of Babylon by Sennacherib and from familiar reminiscences of the total disappearance of Sodom and Gomorrah. Jeremias has pertinently noted the similarity in symbolic phraseology between the "Chedorlaomer texts" and two passages of Hebrew prophetic literature: Isaiah 14:23 and Jeremiah 51:42.[240] It is interesting to follow this analogy more closely. Both passages belong to anonymous prophets of the Exile period, whose works

236. Nedarim 32a; cf. *JE*, V, 589. א = 1, ל = 30, י = 10, ע = 70, ז = 7, ר = 200; total 318.

237. For other possible instances of arithmetical gematria in the Bible, see *JE*, V, 589; Bewer, p. 279; for computative gematria, see Note 242 below.

238. Koehler-Baumgartner, pp. 915, 916.

239. *UM* § 20.1809: *šd* II "acre" || *kmn*; *kmn* (*UM* § 20.929) appears in Nuzu as *kumânu* (and in middle Assyrian as *ku-ma-a-ni*, the smallest unit of area [Weidner, p. 43]).

240. Jeremias (1917), p. 81, n. 2.

were included in the books by their great predecessors.[241] In the first passage—a prosaic insertion into a highly artistic poem about the downfall of the Babylonian king—it is said (Isaiah 14):

> (22) I will rise up against them, says Yahwe Zebaoth, and will cut off from Babylon name and remnant, offspring and posterity, says Yahwe. (23) And I will make it a possession of the hedgehog and pools of water, and I will sweep it with the broom of destruction, says Yahwe Zebaoth.

The second passage pertains to a chapter (Jeremiah 51) which predicts a quick destruction of Babylon by the Medes. This chapter is not unlike the poetic parts of the "Chedorlaomer texts," but what was a matter of mourning and distress for the Babylonians is here described with malignant joy. The ciphering of בבל into ששך[242] imitates the neo-Babylonian play with ideograms to hide the execrable names, samples of which we have seen in our analysis of the "Chedorlaomer texts":

> (41) How Sheshach is taken,
> the praise of the whole earth seized!
> How Babylon has become
> a horror among the nations!
> (42) The sea has come up on Babylon,
> she is covered with its tumultuous waves.

Such descriptions were bound to evoke associations with the ruin of Sodom and Gomorrah—and indeed, the works of the same late-Exilic prophets contain quite clear comparisons:

> (19) And Babylon, the glory of kingdoms,
> the splendor and pride of the Chaldeans,
> will be like Sodom and Gomorrah
> when God overthrew them. (Isaiah 13)

> (39) Therefore wild beasts and jackals shall dwell in Babylon, and ostriches shall dwell in her; she shall be peopled no more for ever, nor inhabited for all generations. (40) As when God overthrew Sodom and Gomorrah and its inhabitants,[243] says Yahwe, so no man shall dwell there, and no son of man shall sojourn in her. (Jeremiah 50).

These passages give us the clue to the formation of Genesis 14, which we attributed, on the ground of its close connection with the so-called Second Deuteronomist, to the same years and place. Jewish authors of this period were doubtless well acquainted with the Babylonian moralistic literature about the past catastrophes suffered by Babylon, like the priestly narrative of Esarhaddon quoted above and our "Chedorlaomer texts." The resemblance with the familiar history of the destruction of Sodom and Gomorrah

241. Lods, pp. 461ff.; Pfeiffer, p. 443.

242. By the device called אתבש (substituting the last letter of the alphabet for the first, the last but one for the second, and so on); another example is לב קמי = כשדים, Jeremiah 51:1.

243. Also referred to in Note 40 above.

was striking for them. What for the Babylonians was bitter memory and an appeal to improve themselves lest the troubles return, was for the exiled Jews a source of satisfaction and anticipation of Babylon's definitive ruin. From equating Babylon with Sodom and Gomorrah it was only one step to transferring to Sodom and Gomorrah some catastrophic events of Babylonian history. That is what was done by the author of Genesis 14. He gave the symbolic astral name of Babylon to the valley of Sodom and Gomorrah and, before he let the cities be incinerated in fire and swallowed by the Dead Sea, he inserted into the patriarchal tales his own version of their full defeat and sack by the very same four kings who, according to the "Chedorlaomer texts," had plundered and oppressed Babylon. We have already seen how skillfully and felicitously he utilized this subject to present the idea of the legal rights of Abraham and his progeniture to possess all of Canaan with Transjordan and Negeb, and of the primordial authority of the Jerusalem temple and its priesthood.

In 1898, L. W. King wrote disdainfully about the three Spartoli tablets: "In fact, they can hardly be said to possess a context at all."[244] Our preceding study showed that they do possess a perfectly intelligible context referring to events written down in chronicles and annals, and to historical figures well known from the history of Babylonia, Assyria, Ḫatti, and Elam. This alone would have been worth the trouble of the lengthy investigation that had to be undertaken. But it also provided, in addition, a clue to "the most tantalizing historic problem of the Bible."[245] Although many Biblicists might wish the problem to have been solved differently,[246] the

244. King (1898), I, lii f.

245. "Until the actual personages of Genesis 14 are encountered in other documents, we cannot be sure of the situation. Meanwhile the chapter will remain the most tantalizing historic problem of the Bible" (Gordon, p. 87).

246. The latest achievement in this field is a short but amazing article by Cornelius (1960). In it, Amraphel is equated with the "deified Ḫammurabi-El" (see Note 65, above) and Tidal, with Tudḫaliaš I; these two monarchs allegedly concluded an alliance with an imagined Hurrian Arriwuk of Alzi and a king of Elam in order to capture Palestine from the Pharaohs of the XIIIth Dynasty. Now Ḫammurapi, according to the author's own chronology (known as the Albright-Cornelius chronology), reigned from 1728 to 1686, while Tudḫaliaš I can by no means be placed, within the same chronology, earlier than 1635–1620, three generations before Muršiliš I, who conquered Babylon in 1530 (see the chronological tables of Moortgat and Helck, both of whom adhere to the Albright-Cornelius chronology). And if the real enemy of the four kings was the Pharaoh, why did Genesis 14—Cornelius' only source—forget precisely him, though it remembered the Zuzim and the Emim? But the coalition turned out to be a grave mistake committed by the senile Ḫammurapi: "It was not Babel who reaped the success [what success? Were not the four kings totally *defeated* by Abrahām?], but a Hyksos [the Hyksos are made Hittites by Cornelius] took possession of Egypt itself... and the Hurrians settled in the region of the Euphrates bend ... and it even opened the road to Babel to the Cassites" (p. 5). Thus, a new history of the ancient Near East is being created on the sole basis of Genesis 14, but, ironically, the data of Genesis 14 are completely reversed to fit the author's imagination.

results of our investigation were not totally disappointing. By unraveling the meaning of some obscure Babylonian texts, it helped to follow the survival and evolution of their political and cosmic symbolism in Jewish literary creations of the Captivity period, and to catch a glimpse of the Jewish-Babylonian spiritual connections at that time.

BOOKS AND ARTICLES CITED

Albright (1921): William F. Albright, "A Revision of Early Hebrew Chronology," *Journal of the Palestine Oriental Society*, 1:49–79 (1920–21).

——— (1926): "The Historical Background of Genesis XIV," *Journal of the Society of Oriental Research*, 10:231–269 (1926).

——— (1931): "Mitannian maryannu 'Chariot-Warrior,' and the Canaanite and Egyptian Equivalents," *Archiv für Orientforschung*, 6:217–219 (1930–31).

——— (1939): "The Babylonian Matter in the Predeuteronomic Primeval History (JE) in Gen. 1–11," *Journal of Biblical Literature*, 58:91–103 (1939).

——— (1942): "A Third Revision of the Early Chronology of Western Asia," *Bulletin of the American Schools of Oriental Research*, no. 88 (1942), pp. 28–36.

——— (1943): "Two Little Understood Amarna Letters from the Middle Jordan Valley," *Bulletin of the American Schools of Oriental Research*, no. 89 (1943), pp. 7–17.

——— (1944): "A Prince of Taanach in the Fifteenth Century B.C.," *Bulletin of the American Schools of Oriental Research*, no. 94 (1944), pp. 12–27.

——— (1951): "The Old Testament and the Archaeology of Palestine," in H. H. Rowley (ed.), *The Old Testament and Modern Study* (Oxford, 1951), pp. 1–26.

ANET: James B. Pritchard (ed.), *Ancient Near Eastern Texts Relating to the Old Testament*, 2nd ed. (Princeton, 1955).

AR: Daniel David Luckenbill, *Ancient Records of Assyria and Babylonia*. 2 vols. (Chicago, 1926–27).

ARM: *Archives royales de Mari*, ed. André Parrot and Georges Dossin. 12 vols. to date (Paris, 1950–).

Benzinger: Immanuel Benzinger, "Zur Quellenscheidung in Gen. 14," in *Vom Alten Testament, Karl Marti... gewidmet* (*Beihefte der Zeitschrift für Alttestamentliche Wissenschaft*, 41:21–27 [Giessen, 1925]).

Bereschit Rabba, ed. J. Theodor. 2 vols. (Berlin, 1912).

Bewer: Julius A. Bewer, *The Literature of the Old Testament*, 3rd ed., revised by Emil G. Kraeling (New York, 1962).

Bezold: Carl Bezold, *Babylonisch-assyrisches Glossar*, posthumously published by Albrecht Goetze (Heidelberg, 1926).

Böhl (1916): Franz Marius Theodor de Liagre Böhl, "Tud'alia I, Zeitgenosse des Abraham, um 1650 v. Chr.," *Zeitschrift für Alttestamentliche Wissenschaft*, 36:65–73 (1916).

——— (1924): "Die Könige von Genesis 14," *Zeitschrift für Alttestamentliche Wissenschaft*, 62:148–153, N.S. 1 (1924).

——— (1930): *Das Zeitalter Abrahams* (published in *Der Alte Orient*, 29:1) (Leipzig, 1930).

——— (1953): *Opera Minora. Studies en Bijdragen op Assyriologisch en Oudtestamentisch Terrein* (Groningen-Djakarta, 1953).

Breasted: James Henry Breasted, *Ancient Records of Egypt*. 5 vols. (Chicago, 1906).

Brünnow: Rudolf E. Brünnow, *A Classified List of All Simple and Compound Cuneiform Ideographs*... (Leiden, 1889).

B. u. A.: Bruno Meissner, *Babylonien und Assyrien*. 2 vols. (Heidelberg, 1920, 1925).

CAD: *The Assyrian Dictionary of the Oriental Institute of the University of Chicago*. 8 vols. to date (Chicago-Glückstadt, 1956–).

Cameron: George G. Cameron, *History of Early Iran* (Chicago ,1936).

Cassuto: Môše David Cassuto, "Berêšît," *'Enṣiqlôpedîyā miqrā'ît*, II (Jerusalem, 1954), 318–335.

Clay: Albert T. Clay, *Personal Names from Cuneiform Inscriptions of the Cassite Period.* Yale Oriental Series, vol. I (New Haven, 1912).

Cornelius (1956): Friedrich Cornelius, "Die Chronologie des Vorderen Orients im 2. Jahrtausend v. Chr.," *Archiv für Orientforschung*, 17:294–309 (1954–56).

——— (1960): "Genesis XIV," *Zeitschrift für Alttestamentliche Wissenschaft*, 72:1–7, N.S. 31 (1960).

Deimel: Anton Deimel, *Pantheon Babylonicum* . . . (Rome, 1914). See also *ŠL.*

Delitzsch (1896): Friedrich Delitzsch, *Assyrisches Handwörterbuch* (Leipzig, 1896).

——— (1914): *Sumerisches Glossar* (Leipzig, 1914).

Dhorme (1951): *Recueil Édouard Dhorme*: *Études bibliques et orientales* (Paris, 1951).

——— (1956): *La Bible*: *L'Ancient Testament.* Bibliothèque de la Pléiade. 2 vols. (Paris, 1956).

Dossin: Georges Dossin, "Le Site de Reḫobot-'Ir et de Resen," *Le Muséon*, 47:107–121 (1934).

Dupont-Sommer: A. Dupont-Sommer, *Les Écrits esséniens découverts près de la Mer Morte* (Paris, 1959).

Ebeling: Erich Ebeling, "Bruchstücke eines politischen Propaganda-Gedichtes," *Mitteilungen der altorientalischen Gesellschaft*, vol. XII, no. 3 (1938).

Friedrich: Johannes Friedrich, *Aus dem hethitischen Schrifttum.* Published in *Der Alte Orient*, 24:3; 25:2 (Leipzig, 1925).

Gardiner: Alan H. Gardiner, *Ancient Egyptian Onomastica*: *Text*, 2 vols. (Oxford, 1957).

Glueck: Nelson Glueck, "Three Israelite Towns in the Jordan Valley: Zarethan, Succoth, Zaphon," *Bulletin of the American Schools of Oriental Research*, no. 90 (1943), pp. 2–23.

Gordon: Cyrus H. Gordon, *The World of the Old Testament* (New York, 1958). See also *UM.*

Gunkel: Hermann Gunkel, *Genesis übersetzt und erklärt* (Göttingen, 1901).

Gurney: O. R. Gurney, *The Hittites* (Harmondsworth, 1954).

Helck: Wolfgang Helck, *Die Beziehungen Ägyptens zu Vorderasien im* 3. *und* 2. *Jahrtausend v. Chr.* (Wiesbaden, 1962).

Hinz: W. Hinz, "Elamica," *Orientalia*, N.S., 22:1–20 (1963).

Hommel: Fritz Hommel, *Die altisraeltiische Überlieferung in inschriftlicher Beleuchtung* (Munich, 1897).

JE: *Jewish Encyclopedia.* 12 vols. (New York — London, 1901–06).

Jensen: Peter Jensen, *Das Gilgamesch-Epos in der Weltliteratur*, vol. I (Strasbourg, 1906).

Jeremias (1917): Alfred Jeremias, "Die sogenannten Kedorlaomer-Texte," in *Orientalistische Studien Fritz Hommel*. . . *beigetragen*, I (*Mitteilungen der vorderasiatischen Gesellschaft*, XXI, Leipzig, 1917), 69–97.

——— (1929): *Handbuch der altorientalischen Geisteskultur*, 2nd ed. (Berlin — Leipzig, 1929).

——— (1930): *Das Alte Testament im Licht des alten Orients*, 4th ed. (Leipzig, 1930).

King (1898): L. W. King, *The Letters and Inscriptions of Ḫammurabi, King of Babylon, about B.C. 2200*, 3 vols. (London, 1898).

——— (1902): *The Seven Tablets of Creation*, 2 vols. (London, 1902).

——— (1907): *Chronicles Concerning Early Babylonian Kings*, 2 vols. (London, 1907).

Koehler-Baumgartner: Ludwig Koehler and Walter Baumgartner, *Lexicon in Veteris Testamenti Libros* (Leiden, 1953; 2nd printing, 1958).

König: Friedrich Wilhelm König, *Geschichte Elams* (published in *Der Alte Orient*, 29:4) (Leipzig, 1931).

Kraeling: Emil G. Kraeling, *Rand McNally Bible Atlas* (New York, 1956).

Kupper: Jean-Robert Kupper, *Les Nomades en Mésopotamie au temps des rois de Mari* (Paris, 1957).

Labat: René Labat, *Manuel d'épigraphie akkadienne*, 3rd ed. (Paris, 1959).

Lambert: W. F. Lambert, "Three Unpublished Fragments of the Tukulti-Ninurta Epic," *Archiv für Orientforschung*, 18:38–51 (1957–58).

Landersdorfer: S. Landersdorfer, "Das Priesterkönigtum von Salem," *Journal of the Society of Oriental Research*, 9:203–216 (1925).

Lods: Adolphe Lods, *Histoire de la littérature hébraïque et juive depuis les origines jusqu'à la ruine de l'État juif (135 après J.-C.)*, posthumously published by A. Parrot (Paris, 1950).

Luckenbill: see *AR*.

Meinhold: Johannes Meinhold, *1 Mose 14* (published in *Beihefte der Zeitschrift für alttestamentliche Wissenschaft*, no. 22) (Giessen, 1911).

Meissner: Bruno Meissner, *Seltene assyrische Ideogramme* (Leipzig, 1910). See also *B.u.A.*

Moortgat: Anton Moortgat, "Geschichte Vorderasiens bis zum Hellenismus," in Alexander Scharff and Anton Moortgat, *Ägypten und Vorderasien im Altertum* (Munich, 1950; 2nd printing, 1959), pp. 193–535.

Nöldeke: Theodor Nöldeke, *Untersuchungen zur Kritik des Alten Testament* (Kiel, 1869).

NPN: Ignace J. Gelb, Pierre M. Purves, and Allan A. MacRae, *Nuzi Personal Names* (Chicago, 1943).

Oesterley: W. O. E. Oesterley, "Early Hebrew Festival Rituals, " in S. H. Hooke (ed.), *Myth and Ritual* (Oxford, 1933), pp. 111–146.

Olmstead: A. T. Olmstead, *History of Assyria* (New York–London, 1923).

Pilter: W. T. Pilter, "Some Amorite Personal Names in Genesis XIV," *Proceedings of the Society of Biblical Archaeology*, 35:205–226 (1913).

Pinches (1897): Theophilus G. Pinches, "Certain Inscriptions and Records Referring to Babylonia and Elam and Their Rulers,and Other Matters," *Journal of the Transactions of the Victoria Institute*, 29:43–89 (1897).

——— (1902): *The Old Testament in the Light of the Historical Records and Legends of Assyria and Babylonia* (London, 1902).

Pfeiffer: Robert H. Pfeiffer, *Introduction to the Old Testament*, rev. ed. (New York, 1948).

Procksch: Otto Procksch, *Genesis übersetzt und erklärt* (Leipzig, 1924).

PRU II: Charles Virolleaud, *Le Palais royal d'Ugarit*, II: *Textes en cunéiformes alphabétiques des archives est, ouest et centrales* (Paris, 1957).

RLA: *Reallexikon der Assyriologie*, vols. I, II, ed. Erich Ebeling and Bruno Meissner (Berlin-Leipzig, 1932; 1938); vol. III, ed. Ernst Weidner (1957).

Saggs: H. W. F. Saggs, *The Greatness That Was Babylon* (New York, 1962).

Schaeffer: Claude F.-A. Schaeffer, *Ugaritica III* (Paris, 1956).

Schrader: Eberhard Schrader, ed., *Sammlung von assyrischen und babylonischen Texten in Umschrift und Übersetzung* (Berlin, vol. I, 1889; vol. II, 1890; vol. III, part 1, 1892; vol. III, part 2, 1890).

Schröder: Otto Schröder, *Die Tontafeln von El-Amarna*, 2 vols. (Vorderasiatische Schriftdenkmäler der königlichen Museen zu Berlin, books XI and XII) (Berlin, 1915).

Skinner: John Skinner, *A Critical and Exegetical Commentary on Genesis* (New York, 1910).

ŠL: Anton Deimel, *Sumerisches Lexikon*, 4 vols. in 9 books (vol. IV, book 2, by Felix Gössmann) (Rome, 1927–50).

Thompson: R. Campbell Thompson, *The Reports of the Magicians and Astrologers of Nineveh and Babylon*, 2 vols. (London, 1900).

UM: Cyrus H. Gordon, *Ugaritic Manual* (Analecta Orientalia, vol. XXXV) (Rome, 1955).

Virolleaud: Charles Virolleaud, *L'Astrologie chaldéenne*: *Le livre intitulé "Enuma (anu) ilu Bel"*. . . , 14 fascicles (Paris, 1905–14). See also *PRU II*.

Weidner: Ernst Weidner, *Die Inschriften Tukulti-Ninurtas I* (published in *Archiv für Orientforschung*, Beiheft XII) (Graz, 1959).

Wellhausen (1883): Julius Wellhausen, *Prolegomena to the History of Ancient Israel*, trans. from the 2nd German ed. (1883); offset reprint (New York, 1958).

——— (1889): *Die Composition des Hexateuchs und der historischen Bücher des Alten Testament*, 3rd ed. (Berlin, 1889).

Widengren: Geo Widengren, "Early Hebrew Myths and Their Interpretation," in S. H. Hooke, ed., *Myth, Ritual, and Kingship* (Oxford, 1958), pp. 149–203.

Winckler (1897): Hugo Winckler, *Altorientalische Forschungen*, vol. I (Leipzig, 1897).

——— (1900): *Geschichte Israels in Einzeldarstellungen*, vol. II: *Die Legende* (Leipzig, 1900).

Winckler-Abel: *Der Thontafelfund von El Amarna*, ed. Hugo Winckler, autographed from the originals by Ludwig Abel (Königliche Museen zu Berlin, Mitteilungen aus den orientalischen Sammlungen, books I-III) (Berlin, vol. I, 1889; vol. II, part 1, and II, part 2, 1890).

Wiseman: D. J. Wiseman, *Chronicles of Chaldaean Kings (626–556) in the British Museum* (London, 1956).

Yeivin: Šemū'ēl Yeivin, "Be'ēr-Šeba' 'îr hā-'ābôt," *Zion*, 20:711–721 (1955).

The Date and Circumstances of the Cursing of Canaan

By David Neiman

We find in Genesis 9:25–27 Noah's blessing and cursing, in the course of which the diluvian Patriarch confers blessings upon Shem and Japheth at the expense of Canaan. As the text has been received by us, it reads as follows:

ויאמר ארור כנען עבד עבדים יהיה לאחיו.
ויאמר ברוך יהוה אלהי שם ויהי כנען עבד למו.
יפת אלהים ליפת וישכון באהלי שם ויהי כנען עבד למו.

The passage contains a passionate expression of hatred and anger. Clearly this is intended to be the cursing of Canaan, for it is that which is thrice expressed in this passage. Although the blessings conferred upon Shem and Japheth are important, they are clearly subordinate to the execration of Canaan.

We are led to this violent outburst by a series of stories and ideas, skillfully stitched together in what appears to be a connected narrative. Yet the intrusions and irrelevant addenda, purposefully inserted, clearly stand out.

Beginning with verse 18, we can isolate the following statements.

The three sons of Noah are the ancestors of all mankind (verses 18 and 19). This statement of the author's philosophy of history is clearly a forecast of the Table of Nations in chapter 10, to which these two verses could stand as introductory. Yet at the end of verse 18, and quite irrelevantly, the author insinuates the aside, "Ham is the father of Canaan."

The natural order of the verses should be as follows:

ויהיו בני נח היצאים מן התבה שם חם ויפת.
שלשה אלה בני נח ומאלה נפצה כל הארץ.

That the phrase וחם הוא אבי כנען is intrusive is clear from the failure of the passage to mention any other progeny of the three sons of Noah. Moreover, although the sons of Ham are later named[1] as "Ethiopia, Egypt, Put, and Canaan," it is only Canaan who is brought to the fore in 9:18. And the phrasing of the statement is also peculiar in that it says, "Ham is

1. Genesis 10:6.

the father of Canaan," as if to imply that that is his mark of distinction. Then too, despite the fact that Ham is presented as the perpetrator of the crime of uncovering the father's nakedness, it is his role as the father of Canaan—on whose head the curse is to fall—that is emphasized.

It is obvious that the purpose of the insinuation of the phrase concerning Ham's son at this point is to sustain the interest of the narrative which is unfolding. This phrase is one of the links in the chain of stories which follow, all of which are aligned to lead up to the concluding curse. Thus, the story beginning with verse 20, which is probably the etiological account of viticulture, is worked into the larger composition planned by the author. We read:

ויחל נח איש האדמה ויטע כרם.
וישת מן היין וישכר.

In attempting to render the meaning of verse 20, we realize that it poses verbal problems which have led to such disagreements in reading as the following.

The Authorized Version translates, "And Noah began to be a husbandman and he planted a vineyard."[2] The Revised Version renders, "Noah was the first tiller of the soil. He planted a vineyard." The Revised Standard Version follows the Revised Version word for word. John Skinner[3] reads it as "Noah the husbandman was the first who planted a vineyard," and Hermann Gunkel[4] as "Noah, the first husbandman, also began to plant a vineyard." Gerhard Von Rad, in his commentary on Genesis,[5] accepts the reading of the Revised Version, on which the Revised Standard Version is based.

To the Hebrew of antiquity, agriculture was so accepted a part of existence that the first of men was pictured as being involved in the working of the soil,[6] and when the first two sons of man are described, one of them is a shepherd and the other a farmer.[7] The agricultural element in man's civilization is to the ancient Israelite so indispensable a factor in his concept of life that he could not imagine a world without it; nay, not even the paradise which he postulated in his idealization of his prehuman ancestor. For into the garden of perfection which the Lord God created, man was placed

2. Following the Septuagint and the Vulgate.

3. John Skinner, *A Critical and Exegetical Commentary on Genesis*, International Critical Commentary (New York: Scribner's, 1925), p. 182.

4. Hermann Gunkel, *Genesis, übersetzt und erklärt*, Göttinger Handkommentar zum Alten Testament (Göttingen: Vandenhoeck und Ruprecht, 1902), p. 70.

5. Gerhard Von Rad, *Genesis, A Commentary* (Philadelphia: Westminster Press, 1961), p. 131.

6. Genesis 2:15.

7. Genesis 4:2.

לעבדה ולשמרה to till it and to guard it.[8] Thus, to say that Genesis 9:20 is the etiology of agriculture is rather wide of the mark, and the translators of the Revised Version and the Revised Standard Version and Von Rad cannot be correct in their rendering.

Viticulture, on the other hand, is agriculture with finesse, an added element of sophistication in man's otherwise difficult drudgery in the fields of corn. Since man is involved—for he has no choice—in the work of tilling the soil, his work is made more rewarding by the addition of a product, the work of his hands, which can gladden his heart[9] and lighten his burden after the harvest. If the Lord God said to the first of men, "By the sweat of thy brow shalt thou eat bread all the days of thy life,"[10] Noah could answer (after the events of Genesis 9:21), "Man does not live by bread alone."

Actually, the recognition of man's labor as a curse and the welcoming of wine as relief from drudgery are parts of a story whose elements are found in several separated accounts in Genesis. Combined sequentially, they form an interesting unified whole:

ארורה האדמה בעבורך
בעצבון תאכלנה כל ימי חייך.
(Genesis 3:17b–19)

ויקרא את שמו נח, לאמר:
זה ינחמנו ממעשנו ומעצבון ידינו
מן האדמה אשר ארֲרה יהוה.
(Genesis 5:29)

ויחל נח איש האדמה ויטע כרם
[11]וישת מן היין וישכר.
(Genesis 9:20–21a)

When the Lord God pronounces upon Adam the fate that will befall all men in their human state, He says, "The earth is cursed because of you. In pain shall you eat of it all the days of your life." Evidently the writer of chapter 5 is harking back to this statement when he exclaims, at the time of Noah's birth, "This one shall bring us relief from our work and from the toil of our hands out of the ground which the Lord has cursed." Apparently this statement of Lamech is a recollection retrojecting the hope which will come through the efforts of Noah to relieve the painful lot of humanity on the basis of the legend which is already current among the Hebrews, of Noah being the first to discover the blessings of the fruit of the vine when it is carefully and skillfully treated.

8. Genesis 2:15.
9. Psalm 104:15.
10. Genesis 3:19.
11. This combination of the verses was made by Skinner in his *Commentary*, p. 185.

We have then, in Genesis 9:20–21a, the etiology of the vine and its best product. This tradition — that Noah was the world's first vintner — is dexterously woven into the next story, which is clearly the invention of the writer of the concluding section of the ninth chapter of Genesis, which ends with the imprecation poured out upon the head of Canaan and the Canaanites.

We find several such stories-within-stories in the Old Testament, and not a few in Genesis. Especially are the first eleven chapters laden with etiologies-within-etiologies. Much of what was considered significant and ancient in the world of the early Hebrews was presented as having had its origins within the ten generations after the emergence of the first man. Agriculture, "the working of the earth," was so integral a part of the civilization in which the Hebrews found themselves, that it was clearly the function and task of the first of God's human creatures. The origin of cities, of settled society, is retrojected into the generation of Cain, for he was the first to build a city.[12]

The "calling upon the name of Yahweh" is considered to have been a very early discovery of man, for it is the generation of Enosh which first began to call upon His name.[13] Yet clearly, the calling upon the name of Elohim preceded the calling upon the name of Yahweh. The discovery of metal-working,[14] the invention of musical instruments,[15] and the development of viticulture[16] are all elements of civilized life in its complexity. They are very early acquisitions of man, in the view of the narrators of these accounts. They all were in the possession of man within the first ten generations of his career on earth, or, if we prefer a modern term, all were already a part of man's civiliztion in the prehistoric period.

The curse pronounced upon Canaan by Noah has its own *raison d'être*. Yet in and of itself it has little "body" as a story and its context seems to have been lost or misplaced. The feeling expressed in this passage is genuine, the emotional outburst is real, yet the connection with the preceding is rather too weak for such a pronouncement, and the obvious attempt to make Ham the guilty one and Canaan the one to bear the punishment betrays its artificiality.

The modern commentators have, almost without exception, taken this story to be a reflection of the conditions that existed in Israel during the days of the monarchy. The cursing of Canaan is viewed by them as being the etiology of the low state to which the Canaanites had sunk during the rise

12. Genesis 4:17.
13. Genesis 4:26.
14. Genesis 4:22.
15. Genesis 4:21.
16. Genesis 9:20, 21a.

to power of Israel and the consequent enslavement of the original inhabitants of the land by their conquerors. By relating the story of Noah's inebriation and Ham's disgraceful behavior, the subjugation of Canaan by Israel is presumably justified.

August Dillmann, in his commentary on Genesis,[17] makes this point very clear: "The narrative opens a view into the future position and historical significance of the circle of peoples descended from Noah, and into the final form of their relationships, as that had been developed by the time of our author, and should still further be developed."

Dillman's lengthy comment on the relative moral values of Canaan and Israel as source and justification for this story deserves examination.

> ... The miserable condition into which the peoples of the Canaanitish race had already sunk by the time of our author, was also nothing accidental. It was the necessary consequence and the merited recompense of the moral perversity—especially of the want of chastity in their home life, the licentiousness in sexual matters, and the shameless customs which clung to them from early times—which can be traced back to their very beginnings... Ruined by their vices, they early fell a prey to peoples morally more healthy, above all to the Israelites, and the remnants of them which are left will sink deeper and deeper into servitude; whereas victory will be the final portion of those peoples in whom the true faith of God flourishes, and who allow themselves to be led by His discipline. These thoughts, which history had already made plain, and which the course of the following centuries confirmed, are here shortly and sharply comprised in a few words of curse and of blessing, which the ancestor of these peoples pronounced over his three sons, on the occasion of a domestic occurrence. They are intended to inform us, at the entrance into the wide domain of the history of the peoples, regarding their character and their future, and indelibly to impress upon our minds the lessons which lie in the history of the nations.[18]

Skinner, in his commentary on Genesis,[19] says that "Noah's curse and blessings must be presumed to have been legible in the destinies of his reputed descendants at the time when the legend took shape." He then goes on to relate the origins of agriculture and viticulture to the story of Noah's curse, seeing in the pure, moralistic Hebrews revulsion against the depravity of the Canaanite civilization. The highly developed civilization, says Skinner,

> ... existed in Palestine when it was occupied by the Hebrews. The sons of the desert who then served themselves heirs by conquest to the Canaanitish civilization escaped the protracted evolution of vinegrowing from primitive tillage, and stepped into the possession of the farm and the

17. August Dillman, *Genesis: Critically and Exegetically Expounded* (Edinburgh: T. & T. Clark, 1897), I, 302.

18. *Ibid.*, I, 303–304.

19. Skinner, *Commentary*, pp. 184–185.

> vineyard at once. From this point of view the story of Noah's drunkenness expresses the healthy recoil of primitive Semitic morality from the licentious habits engendered by a civilization of which a salient feature was the enjoyment and abuse of wine. Canaan is the prototype of the population which had succumbed to these enervating influences, and is doomed by its vices to enslavement at the hands of hardier and more virtuous races.[20]

Von Rad, too, takes this to be a reflection of the state of slavery into which Canaan had fallen by the time of the rise to power of the nation of Israel.[21]

Gunkel[22] considers this passage to be an answer to the question, "Why are the Canaanites sunk so low? Why are they enslaved to Isıael and to the sons of Japheth, their neighbors?"

Thus many of the leading commentators on Genesis read the passage the same way and are convinced of its nature: namely, that it is the etiology of Canaan's enslavement by Israel. Coupled with this explanation must be another, elucidating the conditions of the relationship existing between Canaan and Japheth, which would throw light on the statement ויהי כנען עבד למו of verse 27. This problem at first led some commentators very far afield, so that Karl Budde, for example,[23] suggested that the defeat of the Phoenicians and the Carthaginians by the Persians, the Greeks, and the Romans were the events referred to in this passage. Others, notably Eduard Meyer[24] and Dillman,[25] explained this statement as a reflection of a situation parallel to that of the conquest and subjugation of Canaan by Israel in the and of Canaan. Dillman says,

> ... There is no occasion for denying that Canaanite-Phoenician emigrants and settlers on the islands and coast lands of the Mediterranean, especially in Asia Minor, were at an early period, in many cases, though of course not everywhere, overpowered by Japhetic tribes.

Still another problem, no less perplexing than the others here presented, is the clarification of the blessing

יפת אלהים ליפת וישכון באהלי שם.

20. It would be in order to note here the fact that the Hebrews were not "sons of the desert," if by that designation Skinner means someone akin to or resembling the Arab Bedouin.

21. Von Rad, *Genesis*, p. 133: "Canaan is cursed because of his immodesty; therefore the people is sunk in profound weakness and slavery."

22. Gunkel, *Genesis*, p. 70.

23. Karl Budde, *Die biblische Urgeschichte* (Marburg: J. Ricker'schen Buchhandlung, 1883).

24. Eduard Meyer, *Geschichte des Altertums*, 3rd ed. (Basel: Benno Schwabe & Co., Verlag, 1953), 311–312 and 336–337.

25. Dillman, *Genesis*, I, 308.

It is interpreted by many Biblical scholars as an acceptance by the Israelites of the fact that they did not possess the land of the Canaanites entirely, but shared this possession with Japhetites, Hermann Gunkel[26] venturing the opinion that by this declaration, Israel acquiesced to the forcible dispossession of Semites from their territory by the sons of Japheth. Dillmann, who also takes this passage to be a recognition by Israel that others than the children of Shem were also in possession of portions of the land of Canaan, says, "One must not think of the settling of Japheth in the tents of Shem as conquest, but as a peaceable dwelling together."[27]

Gerhard Von Rad, trying to probe a bit more deeply into the thinking process of the writer of this passage, thinks that it was consciously composed in order to explain the fact that Israel was not alone in complete control of the land which had been promised to the fathers.

> That Israel alone did not possess the land of Canaan, as it expected to do according to the promises, was certainly a disquieting question with which other texts of the Old Testament also struggled... Did Yahweh not have enough power, then, to accomplish his plans completely? Did other events, which were not foreseen by him, occur in the meantime? No! Our saying makes it aetiologically clear that it was God's will from the beginning, that it was so arranged according to a plan of history prepared long in advance. Noah had already prophesied it.[28]

This, then, is the generally accepted interpretation of the entire passage of the Curse and Blessing of Noah which we find in Genesis 9:25–27. Most scholars are convinced that it is a presentation of the state of affairs that existed at a certain time in Israelite history, after the conquest of Canaan. The statements attributed to Noah are illustrative of the fact that Israel subjugated Canaan and that another nation — probably the Philistines — shared the land of Canaan with Israel.[29]

Despite the great weight of scholarly authority, I feel that the explanations given thus far for the three verses constituting the Curse and Blessing of

26. In his *Genesis*, p. 71.

27. Dillmann, *Genesis*, I, 310.

28. Von Rad, *Genesis*, pp. 134–135.

29. Yehezkel Kaufmann, *Toldot Ha-'Emunah Ha-Yisre'elit*, (Jerusalem/Tel-Aviv: Mosad Bialik, 3rd printing, 1955), rejects the view that the Curse of Noah represents a reflection of the subjugation and enslavement of the Canaanites, contending that there were few Canaanites left in Israel after the Conquest. He says (vol. I, book 3, p. 651), "It is a historical fact that there was no recognizable group of Canaanite slaves." See also the English translation and abridgement by Moshe Greenberg, *The Religion of Israel* (Chicago: University of Chicago Press, 1960), pp. 251f.

Kaufmann dismisses the Curse of Noah in a footnote as of little significance. He can find no historical context for the statement ארור כנען, עבד עבדים יהיה לאחיו and so he asserts that it may be "a reflection of the Tyrian slave-trade," which is mentioned in Ezekiel 27:13. Kaufmann also admits his failure to make sense out of this passage because its content does not seem to fit into a historical situation which he can identify.

Noah must be rejected. There is a fault inherent in this explanation which has so far defied plausible solution, if the interpretation is to be taken as it has been in the past. The student examining the history of Old Testament times would find it difficult to accept this passage as a reflection of a particular stage of Israelite history. There is an obvious contradiction between the general assumption that Israel enslaved Canaan and the true historical events. For at no time was Canaan subjugated by Israel and reduced to slavery. Many Canaanite cities were conquered by Israel, and Canaanites were taken into bondage. Large areas of Canaan — especially southern Canaan, the land that ultimately became the land of Israel — were conquered and occupied.[30] But Canaan was never defeated or subjugated completely. On the contrary; the larger part of Canaan remained free and independent of Israelite dominion.

One of the more remarkable peoples of the ancient world, the Canaanites showed exceptional resilience and extraordinary powers of adjustment to adverse conditions. Like the fabled phoenix, this phoenix people rose to greater heights from amidst the flames that apparently spelled their downfall. Driven out of southern Canaan by the successful two-pronged invasion of Israel from the arid east and the Philistines from western waters, they succeeded in wresting delayed victory from very serious defeat. They more than compensated for their great losses by a new efflorescence — one might well call it a renaissance — in the north and an expansion westward into the Mediterranean which made them the masters of the sea from whence their erstwhile Caphtorian conquerors had emerged.[31]

Canaan and the Canaanites remained powerful and independent long after the establishment of Israel and even after the fall of the two Israelite kingdoms. Throughout the period of time encompassed by the historical writings of the Old Testament, there was a respectable Canaanite entity in the power structure of the Mediterranean world.[32]

There are no etiologies of nonexistent things or conditions, and little could be more ridiculous than an Israelite claim to being the masters of an enslaved Canaan at a time when Canaan was strong and flourishing. Since Canaan during the Biblical period was never in fact completely — nay, nor even for the most part — עבד עבדים לאחיו this passage could

30. Joshua 9; Joshua 17:13; Judges 1:28–35; I Kings 9:20–21.

31. It is assumed by the writer that everyone reading this paper is aware of the fact that the Canaanites are identical with the Phoenicians. See Meyer, *Geschichte des Altertums*, vol. II, part 2, p. 63, n. 2. See also my Note 32.

32. William Foxwell Albright, "The Role of the Canaanites in the History of Civilization," in *The Bible and the Ancient Near East: Essays in Honor of William Foxwell Albright*, ed. G. Ernest Wright (Garden City, N.Y.: Doubleday and Co., 1961), pp. 328–362: "Forced out of Palestine and most of Syria in the 13th and 12th centuries, the Phoenicians turned their energies seaward and became the greatest mariners and traders of all time, if we may relate their accomplishments to the extent of the known world."

not be the explanation of the origin of this nonexistent state of affairs.

The Curse of Canaan is not, therefore, an etiology.

A new approach to the solution of the problem of the Cursing of Canaan is in order, and I would propose at the outset a new examination of the three verses in question, based on the following analysis.

The situation reflected in these three verses clearly sets before us the following set of relationships:

(1) Canaan is inimical to Shem and Japheth;

(2) Shem and Japheth are friendly and obviously allied;

(3) they are allied against Canaan;

(4) they are at war with Canaan, and

(5) from the angry tone of the curse in verse 25, we can conclude that they are engaged in bitter conflict.

The conditions we have reflected in the three verses which contain the Cursing of Canaan and the Blessings of Shem and of Japheth are conditions of war. The three verses constitute a battle cry, the cry of a belligerent engaged in combat against a detested enemy. The curse directed at Canaan expresses not a historical situation, not a state of being, but a hope, a wish, a desire.

The tone and content of the Curse and Blessing of Noah are not unlike expressions of a similar nature found throughout the course of history. From Homer's *Iliad*, through the Song of Deborah, to eyewitness accounts of the two World Wars, similar execrations of the enemy are expressed by soldiers in the heat of combat.

The curses are of different kinds. One curses or threatens an ally or kinsman who does not help in the struggle, as we find in passages from the *Iliad* and Deborah's War Song that are very close in meaning and intent:

> Never shall that man from Troy return,
> But here become for dogs a thing of play,
> Who chooses, of his own free will, to spurn
> His duty on the battlefield this day![33]
>
> Cursed be Meroz! says the angel of the Lord,
> And damned be its inhabitants;
> For they came not to help the Lord
> Together with His champions.[34]

Both these passages express a curse as well as a threat to the members of the poet's own group — either a city of his nation or the allies of his confederation — who fail to join in the great struggle.

Taunting the enemy is another favorite means of expressing hatred and

33. Homer, *The Iliad*, book XIII, lines 232-234.
34. Judges 5:23.

contempt for one's enemies in time of war. The taunt is rarely absent from literary descriptions of men in conflict. Again we find a close parallel between the *Iliad* and the Song of Deborah. The former says:

> Ah! Asios not unavenged lies dead !
> I think that now his journey to the grave,
> The realm of mighty Hades, will be sped
> With joyful company, another soldier brave,
> Whom I have sent as escort on ahead,
> To cheer the way to his eternal bed.[35]

The Song of Deborah taunts the enemy in the following passage, vividly descriptive of the enemy's sad plight:[36]

> Sisera's mother looked out of the window,
> Worried and weeping, she peered through the pane;
> Why does his chariot tarry in coming,
> Why are his carriage-wheels slowed on the way?
> While her ladies-in-waiting cheer her with answers,
> She prays to herself that all will be well.
> "Our heroes will find and divide all the spoil,
> A captive or two for every brave man.
> Beautiful, colorful prizes for Sisera,
> Colored embroidery as spoils of war,
> Double adornments for every man's shoulders."

And then, the final cry of victory:

> So may all Thine enemies perish, Oh Lord!
> But those who love Him shall be as the sun
> Rising in his power!

The outright cursing of the enemy, the wish expressed that he be destroyed, subjugated or oppressed, is also a part of the literature of battle. Again, in the *Iliad* we find, among others, the following passage:

> Thus, by falling dead into the dust,
> You'll bid goodbye to our Danaän ships,
> Arrogant Trojan beasts! Your famished lust
> For constant clash and clang of arms at war
> Can never be appeased, yet some day must,
> When mighty Zeus repays you for your crime,
> Your vile insult, when you betrayed my trust.
> You evil dogs! You have no fear of God,
> Who soon will grind your city into dust.[37]

The passionate war cry is a part of battle; it is a necessary element in any account of war. This is the nature of the Curse of Canaan placed in the mouth of Noah. It is a battle cry, a cursing of the enemy in the heat of the

35. *Iliad*, book XIII, lines 414–416.
36. Judges 5:25–31.
37. *Iliad*, book XIII, lines 620–625.

struggle. In the manner of the passages cited, and many others to be found in world literature, it calls down upon the heads of the enemy the curse of the gods.

ארור כנען. עבד עבדים יהיה לאחיו!

Our task now is to find the occasion, the war in question, during which these conditions obtained.

It is clear from our knowledge of Israel's history that there were no wars between Israel and Canaan after the defeat of the Canaanites at the Battle of Taanach.[38] Certainly the state of affairs governing the relationshhip between Israel and the Canaanites after the rise of the Israelite monarchy was one of friendship and harmony.

The commercial treaties entered into between David and Hiram of Tyre were definitely on a "most favored nation" basis.[39] This state of amity and mutual cooperation continued throughout the reigns of David and Solomon[40] and through the ninth century B.C. There was no occasion during the histories of the two kingdoms of Israel when a war of any significance or duration took place which pitted Israel or Judah against the Canaanites. And never, to the best of our knowledge, were the Israelites and the children of Japheth allied against the Canaanites at any time following the twelfth century B.C.

However, on two occasions, separated by a span of about fifty years, the Hebrews and the sons of Japheth were allied in a bitter struggle against the Canaanites. The first conflict took place during the years ± 1230–1220 B.C.; the second, in the years ± 1195–1180 B.C.

Before we proceed to a detailed chronology of these events, let us fix the identity of the groups of peoples involved in this historical confrontation: the people identified by the writer of this account as "Shem" and "Japheth."

The Hebrews were children of Shem; that is, they were descendants of an ancestor — whether real or imaginary is not significant — who was remembered as Shem.[41] This relationship to a presumed ancestor was very important to the Hebrews, who were a people of patriarchal tradition to whom ethnic or blood relationship was very significant. The Hebrews of antiquity thought patriarchally, and therefore, they thought genealogically.

38. Circa 1180 B.C. Kaufmann, Vol. I, book 3, p. 650, makes the following comment: "The Canaanites are not to be found as a military factor in the history of the Judges and the early kings. In the book of the wars of the Judges (from Judges 2 on), there is an account of but one war against the Canaanites: that of Deborah and Barak (Judges 4 and 5)... But from that time and thereafter there is no account of any war against the Canaanites. There is this basic difference between the accounts of the wars of Joshua and those of the Judges. The former were wars of Israel against the Canaanites, the latter were not wars fought against Canaan." See Greenberg's English abridgement, pp. 251f.

39. II Samuel 5:11.

40. I Kings 5:15–31.

41. Genesis 10:21, 25; 11:14–26.

They viewed history in terms of the ethnic relationships among peoples and they recorded history in terms of genealogical relationships.

Many problems of identification in the tenth chapter of Genesis can be solved if this central criterion is borne in mind. It is on the basis of this criterion that the writer of the tenth chapter of Genesis organized the data at his disposal in his construction of the map of the world which we call the Table of Nations. If we try to impose our own criteria on his arrangement, we must either destroy his reasoning as unsound or consider him to be in error.

But if we could refrain from imposing our own cherished definitions upon a work which was constructed on the basis of definitions other than those we consider valid, we would gain much more of that which the original writer was trying to convey.

The basic criterion of relationship among nations which is presented by the tenth chapter of Genesis is that of family relationship; that is, ethnic relationship or genealogy. Thus, when he states that Canaan was the son of Ham, he knew this to be a fact. The Canaanites were ethnically related to the Hamites; they were descended from ancestors whom they shared in common with the Egyptians and the Ethiopians. When the compiler of the Table of Nations in Genesis states that the descendants of Ham are "Ethiopia, Egypt, Put, and Canaan,"[42] he is making this statement on the basis of his knowledge of the genealogies of these peoples, preserved in their own traditions, or apparently obvious to all.

The Hebrews — later the Israelites — were descendants of Shem.[43] Nations related to them in an ethnic, genealogical relationship were Asshur and Aram, among others.[44] The Hebrews themselves were descendants of an eponymous ancestor whom they called Eber.[45]

One thing is certain and significant. The terms "Semite" and "Semitic" as used by modern scholars are not the equivalent of the concept expressed by the term בני שם used by the Biblical writer. Our term "Semitic" is a linguistic term, defined according to linguistic criteria.[46] The term בני שם as used in Genesis is a genealogical term with ethnic meaning.[47]

If there are linguistic relationships as well as ethnic relationships between

42. Genesis 10:6.

43. Genesis 10:21, 24; 11:10–32.

44. Genesis 10:21.

45. Genesis 10:24.

46. Louis H. Gray, *Foundations of Language* (New York: Macmillan, 1939), pp. 74, 302–303. and 357–359.

47. Note the constant use of the terms ויולד and בן throughout chapters 10 and 11, and the arrangement of the names of the nations as if they were members of tribes or families.

two peoples or two groups of peoples, then the modern and the ancient terms coincide. But there are instances of two nations who speak languages identical with or cognate to each other, yet who are not related genealogically or ethnically.[48] In this case, the terms used by modern linguists indicating relationship would not coincide with the term used by the writer of the Table of Nations of Genesis. On the other hand, there may be an instance of two nations who are ethnically related but whose languages differ radically.[49] Here, too, the modern linguist would speak of no relationship existing between the two peoples, whereas the writer of Genesis might see a relationship.

It is on the basis of this genealogical system which dominates the method of the Biblical writer that we can understand his accounts in the Table of Nations and in the other genealogies of nations which appear in Genesis. If his statements correspond with the modern linguists', the latter stand on firm ground and know that they have verifiable data at their command. If the classification of a nation in Genesis does not correspond to that of the modern linguist, then a "problem" exists, for there are evidently data missing which the modern scholar may never be able to recover. The classic example which has puzzled scholars of the Old Testament has been the listing of Canaan among the sons of Ham. Yet Canaan was a Hamite, according to the defined criterion of the Biblical writer, although the Canaanites spoke a Semitic language. On the other hand, we do not quibble with the compiler of the Table of Nations when he lists Ethiopia among the sons of Ham, although the Ethiopians, too, like the Canaanites, spoke a Semitic language.

Who were the sons of Japheth? The sons of Japheth were, among others, the Hellenic peoples. Like the Hebrews of the second millenium B.C., the Hellenes were also a people to whom genealogical relationship was the significant criterion of kinship; among them, the tribal system predominated. The *Iliad* and the *Odyssey* are filled with patronymics and genealogies.[50] Although the patriarchal system of social organization had been modified by a form of monarchy, the patriarchal concept of kinship was still dominant.

In the genealogies of the Hellenic people, the eponymous ancestor of the Greeks was Hellen. However, if a "researcher" in antiquity persisted in

48. For example: Persia and India; Jamaica and England; Haiti and France; Martinique and France.

49. Nigerians and American Negroes.

50. Hardly a name appears in the *Iliad* which is not accompanied by its patronymic or for which the patronymic is not occasionally substituted. Thus, for example, we meet Odysseus, who often appears as Laertiades, Agammemnon as Atreides, Achilles as Peleides, Diomedes as Tydeides, and even Zeus appears as Cronides!

trying to find out the name of the father's father as far back as the memory of the people could reach, he might be rewarded. The primeval ancestor of Hellen was Prometheus, the immortal who related himself to mankind and sacrificed himself to the welfare and the interests of men. The father of Prometheus was the Titan Iapetus.[51] The figure of Iapetus was evidently considered to be the earliest identifiable ancestor of the Hellenic people — identifiable by name only, of course, and (in keeping with Greek concepts that are beyond the scope of this discussion) an immortal.

The writer of the tenth chapter of Genesis, in compiling his Table of Nations, did such "research." To him, the peoples who dominated the northern tier of his world, from the Aegean Sea (איי הגוים)[52] to the highlands of Iran[53] and northward to the steppes beyond the shores of the Black Sea,[54] were all related to the Hellenic peoples of the Aegean coastlands and islands. Those best known to him and with whom he had most contact were the Greeks of the eastern Mediterranean–Aegean Sea area. Since they were the dominant people of the region in his time, and the other peoples of the northern tier he considered to be related to them, the primeval ancestor of the Greeks would be the primeval father of all of these nations and peoples.

Since the early Hebrew tradition (from the days of Terah and Abraham, at least until the days of the generation of the Israelite eisodus into Egypt) was dominated by Babylonian concepts and historical tradition, and the universal Deluge was a very significant episode in this tradition, the separation of mankind into its component families of nations could only date from the Flood. Since everything within the experience of mankind had to begin from the Flood, the ancestors of all men were considered to be the children of the one family that survived the Flood. The Flood is, in the Hebrew retelling, a significant moment in the history of mankind.

The Hebrew writer conceived of the world as being divided into three parts. His tripartite division consisted of Africa, the Fertile Crescent and Arabia, and the mountains surrounding the Fertile Crescent in a larger concentric arc stretching from the Aegean Sea to the Persian Gulf. The Africans, in the opinion of the Hebrew writer, were the children of Ham;[55] the dominant peoples of the Fertile Crescent were children of Shem;[56] the

51. Apollodorus, *The Library*, I, 2, 3; ed. Sir James G. Frazer, Loeb Classical Library (Cambridge, Mass.: Harvard University Press, 1921), p. 12; Hesiod, *Works and Days*, lines 50, 54; *Theogony*, lines 507–512, 543; ed. H. G. Evelyn White, Loeb Classical Library (Cambridge, Mass.: Harvard University Press, 1914), pp. 6, 116, and 118.

52. Genesis 10:5.

53. Genesis 10:2.

54. Genesis 10:2, 3: Gomer, Ashkenaz, and Togarmah.

55. Genesis 10:6.

56. Genesis 10:21ff. and 11:10ff.

Greeks (the best-known and dominant element in the outer ring) were the children of Japheth (by their own tradition).[57]

Although this seems to have been the general configuration of the parts of the world in his concept of the home of mankind, let us not forget that we must not impose our own rigidity of definition upon his system. His criterion was not the geographical distribution of mankind, nor was it linguistic relationships; his criterion was always ethnic or genealogical. We find, therefore, significant exceptions to any system other than his own. Thus, Semitic-speaking Canaanites, although they live in the lands dominated by the children of Shem, are Hamites as far as the Biblical writer was concerned.[58] The Philistines, too, are children of Ham,[59] although geographically they inhabit the islands of the peoples who are predominantly children of Iapetus. Semitic-speaking Ethiopians are children of Ham[60] for they are genealogically considered so. They also happen to inhabit the land of the children of Ham, but this is not the decisive factor.

The Curse of Canaan is directed against Canaan at a time when the children of Shem are at war with the Canaanites. The allies of the Shemites are the children of Japhet, the Greeks of the Aegean Sea area. The historical circumstances fulfilling these conditions took place only during a period of fifty years which opened and closed to the clash of arms. There were two great wars, accompanied by large invasions, that were fought at the beginning and at the end of this period of time. The first was in the decade circa 1230–1220 B.C., the second, circa 1190–1180 B.C.

Let us examine the two wars in question and observe some of their elements. The first great battle of which we are aware is the invasion of southern Canaan by the Israelites, coming into the land from the Transjordanian region under the leadership of Joshua. This event, as clearly fixed by extensive archaeological data, took place around 1230 B.C.[61]

57. Genesis 10:2–5.

58. Genesis 10:6.

59. Genesis 10:14.

60. Genesis 10:6.

61. David Noel Freedman and Edward F. Campbell, Jr., "The Chronology of Israel and the Ancient Near East," in *The Bible and the Ancient Near East*, p. 222. W. F. Albright, *From the Stone Age to Christianity* (Garden City, N.Y.: Doubleday-Anchor, 1957), p. 278; *The Archaeology of Palestine* (Harmondsworth: Penguin Books, 1960), p. 109; *The Biblical Period From Abraham to Ezra* (New York: Harper & Row, 1963), p. 27 and most of chap. iii, "The Conquest of Palestine."

I cannot but agree with Yehezkel Kaufmann, who maintains that there was but one massive invasion and conquest of Canaan by the Israelites. In *Toldot Ha-'Emunah Ha-Yisre'elit*, vol. I, book 3, pp. 624–625, he says, "According to the tradition preserved in the Biblical account of the Conquest, the tribes of Israel constituted a nation before their entry into the land. The tribes of Israel invaded Canaan as one group, as one army. The conquest was a military conquest, carried out by an organized military force at whose head was a single commander: namely, Joshua. The invaders were bound by an oath to rid the land of its inhabitants (the *ḥerem*) either by destruction or by dispossession. After

At the same time — perhaps even within the year — the Sea Peoples attempted invasions of the Delta region of Egypt and of Egyptian-ruled territories in Hither Asia. The inscriptions of Pharaoh Merneptah, which date from about 1230 B.C., give an account of this war, the repelling of the invasion, and the tale of the Pharaoh's victories.[62] Among these victories is one over the People of Israel, whom he dismisses from further consideration with the couplet now made famous by constant reiteration: "Israel is desolated; his seed does not exist."[63] The determinative for Israel, as has also been mentioned innumerable times, is not that used for "land" or "settled people," but that which signifies "people" in the sense of "unsettled nomads." This would indicate that Merneptah is not talking about a "Land of Israel," but about a landless "People of Israel."[64] This would be the perfect description of Israel in 1230 B.C., when they were a landless, desert-wandering people, just one generation removed from bondage, who had only then invaded the land of Canaan.[65]

The events that took place in the fifth year of Pharaoh Merneptah (circa 1230 B.C.) are the following: Egypt is invaded from the west and from the north by a coalition of Libyans and Sea Peoples, among whom are the Achaeans, Tyrrhenians, Lycians, Sardians, and Sicilians. At the very same time, Canaan, which is under Egyptian suzerainty, nominal though it may be,

the land was conquered by war and wrested from the grasp of the kings who had ruled over it, it was divided among the tribes by lot.

"But the school of Biblical researchers which follows the trail blazed by Stade, Kuenen, Eduard Meyer, Wellhausen, *et al.*, considers this traditional account as unhistorical. Although there is no internal agreement on details, the prevailing opinion of the critical school maintains that the tribes of Israel entered the land singly or in small groups, and settled the land wherever they could find a suitable place, either by force of arms or peaceably. The union of the tribes into one nation was the fruit of their history in the land of Canaan and was not completed until the rise of the monarchy." See the English abridgement, *Religion of Israel*, p. 245.

62. James Henry Breasted, *Ancient Records of Egypt* (Chicago: University of Chicago Press, 1906–1907), III, 241, 243, 249, and 255.

63. The so-called "Israel Stela," a poetic rendering of the events recorded in more prosaic, historical fashion in the other inscriptions. See Breasted, *Ancient Records of Egypt*, vol. III, and John Albert Wilson's recent translation and interpretation of this stela in James B. Pritchard's edition of *Ancient Near Eastern Texts Relating to the Old Testament*, 2nd ed. (Princeton: Princeton University Press, 1955), pp. 376–378.

64. The determinative used for the People of Israel in the Victory Hymn of Merneptah (the "Israel Stela") proves that the People of Israel were an unsettled, nomadic, landless people at that time. Wilson, in his translation and commentary on this document, points out that "determinatives should have meaning, and a contrast between determinatives in the same context should be significant." *Ancient Near Eastern Texts*, p. 378.

The description of the tribes of Israel as a nomadic, landless people would be very fitting in 1230 B.C., when they had just emerged from the desert, had conquered the land of Canaan, and had not yet settled themselves in it.

65. The archaeological data supporting the date circa 1230 B.C. for the conquest of Canaan by the Israelites agrees quite closely, it appears, with the invasions of the Sea Peoples during the reign of Merneptah, which occured in 1230 B.C. (the fifth year of his reign). To consider these two events as separate and unrelated puts too great a strain on historical perspective.

is invaded by an army of Israelite tribes from the desert of Transjordan. The king of the Hittites is giving aid and comfort to this attack against Egyptian power.

Merneptah, faced with this emergency, must direct his greatest force to the immediate defense of Egypt's own homeland. He must direct his greatest thrust, therefore, against the armies of Meryey, King of Libya, and against his allies, the Achaeans and the other peoples of the islands of the sea who are attempting to establish themselves in the Delta of Egypt.

He would perhaps have liked to help Canaan, too, and retain a measure of Egyptian control over the region, but he evidently could not because of his limited strength and resources. But in keeping with a political commitment which Egypt had in Canaan, he made a *pro forma* gesture of help in the direction of Canaan and sent a token force, whose help was to no avail.

We know that his efforts in Canaan were ineffectual, for we are certain that the "People of Israel" mentioned in his Hymn of Victory were securely settled in the land of Canaan after the date of this inscription and that the seed of Israel did continue. Yet his failure to destroy Israel and prevent the successful invasion of Canaan was no hindrance to his publishing the Hymn of Victory.

At this time — during the invasion of Canaan which took place in the year we call 1230 B.C. — Israelites and Greeks were allied against Canaan in a desperate battle. The Israelites were marching upon Canaan from the east and the Greeks were launching a seaborne invasion from the west. Canaan was the common enemy of both. There is no suggestion that the attacks or the invasions were coordinated or planned in concert. On the other hand, it would be wrong to assume that either the Israelites or the Sea Peoples were ignorant of the existence or activities of the other group.

When we turn to the later date, 1190–1180 B.C., the following picture emerges. The Sea Peoples are again on the move, but in much greater force than in the earlier war. This time, the Sea Peoples, including the Philistines, the Sicilians, the Weshesh, and the Danaäns, move in a many-pronged invasion against all of the three great "central powers" of the eastern Mediterranean world. On the defensive are Egypt, Canaan, and the empire of the Hittites. These invasions are recorded in many sources of the time, among which are the following.

The assault upon Egypt and its repulsion are recorded in the inscriptions of Pharaoh Ramses III.[66]

The invasion of the lands controlled by the Hittites and the frontal assault

66. John A. Wilson and William F. Edgerton, *Historical Records of Ramses III: The Texts in Medinet Habu*, vols. I and II, trans., with explanatory notes (Chicago: University of Chicago Press, 1936), no. 12 of Studies in Ancient Oriental Civilization; also in Breasted, *Ancient Records of Egypt*, III, 241.

against one of its mightiest fortresses is recorded in great detail in Homer's *Iliad*.

The attacks of the Sea Peoples against the land of Canaan are also recorded in letters from Ugarit recently published by Charles Virolleaud. In these letters — diplomatic correspondence found at Ugarit — there is clear indication of attacks by enemies emerging from the sea against the lands in the northern reaches of the Mediterranean's eastern seaboard: specifically, against Ugarit, her allies, and her neighbors. In these documents, the role of the Hittites as friends and allies of Ugarit and Cyprus (= Alashiya) is dramatically revealed. Among these letters is one from the king of the Hittites to 'Amurapi, the last king of Ugarit.[67]

Israel is involved in this war too, but this time as an object of invasion and attack, rather than an invader. One can only speculate as to the reasons for the invasion launched against the tribes of Israel by the Canaanites at the time that the Sea Peoples were attempting to invade the lands of Canaan from the west. Were the Canaanites attempting to regain their lands lost to the Israelites fifty years earlier because they were being beaten by the invaders from the sea? Were they launching a "preventive war" for fear that the Israelites might aid the Sea Peoples by applying pressure against their rear on a "second front"? Perhaps the Canaanites felt that they could eliminate Israel first and then turn their full attention to the seaborne invaders. All of these speculations are purely conjectural. What is more likely is that the Canaanites, now driven to war by the massive assault of the Sea Peoples, took this occasion to renew the war against Israel, which had ended in Canaanite defeat a half-century before, and to try to regain their lands, at the same time uprooting and destroying a people who had been allied with the Sea Peoples before and who might want to enter the conflict on their side again.

And so Canaan finds itself fighting a war on at least two fronts. In the west Canaan is trying to repel the invasion of the Peoples from the Sea, and in the south and east, Canaan invades the territory of Israel. It is at this point that Deborah rises to prominence. She evidently was the only one able to rally the tribes of Israel to withstand the Canaanite attack. When the hastily mobilized armies of Israel defeated Sisera's forces at the Battle of

67. Charles Virolleaud, *Le Palais royal d'Ugarit*, V, Tome XI of "Mission de Ras Shamra" (Paris: Imprimerie Nationale, 1965), 81ff. Letter 60, p. 84, is written by the king of the Hittites ("The Sun") to '*Amrpi*, who is elsewhere identified as the last king of Ugarit. This is the first instance we have of the name Hammurabi/pi being written out in an alphabetic script where the original consonants are clearly indicated. We now know with certainty, therefore, that the original of Hammurabi was '*Amurapi*.

That these letters were written during the last days of Ugarit is proven by many archeological indications. Most interesting is the fact that many tablets were found in a tablet-kiln where they had been put for baking and preservation. The city fell before they could be removed from the oven for transmission or for filing.

Taanach "by the waters of Megiddo,"[68] Canaan was driven out of Israel forever. That was the last attempt of the Canaanites to regain the former southern region of their country.[69]

But the Battle of Taanach was taking place at the same time as the siege of Troy.[70] The armies of Israel, led by Deborah[71] and Barak, were inflicting a defeat on the Canaanites at the same time that the Greeks were striking decisive blows against them from the west and bringing the Hittite Empire to its knees with their destruction of the fortress of Ilium. The Greeks and the Israelites, willy-nilly, were allies against the Canaanites and the Hittites during that great world conflict which came down through the historical memory of many peoples by many different names.

It is at this time that the Curse of Canaan as we have it recorded would be a most appropriate expression. "Cursed be Canaan! Bless Yahweh, the God of Shem! May God enlarge Japheth and may he dwell in the tents of Shem, and may Canaan thrice be enslaved to them!"

The phrase "and may he [Japheth] dwell in the tents of Shem" has been interpreted variously.[72] I would offer the following suggestion. In these wars of the Sea Peoples against Egypt, Canaan, and the Hittites, the object

68. Judges 5:19.

69. The story and the Song of Deborah (Judges 4 and 5) clearly indicate that Sisera is to be identified with the Canaanites. The fact that his name does not sound Canaanite is meager proof that he was not a Canaanite warrior. Albright, *The Biblical Period from Abraham to Ezra*, p. 40, attempts to reconstruct the political and military situation surrounding the events of the Battle of Taanach as an alliance of Sea Peoples and Canaanites against Israel There is no evidence in the Song itself to support such a supposition, nor is there a historical context to warrant such an assertion.

70. The Battle of Taanach was fought circa 1180 BC., and the Siege of Troy took place circa 1190–1180 B.C.

71. W. F. Albright, in articles in the *Bulletin of the American Schools of Oriental Research*, 62:26ff. (1936) and 68:24ff. (1937), proposes dating the Song of Deborah to 1125 B.C. or later. This chronology I find unacceptable. His argument that "at Taanach, by the waters of Megiddo," of verse 19 refers to a historical situation which can be attested to archeologically is unconvincing. I view this phrasing as no more than the poetic desire to achieve balance and imagery without identity in parallelism. Albright's conjecture that the phrase indicates that Taanach was standing while Meggido was in ruins is further weakened by the testimony of the latest evidence uncovered at Taanach by the Joint Concordia Seminary and American Schools of Oriental Research Excavations conducted during the season of June 17—August 10, 1963, as reported in a recent issue of the *BASOR*. These discoveries indicate that Taanach fell "in the last quarter of the twelfth century and ended in a violent destruction." This would prove conclusively that Taanach and Megiddo both fell at the same time. See the Report by Paul W. Lapp, "The 1963 Excavation at Taanek," in *BASOR*, 173 (February 1964). I believe, with Martin Noth (*The History of Israel*, revised English ed., New York: Harper & Bros., 1960, p. 151 and footnote), "we have no evidence at all on which to assign a date to the victory over Sisera, even roughly." His footnote says, "As this victory does not appear to have had any direct and tangible effects on Canaanite cities, it is impossible to date it archaeologically —for example from the historical vicissitudes of the city of Megiddo."

72. See Gunkel, *Genesis*, pp. 70, 71; Budde, *Die biblische Urgeschichte*; Meyer, *Geschichte des Altertums*, I, 311–312, 336–337; Dillmann, *Genesis*, I, 308, 310; Von Rad, Genesis, pp. 134–135.

of the invaders was to conquer the coastlands of the eastern Mediterranean world and to annex territory which they would proceed to occupy. They were seeking homes for themselves, for the pressures in the Aegean lands were too great. This factor in the Sea Peoples' movement is referred to by Ramses III in his accounts,[73] and by Herodotus, in his account of the Lydian-Tyrrhenian cleavage.[74]

Since the object of the invaders was known, the phrase וישכון באהלי שם becomes understandable. It is another wish expressed at the same time as that which is embodied in the Curse of Canaan. That is to say, the Israelite is saying to the Hellenes, "If we succeed in defeating our common enemy, there will be room for you to enter into and to dwell in the tents of Shem. We will not oppose your colonizing within the territory we now occupy." This might have been a rash promise to make, but then, such are the passions of war that rash promises often are made only later to be rued.

One more question remains. Why, if this curse was uttered at the time of the invasion of Canaan, circa 1230 B.C.—that is, during the days of Joshua — or alternatively, if it were an expression of the time of the Battle of Taanach, in the time of Deborah, circa 1180 B.C., was it retrojected so far into the past? Why should it have been attributed to Noah, the primeval ancestor of the nations of mankind?

The answer seems to lie in an all too human trait. If one is enraged at an enemy and desires to kill him, one usually justifies one's feeling in a conviction that the enemy is not only evil in this instance, but is inherently bad. Not only do we feel this way, we even publish these ideas and thoughts in official communiques. Nations friendly and allied in war will suceed in finding historical support to prove their continued friendship through the ages. Those opposed to each other find fault, not only with the political policies of their enemies, but in the very fabric, the character and make-up of their antagonists.

The alliance of the Hebrews and the Greeks against Canaan and her allies in the two wars of the Sea Peoples led the Hebrews to seek and find an ancient source for their latter-day friendship. The genealogical tracing through the eponymous ancestors of the two peoples — as far back as they could be traced — led to the conclusion that Iapetus, the ancestor of the Hellenes, and Shem, the ancestor of the Hebrews, as brothers, sons of the one father Noah, would be the best proof of their long-lasting feeling of fraternal ties for each other. This would be the "proof" of their "natural" alliance at this critical juncture of their history.

73. Wilson and Edgerton, *Historical Records of Ramses III*, p. 58; also in Breasted's *Ancient Records of Egypt*, IV, 37.

74. Herodotus, *The Histories*, I. 94; ed. A. D. Godley, Loeb Classical Library (Cambridge, Mass., 1920–24), I, 124.

The story of Noah, the Flood, and his three sons was old at the time in question, and the identity of the three sons of Noah had been set before that time. But by referring back to that remote period in the past they were able to strengthen their own conviction as well as the belief of others, that their alliance was ancient.

Many commentators on Genesis, beginning with Wellhausen and continuing through the latest,[75] put forward the idea that the original triad of Noah's sons consisted of Shem, Japheth, and Canaan. Thus, the phrase וחם הוא אבי כנען would be explained as an interpolation necessary to bring the story of Noah's curse into harmony with the genealogies in the so-called P-document, where the three sons of Noah are mentioned as Shem, Ham, and Japheth.[76] Skinner, in his *Genesis*, presents this theory in full.[77]

I believe that this theory is untenable. Canaan is the name of a nation; Shem and Japheth are not the names of nations. Shem is the earliest ancestor common to the peoples related to the Hebrews. He, therefore, is taken to be the son of Noah (not Aram, not Ashur, not Eber). Iapetus is, in the Greek tradition, the ancestor of all the Hellenic peoples. Japheth is, therefore, taken as the son of Noah and father of all the peoples related to the Hellenes. Ham, too, is not a nation, but a father of nations. He is, therefore, one of the sons of Noah. Canaan does not fit into this pattern. Canaan is a nation, a contemporary of Israel and *Iawan*. It is Canaan, therefore, who is retrojected to the days of Noah. But he is described as a son of Ham, the only son of the three mentioned in this passage in Genesis 9, because of the date and circumstances of this curse. I believe that וחם הוא אבי כנען is a gloss, but that it was inserted to harmonize the historical displacement of the curse with the generation of Noah's sons. Canaan is being cursed — for Israel and the children of Japheth are at war with Canaan — but the curse must be attributed to a far earlier period than the moment under consideration. Just as the friendship between the allies, the Shemites and the Japhetites, is made to appear so ancient, so must the enmity between the two of them vis-à-vis Ham be made to appear as ancient. If Canaan is to be cursed and Noah is the one who pronounces the imprecation, then a close tie must be found between Noah and Canaan. This is done by attributing the sin for which Canaan is to be forever punished to his father, Ham.

The Curse of Canaan is the core of the story; of that there can be little doubt. The cause of this cursing is an enmity which leads to war. But if the friendship of the allies was presented as being as old as the time of Noah, the inherent evil of the enemy had also to be placed in that remote period.

75. E.g., Von Rad, in his *Genesis*, pp. 131–132.
76. Genesis 5:32, 6:10, 7:13, and all of Genesis 10.
77. Pp. 182 and 195.

Canaan was the object of hatred and Canaan is being cursed. But in order to harmonize the chronology, Ham had to be accused of the crime which is taken as the cause for the execration of Canaan. This becomes then the etiology of the political picture of the time (end of the thirteenth and beginning of the twelfth century B.C.). The situation faced by the People of Israel was pictured as if it had its roots in remote antiquity.

Postscript

After this article had gone for final editing, the writer received the latest number of *Vetus Testamentum*, vol. XIV (July 1964), in which A. Van Selms, in an article entitled "Judge Shamgar," reached some of the same conclusions arrived at in this study. Among the points he makes are the following: "As long as Israel's political aim was the settlement in Canaan and the occupation of Canaanite territories and towns, the Philistines would be the natural allies of the Israelite tribes... This cooperation has been attested by the ancient blessings and curses, presumed to have originated from Noah, in Gen. ix 25–27."

The central thesis of Van Selms' article, that Shamgar ben Anath was a Canaanite, is convincing and merits serious consideration.

The End of Ecclesiastes: Literal Exegesis and Its Transformation*

By Judah Goldin

In memory of Judith Marcia Lewittes (1934–1957)

The very fact that we have so much difficulty recovering the original meaning and objective of the sayings preserved in *Pirḳe Abot* is of itself a tribute to the achievement of the redactors of this treatise, who apparently regarded all the sentences in the work as maxims of the widest, most elastic application: the idiom of these sayings, you might say, lent itself to multiple, various, beautiful, ever new interpretations, and each generation, indeed every commentator, could discover in the vocabulary of the *Abot* sayings anticipations, observations, striking confirmations of what the commentator and his generation discovered in their own society and times. "Be of the disciples of Aaron, loving peace and pursuing peace, loving mankind and drawing them to the Torah."[1] Was there ever a century to which this exhortation could be irrelevant? Obviously, therefore, Hillel's words were not of an age only but for all time. Hence, more than a millenium later, reflecting on these words, a distinguished scholar could say, "The Sages have said [*Genesis Rabba* 38:6]: Even when Israel worship idols, so long as there is peace in their midst, no people or nation can have dominion over them... Controversy is a terrible thing, for even if Israel carry out all the commandments of the Torah, if there is controversy in their midst, anybody may do with them what he pleases."[2]

And yet, despite the persuasiveness of great exegetes, and despite the surprising iridescences of polished sentences, every statement—every maxim, even—must originally have come into being because of a specific provocation; every statement must originally have been a specific, pointed

* While in no way whatsoever do I seek to shift responsibility for any of the views I express in this paper, I cannot neglect to say that I am deeply indebted to four erudite, original, and dear friends—Professors Elias Bickerman, H. L. Ginsberg, Saul Lieberman, and Shalom Spiegel—who allowed me to discuss my ideas with them, and doubtless by their acute questions and reactions in the course of give-and-take, helped me to bring greater clarity and precision to my thoughts. I want also to thank Dean William C. DeVane and Provost Kingman Brewster, Jr., through whose interest I received a Yale University Grant to return to Cambridge to examine Genizah manuscripts. To the staff at the Cambridge University Library I am grateful for many courtesies; as for the staff of the Yale University Library, it is kindness itself.

1. *Abot* 1:12.

2. *Machsor Vitry*, ed. S. Hurwitz (Nuremberg, 1923), p. 473.

response to some event or challenge, verbal or otherwise. Consider, for example, the very saying of Hillel which we just cited. Geiger[3] and later Louis Ginzberg observed that originally Hillel's saying was directed to priests, and contentious ones at that; in effect Hillel was saying to them, For a priest it is not enough to be merely a descendant of Aaron; the *kohen* ought to strive to emulate his ancestor, he ought to be not just a son but a disciple[4] of Aaron, bringing peace into the world rather than stirring up controversy, drawing men to the Torah, rather than alienating them from it. Or, as Hillel's teachers retorted when a high priest said to them insultingly, "Come in peace, descendants of gentiles": "May descendants of gentiles who act as Aaron acted come in peace indeed; and may there be no peace for a descendant of Aaron who does not act as Aaron acted."[5]

Abot de-Rabbi Natan, the earliest commentary on *Pirḳe Abot*,[6] seems, however, to have no inkling of this literal meaning of Hillel's saying. Both Version A and Version B have lovely explanations[7] of Aaron's devotion to peace and homilies on its high value, but all in general terms, as though this were a maxim altogether independent of time and place from the very beginning.

Or consider the well-known Aramaic saying, also attributed to Hillel: "Moreover he saw a skull floating on the surface of the water. He said to it: 'For drowning others thou wast drowned; and in the end they that drowned thee shall be drowned.'"[8] The commentators (*ad loc.*) have a number of edifying observations,[9] and they take full advantage of the homiletical

3. In *Ḳebuzzat Maamarim* (Berlin, 1877), p. 161; see also L. Ginzberg, *The Legends of the Jews* (Philadelphia, 1909–38), VI, 113, n. 643 (I have been unable to locate the reference in *Legends* to Ginzberg's remarks in Geiger, *Ḳebuzzat Maamarim*, p. 160). And see also L. Finkelstein, *Mabo le-Massektot Abot we-Abot d'Rabbi Natan* (New York, 1950), p. 238, n. 33; A. Kaminka, *Mehḳarim be-Miḳra we-Talmud u-ba-Sifrut ha-Rabbanit*, 2nd ed. (Tel Aviv, 5711), II, 76f.

4. See also E. E. Urbach in *Tarbiz*, 25:276 (1955–56), on the expression "disciples of Abraham."

5. BT *Yoma* 71b. On the tradition of the ancestry of these sages, see also Ginzberg, *Legends*, VI, 195. On how people often felt about certain leading priestly families, see BT *Pesaḥim* 57a. Or, for that matter, see BT *Makkot* 10a for an interpretation of Hos. 6:9. Cf. Josephus, *Antiquitates judaicae*, XX, 8:8, 9:2.

6. Or, more accurately, on an early form of that tractate.

7. Ed. S. Schechter (Vienna, 1887), pp. 48ff., 163.

8. *Abot* 2:6 and Version A of *Abot de-Rabbi Natan*, chap. xii, p. 55; note, however, that Version B, p. 56, attributes the saying to R. Joshua! One more point: the sentence beginning with אף (אף הוא ראה) also seems to be a stylistic mannerism, suggesting that this was one of a series of sayings in somewhat the same spirit; for a such a style, see, e.g., Mishna *Ma'aser Sheni* 5:15 (on which see S. Lieberman, *Hellenism in Jewish Palestine*, 2nd ed. [New York, 1962], pp. 140–143), Mishna *Ḥallah* 4:11, Mishna *Yoma* 3:10, Mishna *Beẓah* 2:7. And note also the reading in *Abot de-Rabbi Natan*, chap. xii, p. 55.

9. Cf. *Machsor Vitry*, p. 497, and also Maimonides (*Abot Commentary*, ed. M. D. Rabinowitz [Jerusalem, 1961], p. 47), who informs us that "this is something borne out by experience at all times and in all places: whoever does evil and introduces violence and corruption, is himself the victim of the harms caused by those very evils he introduced;

possibilities of the saying. Let me quote one which is not typical but passing strange; it is by the grandson of Maimonides, and one cannot help wondering what the rationalist grandfather would have said if he had heard it:

> Hillel, may he rest in peace, saw Pharaoh's skull floating on the water. It was Pharaoh who used to take one hundred and fifty young children of Israel every morning, and another one hundred and fifty every evening, and [after extreme torture]... cast them into the sea. That is why the Lord slew him and drowned him. And the ancients tell us that the Hillel referred to in the Mishna is really Moses our master, may he rest in peace... And he said to the skull, "Because you slew human beings and threw them into the water, the Lord has slain you and cast you into the water"... This is the hidden [mystic] meaning of this statement.[10]

Whatever else the different comments achieve, one thing is clear: the commentators hardly recognize that there is anything noteworthy about the literary style of this saying reminiscent of a particular genre, although of course they do recognize that the saying is in Aramaic. For them it is enough that *Pirḳe Abot* has preserved Hillel's words, which, to be sure, may very well have been prompted by his seeing a skull floating on some body of water. But in this connection the following must surely be of some interest: "Seeing a fly settle on his table, he said, 'Even Diogenes feeds parasites!' " "Seeing a woman learning her letters [= receiving an education], he said, 'Now, there's a sword getting sharpened!' " "Seeing one woman giving advice to another, he said, 'The asp is buying poison from the viper.' " "Seeing a Negro chewing white bread, [he said], 'Look at the night choking [= swallowing] the day!' " "Seeing a Negro defecating, he said, 'Hullo, a split cauldron!' "[11] In other words, our *Abot* maxim is one of those typical

for he himself has taught an occupation which can only bring harm to him and to others. So too, he who teaches virtue and introduces some good activity will be rewarded by the results of that very activity; for he teaches something which will do good to him and to others. And the words of the verse are very apt in this connection, namely, *For the work of a man will He requite unto him, and cause every man to find according to his ways*" (Job 34:11).

10. *Midrash David* of R. David Ha-Nagid, trans. B. Z. Krynfiss (Jerusalem, 5704), p. 34, and cf. Lieberman, *Hellenism*, p. 137, n. 87, paragraph 2.

11. Ἰδὼν μυῖαν ἐπάνω τῆς τραπέζῃς αὐτοῦ εἶπεν. καὶ Διογένης παρασίτους τρέφει. Ἰδὼν γυναῖκα διδασκομένην γράμματα εἶπεν. οἷον ξίφος ἀκονᾶται. Ἰδὼν γυναῖκα γυναικὶ συμβουλεύουσαν εἶπεν. ἀσπὶς παρ' ἐχίδνης φάρμακον πορίζεται. Ἰδὼν Αἰθίοπα καθαρὸν τρώγοντα. ἰδού ἡ νὺξ τὴν ἡμέραν πνίγει. Ἰδὼν Αἰθίοπα δὲ χέζοντα εἶπεν. οἷος λέβης τέτρηται. (P. Jaguet and P. Perdrizet in C. Wessely, *Studien zur Palaeographie und Papyruskunde* [Leipzig, 1906], pp. 157–158.) I have used the translation (of sentences 1, 3, and 5; 2 and 4 are my own) as it is given in H. I. Marrou, *A History of Education in Antiquity*, trans G. Lamb (New York, 1956), p. 156; see indeed Marrou's discussion, pp. 155–157, and his references; on the question of propriety see also Lieberman, *Hellenism*, pp. 33–34. For a number of anecdotes which include pointed comments made by Diogenes, see Diogenes Laertius, VI, 22ff. (trans. R. D. Hicks, Loeb Classical Library, II, 25ff.) — these have the flavor (but not the same stereotypical stylistic structure) of the sentences we have cited. On the first sentence cited above see Diogenes Laertius, VI, 40.

χρεῖαι employed in the instruction of children. Is it too farfetched to suggest that just as in the primary education of the Hellenistic world, aphorisms of Diogenes were recalled and employed, so in the primary schools of Jewish Palestine Hillel aphorisms were similarly used? I do not think so, and this theory may further explain the neatly drawn contrasts in a number of stories about Hillel and Shammai:[12] these were delightful and effective *exempla* for young students.

At all events, even each of the maxims of *Pirḳe Abot* once rose in a specific setting, although it is difficult to recover it, and I am unable to resist the temptation of stating a general proposition, to wit: When do homiletical and even symbolic interpretations appear? When an original meaning is forgotten. Naturally, I do not mean to imply that in no other way can symbolic interpretation arise; but it certainly helps not to know the *peshat*, the immediate, literal meaning. And this can be demonstrated especially clearly by study of what overtook an exceptionally well known *Abot* saying, the very first one in the treatise and attributed to the Men of the Great Assembly.[13] They said, as everyone knows, three things:

הוו מתונים בדין והעמידו תלמידים הרבה ועשו סייג לתורה

and, for a change, I suggest that we begin with the third, rather than the first, part of their saying.[14]

עשו סייג לתורה, "Make a hedge about the Torah." What does this mean? As usual, when one asks about the meaning of an *Abot* sentence, the first place to which to turn is *Abot de-Rabbi Natan*, and what does one find

12. For example, in *Abot de-Rabbi Natan*, both versions, pp. 60ff., BT *Shabbat* 31a. And on *exempla* in education, see also Marrou, *Education in Antiquity*, pp. 169, 235.

13. *Abot* 1:1, *Abot de Rabbi Natan*, both versions, p. 2 (see also p. 150, where the reading היו נתונים[!] is plainly a printer's error, for note immediately thereafter היו מתונין בדין כיצד); cf. *Mekilta Ishmael*, Pisha VI, ed. H. S. Horovitz and I. A. Rabin (Frankfurt, 1931), p. 19 (ed. J. Z. Lauterbach [Philadelphia, 1933–35], I, 46), *Sifre Deut*. 16, ed. L. Finkelstein (Berlin, 1939), p. 25; note also BT *Sanhedrin* 7b.

14. Much as I have learned from his meticulous and thoroughgoing studies, as is evident from the course of my entire discussion, I am unable to accept the view of my teacher Professor L. Finkelstein of the so-called "original" reading of the *Anshe Keneset Ha-Gedolah* saying, already formulated by him in 1940 in *Journal of Biblical Literature*, 59:455ff.; see also his *Ha-Perushim we-Anshe Keneset ha-Gedolah* (New York, 1950), pp. 54f., n. 151 (see also his *Mabo*, p. 28, p. 234, n. 18, and most recently in the third edition of his *The Pharisees, The Sociological Background of Their Faith* [Philadelphia, 1962], II, 580, and 881, n. 12). In addition to what emerges from the body of this paper, I might add one point: the reason the exposition of the third clause of the saying is treated in *Abot de-Rabbi Natan* before the exposition of the second clause is simply this: once הוו מתונים בדין was interpreted as "a man should be patient in his speech [בדבריו]" it was natural to associate with this "make a hedge about thy words [לדבריך]"; indeed observe how *Machsor Vitry*, commenting on the third clause, introduces the *Abot de-Rabbi Natan* citation: ובמשנת ר׳ נתן אמריי׳ בן עזאי אומ׳ הוי זהיר בדבריך מבטלתן ועשה סייג לדבריך כדרך שעשה וכו׳!: Yet in *Abot de-Rabbi Natan* the Ben Azzai statement is given at the end of the comment on "Be deliberate in judgment"!

here? Version B[15] first makes a sensible observation of a general character, that "a vineyard surrounded by a fence is not like a vineyard without a fence; but no man ought to make more of the fence than of the thing fenced in—for if then the fence falls, even what was planted will be ruined, as we find in connection with Adam": he made an excessive fence, and when the fence fell, even what was planted was ruined; that is, God had forbidden only eating of the fruit of the tree of the knowledge of good and evil, but Adam instructed Eve not only not to eat of that fruit, but also to beware of touching it.[16] After this comment, Version B continues in essentials the way Version A reads, to this effect: "And make a hedge about the Torah. [This means:] And make a hedge about thy words the way the Holy One, blessed be He, made a hedge about His words, and Adam made a hedge about his words. The Torah made a hedge about its words. Moses made a hedge about his words. So too Job, and also the Prophets, the Holy Writings, and the Sages—all of them made a hedge about their words."[17]

A hedge about the Torah has manifestly become a hedge about one's words; and the whole discussion of *Abot de-Rabbi Natan*—and it is not a short one!—is built on that understanding, that by a hedge about the Torah is meant a hedge about one's words. Unlike what we frequently find in our classical texts, that along with the homiletical interpretation, a more literal explanation is offered as an alternative (as a דבר אחר), often even as the first of alternatives, in the present instance only that one interpretation is presented, hedge about the Torah equals hedge about one's words.

That the interpretation offered by *Abot de-Rabbi Natan* is more *derush* than *peshat* was already felt by the earliest commentators. Maimonides, for example, ignores it altogether and says simply that the clause "refers to the decrees and enactments [*gezerot* and *taḳḳanot*] of the Sages which keep a man far from transgression; as the Blessed One said, *Therefore shall ye keep what I have given you to keep* [Lev. 18:30, ושמרתם את משמרתי], which the Talmud [*Yebamot* 21a] interprets to mean: Add protection to what I have already given you as a protection."[18]

And although the commentator in *Machsor Vitry* does refer to the *Abot de-Rabbi Natan* explanation (but really in the most abbreviated fashion!),[19] note that first he gives substantially the interpretation which we meet with in Maimonides. And you may surely put this down as a general rule: Whenever the Rishonim either ignore an explanation plainly provided

15. P. 3; cf. the idiom in Tosefta *Ḳiddushin* 1:11
16. Cf. Gen. 2:17 and 3:3.
17. P. 3; note also pp. 151ff.
18. Maimonides on *Abot* 1:1, p. 1.
19. Pp. 464f.

by a classical source, or give priority to an explanation not immediately given by the classical source, the Rishonim are having difficulty with that source.

In the present instance there is still another detail worth attending to. Even as the illustration of "the hedge which the Sages made," *Machsor Vitry* cites neither the reading of *Abot de-Rabbi Natan* nor the reading of the Mishna *Berakot* 1:1, but rather the text of the Mekilta:[20] "All sacrifices that are to be eaten within one day's duration, may indeed be eaten until the dawn of the following day. Why then did the Sages say, 'Up to midnight'? To keep a man far from transgression, to make a hedge about the Torah, and to fulfill the words of the Men of the Great Assembly who had said[21] three things: 'Be deliberate in judgment,[22] and raise many disciples, and make a hedge about the Torah.'" Why cite the Mekilta? But, of course, while the Mishna *Berakot* does speak of "keeping a man far from sin," it says nothing about making a hedge—that is actually the Mekilta's interpretation of the earlier statement recorded in the Mishna.

The more one contemplates these facts, the more inescapable becomes the conclusion that the Men of the Great Assembly were not talking of such things as *sheniyyot le-arayot*, [23] or of adding *gezerot* and *taḳḳanot*, as Maimonides puts it. Please note, by the way, that the very midrash of עשו משמרת למשמרתי although it occurs earlier in the Sifra[24]—as ושמרתם שמרו לי משמרת...—is cited in the Talmud in the names of Babylonian Amoraim,[25] and if *Abot de-Rabbi Natan* makes no mention of such a notion—which by constant iteration and reiteration has become so plausible to us[26]—we are forced to conclude that *Abot de-Rabbi Natan* knew nothing of it, although it is evident that *Abot de-Rabbi Natan* likewise did not know any longer the real meaning of this exhortation.

But as late as the first three-and-a-half decades of the second century at least one man knew what it meant, namely Rabbi Akiba, the very sage who urged his disciple Rabbi Simeon ben Yoḥai to teach his son from a

20. See above, Note 13, for the reference. By the way, this passage does not occur in *Mekilta Simeon*. And note that Aknin (*Sepher Musar*, ed. W. Bacher [Berlin, 1910], p. 3) cites neither *Abot de-Rabbi Natan* nor the Mekilta nor the *baraita* in BT *Berakot* 4b—cf. below, Page 154 — but the Mishna, *Berakot* 1:1. And on this Mekilta passage, see further below Note 107, paragraph 2.

21. Cf. *Proceedings of the American Academy for Jewish Research*, 27:56, n. 51 (1958).

22. See further below, Pages 146 ff.

23. Cf. *Machsor Vitry*, p. 464.

24. End of *Ahare Mot*, ed. I. H. Weiss (Vienna, 1862), 86d. Cf. below, Note 111.

25. Cf. below, Page 155. BT *Mo'ed Ḳatan* 5a (R. Ashi), BT *Yebamot* 21a (R. Kahana). By the way, in the Munich manuscript of *Mo'ed Ḳatan* 5a the reading is עשו משמרת למשמרת.

26. See C. Taylor, *Sayings of the Jewish Fathers*, 2nd ed. (Cambridge, 1897), p. 11, n. 1; R. T. Herford, *Pirḳe Aboth* (New York, 1945), p. 21.

ספר מוגה.[27] Akiba said, "Masoret is a hedge about the Torah."[28] And what *Masoret* means, *Machsor Vitry*[29] tells us plainly: "This is a reference to those Masoretic comments which are added to the margins of Biblical books, and these are known as Masorah magna."[30]

Let us therefore translate all of this into our own idiom. What the Men of the Great Assembly are talking about in their third clause is the proper protection and preservation of the *text* of the Torah (almost certainly the five books of Moses) lest it be corrupted by false or inferior readings. In the words of Rabbi David Kimḥi: "It seems that these words [that is, of the category of *ḳeri* and *kethib*] came into existence because the books were lost or dispersed during the first exile, and the sages who were skilled in Scripture were dead. Thereupon *the Men of the Great Assembly*, who restored the Torah to its former state, finding divergent readings in the books, adopted those which were supported by the majority of copies and seemed genuine to them."[31] What the *Anshe Keneset Ha-Gedolah* are urging for the text of the Torah is just the sort of attention and scholarship that by the middle of the third century B.C.E. Hellenistic scholars, especially in Alexandria but elsewhere, too, were already devoting to and doing with their own classical texts, above all Homer.[32] When the philosopher Timon the son of Timarchus (ca. 320–230 B.C.E.) was once asked by Aratus how he, Aratus, could obtain a trustworthy text of Homer, Timon replied, "You can, if you get hold of the ancient copies, and not the corrected copies

27. See BT *Pesaḥim* 112a.

28. *Abot* 3:13.

29. P. 513. Maimonides says nothing on this sentence (and note therefore the interpretation Aknin—who is so deeply influenced by Maimonides' commentary—cites and then the one he offers as his own!); but cf. R. Jonah Gerondi in his commentary *ad loc.* and Taylor, *Sayings of the Jewish Fathers*, I, 55, n. 33, end.

30. Note also the *'Aruk*, s.v. סג, VI, 14b: מסורת סייג לתורה פי׳ הן סימנין שעשו חכמים לסדר התורה בפיהם. Observe in *'Aruk* the following reading: מעשרות סייג לתורה וכו׳ —obviously reflecting someone having difficulty with understanding Akiba's saying! I have deliberately made no reference to the expression יש אם למסורת (BT *Ḳiddushin* 18b and parallels; cf. Sifra *ad* Lev. 12:5, 58d), for there are several problems with it which I hope to discuss in a subsequent study, and therefore also I refrain from discussion of the literature cited, for example, in B. Gerhardsson, *Memory and Manuscript* (Uppsala, 1961), p. 49 and n. 2. For the time being, cf. *'Aruk*, s.v. אם 2, I, pp. 109, and 110, n. 1. At all events, it is noteworthy that one of the Sages concerned with this theme—and he maintains יש אם למקרא—is none other than Rabbi Akiba. (I am grateful to Professor I. Twersky for urging me to add this brief notation, despite my decision to postpone full discussion to another time.)

31. Cited by Lieberman, *Hellenism*, p. 21, but the italics are mine. Note also Tanhuma *Beshallah* 16, שהוא תיקון סופרים אנשי כנסת הגדולה ..., and cf. Lieberman, *Hellenism*, pp. 30f. And see especially M. Zucker in *Tarbiz*, 27:68 (1958).

32. See J. E. Sandys, *A History of Classical Scholarship*, 3rd ed. (Cambridge, 1921), I, 105–144, but especially Lieberman, *Hellenism*, pp. 20–82, not only for a host of illuminating details but for the picture as it emerges as a whole; this study is indispensable.

of our day [... εἰ τοῖς ἀρχαίοις ἀντιγράφοις ἐντυγχάνοι καὶ μὴ τοῖς ἤδη διωρθωμένοις]."[33]

Note well: in the third century B.C.E. even a Timon speaks of the ancient, untampered-with texts, as the best texts; even in Homeric scholarship what is most highly recommended is the ancient, the carefully preserved text. In Jewish Palestine such preservation was—and how apt is the expression—the hedge. And the carefully preserved and transmitted text was—again, how apt the term—Masorah.

Obviously the text of the Torah had to be carefully kept,[34] at least with no less a diligence than that lavished on the work of Homer,[35] "the prophet of All,"[36] for on the Torah text so much depended,[37]

אין לך בתורה אפלו אות אפלו תיבה ואין צריך לומר פיסוק שאין לו כמה טעמים.[38]

So important an assignment was it to take extreme care of the Biblical text, that there is little wonder when we hear of a "special college of book readers," to use Professor Lieberman's phrase,[39] checking on the text kept in the Temple.

Now, to the second clause in the saying of the *Anshe Keneset Ha-Gedolah*, העמידו תלמידים הרבה, "raise many disciples." And on this occasion too, let us first examine what the earliest source, *Abot de-Rabbi Natan*, and the earliest commentators have to say. To *Abot de-Rabbi Natan*, [40] apparently what the *Anshe Keneset Ha-Gedolah* are pleading for is what the Hillelites in their time—let us say early in the second half of the first century—are affirming: "For the School of Shammai says: One ought to

33. Diogenes Laertius IX, 113 (Loeb Classical Library, II, 523). Cf. E. Bickerman in *Journal of Biblical Literature*, 63:342 (1944): "The earliest commentators of Hippocrates in Alexandria collected the oldest available manuscripts of the author because the current text was supposed to be corrupt through long transmission." See also Bickerman's notes on that page.

34. Cf. Mishna *Mo'ed Ḳatan* 3:4 (note the reading adopted by H. Albeck in the Albeck-Yallon *Mishna*, and cf. Albeck's comment, p. 508), and see Lieberman, *Hellenism*, p. 22, n. 18.

35. See Lieberman, *Hellenism*, p. 46, and note how he takes the statement of BT *Baba Batra* 116a, top line.

36. Cf. Lieberman, *Hellenism*, pp. 20 and 108.

37. Cf. *Gen. Rabba* 1:14, ed. J. Theodor and H. Albeck (Berlin, 1912), p. 12, and on the possibility of Akiba being the author of the famous interpretation of Deut. 32:47a, see Theodor's note to line 6, *Gen. Rabba*, p. 12.

38. *Midrash Tannaim*, p. 205. Cf. E. Bickerman, "Some Notes on the Transmission of the Septuagint," *Alexander Marx Jubilee Volume* (New York, 1950), pp. 167f.; note especially: "To state it briefly: in Oriental philology, the principle for establishing a text was fidelity to the transmitted readings."

39. *Hellenism*, p. 22. See also the additional note by Taylor, *Sayings of the Jewish Fathers*, p. 135. The comments of D. Daube in *Hebrew Union College Annual*, 22:242f. and n. 10 (1949–50) are unsupported by the sources. See further below, Pages 152–154.

40. Chap. iii, pp. 14f.; note, too, Version B.

teach only him who is talented[41] and meek and of distinguished ancestry and rich. But the School of Hillel says: One ought to teach every man, for there were many sinners in Israel who were drawn to the study of Torah, and from them descended righteous, pious, and worthy folk."[42]

This thought, by association,[43] even leads to the recalling of how Rabbi Akiba explained Ecclesiastes 11:6; to wit, that even if one has in one's youth already raised disciples, one ought not to neglect raising disciples in one's old age.

These ideas, apparently, struck Maimonides as so self-evident—or perhaps we should say, as so typical of the whole classical tradition—that he did not bother to say anything about the clause in our Mishna.[44] No less significant is the way *Machsor Vitry* explains the clause[45]—to the *Abot de-Rabbi Natan* comments it does not refer at all! It tells us to increase the wisdom (= learning) of disciples and cites, "The more the company of scholars, the more wisdom";[46] it reminds us of that famous remark, "Much have I learned from my masters, more from my colleagues, but from my disciples most of all,"[47] and finally refers to that midrash on Jabez, who prayed for many disciples.[48]

One cannot help wondering, why such turning of the back on the *Abot de-Rabbi Natan* comment? Again observe: the commentary of *Abot de-Rabbi Natan* alludes to a rather early give-and-take, one by Bet Shammai and Bet Hillel. Certainly as Talmudic interpretations go, especially haggadic ones, this interpretation of "raise many disciples," namely, that one ought to attract as many disciples as possible, is hardly farfetched.

Whether or not the early commentators ignored it because they considered it farfetched, I would like to suggest that indeed by the time *Abot de-Rabbi Natan* was "composed," the original meaning had already been forgotten. And what the *Anshe Keneset Ha-Gedolah* had in mind was something else.

In pre-Exilic Biblical classical Hebrew, how would you ordinarily say "many disciples?"[49] Surely תלמידים רבים! Note for example the frequently recurring ימים רבים, or expressions like עמים רבים, בתים רבים, and so on and

41. Cf. J. Goldin, *The Fathers According to Rabbi Nathan* (New Haven, 1955), p. 181, n.2.

42. *Ibid.*, n. 3; Finkelstein, *Mabo*, p. 29.

43. Cf. *Abot de-Rabbi Natan*, both versions, pp. 15f. Observe, incidentally, that Aknin, p. 2, cites only this part of *Abot de-Rabbi Natan* for his comment on raising many disciples and cf. his reading with that of *Abot de-Rabbi Natan*.

44. See preceding note and also above, Note 29.

45. P. 464.

46. *Abot* 2:7.

47. BT *Makkot* 10a and parallels.

48. BT *Temurah* 16a; cf. *Abot de-Rabbi Natan*, chap. xxxv, p. 105, and parallels.

49. On *talmid* spoken of in I Chron. 25:8 see E. Bickerman, "La Chaine de la tradition pharisienne," *Revue Biblique*, 59:53 (1952).

on.[50] Why is it, then, that the *Anshe Keneset Ha-Gedolah* speak of תלמידים הרבה? The literature of the Dead Sea Scrolls, for example, still does not resort to that adjectival use of *harbeh*; why then do not the Men of the Great Assembly speak of raising[51] *talmidim rabbim*?

That I am not the first to raise this question is evident from a comment preserved in *Midrash Shemuel*:[52]

ואמר הרבה ולא אמר רבים, הכוונה שומן הרבה יספיקו להם מזונותיהם, ואינו כינוי אל רבוי התלמידים רק אל רבוי הזמן.

So then our clause supposedly means, "Furnish students with support for a long time!"—a charming anticipation of our contemporary grants to graduate students and Ph.D. candidates.

Doubtless this is *derush*, but this should not prevent us from appreciating that someone has been struck by a *fact*, the fact of the textual reading. And he is not the only one to have observed that reading. In the Taylor-Schechter Genizah collection in the Cambridge University Library there is a one-leaf manuscript,[53] which, as the compiler of the hand list has already noted, is a kind of talmud to *Pirḳe Abot*, at least to the first mishna of the treatise. A number of lines on the obverse side are legible, but not enough to warrant detailed analysis in our present discussion. On the reverse side, however, occur only two lines, quite pertinent to us. Here they are:

תלמודייהו דיקא נמי דקתני [תלמידים הרבה]
ולא קתני הרבה תלמידים

And that is all. I am not a paleographer and therefore, alas, cannot even conjecture place or date of that manuscript. Whether earlier than Samuel of Uçeda or later—and in my unprofessional opinion, it is earlier—one thing is clear: the author has noted that *talmidim harbeh* is a reading not to be taken for granted, and that it requires some kind of explanation. I think so, too.

Not long after about 250 B.C.E.,[54] an attentive reader of the Book of

50. E.g., Amos 3:15, Isa. 5:9, 2:3, Mic. 4:3; cf. indeed S. Mandelkern, *Hekhal ha-Kodesh* (Tel Aviv, 1959), pp. 1065ff., s.v. .רב, רבים. In no way, of course, is this meant to ignore the behavior of the Biblical הרבה מאד.

51. Am I right in thinking that the *hiphil* of עמד in Biblical Hebrew does not yet occur in the *general* sense of "raise" (train, develop, attract) (disciples)?

52. Of Samuel ben Isaac of Uçeda. In the edition of New York, 5705, the comment occurs on p. 8—I am unable to decide whether Samuel is giving his own views or is citing someone else's.

53. TS 20.56.

54. On the following, including dates, see H. L. Ginsberg's commentary, *Koheleth* (Tel Aviv-Jerusalem, 1961). On the date see also Ginsberg's *Studies in Koheleth* (New York, 1950), pp. 40–45.

Ecclesiastes, who was deeply disturbed by its contents, appended to the book a kind of caveat, part of which cautioned against עשות ספרים הרבה אין קץ:[55] that is, he warned against the composition of many books, for there is no limit to such activity. The words עשות ספרים הרבה in that clause deserve some attention.

In his brilliant commentary on Ecclesiastes, Professor H. L. Ginsberg interprets the clause as follows, כתיבת הספרים רבה לאין שיעור,[56] "the composition of books is an endless undertaking."[57] I do not necessarily or at all disagree with his grammatical explication of the clause, but in addition to establishing strict syntactical requirements in this connection, we should, I feel, attend also to the way some of the earliest readers we know of understood that clause. Observe that in Tannaitic Hebrew the Biblical adverb הרבה is used very often in an adjectival sense,[58] and therefore in many (not all!) instances is located after the noun it modifies: in other words, treated like a regular adjective.[59] This explains of course the Septuagint reading, υἱέ μου, φύλαξαι ποιῆσαι βιβλία πολλά.[60] The character and probable date of the Septuagint translation of Ecclesiastes being what they are,[61] the translation naturally cannot constitute either independent or additional evidence. At least, however, it does demonstrate that in the second quarter of the second century, in Akiba's time, עשות ספרים הרבה was already rather widely taken as "the making of many books." But Professor Ginsberg too, who says[62] that in Ecclesiastes *harbeh* is to be taken as a term accompanying (מלווה) the verb, nevertheless calls attention to the fact that when *harbeh* has some association with the noun (מסונף לשם עצם), *harbeh* follows the noun. Even if one does no more than check a concordance, one will find how

55. Eccles. 12:12. See Ginsberg's commentary, pp. 134f.

56. Commentary, p. 135; but see also his comment on 1:16 (p. 64) and check all the passages he cites.

57. Note too his addendum on the unnumbered page at the end, which follows p. 137.

58. Or מרובים, etc.; see, e. g., the *Oẓar Leshon ha-Mishna* of Rabbi Chayim Yehoshua Kasovsky on the relevant forms, s.v. רבב, pp. 1644f. For the expression ימים רבים which seems to appear only once in the Mishna (*Menaḥot* 11:8), see Kasovsky, p. 1643; but the Mishna, as edited by Loewe, and the Kaufmann codex do not read רבים! The Naples edition does. Even with ימים the Mishna will say ימים הרבה; see, e.g., Mishna *Niddah* 1:1 (the time of Shammai and Hillel!).

59. In the literature of the Dead Sea Scrolls (thus far published), which strives so hard to emulate and imitate the classical Biblical style, apparently הרבה is not used "adjectivally."

60. Hence also the Vulgate: "Faciendi plures libros nullus est finis." By the way, although it proves nothing, cf. the *teamim* in this verse with the *teamim* at the end of MT Eccles. 9:18.

61. See the discussion in G. A. Barton, *The Book of Ecclesiastes*, International Critical Commentary (New York, 1908), pp. 8–11. On the association of Eccles. 12:12 with Akiba's view in Mishna *Sanhedrin* 10:1, see the passages cited and discussed by Lieberman, *Hellenism*, pp. 108ff.

62. Commentary, p. 64.

prominent and recurrent is this feature of *harbeh* after the noun in Ecclesiastes above all.[63]

I would like to call this use of הרבה the adjectival *harbeh*. And if we now recall what the *Anshe Keneset Ha-Gedolah* said—namely, והעמידו תלמידים הרבה—I do not see how we can escape the conclusion that this clause is an echo of or comment on or response to עשות ספרים הרבה. What the *Anshe Keneset Ha-Gedolah* are saying is, "It is not the composition of many books we should strive for, but the raising of many disciples!" As a medieval scholar might have put it: מפי סופרים ולא מפי ספרים. Or more precisely: we are listening to one of the earliest exhortations to develop the system and discipline and tradition of an Oral Torah. There is a Written Torah; it is all the Writing, the Scripture we require; that is why it is absolutely imperative that its text be properly preserved. And to advance its teachings what is called for is not additional books, *many books*, but the raising of *many disciples*![64]

We come now to the first clause of the saying by the Men of the Great Assembly, הוו מתונים בדין, and as with the other two clauses, we will look first to the classical sources and then examine the comments of the *Rishonim*. This time, however, we shall start not with *Abot de-Rabbi Natan*, but with a passage in a Tannaitic midrash, the Sifre on Deuteronomy,[65] commenting on Deuteronomy 1:16:

> *And I charged your judges at that time, saying*: *Hear the causes between your brethren, and judge righteously*. [That is,] I said to them "Be מתונים בדין": to wit, if some case has come before you once or twice or thrice, do not say, Such a case has already come before me again and again [and therefore it is unnecessary for me to deliberate and I can pass sentence at once]. Instead, "be deliberate in judgment"; and so indeed did the Men of the Great Assembly say: "Be מתונים בדין, and raise many disciples, and make a hedge about the Torah."[66]

As is manifest, we are dealing with an interpretation of the saying of the *Anshe Keneset Ha-Gedolah*, and as we read this interpretation, how eminently sensible it seems: certainly just the kind of counsel that should be directed

63. And it is not as though Ecclesiastes is no longer familiar with the adjective רבים; cf., e.g., 7:29.

64. Cf. W. Jaeger, *Paideia* (New York, 1960), III, 194ff. And see Saadya's commentary on Eccles. 12:12, *Hamesh Megillot*, ed. J. Kapah (Jerusalem, 5722), p. 295:
ואפשר עוד לומר בו שהוא זירז על הלמוד מפי הרבנים וקבלת הלמודים מפיהם כי זה יגיעתו קלה ותועלתו קרובה ולמודו מהיר, ולהתרחק מללמוד [רק] מן הספרים ולשקוד בקריאתם [בלבד] לפי שהם מטרידים וצורכים זמן רב, והלמוד בדרך זה קשה ומיגע את הגוף.
I fear, from his addition of the words רק and בלבד in the translation, that the editor has missed Saadya's point.

65. Ed. Finkelstein, p. 25; cf. *Midrash Tannaim*, p. 9.

66. And see, too, the manuscript, TS C2, fragment 181, in the Cambridge University Library.

to judges, "And I charged your judges... judge righteously." Maimonides, for one, appreciated this; this is how he explains הוו מתונים בדין—"Proceed slowly in sentencing, and do not be hasty with the handing down of decision, [wait] until the matter is thoroughly understood; for it is possible that certain details will be revealed which at first thoughts were not manifest."[67]

And before Maimonides, *Machsor Vitry*,[68] even more explicitly, refers to our Sifre passage. But one look into *Abot de-Rabbi Natan* discloses immediately not only why we have a problem on our hands but also why *Machsor Vitry* reads as it does. Here is a paraphrase of the Vitry commentary: The word מתונים is to be understood as in the expression at the end of the treatise *Horayot*, דמתין מסיק,[69] "taking his time he arrives at a conclusion"; that is to say, they take their time to get to the very bottom of the law, of the case (עומק הדין). Then follows the substance of our Sifre passage. Only then comes the following from *Abot de-Rabbi Natan*:[70] "And in the Baraita of Rabbi Natan occurs this interpretation: 'For thus we find concerning the *Anshe Keneset Ha-Gedolah*,[71] that they were מתונין בדין, as it is said, *These also are the proverbs of Solomon which the men of Hezekiah king of Judah copied out* [Prov. 25:1]: it is not that they copied, but that they took their time.' "[72] *Machsor Vitry* does not stop with this, but concludes with a reference to Bar Kappara's midrash in the treatise *Sanhedrin*.[73]

Is the author of the *Machsor Vitry* commentary, perhaps, not entirely happy with *Abot de-Rabbi Natan*? It would seem so.

For two most striking facts are revealed by the *Abot de-Rabbi Natan* commentary. First, neither in Version A nor in Version B is there a word of that interpretation of the Sifre which we found to be so reasonable. Second, when we examine what *Abot de-Rabbi Natan* does do with הוו מתונים בדין, at first we are hardly enlightened and then we discover that we have been diverted to some other theme. Here is the *Abot de-Rabbi Natan* passage: Be מתונים בדין "teaches that a person should take his time in judgment

67. On *Abot* 1:1, ed. Rabinowitz, p. 1: שיאחרו לחתך הדין ולא יפסקוהו מהרה עד שיבינוהו שאפשר שיתגלו להם הענינים שלא היו נגלים בתחלת המחשבה.

68. P. 464.

69. Cf. the note in *Machsor Vitry ad loc.*

70. Cf. *Abot de-Rabbi Natan*, pp. 2 (both versions) and 150.

71. See next note.

72. The *Abot de-Rabbi Natan* text is somewhat difficult; note Schechter's n. 22, p. 2, and Goldin, *Fathers According to Rabbi Nathan*, p. 176, n. 22. I have begun to doubt the validity of the correction, for everywhere the reading *Anshe Keneset Ha-Gedolah* keeps recurring (note also the reading in the Schechter edition, p. 150), and I am now inclined to accept that reading, even though the sense of the *Abot de-Rabbi Natan* citing Prov. 25:1 is not too smooth. See also Finkelstein, *Ha-Perushim*, p. 74, n. 223.

73. BT *Sanhedrin* 7b, and see further below, Page 151. Bar Kappara is a fifth-generation Tanna (cf. H. L. Strack, *Introduction to the Talmud and Midrash*, 5th ed. [Philadelphia, 1931], pp. 119, 316); in other words, he lived at the end of the second century or the beginning of the third century, at least 450 years after the Men of the Great Assembly!

[שיהא אדם ממתין בדין][74] for whoever takes his time in judgment is unruffled in judgment [מיושב בדין]." Then the verse in Proverbs is cited and explained as we observed it in *Machsor Vitry*. Seriously now, how much clarity has one gained from the remark שכל הממתין בדין מיושב בדין? And how apt after all is that Proverbs proof text? Then מיושב seems to have been forgotten, and we are informed, ולא שהעתיקו אלא שהמתינו.[75]

Next we are off to a statement by Abba Saul on what was almost the fate of Proverbs, Song of Songs, and Ecclesiastes, which illustrates לא שהמתינו אלא שפירשו.[76] And then to our amazement we learn that "Be מתונים בדין" may also (דבר אחר) "teach that a man should be even-tempered, patient in his speech [שיהא אדם ממתין בדבריו] and not be short-tempered in his speech [ואל יהי מקפיד על דבריו], for whoever is short-tempered in his speech forgets what he has to say." And this is proved by what happened once to Moses; and if it could happen to Moses, can you imagine what it would be with the likes of us![77]

So *din* has become דברים, and we are not speaking of conduct in rendering judgment, but of controlling one's temper in general![78]

Is there any wonder Maimonides does not refer to this at all, and that *Machsor Vitry* refers to so little of this, and even that neither as the first nor the last explanation? Above all, let us repeat, why with so sensible a comment as the Sifre's available, did not *Abot de-Rabbi Natan* at least allude to it too, even if *Abot de-Rabbi Natan* wanted to suggest more homiletical ideas?

That we are not getting literal exegesis in *Abot de-Rabbi Natan* is evident; that the *Rishonim* are, to say the least, perplexed by the *Abot de-Rabbi Natan* exegesis, is likewise evident; that the Sifre comment should be absent from *Abot de-Rabbi Natan* is again, to say the least, most puzzling.

Here therefore once again I am forced to the conclusion that if *Abot de-Rabbi Natan*—the earliest commentary we have on the sayings of *Pirḳe Abot*, and an early draft of that Mishna, by the way—if *Abot de-Rabbi Natan* shows no awareness of any explanation more or less plain, it must be because it no longer knew the real meaning of the text it was interpreting. *Abot de-Rabbi Natan* was guessing; the guesses were charming but had nothing to do with what the *Anshe Keneset Ha-Gedolah* were talking about, and I believe I can

74. Cf. Finkelstein, *Mabo*, p. 172.

75. The difficulties I have mentioned are not the only ones encountered; see above, Note 72, and also Finkelstein, *Mabo*, pp. 234f., n. 18.

76. Cf. also Version B of *Abot de-Rabbi Natan*, p. 3, and see Finkelstein, *Mabo*, pp. 126f.

77. On the word מתונים see also *Sifre Deut*. 323, p. 374 (cf. *Midrash Tannaim*, p. 200); on the word מותן cf. *Midrash Tannaim*, p. 201, but in *Sifre Deut*. 325, p. 377, line 8, the reading is אלא ממתין.

78. To try to interpret דין as though it were part of the expression דין ודברים is no longer *peshat* but *derush*!

show that even the Sifre, reasonable as is its comment, is not furnishing us with the original meaning of that first clause in the saying of the Men of the Great Assembly. To recover that, let us return to the verse in Ecclesiastes which has already opened one door for us.[79]

That verse begins: ויתר, and what is more, מהמה בני הזהר, "Take it easy, my son, take warning." Even those who would like to quibble with H. L. Ginsberg's extraordinarily brilliant reading מְהֻמָּה surely cannot overlook the word הזהר and the fact that it is followed by the clause עשות ספרים הרבה אין קץ. The verse evidently opens with an exhortation to "my son": "Take care, my son, take warning, it is an endless and profitless exhaustion to compose more and more books."[80] And I submit that the saying of the *Anshe Keneset Ha-Gedolah* originally also opened in this fashion: הוו מתונין בנין, "Careful, careful, children, instead of composing more literary works, raise many disciples;[81] for there is only one text we need, the Torah, and because without that Writing in a proper state there can be disastrous consequences, preserve the carefully edited readings furnished by the Masorah." The whole sentiment of this saying is like the first signs of the dawn of that intellectual day which is familiar to us as the Talmudic period; here are the first explicit signals of the development of תורה בעל פה as a conscious undertaking. And note, quite independently of all this, Professor Ginsberg says of the peroration of Ecclesiastes, our verse and the two that

79. Once again, for what follows one must consult the Koheleth commentary, *ad loc.*, by H. L. Ginsberg and see also the unnumbered page of his supplementary comments.

80. On the meaning of the word מתונים see H. L. Ginsberg in his commentary, *ad* 7:7, p. 98, and S. Lieberman, *Tosefta ki-Fshutah* (New York, 1955), Long Commentary on *Berakot* III, p. 47, s.v. קלות ראש and *Tosefta ki-Fshutah* (New York, 1962), Long Commentary, p. 1339. But this does not preclude, in my opinion, the use of the word in the meaning of "go slowly, take care"; see Targum on Cant. 5:12 (cf. *Midrash Shir Ha-Shirim*, ed. Grünhut, 40a–b) where, to be sure, the expression מתינין בדינא is based on what we may call the *Sifre–Abot de-Rabbi Natan* interpretation of מתונים בדין, but at the same time it reveals the potential meaning to which מתון could be extended. And on מתונים in the sense of "restrained," see Lieberman, *Tosefta Ki-Fshutah ad* Tosefta *Shabbat* 7:24, Long Commentary, p. 105.

81. The following communication (of March 10, 1961) to me from Professor Ginsberg will be of interest: "(1) First of all there is of course Ps. 34:12, לכו בנים שמעו לי. (2) Secondly, I wonder if בנין couldn't be an Aramaism for '*our* sons.' The suffix for 'our' is still נא as a rule at that time, but the shorter ־ן may very well have been used even then in a familiar expression like 'our sons.'—The title רבן must be pretty old, yet it is רבן and not רַבַּנָא.—(The 5th century Elephantine papyri write ־ן nearly always, but they may have pronounced a short vowel at the end all the same.) (The syllable in question was unstressed.)"

Even at the risk of protesting too much, I should like to say that I well understand the foreseeable and likely strong reluctance to accept this "emendation," and (for four years) I have myself done everything I could to resist taking liberties with so long established a text. But, as I say, I am left with no alternative. At all events, even if this "emendation" is found unacceptable, I hope that at least these two *facts* will not be overlooked; one, the real difficulty with ממתין בדין = מיושב בדין; two, the clear statement in Eccles., בני הזהר...

follow, that it summons up the traces of the religio-intellectual climate of the Mishnaic Sages rather than those of the Biblical climate.[82]

In the saying of the Men of the Great Assembly, then, I suggest we have preserved a kind of commentary on or response to Ecclesiastes 12:12. But at an early time the original meaning was forgotten; maybe it was this that caused the mistaken change from בנין to בדין;[83] maybe the text was accidentally corrupted from בנין to בדין, and since as a result הוו מתונים בדין was puzzling, *Abot de-Rabbi Natan* had only its own resources—hence guesses—to draw upon, and could not really grasp what the clause meant. I would rather not try to add guesses of my own and am especially uneasy with the fact that I have to suggest an emendation of a text at all, and of a text at that which has had so long and well established a history. No one is more reluctant than I to engage in textual emendations or in speculations which cannot be controlled by something concrete, like a text or some preserved hidden-away reading. But I have no alternative—the data force me to conclude that the literal meaning of the saying of the Men of the Great Assembly can be understood only in the context of the sentences appended by that pious soul to the book of Ecclesiastes.

Once the literal meaning was forgotten, it was inevitable that the intent of the words of the *Anshe Keneset Ha-Gedolah* should be transformed. First, each of the clauses in the saying came to be treated as a unit by itself;[84] and then in each unit, even as early as Tannaitic times, each generation discerned what was congenial to its own spirit or needs. A fifth-generation Tanna, for instance, already undertakes to support the first clause with a midrash of Pentateuch verses. Note the idiom carefully:[85]

82. ברור שהמפטיר שלנו, בעל פס׳ יב־יד, קרוב ברוחו לחכמים ההם [ז.א. לחכמים ראשונים כבעלי המקראות תה׳ קי״א, י׳, משלי א׳, ז׳; ט׳, י׳. איוב כ״ח, כ״ח] יותר מקוהלת; אבל עושה הוא רושם פחות ״מקראי״ מהם, ויותר ״יהודי״, באשר אינו מבליט כל כך את החוכמה (אינו נוקב את שמה, ו״סוף דבר״ הוא אומר תחת ״ראשית חכמה״) אלא מדגיש מצוות ודין, ושכר ועונש... מזכירים דבריו את שני מאמרות רבי חנינא בן דוסא (משנה, אבות ג׳, ט): כל שיראת חטאו קודמת לחכמתו חכמתו מתקיימת; וכל שחכמתו קודמת ליראת חטאו, אין חכמתו מתקיימת... כל שמעשיו מרובין מחכמתו חכמתו מתקיימת; וכל שחכמתו מרובה ממעשיו, אין חכמתו מתקיימת.

83. Because people no longer understood what that could mean.

84. In a future study I hope to show that the three-clause structure of almost all the early sayings preserved in *Abot* (say, at least down through the disciples of Joḥanan ben Zakkai) is not intended to suggest individual and independent clauses, but clauses directed to a single thought. For the time being, this should certainly be clear in the following: 1:2, 3, 8, 9, 11, 12 (cf. above, Pages 135–136), 18; 2:8a (Joḥanan ben Zakkai's saying), 11, 14 (cf. the Hebrew paper on the academy of Joḥanan ben Zakkai in the forthcoming *Wolfson Jubilee Volume*); 3:1. Moreover, cf. *Proceedings*, *AAJR*, 27:53 (1958).

After the present paper was read (March 20, 1963), Professor A. Altmann raised a question regarding the specific statement of the Mishna, "they said *three things*" (*sheloshah debarim*), which would by itself certainly not suggest that the sentence is directed to a *single* thought. The answer of course is that "they said three (different) things" is the editor's interpretation of those clauses both in 1:1 and 2:10—on which see further the paper in the *Wolfson Jubilee Volume* referred to.

85. See above, Note 73.

דרש בר קפרא, מנא הא מילתא דאמרי רבנן [Rabbanan, no less!] הוו מתונין בדין דכתיב לא תעלה במעלות. וסמיך ליה ואלה המשפטים.
Perhaps in the latter half of the second century,[86] when discussion of the right behavior of judges was being described in midrashic moralizing terms, "Be deliberate in judgment" naturally suggested of itself a directive to judges to ponder carefully before arriving at a decision, regardless of how familiar the case seemed to be.

When in the latter part of the first century the original intention of "Raise many disciples" was no longer recalled, it seemed indeed that the *Anshe Keneset Ha-Gedolah* must have had in mind what was obviously preoccupying the sages of that age: Is everyone to be admitted as a student to the rabbinic academy, or only a select group? As is evident, the Shammaites did seek to limit admissions; [87] let us not forget that Hillel (according to the story)[88] was on one occasion unable to scrape together enough funds for the admission fees; Rabban Gamaliel the Elder did not look with the same eye on rich and poor students.[89] Rabban Gamaliel II would have certain students kept from entering the academy.[90] *Abot de-Rabbi Natan*, which I seem to be belaboring for forgetting so much, certainly recalls the possibility of a student paying fees! "Another interpretation of 'Let thy fellow's property be as dear to thee as thine own':... When a scholar comes to thee saying, 'Teach me,' if it is in thy power to teach, teach him. Otherwise, send him away at once and *do not take his money from him*, as it is said, *Say not unto thy neighbor, Go, and come again, and tomorrow I will give; when thou hast it by thee*" (Proverbs 3:28).[91]

And when as a result of the impetus created by Joḥanan ben Zakkai and his leading disciples in Jabneh, study of Torah came to be elevated as a primary obligation on the part of every member of Jewish society,[92] what was more natural than to see in the formulation of the *Anshe Keneset Ha-Gedolah* the urgent duty which, for example, Rabbi Akiba felt: "If thou hast raised many disciples in thy youth, do not sit back and say, It is enough for me. On the contrary raise them in thine old age [too] and increase the

86. Note, for example, the names of the authorities cited in *Abot de-Rabbi Naian*, chap. x, p. 43. I hope to discuss this more fully in a future study.

87. *Abot de-Rabbi Natan*, both versions, pp. 14f., 154.

88. BT *Yoma* 35b.

89. *Abot de-Rabbi Natan*, chap. xl, p. 127; see Goldin, *Fathers... Rabbi Nathan*, p. 218, nn. 15–17, and particularly the study by G. Allon to which I refer there.

90. BT *Berakot* 28a. See also the statement by R. Simeon ben Yoḥai in *Mekilta Ishmael*, Beshallah I, ed. Lauterbach, I, 171.

91. *Abot de-Rabbi Natan*, chap. xvii, p. 65 (and cf. chap. vi, p. 27). Is there a similar thought behind the statement in chap. xvi, p. 63?

92. Cf. *Proceedings, AAJR*, 27:51–56 (1958).

study of Torah";[93] or Rabbi Ishmael: "If thou hast studied Torah in thy youth, say not, I shall not study in my old age. Instead study Torah [at all times]";[94] or Rabbi Meir: "If thou hast studied with one master, say not, Enough for me. On the contrary, go to another sage and study Torah."[95] Thus by association one thought on this theme stirs up another thought, and just as one urges the master at all times to raise many disciples, so one then goes on urging the disciples at all times and in many ways to keep studying.

As to the *seyag*—here, too, all is not of one piece; here too, we are not dealing with a static concept. When Taylor in his splendid edition and commentary writes,[96] "The סייג (III.20; VI.6) lies at the root of the Rabbinic system," or when Moore says[97] that making "a barrier about the law" (to use his translation) refers to "a body of legislation supplementary to the written law in the Pentateuch... [and] enactments meant to guard against any possible infringement of the divine statute,"[98] he is not unjust to the rabbinic attitude or zeal. The question is, however: did the expression *seyag la-Torah* always and uniformly mean, as the *Rishonim* and modern scholars assume, extending obligation or prohibition even into provinces not specifically demanded by the Torah? Let us see.

A *baraita* cited by the Talmud (not once but twice, by the way)[99] reports the following: "*Tanya*—Rabbi Eliezer ben Jacob[100] says: I heard that the *Bet Din* [a court] may impose flagellation and corporal punishments even in [cases where] the Torah does not do so, not thereby transgressing the view of the Torah, but in order to make a hedge about the Torah. Thus, it happened in the time of the Greeks that someone rode on a horse on the Sabbath. He was brought to the *Bet Din* and sentenced to be stoned—not because that was the proper [legal] penalty, but because שהשעה צריכה לכך, the times demanded it."[101]

Here then is a Tannaitic source expressly declaring that something was imposed כדי לעשות סייג לתורה. If a Tannaitic source so plainly uses *seyag*

93. Version B of *Abot de-Rabbi Natan*, chap. iv, p. 15; cf. Goldin, *Fathers... Rabbi Nathan*, p. 28, and n. 15, p. 181.

94. *Abot de-Rabbi Natan*, chap. iii, p. 16.

95. *Ibid.*; cf., however, the view attributed to R. Meir, chap. viii, p. 36.

96. *Sayings of the Jewish Fathers*, I, 11, n. 1; see also pp. 134f. (the numbering of the *Abot* paragraphs is Taylor's).

97. *Judaism in the First Centuries of the Christian Era*, I (Cambridge, Mass., 1927), 33.

98. Cf. also J. Bonsirven, *Le Judaïsme palestinien* (Paris, 1934), I, 265ff.

99. BT *Yebamot* 90b and BT *Sanhedrin* 46a. By the way, the reading of the Munich manuscript in BT *Yebamot* is simply לעשות סייג (no לתורה)!

100. On the problem of his identity see A. Hyman, *Toledot Tannaim we-Amoraim* (London, 1910), I, 183, col. b.

101. Cf. the second story in the Talmud, BT *Yebamot* 90b and *Sanhedrin* 46a, also illustrating "that the times demanded it."

la-Torah, how dare we, you may ask, depart from the generally accepted explanation of עשו סייג לתורה in the saying of the *Anshe Keneset Ha-Gedolah*?

But note attentively how the *baraita* itself describes its examples: שהשעה צריכה לכך, in unembroidered current English usage, means, It was an emergency measure; that is, at a particular, critical time, Rabbi Eliezer ben Jacob reports, apparently a *Bet Din* imposed an exceptionally severe penalty, and it never entered anyone's mind to say that as a result of that emergency, whenever in the future a Jew was found riding an animal on the Sabbath, he was to be sentenced to be stoned.[102] But when we speak of the prohibition of שניות לעריות or of שבות, that is a permanently binding regulation. Evidently then the expression לעשות סייג לתורה can be used to express a thought not strictly speaking what the commentators say "making a hedge about the Torah" means.

And now we can understand something which would otherwise be utterly eccentric. Not one of the classical commentators, neither *Abot de-Rabbi Natan* nor *Machsor Vitry* nor Maimonides nor any of the *Rishonim* before Duran (1361–1444)[103]—at least of the published *Rishonim*—not one, in commenting on the last clause of the *Anshe Keneset Ha-Gedolah* saying, refers to that Talmudic *baraita*, though as I have already remarked, that *baraita* appears not once but twice in well-known Talmudic treatises: there is nothing recherché about that *baraita*. But of course the early *Rishonim* shy away from that *baraita*, although the very terms לעשות סייג לתורה occur in it, because they know it is not speaking of what they are speaking of. And even Duran, note carefully, refers to it in connection with still another idea, which is at still another remove from what we generally apply to *seyag la-Torah*. Here is how Duran speaks:

וכן בכלל זה (של עשו סייג לתורה) הוא מה שאמרו בסנהדרין פ׳ נגמר הדין וביבמות פ׳ האשה׳ בית דין מכין ועונשין שלא מן הדין ולא לעבור על דברי תורה אלא כדי לעשות סייג לתורה וחכמי ישראל לא היו רוצים לגלות לכל אדם טעמי אלו התקנות לפי שהם סתרי תורה כמו טעמי המצות כמו שנזכר במדרש חזית!

So we are already off to the world of "esoteric" teachings and their restriction to the qualified few![104]

102. Cf. indeed the commentary of R. Hananel in B.M. Lewin, *Oẓar Ha-Geonim*, VII (Jerusalem, 5696), 322: התם דוקא משום מיגדר מילתא לעשות סייג ותקנה כי התם שהשיבן ע״י כך מעבודה זרה, וכן לקמן מפני שהיו פרוצים בעריות או שהיו מזולזלין בשביתת שבת, אבל בעלמא לא.

103. *Magen Abot* (Leipzig, 1855), p. 4a.

104. Cf., e.g., *Cant. Rabba* on 1:2b, 5c. On this last point made by Duran, see also Lieberman, *Hellenism*, pp. 139ff. I have put the word "esoteric" in quotes deliberately, for explanations were often withheld not only in esoteric lore, strictly speaking, but in legal matters, too, as the Lieberman reference shows. Note the interesting conjunction in the text of *Mekilta R. Simeon*, ed. J. N. Epstein and E. Z. Melamed (Jerusalem, 1955), p. 158.

So much, therefore, for that *baraita*. There is, however, another *baraita* (*ke-de-tanya*)[105] which is not irrelevant to our discussion. This *baraita* instructs us that in the evening when a man returns from his work, before he sits down to his meal he should recite the evening *Shema*‘; otherwise he might discover that he has eaten and fallen asleep, and the time for the recitation of the *Shema*‘ will have passed, and thus he will have been guilty of transgressing the injunction of the Sages. And this is the reason why the Sages made a hedge about their words. Note well, **חכמים עשו סייג לדבריהם**: the sages made a hedge about *their words*. This *baraita*, then, is the same[106] as the one in *Abot de-Rabbi Natan*, either drawn from that treatise, or perhaps both the Talmud and *Abot de-Rabbi Natan* have drawn on the same source. At all events, this source is illustrating not **עשו סייג לתורה** but **חכמים עשו סייג לדבריהם**, the homiletical extension of the original saying, "Make a hedge about the Torah," as we observed earlier in our analysis, the homiletical extension which can hardly represent the meaning of what the *Anshe Keneset Ha-Gedolah* had in mind, as we have already seen.[107]

Something there is in Talmud that does love a wall, because it knows quite well what it is walling in and walling out, and what is likely to give

105. BT *Berakot* 4b.

106. On the readings of the two versions of *Abot de-Rabbi Natan*, see Finkelstein, *Mabo*, pp. 24f., and *HUCA*, 19:102–104 (1945/46). The two *Abot de-Rabbi Natan* versions (cf. also *Abot de-Rabbi Natan*,p. 154) and the reading of BT *Berakot* 4b, if set side by side and compared, would reveal some interesting variants; but this is not the place for such discussion.

107. See above, Pages 139 ff. Note also the Baraita in BT *Niddah* 4b (cf. PT *Niddah* 1, 48d) where we are told that Hillel would not accept Shammai's view because he, Shammai, would not make a hedge to his words, שלא עשה סייג לדבריו. As for the give-and-take between Shammai and Hillel in BT *Niddah* 3b, where Hillel is reported as criticizing Shammai ומיהו עשה סייג לדבריך דמאי שנא מכל התורה דעבדינן סייג—not only do we meet here too with עשה סייג לדבריך, but more important: I do not believe that the Talmud BT *Niddah* 3b (compare, indeed, the whole *sugya*) is saying that the words דמאי שנא מכל התורה דעבדינן סייג are the *ipsissima verba* of Hillel; rather this is what the *Amoraim* conceive to be part of the exchange which lay behind the different views of Hillel and Shammai reported in the Mishna. Observe the very style of this sentence! Cf. below, Note 110.

And in the light of our analysis the *Mekilta Ishmael*, Pisha VI, passage cited above, Page 140, should now be clear at a glance: that passage is really discussing a hedge the Sages made about *their words*, that though strictly speaking the sacrifices supposed to be eaten within one day's duration might indeed be eaten until the dawn of the following day, once again the Sages set a time limit in the night. And by citing the saying of the Men of the Great Assembly and calling this limitation a hedge about the Torah, the Mekilta is adopting the approach of *Abot de-Rabbi Natan* that "hedge about the Torah" equals "the Sages made a hedge about their words." Note the idiom carefully:

בלילה הזה, שומע אני כל הלילה, ת״ל לא תותירו ממנו עד בקר... עד בוקר למה נאמר, לא בא הכתוב אלא ליתן תחום לבוקרו של בוקר, ואיזה זה עמוד השחר, מכאן אמרו אכילת פסחים וכו׳... עד שיעלה עמוד השחר, ולמה אמרו חכמים עד חצות להרחיק וכו׳.

offense.[108] As we noted above,[109] the way Talmudic sources express the idea of extending obligation or prohibition even into provinces not specifically demanded by the Torah is שמרו לי משמרת (Sifra) or עשו משמרת למשמרתי.[110] Is it not noteworthy that when this formulation is cited, no one in the primary sources bothers even to make use of the expression לעשות סייג לתורה?[111]

In other words, there is absolutely no need to assume that the notion of a hedge about the law, as we speak of it familiarly, appears late in the Talmudic tradition.[112] All I am trying to demonstrate is that this notion is *not in the beginning* suggested by the third clause in the saying of the *Anshe Keneset Ha-Gedolah*, for indeed originally no one thought of עשו סייג לתורה in that sense. In my opinion, the equation of עשו סייג לתורה with עשו משמרת למשמרתי was first made in Geonic times,[113] and perhaps the Geonim were led to that equation because they remembered that the one who spoke of רמז לשניות מן התורה[114] was the same Amora—namely, Raba—who interpreted Ecclesiastes 12:12[115] as

בני, הזהר בדברי סופרים יותר מדברי תורה, שדברי תורה יש בהן עשה ולא תעשה, ודברי סופרים כל העובר על דברי סופרים חייב מיתה; שמא תאמר אם יש בהן ממש מפני מה לא נכתבו? עשות ספרים הרבה אין קץ.

But of course this is only guesswork on my part, and I would hardly press it.

At all events, the *Rishonim* certainly took up the suggestion of this equation and they have made the most of it. So let us return to the main point.

What therefore were the *Anshe Keneset Ha-Gedolah* saying? This: We

108. Note not only *Abot de-Rabbi Natan*, chaps. i and ii, but Tosefta *Ḳiddushin*, cited above, Note 15; see too *Oẓar Ha-Geonim*, *Yebamot*, VII, p. 24 and Lewin's note 1 (but observe that this is wanting in *Mekilta Simeon*, ed. Epstein-Melamed). Of course the Rabbis objected to excessive hedges; see above, Page 139. On the figure of hedge and vineyard see also *Mekilta Ishmael*, Pisha I, ed. Lauterbach, I, 15.

109. Page 140.

110. But apparently in Amoraic times, the thought of extending prohibition could be expressed sometimes by "make a hedge"; see the clause מאי שנא מכל התורה דעבדינן סייג in Note 107 above: note that we still do not get דעבדינן סייג לתורה! In other words, that has still not yet become the commonplace formula for what we mean by "a hedge about the law."

111. Nor does R. Hillel in his commentary on Sifra, end of *Ahare Mot*, say anything about making a hedge. Rabad, *ad loc.*, says nothing.

112. See some fine remarks by A. Goldberg, "The Place of *Shevut*... in the Pattern of Sabbath Observance," in *Conservative Judaism*, Winter-Spring Issue, 1962, pp. 71–78 (an expanded version appeared in *Sinai*, 46:181–189 [5720]).

113. Cf. *Oẓar Ha-Geonim*, *Yebamot*, VII, p. 24 ... אילו שאסר הקב״ה בתורה ובאו חכמים ועשו סיג לתורה ואסרו עוד שמונה וכו׳.

See also Note 110 above.

114. BT *Yebamot* 21a; but cf. marginal reading in the Talmud *ad loc.* and *Diḳduḳe Soferim ad loc.*

115. BT *Erubin* 21b.

must be careful; the way to inculcate right teaching and piety is not through the multiplication of more and more books, but through the raising of many disciples to whom one will teach the Torah, that singular literary work which is at the root of all true wisdom and right conduct. And because that text is so fundamental, be sure to preserve it with greatest care. Or as that pious reader of Kohelet put it:

ויתר, מהמה בני, הזהר, עשות ספרים הרבה אין קץ ולהג הרבה יגעת בשר; סוף דבר הכל נשמע, את האלהים ירא ואת מצותיו שמר, כי זה כל האדם.

This is what the closing verses of Kohelet speak of, and this is what the *Anshe Keneset Ha-Gedolah* are talking about. But all generations, even conservative ones, have their own problems. And great words are always hospitable. As new problems and new preoccupations arose, new thoughts were first inserted into these fine words and then in all innocence and great imaginativeness these very thoughts were re-extracted from those words, as though from the outset these words had had the new thoughts in mind. The active intellect will always reinterpret; but it is also said **אין מקרא יוצא מידי פשוטו**.

* * * *

So much for the analysis and interpretation of the saying of the *Anshe Keneset Ha-Gedolah*, which is the only purpose of this study.[116] But one cannot study what these men said without at the same time being forced to consider again their identity and date. For my present purpose it is certainly unnecessary to review all the secondary literature on the subject of the Men of the Great Assembly. Those interested in that subject will find a comprehensive collection of all the early sources referring to the *Anshe Keneset Ha-Gedolah*, and a bibliography of all the major secondary studies, in Professor Louis Finkelstein's *Ha-Perushim ve-Anshe Keneset Ha-Gedolah*, pages 45–52. To add to the mass of speculations seems to me unnecessary, or, perhaps more accurately, is beyond my powers. But several brief observations are inevitable as a result of the reflections thus far.

First, while all kinds of reports about the achievements of the *Anshe Keneset Ha-Gedolah* are made in Midrashic-Talmudic sources, note that the only saying of which they are presumably the authors is the saying in the first mishna of *Abot*. So that if we are to be on comparatively safe ground,

116. Obviously, with the interpretations, delightful as they are, in *Kohelet Rabba ad* Eccles. 12:12ff. (and parallels) this paper need not concern itself: once the haggadic homilist gets to work, the only limits are the richness or poverty of his wit (in the seventeenth-century sense of the word, no less than the modern). See also Lieberman, *Hellenism*, pp. 108ff., and especially p. 109, n. 58.

I think it best to come to conclusions (if such are possible) on the basis of what these men themselves said, and not on what later authorities credited them with.[117] The primary interest of the Tannaim and Amoraim was not historical study or research. As Bickerman pointed out with engaging lucidity and charm more than a decade ago,[118] neither the Synagogue Fathers nor their contemporaries among the pagan scholars—except for "quelques érudits moroses"—displayed strong historical interests, and of the past they knew accurately only some minor facts. Hence, methodologically I believe it would be wisest if scholarship, like urbane wit, aimed rather at understatement when reliable sources are so meager. It just will not do to project the *Anshe Keneset Ha-Gedolah* back to the age of Ezra and Nehemiah, and then in order to justify this and at the same time to try to make sense of the material at our disposal, to project hypotheses about successive generations of such an *institution*, the last of which functioned in the time of Simeon the Righteous, who was one of their last survivors.

Second, if we content ourselves with the so-called facts regarding the Men of the Great Assembly, we shall have to admit that we have only two: namely, one, that these Men were the authors of the saying we have been examining, and, two, that Simeon the Righteous was one of the last survivors (משיירי) of that group.[119] The date of Simeon we know—about 200 B.C.E.[120]—and, remember, he was a high priest.[121]

Now, while the first part of the first chapter of *Abot* can hardly be set up as a paradigm for chronological fastidiousness, one thing is by and large clear: the *Zugot* are introduced in chronological sequence; if the first of these Pairs took over from Antigonus of Soko (or from him and Simeon),[122] and he in turn took over from Simeon the Righteous, we are dealing in time spans of a generation more or less. Whatever the time span between the authorities quoted in each instance, it is certainly not one of centuries. *Abot* does not say that Simeon was a member or survivor of some so-to-speak "original" or "final" *Keneset Ha-Gedolah*, and it is certainly plainest of *peshat* to assume that he was the survivor of that *Keneset Ha-Gedolah* cited in the mishna preceding the one citing *him*.

117. I hope to write on some future occasion on the historicity of the various attributions.

118. In his paper, *RB*, 59:44–47 (1952).

119. Note the reading משיירי כנסת הגדולה in Version B of *Abot de-Rabbi Natan*, chap. v, p. 18; see also Taylor, *Sayings of the Jewish Fathers*, II, 70 (from the Loewe ed.), and Codex Kaufmann and the Naples ed.

120. See G. F. Moore, "Simeon the Righteous," in *Israel Abrahams Memorial Volume* (Vienna, 1927), pp. 348–364.

121. See the data in Moore, "Simeon the Righteous," pp. 348–364, and cf. below Page 158 and also my Note 124.

122. Cf., e.g., *Machsor Vitry* and Rabbi Jonah Gerondi *ad Abot* 1:4.

We are therefore less likely to exaggerate if we assume that the authors of the saying in *Abot* 1:1 began to function about fifty to thirty years before Simeon, who was משיירי that group of Men. And that date fits most admirably with the date of Kohelet.[123] As the discussion above also suggested, the concern reflected by the statement of the *Anshe Keneset Ha-Gedolah* fits best what we know of the religio-intellectual climate and preoccupations of the mid-third century B.C.E. and is to be understood against the background of Kohelet's last words.

Whether there was a *Keneset Ha-Gedolah* before that, I cannot say, nor do I necessarily deny that some such body or some authoritative assembly could have existed in the days of Ezra and Nehemiah and after. But if such a body existed then, it was not the author of the saying in *Abot* 1:1. That saying belongs to the *Anshe Keneset Ha-Gedolah* of the latter half of the third century B.C.E., not too late (about a decade?) after 250.

But who were they? This is much more difficult to answer. Perhaps they were one of the synods the Ptolemies liked to convene from time to time.[124] "Les Ptolémées, on le sait," writes Bickerman, "avaient souvent convoqué des synodes du clergé égyptien."[125] Perhaps we have in *Pirke Abot* a record of a Jewish general council summoned by Ptolemy III (247–221 B.C.E.), who hoped in this way to strengthen Jewish allegiance to his cause. But here again we are on the border of conjecture, and "I cannot see what flowers are at my feet";[126] it is best therefore to stop right here.

123. See above, Note 54.

124. See E. Bevan, *A History of Egypt under the Ptolemaic Dynasty* (London, 1927), p. 180, and esp. pp. 208ff., for the text of the decree passed by the synod at Canopus in March, 237 B.C.E.; see also A. Bouché-Leclercq, *Histoire des Lagides* (Paris, 1906), III, 20–21; I, 265ff. Cf. *RB*, 59:48, n. 2. By the way, of synods in general, in C. V. Daremberg and E. Saglio, *Dictionnaire des antiquités grecques et romaines*, (Paris, 1877–1919), vol. IV, part 2, p. 1588b, s.v. "Synodos," it is said by G. Colin, "Les plus importantes sont les associations réligieuses vouées au culte d'un dieu ou d'un prince divinisé."

125. *RB*, 59:48, n. 2.

126. J. L. Maimon's "Who Were the Anshe Keneset Ha-Gedolah" (Heb.), in *Mazkeret, Kobeẓ Torani le-Zeker Rabbenu Geon Yisrael Maran Ha-Rav Yiẓḥaḳ Eisik Halevi Herzog* (Jerusalem, 5722), pp. 565–569, is of no help.

Apologetic Motifs in the Targum to the Song of Songs*

By Raphael Loewe

The term allegory, introduced into the vocabulary of Biblical exegesis by Philo and maintained there by Christian practitioners of the art, has been retained by modern students of their productions and in turn borrowed, as a descriptive category, by those concerned specifically with the study of Jewish Biblical exegesis. Its application to the Jewish—more precisely, rabbinic—field is in itself reasonable, but it involves the risk of giving rise to two misconceptions of contrast against which we shall do well to be on our guard. First, patristic exegesis and subsequent scholasticism sees the allegorical sense as contrasted to the literal.[1] The allegory may, indeed, presuppose the letter as a base, but it normally transcends it, so that the relevance of the literal to the allegorical meaning will prove, in the event, to be negligible or scant. True, a feature included in the literal meaning may sometimes be laid under contribution in order to enhance the allegory,[2] but such application is casual, and, far from stressing it, the allegorist normally finds it convenient to ignore his own debt to the depreciated letter—in Christian eyes the preserve of Jewish purblindness to deeper meanings. On the other hand, we ought not to expect rabbinic literalism to admit a distinction between literal and allegorical senses as supposedly being mutually exclusive, precisely because it exploits the resources of the letter in order to reinforce its own variety of allegorical interpretation by adding thereto colorful verisimilitudes, and these are sometimes discovered by a remorseless insistence upon one literal (or possible) meaning of a single word, in a sense paradoxical to the context as naturally understood. In discussing rabbinic exegesis, therefore, we ought perhaps to distinguish the idiosyncratic meaning of the term "literal" here by putting it into quotation marks, for the letter is not, as in Christian exegesis, the potentially jealous stepmother of allegory, but rather her willing handmaid or research assistant. The other fallacy consists in an identification of the two

* A preliminary bibliographical note will be found as an Appendix on Page 196.

1. See my article, "The Jewish Midrashim and Patristic and Scholastic Exegesis of the Bible," *Studia Patristica*, 1: 492 ff. (1957) (*Texte und Untersuchungen*, 63,i), esp. pp. 504f. See also H. de Lubac, *Exégèse médiévale: Les quatre sens de l'Écriture* (Paris, 1959), I, 110, 384, and esp. pp. 489f.

2. E.g., Theodoret's interpretation of the words *gazelle* and *young stag* in the concluding verse of the Song of Songs, quoted below, Note 111.

categories, allegorical and "literal" (or even more confusing, literal without the necessary reservations just sketched), with the native Jewish categories of *derash* and *peshaṭ*. A differentiation between these two which would equate *peshaṭ* with a literalism that is to be contrasted to something else is a medieval development within Judaism, perhaps first stimulated by Saʿadya, and the Talmudic usage of the two terms will not sustain such a contrast. The early sources appear to use the term *peshaṭ* merely to designate that aspect of a given Biblical text which, in the view of the rabbi concerned, conveyed its *primary importance*.[3]

The Targums are an excellent example of the breakdown of the conventional terminology if it is applied without any of the qualifications here outlined. It is, of course, quite unexceptionable to classify the Targum to the Song of Songs as an allegory, and we may indeed recognize in it the most sustained piece of allegorical interpretation to be found in what survives of this Jewish literary genre. Nor can one fail to take note of the circumstance that this Targum differs in a number of respects from that of 'Onqelos to the Pentateuch. But what we have no justification for doing is to label 'Onqelos on the basis of such differences, as a literal Targum. 'Onqelos does, indeed, avoid prolixity for the most part, but he introduces his own slant by subtle yet unmistakable touches of syntax, prepositional usage, et cetera, and he is at no pains at all to conceal his concern to spell out those alleged halakic implications of the text which, in his own view, enjoy primacy of importance. Insofar as *peshaṭ* is an appropriate term by which to describe this sort of treatment of a Biblical text, it is surely no less applicable to the method in which the author of the Targum to the Song of Songs has handled his material —seeing that the allegorical theme embodied therein has been regarded in rabbinic circles, since at least Tannaitic times, as conveying the primary, or even the sole true significance of the book.

This brings us to the history of the exegesis of the Song of Songs,[4] which for our purposes has to begin with a glance at the well-known passage in the Mishnah[5] in which the canonicity of the Song of Songs, and/or Ecclesiastes,

3. For a full study of this problem see my article, "The 'Plain' Meaning of Scripture in Early Jewish Exegesis," in the *Annual of Jewish Studies*, pp. 140ff., published by the Institute of Jewish Studies, London.

4. The exegetical history of the book, in both Judaism and Christianity, was surveyed by H. H. Rowley in an article in *Journal of Theological Studies*, 38: 337f. (1937), reprinted in Rowley's *The Servant of the Lord and Other Essays on the Old Testament* (London, 1952), incorporating material from the same writer's article in *Journal of the Royal Asiatic Society* (1938), pp. 251f. (The following works have, regrettably, not been available to me: S. Salfeld, "Das Hohelied bei den jüdischen Erklärern des Mittelalters," *Magazin für die Wissenschaft des Judenthums*, 5: 110ff. [1878], also published separately, Berlin, 1879; P. Vuillaud, *Le Cantique des Cantiques d'après la tradition juive* [Paris, 1925]; F. Ohly, *Hohelied-Studien, Grundzüge einer Geschichte der Hoheliedauslegung des Abendlandes bis um* 1200 [Wiesbaden, 1958]).

5. *Yadhayim*, iii, end; H. Danby's English translation (London, 1933), pp. 781f.

is questioned and receives an emphatic vindication from R. ʿAqibha. ʿAqibha, we may note, there insists merely on the outstandingly "holy" character of the Song of Songs, and probably also on its having been "given" (that is, published), perhaps by the Deity Himself, at Sinai—or, according to a variant reading, on its (then) having been (begun to be) studied as a piece of traditional lore (*mishnah*).[6] Nothing is here explicitly stated regarding the supposed allegorical meaning of the Song: but since there survive examples of exegesis by named Tannaitic figures, including R. ʿAqibha himself,[7] in which the reading of the Song as a dialogue between God the lover and Israel the beloved maiden is taken for granted, we may assume that the mishnaic account of ʿAqibha's defense of its canonicity presupposes the allegorical interpretation. A trace of the same exegetical approach is to be found likewise in II Esdras (IV Ezra) 5:24–26, a text which is dated with confidence to 100 C.E.[8] That interpretation was of course to become all but universal in the midrashic treatment of the Song, the exegesis of which ascends largely to Amoraic times. I say "all but universal" in order to take note of the fact that, for example, 2:14, *for your voice is sweet*, and 6:5, *your hair is like a flock of goats*, are adduced by Samuel and R. Shesheth respectively as evidence that voice and hair are to be reckoned, for halakic purposes, as part of a woman's physical charms (*ʿerwah*) regarding which circumspect behavior is called for in men.[9] Midrashic exegesis offers examples of the allegorical handling of both the named features;[10] are we, therefore, to see in their application in their literal sense as here cited an implicit disavowal of their allegorical interpretation? If that is so, we would then perhaps be confronted with a parallel to the case of Theodore of Mopsuestia in the latter half of the fourth century, who denied that the Song contained any prophetic message regarding the welfare of the Church, and read it as Solomon's rejoinder to popular

6. S. Lieberman, in Gershom G. Scholem, *Jewish Gnosticism, Merkabah Mysticism, and Talmudic Tradition* (New York, 1960, with an appendix [D. pp. 118ff.] in Hebrew, *Mishnath Shir ha-Shirim*, by Lieberman), p. 118, n. 3, quoting from E. Porath, *Leshon Ḥakhamim* (Jerusalem, 1938), p. 184, n. 1, a Genizah reading כיום שנשנתה בו שיר השירים for the *textus receptus* ניתנה. See Note 197.

7. Chapter 2, verse 14: *Let me see your face* is understood by ʿAqibha to have been addressed by God to Israel at Sinai: *Mekhilta de-R. Shimʿon b. Yoḥai*, ed. J. N. Epstein and E. Z. Melamed (Jerusalem, 1955), p. 143, quoted by Lieberman in Scholem, *Jewish Gnosticism*, p. 119. R. Eliezer there identifies the occasion not with Sinai but with the crossing of the Red Sea, and it is the latter view which is adopted by the Targum *ad locum*.

8. The *lily* symbolizes Israel among the nations (compare Song 2: 1, 2) as do also, among other things, the *stream* (? Song 4:15. Isaiah 8: 6) and the *dove* (Song 2: 14, Psalm 74:19). For the date of II Esdras, see G. H. Box in R. H. Charles, *Apocrypha and Pseudepigrapha of the Old Testament* (London, 1913), II, 553; L. H. Brockington, *A Critical Introduction to the Apocrypha* (London, 1961), pp. 27, 31; the provenance is regarded as being Palestinian. The relevance of the passage for present purposes was noted by Wilhelm Riedel, *Die Auslegung des Hohenliedes in der jüdischen Gemeinde und der griechischen Kirche* (Leipzig, 1898), p. 4, following G. Wildeboer, *Die Litteratur des AT*, trans. F. Risch (Göttingen, 1895), p. 426.

9. BT *Berakhoth* 24a; similarly, R. Ḥisda in *Kethub.* 75a, also *Niddah* 31b.

10. See Note 7.

indignation aroused by his uncanonical marriage to Pharaoh's daughter—*I am very dark, but comely, O daughters of Jerusalem.*[11] It is more probable, however, that the rabbis concerned did endorse what had become a conventional Jewish allegorical approach to the Song, and that in thus citing references to the maiden's voice and hair, they were merely indicating that the very fact that these words could "carry" an allegorical interpretation that does not studiously ignore the plain meaning of the text shows that the features named are easily prone to upset the male equilibrium.

By the time, then, that the Targum to the Song of Songs was being edited in its present form, and probably, indeed, by the time that it was beginning to take shape—separate questions, to which we shall revert shortly—there was apparently already in existence a substantial corpus of midrashic treatment of the text on allegorical lines. Some of it is paralleled in the Targum,[12] and in a few elliptical cases the Targum's own link with its underlying text is not intelligible without knowledge of a midrashic application of it. For example, at 7:9(8), *I say I will climb the palm tree and lay hold of its branches* becomes, in the Targum, "...the Lord *did declare*, *I will go up* and test Daniel... Hananiah, Mishael, and Azariah."[13] This reflects the treatment in the *Siphra*[14] of the preceding verse, *your eyes are stately as a palm tree*, which is applied to the three Biblical heroes: these, it is declared, remained standing bolt upright like palm trees rather than bow down to Nebuchadnezzar's golden image. In other cases the Targum diverges from traditional exegesis for reasons that we may sometimes surmise.[15] Most striking, perhaps, in this

11. 1:5. See Theodore, *PGL*, LXVI, 699C; 700CD: "...Unde nec Judaeis, nec nobis publica lectio umquam Cantici canticorum facta est, tamquam domesticus et nuptialis Salomonis conviviis cantus opprobria sponsae sonans." Theodore's dates are *ca.* 350–428. His view of the Song of Songs was condemned by the Council of Constantinople in 553 (see *PGL*, LXVI, 634).

12. Thus, to cite merely the closer parallels with the *Gemara:* 1:2 and 7:10 with PT *ʿA.Z.* ii, 7, 15a, and *Sanh.* xi, 4, 40b (Simeon b. 'Abba in the name of) R. Yoḥanan; 1:12 with BT *Shabbath* 88b, *Giṭṭin* 36b (R. Mari, grandson of Samuel, in the name of) Rabh; 2:8 with *R.H.* 11a, R. Eliezer; 5:11 with '*Erubhin* 21b (R. Ḥisda in the name of) ʿUqba; 7:2 with *Ḥag.* 3a, Rabha; 8:13 with *Shabbath* 63a, Resh Laqish, and *B.B.* 75a, R. Yoḥanan.

13. אמר ייי במימריה אסק ואנסייה לדניאל... ובכין אנסינון לחנניה מישאל ועזריה אי כהלין למקם בנסיוניהון וכו׳

14. '*Aḥarey Moth*, on Leviticus 18:5 (ed. I. H. Weiss [Vienna, 1862], f. 82a, col. b [14]); somewhat differently, but implying the same allegorizing of the palm tree, in BT *Sanh.* 93a (R. Jonathan).

15. For example, 3:11: ... *behold King Solomon, with the crown with which his mother crowned him*, as exegetically treated by R. Eleʿazar b. Yosey in *Pesiqta de-R. Kahana*, on *Wayehi beyom kalloth mosheh* (ed. S. Buber [Lyck, 1868], f. 4a), and parallels there given. According to this interpretation "Solomon" — that is, the Deity — out of inordinate affection, calls Israel His mother (on this see Leo Baeck, "Haggadah and Christian Doctrine," *HUCA*, 23, part 1 [1951–52]: esp. pp. 553f.). The Targum turns "his mother" ('*immo*) into "his people" ('*ummo*: עמא בית ישראל). R. Eleʿazar b. Yosey's exegesis was doubtless felt by the author of the Targum to be too liable to misinterpretation for him to adopt it in a version intended for popular circulation amid an environment in which the Virgin Mary was venerated as *Theotokos* — a title which had originated among Alexandrian theologians at the end of the third century, and which became frequent in the fourth.

respect is its disregard of the principle that all references in the Song to "Solomon," except that at 8:12, and possibly also that at 3:7, are to be construed as referring to God, "the King unto whom belongeth peace."[16] Both of these verses are taken by the Targum as referring to King Solomon himself, but so also are 1:1, 3:9, and 3:11. One passage only (8:11) assumes the equation Solomon = "the Lord of the world to whom belongeth peace," and in the sole remaining reference *the curtains of Solomon* (1:5) become the curtains of the tabernacle, in consideration of the erection of which Moses finally restored *peace* between Israel, penitent after the sin of the golden calf, and "the King": that is, God.[17] It is clear, then, that the Targumist (or the final editor of the present Targum to the book) allowed himself considerable freedom of selection from traditional material, in arrangement, and in independent interpretation, in order to make the Song of Songs convey a message of which the sense was quite clear in his own mind before he took up his pen.

The Date of the Targum

We have now to consider date and provenance. That this Targum stems from Palestine is not only inherently probable, but is confirmed, possibly by external and certainly by internal evidence: for it may be cited by the *ʿArukh* as *targum yerushalmi*,[18] and Alexander Marx[19] pointed to both its mention of the specifically Palestinian title *'abh beth din*[20] and its eulogy of the Palestinian Gaonate ("Sanhedrin"),[21] in contrast to the praise accorded to the academies of Sura and Pumpeditha by a fragmentary midrash to the Song of Songs preserved in the British Museum.[22] I note further in the Targum to the last verse of the book, the reference to the defiled state of "this land" (*'arʿa hadha mesa'abhta*), presumably Palestine, the condition of which (presumably meaning its continued occupancy by gentiles) is adduced as a temporary bar to God's own reoccupation of it.[23] Such sentiments are per-

16. BT *Shebhuʿoth* 35b, on 8:12; *Massekheth Sopherim* 5, 21 (ed. M. Higger [New York 1937], p. 163f.). An alternative view (י״א) holds that in 3:7 the name Solomon is likewise "secular."

17. ועל דעבדו יריעתא למשכנא ושרת ביניהון שכינתא דייי ומשה רבהון סליק לרקיעא ויהב שלמא ביניהון ובין מלכא

18. *S.v.* פלטיא (ed. A. Kohut, VI, 342, col. i; noted by Riedel, p. 8). Kohut, however, on the evidence of manuscripts of the *ʿArukh*, omits the word ירושלמי, which he regards as an error; see his n. 5.

19. *JQR*, N. S., 1: 65–66 (1910–11), on 7: 3, 5, and 8: 13; cf. J. Mann in *HUCA*, 14: 333 (1939), and also Mann, *The Jews in Egypt and in Palestine* (London, 1920), I, 274.

20. At 7: 5.

21. At 7: 3, also 5: 12 (perhaps also 4: 4, 7: 14).

22. MS. Or. 5554a, f. 12a, on the ultimate verse.

23. For the rendering of the verse by the Targum see below, Note 114. I do not suppose that ארעא, in the phrase quoted in the text here from that rendering, means the whole earth.

haps more likely in a Palestinian resident than a Diaspora Jew, and the nearer demonstrative adjective seems indeed to postulate a writer on Palestinian soil.

Raphael Hai Melamed,[24] in referring the redaction of the Targum to the Hagiographa in general to the period between the fifth and eighth centuries, followed S. Landauer[25] in assigning the Targum to the Song to the latter part of that period, on the grounds of its inclusion of Arabic terms for the jewels in the High Priest's breastplate cited at 5:14 from Exodus 28:17–21 and 39:10–14. This argument is not, in itself, very substantial, since where no questions of textual sacrosanctity are involved it is not unusual for terms strange to Jewish scribes to be replaced by more familiar ones— for example, the replacement, in some Rashi manuscripts, of the French glosses by glosses in other vernaculars. Such a process is particularly likely in the case of jewels, the supposed magical properties of which interested lapidarists, and in point of fact, in some of Melamed's own Yemenite manuscripts the Biblical Hebrew names for the stones are restored.

Nevertheless, the assignment of the redaction to the early Islamic period may perhaps be substantiated on other grounds. The Aramaic in which the Targum has come down to us mixes Palestinian and Babylonian forms on a generous scale.[26] There are also two references to Esau and Edom,[27] but although at least one of these refers to the Jewish Diaspora in the Roman world, they afford us no significant dating material. Ishmael, who generally represents the Arabic world, is mentioned twice. The sixty queens and eighty concubines (6:8) are allegorized as sixty "Edomite" cavalry contingents and eight "Ishmaelite" contingents mounted on elephants which advance on Jerusalem under command "of Alexander." Although a Spanish version[28] of the Targum reads, a degree less fantastically, "Antiochus," the two names mean no more than "the entire gentile world." Even before the rise of Islam, and (if the transmission is accurate) as early as the time of Rabh (early third century C.E.),[29] the name "Ishmael" could be contrasted, as a gentilic, with the (eastern) Roman Empire. More promising, at first sight, is the reference to the sons of Esau and Ishmael introduced into the Targum at 1:7, in explanation of the text *why should I be like one who covers herself* (*? who wanders*)

24. See pp. 5, 19.

25. *Orientalische Studien*, pp. 505f.

26. Particularly so in the Yemenite recension edited by Melamed: see his introduction, pp. 25f., 37f., 42f., 49f., and 54f. For the relationship of this recension to the *textus receptus* of the Targum to the Song of Songs (that is, Bomberg's Rabbinic Bible of 1517 [Venice] and its descendants) see Melamed, pp. 15–16. The latter is on the whole a superior text to the Yemenite recension.

27. 6:8, 7:12.

28. See below, Note 218.

29. BT *Shabbath* 11a, *top*. The contrasted term *nokhri* is clearly a change occasioned by considerations of censorship, and it there stands for the Byzantine empire: compare Rashi *in loco* and R. N. Rabinovicz, *Diqduqey Sopherim* (Munich, 1867–97), *Shabbath*, p. 8a, n. 80.

beside the flocks of your companions?[30] The Targum, which here pictures Moses as questioning God regarding the leadership and provision (*parnasah*) for Israel after his own death, paraphrases this clause as follows:[31] "For why should they be harassed amid the herds of the sons of Esau and Ishmael, who associate their [idolatrous] errors with Thee as companions in divinity?" In view of the monotheistic emphasis of the slogan with which Islam proclaims its faith, it is tempting to argue that the attribution by the Targumist to "Ishmael," no less than to "Esau," of a theology that compromises absolute monotheism is to be placed during the *jahiliyya*, and that he cannot, therefore, have written later than 622 C.E.[32] It is, however, perhaps more circumspect to conclude merely that his formulation implies a *Sitz im Leben* in which Jewry had not yet come to appreciate the monotheistic insistence of Islam, and conversely one in which the Targum was as yet unlikely to come to the notice of Islam's own apologists or propagandists.

As it happens, however, there is a further piece of internal evidence which seems to me well-nigh conclusive evidence that this Targum is to be dated after the beginning of the Islamic expansion, or more precisely after the conquest of Palestine in 636–638. I refer to the exegetical handling of 8:8–10, *We have a little sister, and she has no breasts. What shall we do for our sister, on the day that she is spoken for? If she is a wall, we will build upon her a battlement of silver... I was a wall, and my breasts were like towers...*[33] The Targum reads into this dialogue the anxiety of the angels for Israel: their merits are exiguous, and they lack royal leadership; how, then, will they fare in the eschatological war? The Archangel Michael provides the answer: "If she is bracing herself, all prepared like a rampart, amongst the peoples, and if she is ready to pay out her silver to acquire permission to assert the uniqueness of the Name of the Master of the world, then shall we, both you and I, be at the side of Israel's scribes ... but even though she prove poor in merits derived from obedience to the commandments, nonetheless we shall seek pity on her behalf before the Lord." Israel replies, "I am mighty as a wall, through the words of the Torah, and my sons are sturdy as a tower."[34]

30. שלמה אהיה כעטיה על עדרי חבריך. A reading כטעיה, that is, wandering [maid], apparently underlies the Septuagint περιβαλλομένη, and conceivably also the Targumic מטלטלין (see next note).

31. ולמא דין יהון מטלטלין ביני עדרי בנוי דעשו וישמעאל די משתתפין טעוותהון לחבריא (ed. Lagarde and 1 Yemenite MS., משתפין)

32. Professor S. D. Goitein, in an oral communication, would endorse this argument; Professor Saul Lieberman, however, likewise orally, queries it, on grounds of the earlier occurrence of "Ishmael" = the Arabic-speaking world (as a political bloc). See Note 29.

33. אחות לנו קטנה ושדים אין לה מה נעשה לאחותנו ביום שידבר בה (9) אם חומה היא נבנה עליה טירת כסף ואם דלת היא נצור עליה לוח ארז (10) אני חומה ושדי כמגדלות וגו׳

34. (9) אמר מיכאל רבהון דישראל אן היא מתעתדא באושה (ed. Lagarde, כאושא) ביני עממיא ויהיבא כספהא למקני ייחוד שמיה דמרי עלמא נהא אנא ואתון עם ספריהון סחרין לה כנדביכין דכסף ולית רשו לזחלא למשלט בכספא ואפילו היא מסכינא נבעי רחמין עלה קדם ייי... (10) מתיבא כנישתא דישראל ואמרא אנא תקיפא בפתגמי אוריתא כשורא ובני חסינין כמגדלא וכו׳

The source of the exegesis here provided for the words *If she is a wall* can be identified. It occurs in the *Midrash Tanḥuma*,[35] being probably there attributed to R. Berekhiah, a Palestinian Amora of the fourth century. He linked the whole passage with Abraham, whose steadfastness in faith was tested by his being cast by Nimrod into a fiery furnace: would he measure up to the test? "*If she is a wall, we will build upon her a battlement of silver:* this means that if, like a wall which stands up to many a war, he gives up his life for the sake of the sanctification of the divine Name, *we will build upon her a battlement of silver*. Those referred to here are Israel, Psalm 68:14 (13) being the proof text. *But if she is a door* [deleth], *we will enclose her with boards of cedar:* if he is made of too poor [*dal*] stuff to give up his life for the sake of the divine Name, *we will enclose her* ... Abraham said, I am indeed a wall, steadfast to give up my life for the sanctification of the divine Name, aye, my descendants also ... including R. Ḥananiah b. Teradion and his fellows, who will in their own times give up their lives for the sanctification of the divine Name." It will be observed that the crucial phrase in the midrash, giving up one's life for the sanctification of the divine Name, has been replaced in the Targum by the words *we-yahibha kaspeha le-miqney yiḥudh shemeh de-marey ʿalema*, which have, I think, to be translated, "and she lays out her money to acquire the right to proclaim the uniqueness of the Name of the Master of the world." For the courting of martyrdom and the specific mention of victims of the Hadrianic proscription of Judaism, there has been substituted the securing, against payment, of the right to practice it. Now, the payment of poll tax by Jews to non-Jewish governments has a long history,[36] which for our purposes may be taken as beginning with the diversion by Vespasian of the equivalent of the *sheqalim*, formerly paid to the Jerusalem Temple, to that of Jupiter Capitolinus at Rome. That payment was regarded essentially as a war indemnity, and in no sense as a license to practice Jewish rites, which in the Diaspora were never questioned by the Romans, and even in Palestine itself it was for a short time only, under Hadrian, that the practice of Judaism was ever proscribed, and no non-Jewish testimony for such proscription is in point of fact extant. After this *fiscus judaicus* had fallen into desuetude it was reintroduced by Theodosius II in 429,[37] on the abolition of the Patriarchate in Palestine, but, once

35. *Lekh lekha*, 2, Warsaw ed. (Levin Epstein, n.d.), f. 18a–b: אם חומה היא נבנה עליה טירת כסף אם נותן נפשו כחומה זו שהיא עומדת בפני מלחמות הרבה וימסור עצמו על קדושת השם נבנה עליה טירת כסף אלו ישראל שקראם כנפי יונה נחפה בכסף (תהלים 68:14) ואם דלת היא אם דל הוא מלמסור נפשו על קדושת השם נצור עליה לוח ארז... אמר אברהם אני חומה למסור נפשי על קדושת שמך ולא אני בלבד אלא ושדי כמגדלות בני בניו חנניה מישאל ועזריה ודורו של ר׳ חנניה בן תרדיון וחבריו שיתנו נפשם על קדושת שמך וכו׳

36. See H. Loewe, *Render Unto Caesar* (Cambridge, 1940), pp. 38ff., esp. p. 41. S. W. Baron, *A Social and Religious History of the Jews*, 2nd ed. (New York, 1952–60), I, 411, n. 20; II, 105f., 185f., 373, n. 21; 399, n. 18.

37. Baron, II, 186.

again, there is nothing in the language of the relevant imperial rescripts[38] to imply that the tax is to be considered a license fee. On the other hand, precisely that is the presupposition of the legitimizing jurisprudence by means of which expanding Islam came to terms with certain religious minorities that it had perforce to absorb politically:[39] Jews, Christians, and certain others, as each of them constituting an *ahl al-kitáb*, became, by payment of poll tax (*jizya*), licensees, and as such were exempted from the choice between Islam or the sword. Even if the arrangement may not always, in strictly legal terms, have rested on a contract of the type here outlined,[40] it was so construed by members of the Jewish and other taxed minorities. The economic and social effects of the Islamic conquest of Palestine, beginning with the battle of the Yarmuk in 636 C.E., consequently meant more to the Jewish taxpayer than a mere change of taxgatherer, and the new situation provides us with a plausible enough historical context in which to place the Targumist's modification of R. Berekhiah's exegesis of the phrase *If she is a wall*.

But to assign the Targumist to the seventh century is merely to postulate a

38. C. and M. Pharr, *The Theodosian Code* . . . (Princeton, 1952), pp. 468 (xvi, 8 §14), 469 (§ 17), and esp. 471 (§ 29, *Corpus juris*, i, 9 17).

39. The *locus classicus* is in the Qur'an, *Sura* ix, 29. See C. H. Becker, "Djizya," *Encyclopaedia of Islam* (London, 1913), I, 1051f., and, for later bibliography, *The Shorter Encyclopaedia of Islam*, ed. H. A. R. Gibb and J. H. Kramers (Leiden, 1953), p. 92. I. Goldziher, "Islam," *Jewish Encyclopedia*, VI, 655f.; Baron, III, 80, 90, 96, 101 foot (for Palestine), 108–110, 115, 120, 123, 127f., 130, 161–170, esp. 164; 274, n. 28; 309, n. 49. S. D. Goitein, *Jews and Arabs, Their Contacts Through the Ages* (New York, 1955), p. 97, also pp. 62f.

Dr. J. Neusner has suggested to me, as an alternative, a Sassanid background and the payment of *kharaj*. Since the origin of this Targum is Palestinian (see above, Page 163), this seems less probable. Although it is true that the Arsacid and Sassanid imposition of *kharaj* on Jews and other religious minorities worked in a manner somewhat similar to that of the *jizya* of the Arabs, no evidence known to me indicates that it was construed, analogously to the *jizya*, as a license fee by Jews who had to pay it. On the contrary, if Rabha be assumed to use the terms אכרגא and טסקא indiscriminately (see BT *Nedarim* 62b and *B. M.* 73b), he construed it jurisprudentially as a royal entitlement to the person of the subject, resting on something analogous to title by capture (so R. Solomon b. Adreth; see E. E. Urbach's article on the Talmudic laws of slavery, *Zion*, 25, part 3–4 [1960], in Hebrew; an English translation by me will be found in the *Annual of Jewish Studies*, published by the Magnes Press, Jerusalem, for the Institute of Jewish Studies, London, p. 88). Rabha's concession to a budding rabbi (צורבא מרבנן) to evade, by posing as a Zoroastrian, claims for *kharaj* advanced by gentile (but not by Jewish) tax-collectors rests on the fact that Zoroastrian priests, among other classes, were exempted. On the subject see R. N. Frye, *The Heritage of Persia* (The World Histories of Civilization; Cleveland, 1963), pp. 187, 219, and 270, n. 65, with references to recent bibliography; Baron, *Social and Religious History of the Jews*, II, 184.

In maintaining that the language of the Targum here is not easily intelligible except in terms of the *jizya*, I ought to state that Professor S. D. Goitein, who has been good enough to discuss this point with me, disagrees and considers that the emphasis evinced by some Genizah documents on the "holy character" of certain Jewish communal obligations involving pecuniary sacrifice, such as the redemption of captives (see, for example, Mann, *The Jews in Egypt*, II, 345), is adequate as an explanation. If in spite of this I remain unconvinced, it is because of the occurrence in the Targum of the phrase למקני ייחוד שמיה, and particularly of the verb.

40. Baron, III, 128, states that the Caliphate never precisely defined the position of religious minorities.

date by which the Targum had, so to speak, crystallized out. As I have observed above,[41] it contains exegesis for which midrashic parallels are extant, some of them in Tannaitic sources: can we, then, say anything regarding the coming into being of the particular exegetical line which the Targum follows? Such conclusions as I am for the moment prepared to advance are quite tentative only, but it may be noticed that in several passages[42] the Targum presents exegesis recorded elsewhere in the name of R. Yoḥanan. It is perfectly true that the homiletical treatment by R. Yoḥanan (as collected by W. Bacher)[43] of the Song of Songs contains much that is not reflected in the Targum. But several of his sayings[44] linked to passages in it emphasize the significance of Torah, and particularly of the Oral Torah, in God's relationship to Israel as allegedly set forth in the Song, and this, as will appear below, is one of the main themes of the Targum. Moreover, Yoḥanan's principle[45] of the literal treatment to be accorded to the name "Solomon" in the Song is likewise on the lines of the Targum, and contrary to the general rabbinic view[46] that throughout the book "Solomon" is, with one exception, a cipher for the Deity. Should further research confirm the suggestion that the Targumic handling of the Song owes something to R. Yoḥanan, or extend it so as to include also Resh Laqish,[47] who was R. Yoḥanan's brother-in-law, and other contemporaries, an interesting pattern would then emerge: for, as G. Scholem has shown,[48] it was the late Tannaitic period that witnessed the development, within Jewish circles, of an advanced mystical reading of the Song of Songs that remained within the framework of Torah and its practical implementation. We should, in that case, be led to the conclusion that what I shall interpret below[49] as the Targum's own line of rejoinder to this type of esotericism had already been adumbrated in the early third century, or in other

41. See Pages 161, 162, Notes 7, 12.

42. With the Targum to 1: 2 (מיין) compare PT *ʿA.Z.* ii, 7, 15a, and similarly (on 7: 10) *Sanh.* xi, 4, 40b. With 1:6 (בני אמי), compare *'Eliyyahu Rabbah* 30 (28), ed. M. Friedmann, p. 149 (R. Yoḥanan transmitting an earlier source). With 4:11 (נפת תטפנה) compare *Tanḥuma, Ki Tissa'*, 18 (Warsaw ed. f. 122b; Buber's text, 56a). With 7: 10 compare *Canticles Rabbah in loco*. With 8:13 (השמיעני) compare BT *B.B.* 75a (in *Shabbath* 63a, this is attributed to Resh Laqish).

43. *Die Agada der palästinensischen Amoräer*, I (Strassburg, 1892), 313f.

44. To those listed in Note 42 to 1: 2 and 8: 13 may be added the story concerning R. Yoḥanan rehearsed in *Canticles Rabbah* on 8: 7 (Wilna ed., f. 40a, col. i), since it probably implies that he himself endorsed the exegesis which precedes the anecdote whereby באהבה is taken (the *beth* being regarded as *beth pretii*) as meaning [all worldly wealth] *in exchange for Torah*. For passages elsewhere in the Bible applied by R. Yoḥanan to inculcate the significance of the study of Torah, see Bacher, I, 234f.

45. *Canticles Rabbah* on 1: 1, *end* (Wilna ed., f. 4a, col. i).

46. See above, Note 16.

47. The material on the Song of Songs listed for him by Bacher, I, 401f., does not look promising, but see the end of Note 42.

48. *Jewish Gnosticism*, pp. 40f., 58f.

49. See Pages 184f.

words but shortly after the emergence of the very mystical extravagances that it set out to combat.

SUMMARY OF THE CONTENTS OF THE TARGUM

I shall here summarize the motifs and emphases of the Targum to the Song of Songs, and outline what may be termed, without incongruity, the symphonic construction in which they are presented.

The Targum is a *Heilsgeschichte*, and it announces itself as such in an excursus attached to the very first verse, detailing the Ten Songs[50] that form the milestones of all human or Jewish experience, from Adam's composition of Psalm 92 when his sin was pardoned through the intervention of the Sabbath, past the Song of Songs itself—the ninth in the series—uttered by "Solomon, king of Israel, in the holy spirit, before the Sovereign Power of the world,"[51] to that Song referred to in Isaiah 30:29,[52] which the Targumist elaborates into an eschatological marching-song: "for thus it is written, aye, and interpreted, by Isaiah the prophet— '*This song shall be for you* for joy, *as on the night when the feast* of Passover *is sacramentally kept, and joy of heart, as of* a people *who go* to appear before the Lord three times a year... *before the Mighty One of Israel.*' "[53] If the climax is here expressed in conventionally Jewish messianic idiom, the construction of the whole design seems strangely out of character; and it immediately recalls the majestic architecture of Milton's proem:

> Of man's first disobedience, and the fruit
> Of that forbidden tree, whose mortal taste
> Brought death into the world, and all our woe,
> With loss of Eden, till one greater man
> Restore us, and regain the blissful seat,
> Sing, heav'nly Muse...[54]

In point of fact Origen likewise, in his introduction to the Song of Songs,[55] had rehearsed a history of progressive revelation, consummated in intimacy with Christ, in terms of a series of six songs all included in the Old Tes-

50. On the midrashic theme of the Ten Songs see J. N. Epstein in *Mimmizraḥ umimmaʿarabh* 1 (Vienna, 1894), i, pp. 85–89 (this article was unfortunately not available to me), supplemented by S. Schechter, *Agadath Shir Hashirim*, p. 52 (*JQR* 6: 672ff. [1893–94]).

51. שירתא תשיעיתא אמר שלמה מלכא דישראל ברוח קודשא קדם ריבון עלמא ייי

52. השיר יהיה לכם כליל התקדש חג ושמחת לבב כהולך בחליל לבוא בהר ה׳ אל צור ישראל

53. דהכין כתיב ומפרש על יד ישעיה נבייא שירה הדין יהי לכון לחדוא כלילא יתקדש חגא דפסחא וחדות ליבא כעמא דאזלין לאתחזאה קייי תלת זמנין בשתא במני זמר וקל טבלא למיעל לטורא דייי ולמפלח קדם תקיפא דישראל

54. Although the beginning of *Paradise Lost* is modeled on that of the *Iliad*, it is not inconceivable that Milton may have known of the motif of the Ten Songs of Jewish history, with their messianic climax, from the Targum to the Song of Songs itself; it was available to him, at the time when he was working on the epic, in Latin translation both in the Royal Polyglott (Antwerp, 1569–73), and in the polyglot edition of Brian Walton (London, 1655–57).

55. Ed. Baehrens, p. 28, lines 1f. (*PGL*, XIII, 37); compare Theodoret, *PGL*, LXXXI, 49.

tament,[56] which find their climax in Solomon's Song. I am not now claiming any specific connection between the midrashic conceit of the Ten Songs utilized by the Targum and Origen's scheme of six. But the following summary does, I think, fairly represent the whole *Tendenz* of the Targum, which evinces a marked emphasis on Israel's potential perfectness, combined with stress on the inhibiting effects, upon the divine scheme of messianic redemption, of Israel's proclivity to sin. And I shall attempt below[57] to adduce support for the suggestion that this tendency owes something to a stimulus originating outside Judaism.

Introduction (1:1): The Ten Songs, from Adam's to that of the (future) redeemed exiles.

First Movement (1:2–3:6)

(a) (1:2–1:17) The Exodus, Sinaitic revelation, the sin of the golden calf; atonement is effected by Moses' intercession, the merits of the patriarchs, and the construction of the tabernacle, which prefigures the Temple.

(b) (2:1–3:6) The theme is repeated, Israel's triumphal entry into Canaan forming the climax.

"Contrapuntal" hints, to be taken up in subsequent movements, are: (i) God's choice of Israel evinced through gift of Torah, particularly the Oral Torah (1:2). (ii) Exile is a necessary proving experience for Israel (1:7–8). (iii) Solomon's Temple is but a shadowy prefigurement of the glory of the Temple that will be rebuilt in messianic times (1:17).

Second Movement (3:7–5:1)

Solomon's Temple and its dedication (3:7–4:1); the devotion of the priests,

56. Exodus 15; Deuteronomy 32; Judges 5; II Samuel 22 (= Psalm 18); Isaiah 5: 1f.; and the Song of Songs. It may well be that R. Jonathan's view of the order of Solomon's composition of the books canonically accredited to him (Song of Songs, Proverbs, Ecclesiastes), according to which they represent his progress from youthful ardor to mature wisdom, or rather senility (דברי הבלים), is oriented not so much against R. Ḥiyya Rabbah's order (Proverbs, Song of Songs, Ecclesiastes: see *Canticles Rabbah* on 1: 1, Wilna ed., f. 3b, col. i), as with the object of tacitly repudiating the Christian canonical order (Proverbs, Ecclesiastes, Song of Songs), which reflects Origen's view of these three books as forming a climactic series: after the ethical teaching of Proverbs and training in natural philosophy of Ecclesiastes, the student is introduced to the "contemplative" (*theoreticen, inspectivum*) teaching of the Song of Songs. "Ideo enim novissimum locum tenet hic liber, ut tunc ad eum veniatur, cum et moribus quis fuerit defaecatus et rerum corruptibilium atque incorruptibilium scientiam distinctionemque didicerit, quo in nullo possit ex his figuris, quibus sponsae ad sponsum caelestem, id est animae perfectae amor ad Verbum Dei, describitur ac formatur, offendi. Praemissis namque his, quibus purificatur anima per actus et mores et in rerum discretionem naturalium perducitur, competenter ad dogmatica venitur et ad mystica atque ad divinitatis contemplationem sincero et spiritali amore conscenditur" (Baehrens, p. 75, line 2, to 78, line 19, of which I quote the concluding portion here; *PGL*, XIII, 73A–76A). Contrast the emphasis of R. Yannai — somewhat earlier than Origen — regarding the unanimity of tradition that Ecclesiastes was the last Solomonic book.

57. See Pages 173f.

et cetera, to the cult (4:2–4:5), and the physical protection that the cult affords Israel so long as she remain steadfast in piety and devoted to her ancestral institutions (4:6–7). On taking up occupancy of the Temple, God invites Israel to share it with Him, comparing Israel's chastity to that of a bride; He accepts favorably the holocausts offered Him, and confirms the right of the priesthood to their own perquisite portions (4:8–5:1).

Third Movement (5:2–6:1)

Israel's sin, countered by God's own ineffective plea (communicated through the prophets) for Israel's penitence and praise of Him; after the loss of the two-and-a-half tribes, Israel's half-hearted and thus futile remorse is succeeded by a true repentance, but too late to stave off the punishment of exile (5:2–7). When Israel confides to the prophets her lovesickness for God, a skillfully posed question elicits from her her love poem, the scriptural phrases in this regarding the lover's physical charms are converted into a panegyric of the Deity's expertise as a Jewish scholar, an assertion of the cosmic significance of Torah, and of God's concern for the welfare of Jerusalem and that of Israel's sages (5:8–16); Israel confesses that it is her own refractoriness that has alienated God from her, and the prophets offer to aid her in recovering His love through penitence (6:1).

Fourth Movement (6:2–7:11)

(a) (6:2–6:12) God accepts her prayer, effects the rebuilding of the Temple by Cyrus, Ezra, et cetera, and reoccupies it in a spirit of reconciliation. He praises Israel's devoted maintenance of the cult and of rabbinic scholarship, which finds its recompense in a secure prosperity that impresses the gentiles. The climax is the divine guarantee of Israel's future well-being, in recognition of the devotion of the restored community to Torah.

(b) (7:1–11) The theme is repeated, with variations of order. God's praise of Israel is prefaced by an appeal for her return to Him, to Jerusalem, to the house of study, and to a receptivity toward true prophetic teaching and a rejection of the false prophets. It is the steadfastness of Ḥananiah, Mishael, and Azariah under trial that leads to God's decision to redeem Israel from exile (7:9–10). Israel acknowledges that it is obedience to Torah that is the condition of God's continued presence in her midst, and that disobedience would precipitate a further exile.

Fifth Movement (7:12–8:14)

(a) (7:12–8:7) Exiled throughout the Roman Empire, Israel entreats that God remain accessible to her prayers. She attempts to calculate the date of the future redemption, but prognostication is immediately abandoned in favor of description (7:14f.) of the messianic programme that will be initiated in God's own good time. When eventually the Messiah is commissioned to take up his kingdom and reveals himself to Israel, he is welcomed by an invitation to join Israel in proceeding to Jerusalem to attend a Talmudic discourse—the unnamed guest lecturer being presumably the Deity Himself (compare 5:10). The Messiah's own activity is restricted to teaching Israel the fear of God (8:2) and to restraining her from impetuously returning to Jerusalem before the eschatological war shall have burned itself out (8:4). As the resurrected righteous debouch from the Mount of Olives into a Land of Israel now purged of defilement, their merits recall to the gentiles Israel's Sinaitic moment. Israel asks (8:6) that her renewed intimacy with God may now be for perpetuity: God replies (8:7) that his love for her is not dissoluble by gentile hostility, however intense, and that her determined cultivation of Torah in exile will receive compensation from the spoils of the eschatological war.

(b) (8:8–10) The picture reverts to the pre-eschatological situation. The angels, fearful for Israel's fate in the eschatological war because her merits are exiguous, declare that they will themselves afford their support if Israel has been at pains to secure license (from the Moslems)[58] against payment, to practice Judaism: but failing that, they will at least urge on the Deity the merits of the study of Torah by the young. The people of Israel assert their steadfastness, receive God's acknowledgement of their claim, and are accorded the universal acclamation of the gentiles.

(c) (8:11–14) A second flashback, this time concerning the fortunes of the House of David, to whose dynasty Israel—God's vineyard—had been entrusted for safekeeping. Although the split of the kingdom was predestined, Solomon was prophetically assured that his son would retain Judah and Benjamin. Israel, still dispersed in exile, receives God's assurance that He Himself endorses such teaching and decisions as are duly formulated by rabbinic leadership and accepted with proper respect by the Jewish public (8:13). In response, the sages indicate that the Land (of Israel) is as yet defiled, and not fit for God's occupancy. Let Him therefore retire temporarily to heaven, and thence afford His sympathy for Israel's tribulations, until such time as He sees fit to restore her to Jerusalem and re-establish the temple cult.

58. See above, Pages 165, 167.

Four features here seem to me to invite explanation in their context. The first is the prominence accorded to Torah, or rather the Oral Torah,[59] as the symbol of God's love for Israel and of the means by which rabbinic leadership retains God's providential interest for Israel in exile. Secondly, there is the emphasis on Israel's sin—first with the golden calf, and later as twice involving exile from their Land. Third is the stress on the building of the tabernacle as the symbol of the effecting of atonement, and also on the atoning value of the temple cultus,[60] and finally, the very restricted role that is accorded to the Messiah. It is the Deity Himself who effects redemption and only thereafter bids the Messiah take up his kingdom. When he does so he becomes not a leader, but a fellow student, who promotes fear of God among his classmates and dissuades them, by force of character, from over-hasty eschatological irredentism.

It is true that all the foregoing motifs, with the possible exception of this particular method of playing down the messianic figure, can be paralleled from elsewhere in rabbinic literature. The point that I wish to make is that an exegete concerned to allegorize the Song of Songs as the account of God's love for Israel might have been expected to refrain from dragging in reference to Israel's classical occasion of sinfulness; that he could perfectly well, on the basis of the relevant Scriptural accounts, have treated the building of the tabernacle and Temple as expressions of pure devotion on Israel's part, without introducing the ulterior motivation of their efficacy in securing atonement, and that if he regarded the figure of the Messiah as having a place in his story at all, it is a surprisingly circumscribed part that he allows him to play in it. And an explanation for all these tendencies is, I think, forthcoming.

Anti-Christian Apologetic

It scarcely requires demonstration that all of the aforementioned items are integrally involved, as far as the Church is concerned, in the person of Jesus as Messiah: Christ, for Paul, is the summation of the "Law";[61] he is the indispensable antidote to original sin;[62] and for the author of the Epistle to the Hebrews at once the atonement and the officiating high priest.[63] Moreover, the Church had inherited from the Synagogue the allegorical approach to the Song of Songs, replacing God and Israel by Christ and the Church as the two main characters of the dialogue. Although Origen,[64] writing in the

59. See 1: 2.
60. See 1: 14 and 3: 4. Note esp. 4: 3, 11; 5: 5; 6: 2; 8: 14.
61. See W. D. Davies, *Paul and Rabbinic Judaism* (London, 1948), pp. 147f.
62. Romans 5:10, 5: 12f., 3: 25; II Corinthians 5: 19.
63. As sacrifice: 9–10, esp. 9: 11f.; see also Davies, pp. 230f. As High Priest, 4: 14–6:20, esp. 5: 1f.
64. Scholem, *Jewish Gnosticism*, p. 39, n. 11, refers to Ohly, *Hohelied-Studien*, p. 15, which is unfortunately not accessible to me.

middle of the third century, was not the first Christian exegete to adopt this line, he became its classical exponent, and Jerome[65] could even say of him that whereas in commenting on the other Biblical books he had surpassed all others, on the Song of Songs Origen had surpassed himself. Most of his commentary has unfortunately disappeared, but the four books of Rufinus' Latin translation[66] take us as far as 2:15, *Catch us the foxes*, and two homilies in more popular vein, translated by Jerome himself, [67] go up to the previous verse. Origen's influence on the later commentators to the Song—at any rate on those who write in Latin—was substantial, and parallels can be demonstrated between what survives of his work and the complete commentary of Theodoret[68] (*circa* 393–*circa* 458), who wrote in Greek and who acknowledges his own generous borrowings from his predecessors.[69] In what follows I shall therefore refer to Theodoret where Origen is not available.

I ought perhaps to explain here that I do not believe it to be necessary, in order to make good a claim that rabbinic exegesis is apologetically motivated, that one should be able to demonstrate an actual point of contact, or divergence, or a palpable parallel between the Jewish handling of a given text and some extant Christian treatment of the same text. In point of fact I am able, in what follows, to indicate what to me appear to be examples of that process. But I take the following principle as axiomatic: wherever a piece of rabbinic exegesis implicitly emphasizes Jewish repudiation of a notion or belief so prominently associated with Christianity that any Jew, with even slight Christian contacts, might be expected to have heard about it (albeit possibly in a garbled form), anti-Christian apologetic is to be assumed as a main motivation in the Jewish exegete, though not necessarily as his sole motivation. The same will hold good where what the Jewish exegete is putting himself at pains to enunciate is some Jewish notion capable of acting as a counterpart to a well-known Christian idea—that is to say, it is able to convey, in its own idiom, theological truths regarding election, forgiveness of sin, and so on, equivalent in depth to those which Christianity attaches to notions or symbols of its own that are incompatible with Judaism.

First, then, two cases of possible or probable interaction, direct or at one

65. Ed. Baehrens, p. 26, line 3 (*PGL*, XIII, 35, below): "Origenes, cum in ceteris libris omnes vicerit, in Cantico Canticorum ipse se vicit."

66. Ed. Baehrens, pp. 61f. (*PGL*, XIII, 61f.).

67. Ed. Baehrens, pp. 27f. (*PGL*, XIII, 37f.; *PL*, XXIII, 1173f.).

68. *PGL*, LXXXI, 28f. Compare, for example, with Origen, ed. Baehrens, p. 62, lines 22f. (*PGL*, XIII, 63D), his reference to (Jewish) limitation of the teaching of (the lore of) the Song of Songs to mature students only.

69. *PGL*, LXXXI, 48C. Baehrens, p. xxviii, is of the opinion that other post-Origenic commentators who wrote in Greek do not betray the influence of Origen on the Song, and he utters a warning against the assumption that Theodoret may be used as testimony to the original Greek of Origen's own commentary.

remove, between the exegetical ancestry of the Targum and that of Origen and his successors. The text of 1:5 reads *I am very dark, but comely, O daughters of Jerusalem, like the tents of Kedar, like the curtains of Solomon.*[70] The Targumic elaboration of this runs (with slight omissions) as follows: "When...the house of Israel made the golden calf, their faces turned black as the Ethiopians...but when they returned in penitence and their sin was forgiven them, the effulgence of the glory of their faces did increase to be bright as that of the angels, both in virtue of their penitence and because they made curtains for the tabernacle, and so the Presence of the Lord came to dwell amongst them: and [also because] Moses, their teacher, had gone up to heaven and had effected peace between them and their king."[71] The three basic elements in the Targum's exegesis are thus *black* in sin, *fair* in penitence, and the reconciliation effected by means of the *curtains* of the tabernacle with "Solomon"—that is, with the King of peace. Turning to Origen,[72] we find a similar scheme: *black* in sin, but after penitence—which for Origen is the equivalent of conversion—blackness is no longer a defect but a mark of beauty. More circumstantially,[73] Origen pictures the gentile Christians chiding Jewish Christians for reproaching them with their ignoble and pagan antecedents, claiming that they have a beauty all their own, achieved after conversion: so that comparison with Solomon's curtains, so far from being a reproach, is in fact a compliment, the curtains being in fact none other than those of the tabernacle, and "Solomon" standing for Christ, the peacemaker. The argument is directed, be it emphasized, against Jewish Christians, and not (except perhaps obliquely) against Jews. But it seems not improbable that the Targum is here formulating its own rejoinder to what it took to be a rebuke addressed by the Church to the Synagogue itself, and that it counters the implicit Christian claim to have been wholly transmuted through conversion, by asserting the completeness of the reconciliation effected between God and penitent Israel after their own most spectacular act of apostasy.

Or again: into 7:5(4), *Your eyes are pools in Heshbon, by the gate of Bath-*

70. שחורה אני ונאוה בנות ירושלים כאהלי קדר כיריעות שלמה

71. כד עבדו עמא בית ישראל ית עגלא אתקדרו אפיהון כבני כוש דשריין במשכני קידר וכד תבו בתיובתא ואשתביק להון סגא זיו יקרא דאפיהון כמלאכיא ועל דעבדו יריעתא למשכנא ושרת ביניהון שכינתא דייי ומשה רבהון סליק לרקיעא ויהב שלמא ביניהון ובין מלכא

72. Homily I, ed. Baehrens, p. 36, especially line 1f. (*PGL*, XIII, 43B): "Paenitentiam egit a peccatis, speciem ei est largita conversio..."

73. Commentary, ed. Baehrens, p. 113, line 25f. (*PGL*, XIII, 101D): "Haec sponsa, quae loquitur, ecclesiae personam tenet ex gentibus congregatae"; p. 114, line 15 (*PGL*, XIII, 102D): "Sed et pellibus Solomonis comparatis me, quae non aliae sunt quam pelles tabernaculi Dei"; p. 124, lines 4f., 18f. (*PGL*, XIII, 109C, 110A): "Puto ergo quod harum pellium mentio fiat in Cantico Canticorum et istae dicantur esse Solomonis, qui accipitur in pacificum Christum." The same matter is presented, more succinctly, by Theodoret, *PGL*, LXXXI, 68–69.

Rabbim,[74] the Targum reads an eulogy on the scholars of the Sanhedrin who possess the near-esoteric knowledge of astronomy necessary for calculating (*ḥeshbon*) matters of intercalation: "Thy scribes are as full of wisdom as brooks of water, and do know how to count out the calculations for intercalations, and so do they intercalate years and determine the beginning of years and the beginning of months, [holding their deliberations] in the gate of the great Sanhedrin."[75] Aquila, who here rendered the place-name Heshbon by ἐπιλογισμός,[76] doubtless had this same exegetical conceit in mind;[77] and he will presumably have expected Jewish readership to recognize the hint conveyed by his own choice of a suggestive rendering for the word. But the meaning which he intended his readers to catch would obviously elude a gentile public that was not familiar with the importance attached to the calendar by rabbinic Judaism, and we consequently find Theodoret[78] (or his patristic source) taking note of the Aquilan ἐπιλογισμός and foisting on to it exegesis of his own. From the "many gates" (Hebrew *shaʿar bath rabbim*) of the Old and the New Testaments, the Apostles, and the patristic writers, the Church has drawn manifold waters of sound teaching: and the "eyes" of pious souls are the "pools" in which these waters are collected. What the text therefore means is that "the contemplative activity of thy soul, and the multitude of thy pious reckonings [λογισμοί], resemble pools that gather water from many a direction, seeing that just so dost thou receive from many mouths the flowings of doctrine." The Church here got hold of the wrong end of the rabbinic stick, but having done so, it proceeded to whittle it down into a peg, on to which it has then crammed most of its own exegetical wardrobe.

74. עיניך ברכות בחשבון על שער בת רבים

75. ספרין (ספרי[י]ך ed. Lagarde and *Codices*) מלין חוכמתא כפרקטנין דמיא וידעין למנני חושבני עוברי ומעברין שנין וקבעין רישי שנין ורישי ירחין בתרע בית סנהדרין רבא וכו׳

76. Quoted by Theodoret, *PGL*, LXXXI, 192A. Frederick Field's *Hexapla* (Oxford, 1875) has no further evidence.

77. The comment of the *Siphrey* on the verse (*ʿEqebh*, Deuteronomy 11: 41, ed. L. Finkelstein, p. 87) reads בחשבונות שנגמרים בעצה ובמחשבה: similarly *Numbers Rabbah*, 14, 4 (Wilna ed., f. 59a, col. i). Compare also *Canticles Rabbah in loco* (Wilna ed., f. 36b, col. ii, foot): מילי דחושבן, לו מזכין ול״ה מחייבין, על שער בת רבים, זו ההלכה שיוצאה שער וכו׳ The latter clearly, and the *Siphrey* probably, has a wider reference to the business of the Sanhedrin than merely to its responsibility for the regulation of the Jewish calendar, although in point of fact it was the latter that became the only surviving prerogative of the Patriarchate and its associated court in the early Christian centuries. On grounds of social history, therefore, no less than of lexical signification, Aquila's rendering ἐπιλογισμός may be assumed to reflect an interpretation of *ḥeshbon* congruent with that of the Targum. ἐπ. is used of the calculation of *dates* by Dionysius of Halicarnassus, *Ant. Rom.* i, 74.

78. *PGL*, LXXXI, 192AB: Διδάσκει... ὅτι τῶν εὐσεβῶν ψυχῶν τὸ ὀπτικὸν λίμναι εἰσὶ... ἅτε δὴ ἀπὸ πολλῶν πυλῶν, τουτέστι στομάτων... τὰ ῥεῖθρα δεχόμεναι. Καὶ γὰρ παρὰ... Μωσέως, καὶ παρὰ... τῶν... προφητῶν, καὶ παρὰ τῶν θείων Εὐαγγελίων, καῖ παρὰ τῶν ἱερῶν ἀποστόλων... Αἱ γὰρ θεωρίαι τὴς ψυχῆς σου, καὶ τῶν εὐσεβῶν σου λογισμῶν τὸ πλῆθος λίμναις ἐοίκασι πολλαχόθεν δεχομέναις ὕδατα, ἐπειδὴ καὶ ἀπὸ πολλῶν στομάτων ὑποδέχῃ τῆς διδασκαλίας τὰ νάματα.

I turn now to some passages which give the Targumist occasion to launch out into elaborate discussion of Torah and its significance, in order to set them against patristic treatment of the same texts and to inquire whether any dialectical relationship obtains between the two. The Targum states its own position, quite unequivocally, at the very outset (1:2): *O that he would kiss me with the kisses of his mouth! For your love is better than wine.*[79] The following is the paraphrase:[80] "Blessed be the Name of the Lord, who gave us both the Torah through the agency of Moses, the great Scribe, written upon two tablets of stone, and as well the six Orders of the Mishnah and the Talmud by means of oral record: and who did speak to us face to face, like a man who kisses his fellow, out of the magnitude of the love that He bore [for us], more than for the seventy nations of the world" (the numerical value of *yayin* [= wine], the last word of the Hebrew text, is seventy). For Origen,[81] the verse is a plea by the Church for the kiss of her lover's own mouth—how long must she make do with vicarious kisses, mediated by Moses and the prophets? By way of preparation she has been vouchsafed the Law, and the prophets have foretold her espousal to him and have described his beauty: but she is nevertheless still dependent on his intermediaries. Let him come himself and kiss her with his own direct teaching. Or, on another level, so long as the soul was unready for the pure doctrine of the word of God, it had of necessity to receive kisses from those erudite in secular studies. Having now achieved maturity sufficient to interpret their parables and enigmatic sayings, it sees itself as having at length received his own kisses of manifold enlightenment.[82] Theodoret's summary is succinct and explicit:[83] "I have heard thy speech through the medium of the written word, but am desirous of hearing thy very voice as well. I would fain receive the holy doctrine by immediate word of mouth, and kiss it with the lips of my own mind." These patristic citations merely rehearse or allude to the conventional Pauline view of the Law as a dispensation rendered obsolete by revelation in Christ. The specific symbols rendered prominent by post-Biblical Judaism are not singled out for disdainful rejection, but (if they are indeed noticed at all) are subsumed in what is said about the Law and the Prophets. The Targum, on the contrary, insists not merely on the significance of Torah in the theology of election, but specifically on the full apparatus of

79. ישקני מנשיקות פיהו כי טובים דודיך מיין

80. אמר שלמה נבייא בריך שמיה דייי דיהב לן אוריתא על ידוי דמשה ספרא רבא כתיבא על תרין לוחי אבנא ושיתא סדרי משנה ותלמודא בגרסא והוה מתמלל עימן אפין באפין כגבר דנשיק לחבריה מן סגיאות חיבתא דחביב (ed. Lagarde and one *Codex* + לן) יתיר מן שבעין אומיא

81. Ed. Baehrens, p. 30, line 1 (*PGL*, XIII, 59B).

82. Ed. Baehrens, pp. 90, line 8–91, line 24 (*PGL*, XIII, 84D–86A).

83. *PGL*, LXXXI, 57A.

the Oral Torah, and it moreover uses markedly particularistic language in which to enunciate Israel's unique privilege as the recipient of Toranic revelation. Such emphasis is in my view most satisfactorily accounted for by the assumption that it is a deliberate counterattack.

Judaism occasionally shows itself to be explicitly aware of the significance of Torah, or of the history of salvation that Torah records, to the wider world. *Your name is oil poured out; therefore the maidens love you* (1:3)[84] becomes, in the Targum,[85] "At the sound of Thy miracle and mighty acts which Thou didst perform for Thy people, the house of Israel, all the peoples did tremble who heard the report of Thy might and Thy good signs; and Thy holy Name was heard spoken of throughout the world, Thy Name being choicer than the oil of anointing... And for this reason did the righteous ones love to follow the way of Thy goodness..." The name which is diffused ointment is identified by Origen,[86] as one would expect, with Christ's, and more specifically by Theodoret[87] with the world-wide diffusion of the Christian message brought about by his crucifixion. Origen, however, elaborates the idea—it was the preaching of Christ's gospel, and that alone, which brought the Biblical history of salvation to the world:[88] "Now at last is the name of Moses heard about abroad, having been previously confined to the narrow borders of Judea; for none of the Greeks mention him, nor do we find any written reference to him, or to the rest of the Biblical story in any historical treatise of non-Jewish composition. But as soon as Jesus shone forth in the world, he carried the Law and the Prophets out into it with him, and in very truth our text—*thy name is oil poured out*—so found its fulfillment." Origen's negative statement—that Moses was not, previous to the spread of Christianity, a figure of world history—can scarcely be intended to controvert the Targumic exegesis: it is insufficiently explicit. The Targum itself reflects traditions,[89] to the effect that the miracles accompanying the crossing of the Red Sea won proselytes for Judaism, which the Midrash appends to the appropriate Biblical texts.[90] Exegetical allusion to the legend

84. לריח שמניך טובים שמן תורק שמך על כן עלמות אהבוך

85. לקל ניסך וגיברוותך דעבדת לעמך בית ישראל זעו כל עממיא דשמעו ית שימע גבורתך ואתוותך טביא ושמך קדישא אשתמע בכל עלמא דהוא בחיר ממשח רבותא דהוא מתרבי על רישי מלכין וכהנין ובגין כין רחימו צדיקיא למהך בתר אורח טובך בדיל דיחסנון עלמא הדין ועלמא דאתי

86. Ed. Baehrens, p. 33, line 27 (*PGL*, XIII, 41D).

87. *PGL*, LXXXI, 60B.

88. Ed. Baehrens, p. 34, line 1 (*PGL*, XIII, 42A): "Nunc Moysi nomen auditur, quod prius Iudaeae tantum claudebatur angustiis; neque enim Graecorum quispiam meminit eius neque in ulla gentilium litterarum historia de illo seu ceteris scriptum aliquid invenimus. Statim ut Iesus radiavit in mundo, eduxit secum legem et prophetas et vere completum est: 'unguentum effusum est nomen tuum.' "

89. See *Exodus Rabbah* 27, 4 (Wilna ed., f. 48b, col. ii).

90. Exodus 15: 2, 18: 1; Joshua 2: 10; Jeremiah 16: 19.

in connection with this verse[91] could well have been motivated by a desire to refute Origen's assertion that the true message of Israel had to wait for Christ not merely for its fulfillment, but even for its effectual publication.

In the following verse (1:4), *The king brought me to his chambers,*[92] we possibly catch the Targumist picking up an actual word from the patristic tradition and turning it to his own account. For Origen,[93] according to the spiritual (as opposed to the historical) meaning, the "chamber" and "store-room" are the deep sensation of intimacy indicated by St. Paul when he speaks[94] of having *the mind of Christ*, and *understanding the gifts bestowed on us by God.* Following Paul in applying to these gifts the words of Isaiah[95]—*no eye but Thine hath seen, O God*—from which R. Yoḥanan had deduced[96] that the delights of the World to Come surpass even the prophet's powers of description, Origen interprets the text as meaning, "Christ has brought the soul to an understanding of his mind, thereby introducing it into his own royal chamber," and this in turn leads him to Paul's reference[97] to Christ, *in whom are hid all treasures* (θησαυροί) *of wisdom and knowledge.*

Following out its scheme of dramatic history, the Targum[98] assigns the words to the righteous amongst the Israelites who went forth from Egypt. Vocalizing the Hebrew *hebhi'ani* not as a preterite verb, as do the Masoretic

91. R. Yoḥanan (*Canticles Rabbah, in loco,* [Wilna ed. §3, f. 6b, col. ii]) interprets the verse of Abraham, whose reputation became diffused by his migration from his original home even as a vessel of ointment diffuses its perfume when it is moved. Since in rabbinical thinking it is Abraham who is the archetypal evangelist (see, e.g., *Genesis Rabbah* 39, 14, on Genesis 12: 5 [Wilna ed., f. 81a, col. ii; ed. Theodor-Albeck, p. 379], this exegesis may well be a rejoinder to the Christian view represented by Theodoret (*PGL*, LXXXI, 60B), who applies the verse to the Passion and the consequent evangelical endeavors of the Apostles: ὁ... Χριστὸς, πρὸ μὲν τοῦ πάθους ὀλίγοις ἦν γνώριμος· ἐπειδὴ δὲ τὸν σταυρὸν ὑπέμεινε... πλήρεις... οἱ... ἀπόστολοι τῆς εὐοσμίας ἐκείνῆς ἐγένοντο... καὶ τὸ κήρυγμα πᾶσι διαπορθμεύσαντες, ἅπασαν τὴν οἰκουμένην τῆς εὐοσμίας ἐπλήρωσαν.

92. הביאני המלך חדריו

93. Ed. Baehrens, p. 108, lines 20f. (*PGL*, XIII, 98C): "...Hic est secundum propositi dramatis ordinem quasi historicus intellectus. Sed quoniam, cui res agitur, ecclesia est ad Christum veniens vel anima Verbo Dei adhaerens, quod aliud cubiculum Christi et promptuarium Verbi Dei credendum est, in quo vel ecclesiam suam vel animam cohaerentem sibi introducat, nisi ipse Christi arcanus et reconditus sensus? De quo et Paulus dicebat: 'nos autem sensum Christi habemus, ut sciamus, quae a Deo donata sunt nobis.' Haec illa sunt, quae 'oculus non vidit nec auris audivit nec in cor hominis adscendit, quae praeparavit Deus his qui diligunt eum.' Cum igitur animam Christus in intelligentiam sui sensus inducit, in cubiculum regis introducta dicitur, in quo 'sunt thesauri sapientiae ac scientiae eius absconditi.'" Compare Theodoret, *PGL*, LXXXI, 61A: Ἀξιοῦται δὲ... τῶν τοῦ νυμφίου θαλάμων τε καὶ ταμιείων,... λέγει... τὰ κεκρυμμένα αὐτοῦ ἀπεκάλυψέ μοι βουλεύματα· τὸ μυστήριον τὸ ἀπὸ τῶν αἰώνων καὶ ἀπὸ τῶν γενεῶν ἐγνώρισέ μοι· τοὺς θησαυροὺς... ἀνέῳξέ μοι, κατὰ τὴν τοῦ Ἡσαΐου προφητείαν.

94. I Corinthians 2: 16, also verses 9, 12.

95. Chapter 64: 4: עין לא ראתה אלהים זולתך יעשה למחכה לו

96. BT *Berakhoth* 34b.

97. Colossians 2:3: ἐν ᾧ εἰσὶν πάντες οἱ θησαυροὶ τῆς σοφίας καὶ γνώσεως ἀπόκρυφοι.

98. אמרו צדיקי ההוא דרא קדם ריבון כל עלמא נגידנא בתרך ונהי רהטין בתר אורח טובך וקריב יתן לשפולי טורא דסיני והב לן אוריתך מן גנזך דרקיעא וכו׳

text and the Revised Standard Version (*has brought me*), but as an imperative,[99] *habhi'eni*, the Targum makes them say, "Draw us after Thee...and draw us near to the base of Mount Sinai, and give us Thy Torah from Thy treasure-house (*min ganzakh*) of heaven..." The Aramaic (ultimately perhaps Persian) *ganza, ginza* is the exact equivalent of the Greek θησαυρός. Is the language of the Targum here no more than a reminiscence of the phrase in Scripture [100] in which the heavens, as the source of rain, are described as God's "goodly treasury"?[101] I suspect that it is rather a deliberate counter-assertion of the enduring validity of Torah, and of the adequacy of the Sinaitic revelation, against the claims here made by patristic exegetical tradition for a new and superior revelation through Christ: and that the Targumist subtly insinuates his apologia by himself adopting (or reclaiming) Paul's metaphorical reference to *all the treasures of wisdom and knowledge* hidden in Christ. Conceivably, too, an additional motive for the Targumist's identification was provided by the well-known words of Jesus himself[102] regarding *laying up for yourselves treasures in heaven*. The latter passage does not, of course, refer to any source of revelation, but its celebrity might have prompted the Targumist to chose a form of words that could insinuate that the teaching was supererogatory, having been in effect anticipated by the heavenly origin of Torah and the heavenly rewards which, in rabbinic thinking, are the corollary of its observance.

I conclude this section by referring to the two final verses of the Song of Songs. In the treatment of these by Theodoret and the Targum respectively there is no obviously apologetic matter, but comparison can reveal not only how the Church and the Synagogue have each of them integrated the Song into its own variety of messianism, but also the way in which each copes with the awkward circumstance that whatever the messianic beliefs to which one may happen to subscribe, life has for the moment to be lived, willy-nilly, in the midst of an unregenerate society. How is the believer to come to terms with the facts of life? Is he to focus his faith upon the certainty of an ultimate solution brought about by a divine intervention in the affairs of men—the "sending of the Messiah," or his "second coming"—and meanwhile resign himself, quite negatively, to a period during which the utmost personal vigilance and self-control is called for, but during which constructive spiritual

99. For the change, contrast the treatment of the same word in 2: 4, where Origen follows the Septuagint, which construes הביאני as an imperative: the Masoretic text punctuates it, and the Targum construes it as a preterite indicative.

100. Deuteronomy 28: 12: יפתח ה׳ לך את אוצרו הטוב את השמים

101. Targum 'Onqelos to the passage is quite literal; Pseudo-Jonathan, although attaching to the verb יפתח an allusion to the four keys (מפתחין) reserved by God in His own hand, does not expand the meaning of *treasury* in the context ("His goodly treasury that is with Him in heaven, to give rain": ית אוצריה טב דעמיה בשמיא למתן מטר וכו׳)

102. Matthew 5: 19.

activity of any real significance is not a practical possibility? Or is he rather to see his role during the waiting period more positively, and as having some bearing on the feasibility (or otherwise) of advancing the date of the messianic climax of history?

The conclusion of the Song (8:13-14) reads:[103] (13) *O you* (feminine singular) *who dwell in the gardens, my companions are listening for your voice; let me hear it.* (14) *Make haste* (literally, *flee*), *my beloved* (masculine singular), *and be like a gazelle or a young stag upon the mountains of spices.* Theodoret's comment runs as follows:[104]

(13) That is, O thou my bridegroom,[105] who dost take thy rest upon creation—both creation attainable as an intellectual concept and creation subject to the senses, both of which were planted, in the manner of gardens, by acts of thy will: there are others,[106] [of a caliber] beyond [that of] ourselves, who fix their gaze unswervingly on thee, in virtue of their not being distracted through the bondage of the body. Those, that is, of the absolutely immaterial rank of angels. I, however, being subject to bondage of the [aforementioned] kind, am fearful of [sustaining] a change [for the worse].[107] That is the reason why, in eager enthusiasm for thy second coming, I do thus supplicate thee to cause me to hear [that utterance of] thy voice so ardently besought in prayer, *videlicet*, *Come, O blessed of my Father, inherit the kingdom prepared for you.*[108] And so, (14) in summoning the righteous[109]

103. היושבת בגנים חברים מקשיבים לקולך השמיעני: (14) ברח דודי ודמה לך לצבי או לעופר האילים על הרי בשמים

104. *PGL*, LXXXI, 213: (13) ʻΟ καθήμενος ἐν κήποις, ἑταῖροι προσέχοντες, τὴν φωνήν σου ἀκούτισόν με. Εἴτουν, ʹΩ νυμφίε μου, σὺ ὁ ἐπαναπαυόμενος τῇ τε νοητῇ κτίσει, καὶ τῇ αἰσθητῇ, ὡς τοῖς σοῖς θελήμασι δίκην κήπων πεφυτευμέναις· ἄλλοι παρ' ἡμᾶς εἰσιν οἱ ἀμεταστρεπτὶ πρὸς σὲ ἀτενίζοντες, διὰ τὸ μὴ μερίζεσθαι δεσμῷ σώματος, αἱ ἄϋλοι πάντως καὶ ἀγγελικαὶ τάξεις· ἐγω δὲ ὡς ὑποκειμένη τῷ τοιούτῳ δεσμῷ, δέδοικα τὴν τροπὴν, καὶ διὰ τοῦτο τὴν δευτέραν σου κάθοδον ἐπισπεύδουσα, ἱκετεύω σε, ἀκουστήν μοι ποίησον τὴν εὐκταίαν ἐκείνην φωνήν σου, τὸ, «Δεῦτε, οἱ εὐλογημένοι τοῦ Πατρός μου, κληρονομήσατε τὴν ἡτοιμασμένην ὑμῖν βασιλείαν». Καὶ οὕτως· (14) Φύγε, ἀδελφιδέ μου, καὶ ὁμοιώθητι τῷ δόρκωνι, ἢ νεβρῷ ἐλάφων ἐπὶ ὄρη ἀρωμάτων. Προσκαλούμενος γὰρ τοὺς δικαίους εἰς τὴν ἀπὸ καταβολῆς κόσμου ἡτοιμασμένην αὐτοῖς βασιλείαν σου, ἀφίστασαι πάντως τῆς διὰ τῶν αἰσθητῶν προνοίας ἡμῶν, ἐφελκόμενος τοὺς ἀξίους ἐπὶ τὰ ὕψη τῶν πνευματικῶς εὐωδιαζουσῶν αὐτοὺς κατὰ θέωσιν χαρίτων· ἐν αἷς ὥς τις δόρκων, ἢ ἐλάφου νεβρὸς, ἀναιρετικὸς τῶν ἰοβόλων θηρίων, τὰ μαινόμενα καθ' ἡμῶν τῆς πονηρίας πνεύματα νεκροῖς, καταπαύων τὸν πρὸς ἡμᾶς αὐτῶν πόλεμον. Εἴη δὲ καὶ ἡμᾶς διαφυγεῖν τὰ τῶν ὄφεων δήγματα· εἰ δὲ καὶ δηχθείημεν, εἰς τὸν ὑψωθέντα ὑπὲρ ἡμῶν ἀπιδεῖν, καὶ τὴν θεραπείαν ἑλκῦσαι.

I am grateful to Mr. W. R. Schoedel and Dr. W. S. Dietrich, my colleagues while I was at Brown University (1963–64), for advice in connection with the translation of this passage.

105. The Septuagint either read a masculine imperative in their Hebrew *Vorlage* or misrendered the feminine preserved in the Masoretic text.

106. That is, the angels; see below, Note 109.

107. That is, a change from steadfast concentration momentarily achieved.

108. Matthew 25: 34.

109. δικαίους = ἀξίους (worthy) mentioned below: it presumably refers to the deceased righteous, who, being now set free from the bondage of the body, have come to share the rank of the angels, described above. According to Philo, such souls as qualify for immortality revert to the sphere inhabited by angels; see H. A. Wolfson, *Philo*, 3rd ed. (Cambridge, Mass., 1962), I, 402.

to the kingdom prepared for them *from the foundation of the world*, thou dost stand absolutely aloof from [the exercise over us of that type of] providence [which operates] through the objects of the senses, as thou dost attract those worthy [of it] to the heights [that are to be attained through] the graces—graces which, in a spiritual manner of speaking, impart to them sweet-smelling odors:[110] [this being thy method of going to work] in pursuance of [the object of effecting their progressive] divinization. It is through the instrumentality of those graces that thou dost mortify those spirits of evil that rage against us [mere mortals], being thyself, like some gazelle or fawn of the deer, deadly to venom-bearing creatures;[111] [so] putting a stop to the war which they wage against us. May it turn out that we, too, [mere humans and Christians] may escape the bites of the serpents.[112] But should we, after all, be bitten, may we look upon him who was raised up on our behalf,[113] and so draw [thence] the [appropriate] cure.

The exegetical results of the foregoing may be summarized thus. Participation in the kingdom, which ultimately belongs to all Christians as of right through their faith, is (for the present) not achieved except by the departed righteous; these have been found worthy of it, and have therefore—as part of their progressive *theōsis*—been relieved of corporeal obstacles to that concentration on Christ which is necessary in order to achieve the kingdom. They have thus been placed upon the same footing as the incorporeal angels. Under the present dispensation, however, Christians in this life are frustrated by those same obstacles, albeit possessing in Christ an antidote to them. The abrogation of the conditions under which these frustrations are operative is a matter of divine choice, operating through the graces infused into the soul; being, in the case of the departed righteous, already effected by Christ. The remainder of Christendom, however, having at its disposal for the comprehension of Christ merely the physical senses, pray that the waiting period prior to Christ's second coming, during which they are liable to lapse into temptation, may (by an arbitrary divine act) be foreshortened as much as possible.

110. Compare II Corinthians 2: 15f., quoted by Origen, ed. Baehrens, p. 101, line 17 (*PGL*, XIII, 93B).

111. Theodoret refers earlier in his commentary (on 2: 9, *PGL*, LXXXI, 96D) in greater detail to the folk belief, common in classical antiquity and transmitted to medieval Europe through the bestiaries, that deer destroy or devour snakes. See *Physiologus*, ed. F. Sbordone (Milan, 1936), pp. 97f., with a substantial list of ancient sources and references from Theophrastus onward, including Origen on 2: 9, ed. Baehrens, p. 56, line 20 (*PGL*, XIII, 56B).

112. Compare Numbers 21: 6. Serpents are probably here understood as typifying heresy, as elsewhere in patristic writings; see *PL*, CCXIX, *index* (xlvi) *de allegoriis*, art x, 194, below, s.v. *serpens*. The instances there given are all late, and are anticipated by (for example) Jerome, *PL*, XXVI, 622B.

113. That is, the brazen serpent of Numbers 21: 8–9 as identified with Jesus in John 3: 14–15 (cf. also 8: 28, 12: 32).

The following is the Targum's rendering:[114]

(13) At the conclusion of his prophecy, Solomon the prophet did say: "The Master of the world is destined to declare to the Congregation of Israel [at the end of days: 'Thou, O Congregation of Israel], that art comparable to a miniature close-*garden* amid the nations, and dost *dwell* in the house of study alongside the *members* of the Sanhedrin and also with the remainder of the people, who [*do listen*] to the voice of the head of the Academy and so do learn from his mouth the words of the Torah—*do thou let Me hear thy voice*, what time thou art in session to pronounce judgment on what is clean and what unclean: and for My part I will concur with all that thou art doing.'

(14) "In that hour will the elders of [the Congregation of] Israel declare: '*Flee* Thee hence, *O my Beloved*, O Thou Master of the world, away from this defiled Land, and cause Thy Presence to abide in the loftiest heavens. And in the time of our tribulation, when we pray before Thee, *be thou like unto a hart* which, at the time when it is asleep, closes one eye tight but keeps the other open, *or like to a young gazelle of the deer* which, at the time that it is in flight, looks ever and anon to its rear. Even so do Thou be watching over us, and be taking note from the loftiest heavens of our tribulation and affliction, until such time as it may be Thy will to redeem us, [to go] *to the mountains* of Jerusalem: and there shall the priests cause the incense *of spices* to ascend before Thee.' "

This paraphrase, unlike Theodoret's and the Septuagint, takes note of the differing genders of the verbs in the two verses, and assigns each to the relevant character. What are the implications of its exegesis? Like Theodoret's, it acknowledges that the messianic climax of history must be set in motion by a force outside humanity—but by God Himself, and not by a Messiah acting with even quasi-independence. It likewise acknowledges that the time for that climax is not yet; but it neither importunes the Deity to foreshorten the necessary interval, nor regards the period of waiting as being inevitably spiritually barren. On the contrary, it betrays a conviction that the function of Israel in history to implement Torah in its domestic existence, according to the established canons of rabbinic jurisprudence, is both divinely commissioned and able to count on divine endorsement.[115] Being now finally

114. (13) אמר שלמה נביא בסוף נבואתיה עתיד מרי עלמא דיימר לכנשתא דישראל דמתילא
לגינתא קלילא ביני אומיא ויתבא בבי מדרשא עם חברי סנהדרין ושאר עמא דמתילין (דצי[י]תין
(ed. Lagarde and *Codices*, לקל ריש מתיבתא ואלפין מן פומיה פתגמי אוריתא אשמעיני קל מלייך
בעידן דאת יתבא לזכאה ולדכאה (ed. Lagarde and *Codices* ולחייבא) ואיהי מסכים לכל מה דאת
עבדא: (14) בההיא שעתא יימרון סבי ישראל ערוק לך רחימי מרי עלמא מארעא הדא מסאבתא
ותשרי שכינתך בשמי מרומא ובעידן עקתן דאנחנא מצלן קדמך תהי דמי לטביא דבעידן דדמיך
עינא חדא קמיץ ועינא חדא פתיח או כאורזילא דאילא דבעידן דעריק מסתכל בתריה כין את תהי
משגח בן ומסתכל בצערן ובסיגופן משמי מרומא עד (זמן + ed. Lagarde and *Codices*) דתרעי
ותפרוק יתן על טוריא דירוש׳ ותמן יסקון כהניא קדמך קטורת בוסמין

115. The idea of God's confirming the decisions arrived at, in due halakic form, by rabbinic authority is expressed elsewhere, particularly (and significantly: see above, Note 80) in connection with the promulgation of the Jewish calendar. See, for example, *Siphra* on Leviticus 23: 2, ed. I. H. Weiss, f. 99b, col. ii, below,

ת״ל אשר תקראו אותם מועדיי קראתם אותם מועדיי ואם לאו אינם מועדיי וכו״

Compare also Samuel's exegesis of Esther 9: 27 in BT *Meghillah* 7a,

קיימו למעלה מה שקיבלו למטה.

reconciled with God after the cycle of sin, punishment, and true repentance set forth in the Targum to the remainder of the Song, Israel is conscious that if history is indeed not yet mature enough for its messianic climax, the impediment lies no longer with themselves, and the continued defilement of the Land (namely, of Israel) by the presence therein of the bones of the wicked[116] symbolizes the unfitness of an unregenerate world for renewed occupancy on the part of the Deity. It is God—not the Messiah—who is addressed in the last verse. And the reason why the Jewish exegesis discovers the obstructions to His reoccupancy to be outside Israel's control, and therefore bids Israel get quietly on with their own job, whereas the Christian exegesis is dominated by apprehension lest the Christian believer fall victim to the forces of temptation that are in permanent array against him, and therefore prays for the harrowing period of waiting to be arbitrarily foreclosed, lies in the circumstance that Christianity maintains, while Judaism rejects, the doctrine of original sin.

Apologetic Against Jewish Esotericism

If the Song of Songs was a fair maid whom the author of the Targum saw himself as in duty bound to recover from the clutches of her ecclesiastical captor, the Church was not the only one to have attempted a runaway match, and the wry thought may well have struck the Targumist that black hair, no less than red, may spell trouble for its owner. Within Jewry itself, the Song had become involved in a complex of esoteric theology[117] the premises of which could easily be read as compromising some of the fundamental principles of Judaism. The Targumist, it seems, was no less embarrassed by it than were Jewish apologetic writers of the nineteenth century,[118] and it seems as though he felt himself obliged to formulate his own paraphrase of the Song in terms that would convey his own rejection of its interpretation as put forward by devotees of advanced Jewish mysticism, no less than the Christ-and-Church interpretation of patristic tradition.

Saul Lieberman[119] has recently demonstrated that the description, in fantastically exaggerated physical terms, of the mystical "body" of the Deity that goes under the name of *Shi ͑ur Qomah*[120] was originally a midrash, intended for esoteric circulation, on the catalogue of her lover's physical

116. The Targum (to 8:5) describes their ejection at the time of the resurrection of the righteous, who will emerge out of subterranean passages from the Mount of Olives.

117. See Scholem, *Jewish Gnosticism*, pp. 36f.

118. *Ibid.*, p. 36, n. 3.

119. *Ibid.*, appendix D, pp. 118ff.; see also pp. 36f. In what follows here I am summarizing the findings of my own article, "The Divine Garment and *Shi͑ur Qomah*," *Harvard Theological Review*, 58 : 153f. (1965).

120. Printed, from *Sepher Razi'el* and other sources, in Solomon Musajoff, *Sepher Merkabhah Shelemah* (Jerusalem, 1921), pp. 30f. See Scholem, *Jewish Gnosticism*, p. 36, n. 1, on the shortcomings of this text, and manuscripts of it (see also p. 6, n. 12).

charms given by the maiden in the Song of Songs (5:10-16). Scholem has, moreover, pointed to a connection between the *Shi ʿur Qomah* and one of the hymns preserved in the *Heykhaloth Rabbathi*[121]—a literary genre some at least of which, Scholem claims, ascends to the second to third century C.E. This hymn, in its turn, links up with a midrashic passage[122] that bears marks of esoteric transmission regarding the alleged creation of light from the divine garment, and Scholem concludes,[123] on the evidence of the hymn, that the description of the garment was part of the *Shi ʿur Qomah* traditions and consequently an item which the visionary would be taught to expect. It seems to me that this must be the background to the apparently gratuitous introduction by the Targumist of a circumstantial, but nevertheless strictly defined, reference to the divine garment at the beginning of his own paraphrase of precisely that passage in the Song out of which, according to Lieberman, the *Shi ʿur Qomah* has grown.

The maiden begins her praise by saying (5:10) *My beloved is radiant and ruddy, distinguished among ten thousand.*[124] Of this the Targumic rendering runs as follows:[125]

> Thereupon did the Congregation of Israel begin to make rehearsal, showing forth part of the praise of the Master of the world, and thus did she declare: "It is that same God that 'tis my will to serve, who is enwrapped by day in a robe *white* as snow whilst engaged upon the twenty four [canonical] books—the words of the Torah, of the Prophets, and the Sacred Writings—yea, He who by night is engaged upon the Six Orders of the Mishnah: He, [I say,] the *brightness* of the glory of whose face in its effulgence is like fire for its richness of wisdom and insight, forasmuch as each several day He produces new particulars revealed from within traditional learning, and is destined to publish them to His people on the great Day: that same God whose *standard of rank is superior to the myriad* on myriad angels that do minister before Him."

The two Hebrew epithets *ṣaḥ* ("radiant") and *'adhom* ("ruddy") are in their context here virtual synonyms. In the case of the latter, the Targumist explicitly states that the cause of the divine "ruddiness," or effulgence, is the acumen and richness of the Deity's own rabbinic scholarship (*mis-saggi'-uth ḥukhmetha we-sibhra*).[126] The former term, *ṣaḥ*, has been here transformed

121. Scholem, *Jewish Gnosticism*, pp. 61f.

122. *Genesis Rabbah* 3, 4 (Wilna ed., f. 13a, col. ii; Theodor-Albeck, pp. 19–20) (R. Samuel b. Naḥmani).

123. Scholem, *Jewish Gnosticism*, p. 60.

124. דודי צח ואדום דגול מרבבה

125. בכין שריאת כנשתא דישראל למשתעי בשבחא דמרי עלמא וכין אמרת לההוא אלהא רעותי למפלח דעטיף (+ביממא ed. Lagarde and *Codices*) באוצטלא חוור כתלג ועסיק בארבע ועסרין ספרין פתגמי אוריתא ופתגמי נביי וכתיבי ובליליא הוה (read הוא) עסיק בשיתא סדרי משנה וזיו יקרא דאנפוהי זהירין כנורא מסגיאות חוכמתא וסברא דהוא מחדית שמעתן חדתין בכל יומא ועתיד לפרסומינון לעמיה ביומא רבא וטקסיה על רבו רבוון דמלאכין דמשמשין קדמוהי

126. For the alleged effect on the countenance, compare the description of Phineas, whose face, when he was the vehicle of the Holy Spirit, "blazed like torches" (*Leviticus Rabbah*, 1:1 [Wilna ed., f. 2a, col. 1]): בשעה שהיתה רוח הקודש שורה עליו פניו בוערות כלפידים

into a garment (στολή) white as snow. Its dazzling whiteness is not quite so explicitly connected with God's own brilliance as a Biblical scholar, but it is to be observed that the Targumist's formulation suggests that the wrapping on of a garment reminiscent of the "robe [*ḥaluq*] of the rabbis"[127] is a necessary or invariable preliminary to God's delivering a discourse on the Bible. It is, so to speak, a symbol of the Deity's standing as an *Alttestamentler*.

Is this merely a pretty conceit of the Targumist's own, and simply the product of his over-all tendency to glorify the Torah? In order to achieve the latter object, resort to such "stage property" as the garment was certainly not indispensable. I suggest that the association, postulated by Scholem, between the description of the Deity's mystic "body" and that of the Deity's mystic "garment" had become, by the Targumist's time, so established a convention (at any rate within esoteric circles, and perhaps, by whispered rumor, even outside them), that he felt unable completely to bypass it. He consequently reinterprets it, in terms appropriate to the Toranic meaning that he is about to discover running through the whole passage, and in so doing, he by exclusion repudiates the esoteric doctrine of the divine garment as material for the creation of light—a doctrine perhaps the more reprehensible to him because of its nonesoteric prominence in the pagan world, where its roots go deep into the history of Greek religious symbolism.[128]

Until an adequate interpretation has been proposed for the theophoric names, the *nomina barbara* assigned in the *Shi ʿur Qomah* to the divine limbs, and also, perhaps, to the number symbolism of each of their alleged measurements, it seems scarcely possible to correlate the material with the specific physical features mentioned in the maiden's praise in the Song of Songs.[129] There is, however, one available source that can tell us something. It is provided by a collection described as *Twenty-four "Sodhoth"* contained in a manuscript now in London,[130] written in an Italian cursive Hebrew script. An extract of this collection was published by M. Gaster.[131] In this document the Biblical text is construed by the simultaneous application of numerology, the significance of the Thirteen Divine Attributes proclaimed in Exodus 34: 6–7, and scriptural proof texts, in order to establish not only the alleged

127. In my article, "The Divine Garment," n. 28, I have suggested that the evidence for the distinctiveness of the טלית or חלוקא דרבנן ought not to be overplayed.

128. On the subject at large, see A. B. Cook, *Zeus* . . ., I (Cambridge, 1914), lf., 56f., etc.

129. Possibly the sequences beginning אגטיה טחון or אנטייה בוחין cited from *Sepher Razi'el* and the *Razin ʿIlla'in* in *Merkabhah Shelemah* f. 38a, below, immediately after the Biblical passage concerned, may contain a clue.

130. MS. Halberstam 219, item 4a, now at Jews' College, Montefiore MS. 279 in H. Hirschfeld, *Descriptive Catalogue of the Hebrew MSS. of the Montefiore Library* (London, 1904).

131. In *MGWJ* (1893), p. 224, reproducing from f. 28b-29a of the manuscript. Reprinted in M. Gaster's collected *Studies and Texts in Folklore, Magic, Medieval Romance* . . . . (London, 1925-28), II, 1330f.

dimensions of the divine members, but also the function of each.[132] For example, the words (2:14) *let me hear your* (feminine) *voice*[133] not only yield a measurement of 13,800 "parasangs" for the divine ear, but identify it with the seat of the divine Attribute of Mercy (*ḥannun*), on the strength of the quotation *and if he cries to me I will hear, because I am merciful.*[134] Similarly, the whites of the eyes are associated with the Attribute of Compassion (*raḥum*), by calling in aid the Targumic rendering of the text *for you have found favor* (that is, compassion) *in my sight.*[135]

Since the tract works right through the maiden's praise of her lover, we are in a position to compare its author's findings with what is embodied in the Targum to the same passage. In what here follows I therefore set down, in brief form, the result of the deductions of the source of MS. Halberstam. This is followed by the quintessence of the Targum. Since, however, evidence that is in my view sufficient has been set forth above[136] for the suggestion that the Targumist was also on the defensive against the conventional Christological interpretation of the Song of Songs by the Church, I also indicate (in the third column) the focal point of Theodoret's exegesis of the reference to each of the members.

Text	*MS. Halberstam*	*Targum*	*Theodoret*
verse 10: *radiant and ruddy*[137]	Measurements of forehead	White-robed while studying Bible, face shining while prosecuting research in Oral Torah[138]	Jesus white *qua* God, red *qua* earthborn human, and reddened by the sins of humanity[139]
distinguished among ten thousand[140]	————	Superior to myriad ministering angels[141]	Christ's divinity out of reach of suffering to which humanity is subject[142]

132. Gaster, pp. 226f., cites the Anglo-Saxon *Dialogue of Solomon and Saturnus*, a text attributed to the eighth century (pp. 145–153 in the text ed. J. M. Kemble, London, 1848), in which there is some localization of divine functions in certain of the divine members, which are correlated with the Song of Songs description. Thus, the golden fingers of God's right hand hold a golden sword, etc.

133. השמיעני את קולך. For the apparent inversion of the genders, compare above, Note 105.

134. Exodus 22: 27, ושמעתי כי חנון אני

135. Exodus 33: 17. The manuscript reads וכשתשגיח בלובן זה (ר״ל של עינים) כת׳ כי מצאת חן בעיני ומתרגמינן אשכחת רחמין בעיני

136. See Pages 173f.

137. דודי צח ואדום

138. See above, Note 125.

139. *PGL*, LXXXI, 156D – 157D: Λευκὸς τοίνυν ἐστὶν, ὡς Θεός... ἀλλὰ καὶ πυῤῥός. οὐ μόνον γάρ ἐστι Θεὸς, ἀλλὰ καὶ ἄνθρωπος· τὸ δὲ πυῤῥὸν παραδηλοῖ τὸ γήϊνον... Ἔπρεπε γὰρ τῷ τὰς ἁμαρτίας ἡμῶν ἀνειληφότι, αἵτινες ἦσαν πυῤῥαὶ ὡς φοινικοῦν... πυῤῥῷ γενέσθαι καὶ προσαγορευθῆναι κτλ.

140. דגול מרבבה

141. See above, Note 125.

142. *PGL*, LXXXI, 157C: οὐ λέγει κατεῤῥάνθην ἐγὼ, ἀλλὰ κατεῤῥάνθη... τὸ σῶμά μου· ἀπαθὴς γὰρ ἡ θεία φύσις, κτλ.

Text	*MS. Halberstam*	*Targum*	*Theodoret*
verse 11: *head the finest gold*[143]	Equals half the numerical value (*sic*) of the Attribute *YHWH*[144]	Summary or chapter headings of Torah[145]	The divine quality in Christ[146]
locks wavy, black as raven[147]	————	Sages' exposition of words of Torah is white to those who observe, and black to those who reject the commandments[148]	Graces flowing from Christ's head are fruit-growing palm spathes (Septuagint has ἐλάται for Hebrew *taltalim*), and black in that the divine economy works obscurely[149]
verse 12: *eyes like doves*[150]	Whites of eyes "embody" Attribute of Mercy (*raḥum*)[151]	God's eyes permanently focused on Jerusalem (Deuteronomy 11:12), for the sake of the Sanhedrin (*ʿayin*=seventy), who study Torah and administer justice in accordance with it[152]	Doves recall spirit descending in dove's form at baptism of Jesus (Matthew 3:16), whose eyes constantly look forward to baptism, longing for the salvation of all[153]

143. ראשו כתם פז

144. והוא חשבון חצי השם הראשון יהוה (י׳.ג׳. ה׳.מ׳. ו׳.א׳. ה׳.ר׳.) 300,000 myriad + $33\frac{1}{3}$ ול״ג ושליש)

145. רישי אוריתא דהיא רגיגא מדהב טב

146. *PGL*, LXXXI, 157D: Κεφαλὴν δὲ αὐτοῦ τροπικῶς καλεῖ τὸ Θεῖον, ...χρυσῷ καὶ λίθῳ αὐτὴν ἀπεικάζει,... οὐ γὰρ εὗρεν ἕτερον ὄνομα εὐπρεπέστερον.

147. קוצותיו תלתלים שחרות כעורב

148. ופירוש מליא דבה דגזרין (read with ed. Lagarde דגורין) טעמין ופיקודין למן דנטרין להון חוורין כתלגא ודלא נטרין להון אוכמין כאנפי (ed. Lagarde כאגפי) עוריבא

149. *PGL*, LXXXI, 160A: Τὰς ἐκ τῆς κεφαλῆς ἐκείνου προχεομένας χάριτας ἡγοῦμαι βοστρύχους ὀνομάζεσθαι... Αἱ γὰρ ἐλάται, καρπός εἰσι φοινίκων... Ἐπειδὴ τοίνυν τῶν ποικίλων αὐτοῦ χαρισμάτων ἀπολαύοντες οἱ πεπιστευκότες αὐτῷ καρποφοροῦσιν αὐτῷ τῆν εὐσέβειαν, ἐλάταις εἰκότως ἀπεικάζει τοὺς βοστρύχους· μέλανας δὲ προσαγορεύει, διὰ τοῦ... χρώματος... σκοτεινοῦ, τὸ ἀνέφικτον τῶν οἰκονομιῶν παραδηλῶν.

150. עיניו כיונים על אפיקי מים רחצות בחלב ישבות על מלאת

151. See Note 135, above.

152. עינוהי (מסתכל[י]ן + ed. Lagarde and *Codices*) תדירא על ירושלים לאיטבא לה ולברכהא מרישה דשתא ועד סופהא כיונין דקימן ומסתכלן על מפקנות מיא בגין זכוותא דיתבי סנהדרין דעסיקין באוריתא ומנהרין ית דינא למהוי שעיע כחלב ויתבין בבי מדרשא ומתינין בדינא עד דגמרין לזכאה ולחייבא

153. *PGL*, LXXXI, 160BC: ἀναμιμνήσκει ἡμᾶς τῆς ἐν τῷ Ἰορδάνῃ κατελθούσης ἐπ' αὐτὸν περιστερᾶς.... Διηνεκῶς γὰρ εἰς τὴν βαπτίσματος βλέπουσι χορηγίαν οἱ ὀφθαλμοὶ αὐτοῦ, τοὺς σωζομένους ἀναμένοντες, καὶ πάντων τὴν σωτηρίαν ποθοῦντες κτλ.
It may be observed that the term διηνεκῶς (*continuously*) is paralleled by the Targum (תדירא), and that similarly ποθοῦτες (*yearning*) is paralleled by ומסתכלן על, which has been suggested by the similarity of the present text (על אפיקי מים) to Psalm 42:2: כאיל תערג על אפיקי מים וגו׳

Text	*MS. Halberstam*	*Targum*	*Theodoret*
verse 13: *cheeks like beds of spices, lips are lilies*[154]	— — — — Linked to Attribute of Abundance in Mercy (*rabh ḥesedh*) by the providence of God's mouth (Deuteronomy 8:3)[155]	Cheeks (*leḥayaw*) are the two tablets (*luḥey*) of stone; lips of the sages can argue Torah casuistically with complete expertise[156]	Cheeks and lips stand for doctrine and its fair perfume: from its "phials"[157] the doctors of the Church draw their arguments[158]
verse 14: *hands are rounded gold*[159]	Hands linked to Attribute of Truth (*'emeth*) and the location of the divine charity (*ṣedaqah*) evinced in provision of sustenance (Psalm 145: 16)[160]	The Patriarchs and twelve tribes of Israel God's instrumental "hands"[161]	Hands stand for Christ's virtue evinced in actions fulfilled with perfect competence and symmetry[162]
body is ivory work encrusted with sapphires[163]	Gives dimensions from thigh to ankle-bone, corresponding to Attribute of Forgiveness of Iniquity (*nose' ʿawon*)[164]	Israel gleam like ivory in their good deeds[165]	The mystery of the treasury of hidden wisdom and knowledge, an ivory box for those worthy to have it opened[166]

154. לחיו כערוגת הבשם מגדלות מרקחים שפתותיו שושנים נטפות מור עבר

155. ויוצא ממדה ר״ב חס״ד כי על כל מוצא פי ה׳ יחיה האדם

156. תרין לוחי אבנין דיהב לעמיה כתיבן בעסר שטין דמיין לשיטי גינת בוסמא מרבין דקדוקין היי כמא דגינתא מרביא בוסמין וספתי חכימיא דעסיקין באוריתא ולהון (read with ed. Lagarde זלחין) טעמין בכל סטר ומימר פומיהון כמורא בחירא

157. The Septuagint renders ערוגת by φιάλαι: that is, unguent-bottles.

158. *PGL*, LXXXI, 160D - 161A: Σιαγόνας δὲ πάλιν καὶ χείλη τὴν διδασκαλίαν καλεῖ·... φιάλας δὲ ἀρώματος ταύτας προσαγορεύει, διὰ τὸ τῆς διδασκαλίας εὐῶδες· λέγει δὲ ἀυτὰς καὶ φύειν μυρεψικά· ἐκεῖθεν γὰρ τὰς τῆς διδασκαλίας ἀφορμὰς λαμβάνοντες οἱ τῆς Ἐκκλησίας διδάσκαλοι, οἷόν τινες μυρεψοὶ γίνονται τοῦ κηρύγματος, καὶ τὸ μύρον τῆς ὠφελείας κατασκευάζουσι.

159. ידיו גלילי זהב ממלאים בתרשיש מעיו עשת שן מעלפת ספירים

160. *MGWJ* (1893), p. 224: וזהו מדת האמת וכתי׳ ידיו גלילי זהב זו הצדקה דכתיב פותח את ידך ומשביע לכל חי רצון וכתיב תפתח ידך ישבעון טוב ואמת כלם מן הידים וכו׳

161. תרי סר שבטין... דמיין לתרי עסר מזלין בחירן כעששית צחיחן בעובדיהון כשן דפיל כשבזיזין

162. *PGL*, LXXXI, 161B: Χεῖρας δὲ τὴν πρακτικὴν ἀρετὴν ὀνομάζει, ἣν μετὰ πάσης ἁρμονίας μετελήλυθεν, οἷον διατορεύων καὶ ἀπευθύνων πρᾶξιν ἑκάστην.

163. See Note 159, above.

164. *MGWJ* (1893), p. 224: חשבון הנכבד... מירכותיו... מקרסוליו ועד כף רגלו אלף רבבות וה׳ מאות בסוד מעיו עשת שן... והשם הנכבד נושא עון. מירכותיו ועד שוקיו כענין שנאמר מעיו עשת שן

165. See Note 161, above.

166. *PGL*, LXXXI, 161C: Ὁ γὰρ βυθὸς αὐτοῦ τῶν μυστηρίων, καὶ τὸ ταμιεῖον τῆς γνώσεως, ἔνθα εἰσὶ πάντες οἱ θησαυροὶ τῆς σοφίας καὶ τῆς γνώσεως ἀπόκρυφοι, πυξίον εἰσὶν ἐλεφάντινον τοῖς τῆς ἀποκοαλύψεως ἀξίοις.

Text	*MS. Halberstam*	*Targum*	*Theodoret*
verse 15: *legs are alabaster columns*[167]	The Attributes of Maintaining Loving-kindness (*noṣer ḥesedh*) and of Forgiving Iniquity (*nose' ḥaṭa'ah*); the location of divine faculty of righteousness (*ṣedheq*) (Isaiah 11:5)[168]	The righteous, being pillars of the world that was created in six days (*shesh*=alabaster or six)[169]	Christ's firmness and constancy—
set upon bases of gold[170]	The Attribute of Granting Acquittal (*wenaqqeh*)[171]	are supported on gold of Torah[172]	as the evidence of fair deeds[173]
appearance like Lebanon, choice as cedars[174]	————	so as to teach (*mar'ehu, moreh*) and admonish the people to do God's will[175]	Indicates Christ's double nature: the frankincense (λίβανος) standing for his divinity, the imperishable cedar wood for his uncorrupted humanity[176]
verse 16: *palate sweet, altogether desirable*[177]	The Attribute of Forgiveness of Sin (*nose' pesha'*) continues throughout "Body," as far as neck[178]	God's words sweet as honey, His precepts more desirable than gold (Psalm 19: 11)[179]	The divine sayings, for example those which won admiration for Jesus from the High Priest's servants, et cetera (John 7:46)[180]

167. שוקיו עמודי שש מיסדים על אדני פז מראהו כלבנון בחור כארזים

168. *MGWJ* (1893), p. 224: נוצר חסד ממתניו ומעלה כד״א והיה צדק אזור מתניו... והשם הנכבד נושא חטאה מקרסוליו ועד כף רגליו שהם אדני פז

169. וצדיקיא אינון עמודי עלמא בסיסן על סמכי דהב טב אינון פתגמי אוריתא דעסיקין בהון ומוכחין עמא בית ישראל למעבד רעותיה יאי הוא (ed. Lagarde, ואיהו) מתמלי עליהון רחמין כסבא ומחוור חוביהון דבית ישראל כתלג ומתעתד למעבד נצחן קרבא בעממיא דעברין על מימריה כעולים גיבר וחסין כגולמישין

170. See Note 167, above.

171. *MGWJ* (1893), p. 224 (immediately following on the passage quoted in Note 168, ending והשם הנכבד ונקה לגובה. פרסות רגליו ג׳ אלפים רבבות שהוא מלא כל העולם שנ׳ (אדני פז השמים כסאי והארץ הדום רגליו (Gaster *sic*) וכתיב לדכא תחת רגליו כו׳

172. See Note 169, above.

173. *PGL*, LXXXI, 164A: τὸ ἑδραῖον αὐτοῦ, καῖ σταθηρὸν, καὶ μόνιμον, καὶ διαρκὲς, διὰ τῶν μαρμαρίνων στύλων εδήλωσε· καὶ τὰς βάσεις δὲ αὐτῶν χρυσᾶς ὠνόμασε, τὸ τίμιον τῶν πράξεων διὰ τούτων παραδηλῶν.

174. See Note 167, above. 175. See Note 169, above.

176. *PGL*, LXXXI, 164A - B: Πάλιν ἐνταῦθα τὸ διπλοῦν ἑρμηνεύει τῶν φύσεων. λίβανον μὲν τὴν θείαν προσαγορεύει, ἐπειδὴ λίβανος κατὰ τὸν νόμον Θεῷ προσεφέρετο. Κέδρον δὲ καλεῖ τὴν ἀνθρωπείαν, ὡς σηπεδόνα τῆς ἁμαρτίας οὐ δεξαμένην· ἄσηπτος γὰρ ἐν ξύλοις ἡ κέδρος.

177. חכו ממתקים וכלו מחמדים

178. *MGWJ* (1893), p. 224, after the words אזור מתניו in n. 168: עד צוארו לקיים מה שנ׳ חכו ממתקים וכלו מחמדים

179. מלי מוריגוי מתיקן כדובשא וכל פיקודויי רגיגן על חכימויי מדהב וכו׳

180. *PGL*, LXXXI, 164B: «Φάρυγξ αὐτοῦ γλυκασμός»· τί γὰρ τῶν θείων λογίων γλυκύτερον;... Διὸ καὶ οἱ ὑπηρέται τῶν ἀρχιέρων, οἱ ἐπ' αὐτὸν ἀποσταλέντες, καὶ κατακηληθέντες, καὶ ἑαλωκότες τῷ πόθῳ τῆς τῶν λόγων γλυκύτητος, φασὶ τοῖς ἀποστείλασιν· «Οὐδέποτε οὕτως ἐλάλησεν ἄνθρωπος, ὡς οὗτος ὁ ἄνθρωπος».

A paradoxical parallel reveals itself in the foregoing, in that the categories with which the exegesis in MS. Halberstam and that of Theodoret operate are, up to a point, interchangeable. Theodoret, a champion of Antiochian Christology, originally recognized a duality in Christ's nature, although he was later on to repudiate the doctrine.[181] His commentary on the Song of Songs apparently reflects his early views, and physical features which, to Theodoret, allegorically represent the divinity (τὸ θεῖον)[182] in Jesus are by the author of MS. Halberstam identified with the divine Attributes (*middoth*). Obviously, allegorical identifications corresponding to the humanity in Christ will not, as such, find any parallel on the Jewish side: but it is worth observing that Theodoret in some cases makes the features stand for Christ's humanity in action among mankind,[183] and it is precisely such activity on the part of the Deity that is adduced by the Jewish author, in some of the proof texts by which he authenticates the connection of the sundry limbs with the various divine Attributes.[184]

The Targum, on the other hand, in its own application of the maiden's eulogy, succeeds in eliminating every single reference to the person of the Deity except that of the eyes (verse 12), and this is itself rendered innocuous by the citation of a Biblical passage (Deuteronomy 11:12) in which the anthropomorphism passes almost unnoticed—God's eyes being, indeed, so familiar a Biblical expression as scarcely to raise any antianthropomorphic scruples save in the ever punctilious 'Onqelos. And even here, it should be noted, the benevolent activity of God's eyes (*ʿayin*) is correlated to the devotion to Torah displayed by the Sanhedrin, the seventy (= *ʿayin*) members of which are likewise identified by this Targumist in other references to *eyes* occurring in the Song of Songs.[185] For the remainder, the physical description has been transformed into a panegyric on Torah as being at once the Deity's own occupation,[186] the vocation of Israel and of the righteous,[187] the occasion of the divine good will for Israel,[188] and as itself an inherently beautiful thing.[189]

Such exegesis could not only provide (at any rate in the Targumist's own view) a satisfactory account of the outspokenly erotic language of the text.

181. For a brief, recent bibliography of the source material, see F.L. Cross (ed.), *The Oxford Dictionary of the Christian Church* (Oxford, 1957), p. 1341. See, for an example, the passage quoted in Note 176.

182. *PGL*, LXXXI, 157A: τὸ γὰρ θεῖον αὐτοῦ κάλλος ἀσύγκριτον.

183. See above, Notes 153, 162.

184. See above, Note 160.

185. For example at 4: 1, 6: 5.

186. Verse 10 (see above, Note 125), verse 16 (Note 179).

187. Verses 13 - 15, see Notes 156, 161, 169.

188. Verse 12, see Note 152.

189. Verse 11, see Notes 145, 148; verse 16, Note 179.

More important, perhaps, it could also be seen to cut the ground from under the feet of the Christian tradition exemplified by Theodoret, Torah being represented as in effect capable of fulfilling all the functions for which Christianity must rely on Christ. Indeed, one possible point of contact between the Targum and Theodoret has been (but tentatively) pointed out in their respective treatments of verse 12;[190] other possibilities occur on verse 13 (Targum, rabbinic scholarship; Theodoret, ecclesiastical doctrine)[191] and verse 16 (Targum, God's words and precepts; Theodoret, Jesus' expertise in Jewish law).[192] At the same time, the effect of the same line of exegesis was also to indicate, by implication, the supererogatory character of the esoteric Jewish interpretation. Most probably it is not here being obliquely condemned outright. But Jewish tradition had, at least since Tannaitic times, been circumspect about the educational hazards involved in mystical matters concerning such things as the divine Chariot,[193] and, on the evidence of what Origen says[194] about Jewish hesitations in communicating the Song to the young, we may take it that any reservations which the Targumist may have entertained regarding the esoteric interpretation of the Song in Judaism did not begin with himself. He doubtless felt that mystical adventures of this kind were without danger to those only who (to use later rabbinical phraseology) had already had "their bellies crammed" with halakic matter.[195] He may, however, well have gone rather further than this, and have jibbed at the assertion with which MS. Halberstam concludes its treatment of the passage, that "all the aforementioned matters are the foundation of the world, and will be intelligible to those capable of understanding them,"[196] and he was (most probably) out of sympathy with the insistence of the *Shiʿur Qomah* to the effect that such things as these are the path to personal salvation. In the *Shiʿur Qomah* as transmitted in the *Sepher Raziʾel*,[197] R. Ishmael is represented as impressing upon his pupils that he and R. ʿAqibha "stand surety for the fact that whosoever knows this 'physical' description of the

190. See above, Note 153.
191. See Notes 156, 158.
192. See Notes 179, 180.
193. Mishnah, *Ḥaghighah*, ii, 1 (H. Danby's English translation, p. 213); BT *Ḥag*. 11b.
194. See above, Note 68, and Scholem, *Jewish Gnosticism*, p. 38.
195. עד שימלא את כריסו ש״ס ופוסקים Cf. Maimonides, *Hil. yesodhey torah*, 4, 13.
196. *MGWJ* (1893), p. 224: כל אלו הדברים שאמרנו יסוד עולם הן והמבין יבין
197. Musajoff, *Merkabhah Shelemah*, p. 38b (also quoted by Lieberman in Scholem, *Jewish Gnosticism*, appendix D, p. 123): אמר לו רבי ישמעאל לפני תלמידיו אני ורבי עקיבא ערבין בדבר זה שכל מי שהוא יודע שיעור זה של יוצרנו ושבחו של הקב״ה מובטח לו שהוא
See also Lieberman's note (p. 118, n. 3):

בן העולם הבא ובלבד שהוא שונה אותו במשנה בכל יום.

indicating that *mishnah* and its corresponding verb are applied elsewhere also to the mystical study of the Song of Songs: see above, Note 6.

proportions of our Creator, and the eulogy of the Holy One, Blessed be He, is assured of the future life, provided only that he studies [*shoneh*] it in the manner of mishnah teaching every day." The whole burden of the Targumist's own interpretation of the same verses was subtly to insinuate that, on the contrary, in the words of the punning application of Habakkuk 3:6 in the *Tana de-bey 'Eliyyahu*,[198] "whosoever studies [*shoneh*] halakic matters every day is assured of the future life."

Conclusions

What, in summary, are the conclusions to be drawn from the material here studied?

Some—but by no means all—of the sources for the Targum's exegesis of the Song of Songs can be identified in midrashic literature and the Talmuds, in part from Tannaitic sources;[199] and although its validity as an allegory of the relationship of God and Israel was established by R. ʿAqibha and may indeed have antedated him,[200] the surviving midrashic sources do not reveal any over-all picture of how the Song is to be interpreted so as to illustrate that relationship. Detailed interpretation on these lines is introduced by the Targum through its marked emphasis on Torah, and in particular on the Oral Torah, as the universe of discourse between God and Israel[201]—a theme round which is constructed a "history of salvation" from the beginning of the world until its future eschatological climax: a climax for which, anxious though the Deity may be to implement it forthwith, realism compels the Targumist to recognize that the time is not yet ripe.[202] That history is marked, on Israel's own level, no less by Israel's love of God and yearning for communion with Him than by Israel's own marked proclivity to sin, and also by the frustration of their endeavors by gentile hostility. But it is the practical institutions that flow from the notion of Torah—the tabernacle and Temple, its sacrificial cult, and the rabbinic learning and leadership of the Sanhedrin[203]—that effect atonement, provided always that a true repentance is forthcoming in response to God's unflagging appeal for it.[204] The underscoring by the Targum of the abiding value of these institutions constitutes a mute repudia-

198. BT *Niddah*, 73a and parallels: תנא דבי אליהו כל השונה הלכות בכל יום מובטח לו שהוא בן העולם הבא שנא׳ הלכות עולם לו א״ת הלִכות אלא הלָכות See also *Sedher 'Eliyyahu Zuṭa*, chap. 2 (ed. M. Friedmann, p. 173), and also Friedmann's introduction, chap. 5, p. 45, on BT *Meghillah* 28b.

199. See above, Note 14.

200. See Notes 5, 7, 8.

201. See Note 59.

202. See Notes 50f., Page 169, and Note 114.

203. See Notes 59, 60.

204. See Page 171; see 5:2; 7:1.

tion of Christian notions[205] of original sin, and atonement and salvation through Christ, to whose relationship with his Church Christian exegesis had reapplied the allegorical handling of the Song of Songs that it had inherited from the Synagogue.[206] This Christian tradition of exegesis, which ascends beyond Origen, acquired a classical status in the third century through Origen's now incompletely extant commentary to the Song, and is well reflected in the intact one, composed in the early fifth century, by Theodoret,[207] and the Targumist's reaction against it affords an adequate explanation for his own playing down of the role of the Messiah in the eschatological climax. The postulation of anti-Christian apologetic as the Targumist's motivation need not stand or fall with the possibility of indicating actual points of contact with extant Christian exegesis of the Song, even though there are in fact some possible instances of this.[208] Just as Paul's idea of the Church as the "new Israel" was sufficiently "in the air" to earn a counter-attack from Judaism based upon Israel's unique title to possession, in the Mishnah as epitomizing the Oral Torah, of God's "mystery,"[209] even so it would have been strange if, at any rate after Origen, the Synagogue had failed to react apologetically to the notion of the Church, as the Bride of Christ, being allegorically described as the maiden in the Song of Songs. And as in the case of the "new Israel" theme, refutation was, not surprisingly, essayed (possibly in the first instance by R. Yoḥanan)[210] by means of the theme of the Oral Torah, as exegetically discovered to be implicit in the very Biblical document upon which the Church was staking its own claim. But it would seem that by the time—after 636 C.E.[211]—that the Targum to the Song of Songs took shape,[212] the conventional rabbinic circles from which its author-redactor was drawn were viewing with misgivings the extravagances to which esoteric circles in Jewry were pressing their determination to read the praise by the maiden of her lover's physical charms as a description of the mystical "body" of God.[213] Scholem has both proved that the history of this exegetical endeavor goes back to Tannaitic times[214] and has also emphasized,[215] in characterizing it as a gnostic movement, the circumstance

205. See Notes 62f.
206. See Note 64.
207. See Note 68.
208. See Notes 70, 153; see Page 174.
209. *Pesiqta Rabbati*, ed. M. Friedmann (Vienna, 1885), 14b (*Wa-yehi beyom kalloth mosheh*, on Exodus 34: 1 and 27).
210. See Note 42.
211. See Notes 34, 39.
212. See Notes 18, 41.
213. See Note 117.
214. See Note 121.
215. *Jewish Gnosticism*, pp. 10f., 42.

that nevertheless it remained, paradoxically, within the orthodox orbit of Toranic observance (perhaps we ought to speak here rather of orthopraxy). Could it be that, by the time of the Targumist, an antinomian tendency had been manifesting itself within these Jewish circles— a tendency that would recall the distintegration of halakically ordained self-discipline which was one effect of the "eschatological" release of mystical energies within Jewry at the time of Shabbetai Ẓebi? Whether such be the case or no, there is no doubt that the Targumist's own exegesis of the crucial passage in the Song is remorselessly geared to an interpretation of the physical description as an allegory of the metaphysical significance of Torah, and of the functional significance of the Oral Torah in particular.[216] It is difficult to avoid the conclusion that he was, in fact, fighting a *Zweifrontenkrieg*, but fighting it on ground that had been carefully chosen by himself. The theme of Torah and of Israel's unique possession of the Oral Torah provided him, indeed, with the ideal weapon for use on either front, although it is to say the least probable that it was brandished more polemically against one front than against the other. The Christian interpretation had to be repudiated to the point of complete exclusion; Jewish esoteric extravagances had merely to be kept in their place, out of reach of the immature, whose stable diet must ever be the Oral Torah in its aspect of practical Halakhah.[217] The question of this Targum's influence on later Jewish exegesis and, in particular, its relationship to the Zohar are a separate matter and fall outside the scope of the present investigation. But the Targum's abiding influence in its own right is reflected in the various Jewish vernacular folk-versions—in Spanish,[218] Judaeo-Italian,[219] Judaeo-Arabic,[220] even Hebrew,[221] and probably other languages as well—some of which were still being printed in the nineteenth century and are still occasionally to be heard being chanted amid a Sephardic Jewish environment in the twentieth.

216. See Notes 138, 186-189.

217. See Note 195.

218. Frequently printed, mostly in Hebrew characters; for example, Venice, 1644. See A. Yaari, *A Catalogue of Judaeo-Spanish Books . . .* (in Hebrew; supplement to *Kirjath Sepher*, vol. 10) (Jerusalem, 1934), p. 3, who gives Venice, 1619, as the earliest edition known to him; he does not mention that of Venice, 1644.

219. Cecil Roth's manuscript collection, No. 532*, from Corfu, dated 1728 (translated from the Spanish).

220. A. Marx in *JQR*, N.S., 1: 65f. (1910-11), n. 10, describes a manuscript dated 1732 in the library of the Jewish Theological Seminary of America. This is apparently distinct from Melamed's *codices* C and D (see his edition of the Targum, pp. 11–13 [*JQR*, N.S., 9: 387-389 (1918-19)]); Melamed's D corresponds to a fourth manuscript mentioned by Marx, containing the Aramaic original of the Targum without the Arabic version. A text of the Arabic, printed at Leghorn in 1887, is in my possession.

221. MS. Cambridge University Library, Dd. 10.4.3, f. 4a, f; written in an Italian cursive hand. See S. M. Schiller-Szinessy, *Catalogue of the Hebrew MSS. Preserved in the University Library, Cambridge* (Cambridge, 1876), no. 68, p. 219.

APPENDIX

Bibliography and Abbreviations

Passages from the Bible cited in English translation are quoted from the Revised Standard Version (New York: Nelson, 1952), with a few slight changes tacitly introduced which, though required by the context, do not justify elaborate explanation.

The Targum to the Song of Songs

Text. The text I have used here is the critical edition produced by Raphael Hai Melamed (Philadelphia, 1921), which was printed first in the *Jewish Quarterly Review*, N.S., 9:377–410 (1918–19), 11:1–20 (1920–21), and 12:57–117 (1921–22). Melamed prints the text of a Yemenite manuscript in the British Museum (Or. 1302), and in his *apparatus criticus* compares five more Yemenite manuscripts (collectively referred to by me as *Codices*) as well as collating the text of P. de Lagarde's *Hagiographa Chaldaice* (Leipzig, 1873). Lagarde's text, in point of fact, merely re-establishes that of Daniel Bomberg's first Rabbinic Bible, edited by Felix Pratensis (Venice, 1517).

Translations. Latin versions of the Targum were printed in two of the Polyglot Bibles: that of Antwerp, 1569–73, and London, 1655-57.

A German translation was published by Wilhelm Riedel, in his *Die Auslegung des Hohenliedes in der jüdischen Gemeinde und der griechischen Kirche* (Leipzig: A. Deicher, 1898). (I regret that works by Salfeld, Vulliaud, and Ohly, of similar scope — see above, Note 4 — were inaccessible to me while I was preparing this article.)

A French translation by P. Vulliaud is included in his *Le Cantique des Cantiques...*, pp. 67–103 (see Note 4).

An English translation was published by Sir Hermann Gollancz in a miscellaneous volume entitled *The Targum to the Song of Songs . . .* (London: Luzac, 1908), and separately reprinted in 1909. I have prepared a fresh translation, based on Melamed's text, and I have utilized it in this article. It is my intention to publish it with the necessary editorial commentary and notes.

It should be noted that material within square brackets in translations from the Targum and other Hebrew, Greek, or Latin sources is either my own elaboration of what I consider to be implicit in the original document or else a change introduced on the authority of a text other than that here advertised as having been basically followed. The footnotes provide, in each case, the original of any matter cited in translation, together with the evidence, where required, for such changes.

In references to other rabbinic material the standard editions are cited, and critical ones where these exist and were accessible to me.

Patristic sources

PGL and *PL* refer respectively to J.-P. Migne, *Patrologia cursus completus, Series graeco-latina* and *Series latina* (Paris, various nineteenth-century dates).

Origen's *Homilies* and *Commentary* on the Song of Songs, of which the original Greek is extant in fragments only, were in part translated into Latin by Jerome and Rufinus respectively. They were reprinted in *PGL*, volume XIII, which reproduces the edition of Origen's works by C. and C.V. Delarue (Paris, 1733–59). References to *PGL* XIII are accordingly given for the reader's convenience, beside references to the critical text which has been followed here. The latter is cited by the name of its editor, W.A. Baehrens (*Origines Werke. Achter Band* [Die griechischen Christlichen Schriftsteller der ersten drei Jahrhunderte], Leipzig, 1925).

Theodoret's *Commentary* to the Song of Songs is cited from *PGL* LXXXI, which reproduces the edition of Theodoret by J.L. Schulze (Halle, 1769-74).

The Book of Job and Its Interpreters

By NAHUM N. GLATZER

This series of colloquia deals with transformations of Biblical motifs. If we apply the term "motif" to the Joban theme of the innocent sufferer who rises in rebellion against a seemingly unconcerned, unjust, arbitrary God, whom in the end he encounters as the Creator and Lord of the universe, then indeed the history of the interpretation of the Book of Job discloses a variety of types into which the figure of Job was transformed.

It should be said at the outset that the figure of Job, more so than others in the Bible, lent itself to a considerable diversity of interpretations. The reasons for this are to be sought in the variety of views exposed in the Book itself, in its position in the Biblical canon, and, last but not least, in the multifariousness of motifs employed in Talmudic-Midrashic literature in its presentation of Job[1] — a literature that assigns Job to diverse historical periods, and even permits the assumption that "Job never existed but is only a symbolic figure."[2] There are various opinions concerning the origin of Job, Hebrew or gentile, the purpose of his sufferings and the meaning of his query to God, the role of Satan, and the character of Job as compared with that of Abraham. Such latitude permitted remarkable freedom of interpretation and provoked the conception of a number of self-contained compositions in which Job appears as a symbolic representation of a particular attitude to God and world. As in the Biblical text, the change in Job's attitude is induced by the speeches of the Lord, whose argument was anticipated in the speeches of Elihu. In the exposition of these speeches, the medieval interpreters displayed their skill in adjusting the Biblical text to their own philosophical or theological opinions. Rarely was there an attempt to realize the radical nature of the Divine "reply" to the quest of Job; the difference between the view held by the author of the Book of Job and the views of the medieval commentators was too vast to allow serious consideration of the former.

The focusing of attention on the folk story of Job, of which the first two chapters and the prose conclusion are a part, gave rise to a literature in which Job became the symbol of a saint who remains steadfast throughout his

1. Especially BT *Baba Bathra* 14b–16b; Mishnah *Sotah* V, 5: BT *Sotah* 31a; PT *Sotah* 20d; *Tanḥuma Noah* 5, *Tanḥuma Vayera* 5; *Tanḥuma* (ed. Buber), *Vayishlaḥ* 8, pp. 116f.; *Sifre* 32, on Deut. 6: 5, ed. Friedmann, 73a; *Pesiḳta Rabbati* 165a; *Genesis Rabbah* XLIX, 17, *Numbers Rabbah* XIV, 7; *Deuteronomy Rabbah* II, 3; *Aboth de-R. Nathan* II, 14, 43 and 45.

2. *Mashal haya;* BT *Baba Bathra* 15a.

sufferings. Though not in the mainstream of tradition, this treatment is, nevertheless, important in the context of Job interpretation. Some aspects of such a reading of Job are to be found in the commentaries such as Rashi's, Saadya's and Samuel Masnut's.

The major trend of Jewish tradition is represented by the Bible commentators and religious philosophers who acknowledge some form of rebellion, heresy, or, at least, an imperfection on the part of Job; in their interpretations the hero's reform, or conversion, appears then in an exposition of the speeches of Elihu (chapters 32-37) and of God (chapters 38-41).

Apart from these presentations, the cycle of themes is to be considered that forms the Zoharic interpretation of Job. There is also a transformation of the Job motif in the Sabbatian theology,[3] which, however, will not concern us here.

The entire literature covers a wide range of types, from Job the saint, via Job the rebel, Job the dualist, the man lacking in knowledge, the Aristotelian denier of providence, the man confusing God and Satan, the determinist, the man who failed to give Satan his due, Job the scapegoat, to Job the prototype of the Sabbatian Messiah. This study will survey extra-Talmudic Jewish literature, from the "Testament of Job" to about 1600. Obviously both survey and analysis will be extremely brief.

I

Job the saint

The best documentation of Job as saint is the so-called "Testament of Job." Its Hebrew original, composed probably in the first pre-Christian century, is lost; two Greek versions, which incorporate later changes and additions, each represented by one manuscript, became known in the nineteenth century.[4]

The Job of the "Testament" is not on trial because of a pact between God and Satan. This Job, or Jobab, King of Edom, had destroyed a venerated idol, the handiwork of Satan. He knew that by this action he would provoke the wrath of Satan and invite countless afflictions upon himself; he knew as well that God would restore his fortune if he endured. He was ready. "I shall from love of God endure until death all that will come upon me and I shall not shrink back." The friends, fellow kings, seeing Job's misfortune, lost their faith, but Job rose to the defense of God. He rejected the ministrations

3. See Hayyim Wirshubsky, "Ha-theologia ha-shabtait shel Nathan ha-ʿAzati," *Keneseth*, 8: 235f. (1943), and G. Scholem, *Be-ʿiqvoth ha-mashiaḥ* (Jerusalem, 1944).

4. "Testament of Job," edited and translated by K. Kohler, in *Semitic Studies in Memory of Alexander Kohut* (Berlin, 1897).

of physicians, asserting that his cure would come from God. He prohibited a search for the bones of his children, declaring, "They are in the keeping of their Maker." Elihu's role in the "Testament" differs radically from the role assigned to him by the mainstream of traditional interpretation. In the "Testament" Elihu is "imbued with the spirit of Satan."[5] Yet, in passages reminiscent of the Elihu speeches in the Book, he chastises Job for his self-pride. Finally God appears "from a whirlwind and clouds" (as in the Septuagint to 38:1) to pardon the three friends and to condemn Elihu, "for he has loved the beauty of the serpent." Job is returned to his original state.

Job as the exemplar of perfect faith appears also in *Aboth de-Rabbi Nathan* (Version I, Addendum II). The version of the Job folk tale as related there is a compilation from various sources. As in the Biblical story, Satan is given permission to test Job's faith; as in the "Testament of Job," the hero remains steadfast, "acknowledging and praising the Lord for all his attributes," until "all the world believed that there is none like him in all the land." "He has not sinned, not even with the words of his mouth and has not turned his heart" from God. This latter motif seems to be a repudiation of the tradition (*Baba Bathra* 16a) that Job, though he "did not sin with his lips," as the Biblical text indicates (2:10), did sin with his heart. The tradition upholding Job as a symbol of unquestioning faith had to assert itself against the tendency of those interpreters who were impelled to insist on the sinfulness of Job in order to justify the acts of God.

The conclusion of the Job story in *Aboth de-Rabbi Nathan* comes from a third source. Satan, who has failed to alienate Job's faith, was condemned by God and cast down from heaven. God in his mercy cures Job, whose afflictions last one full year — symbolic of a perfect unit of time.

The early Christian church seems to have followed the motif of Job the saint. The Epistle of James, head of the Church of Jerusalem, cites Job (and the prophets, but not Jesus) as prototypes of patient endurance (5:11). The Syriac version of the "Apocalypsis Pauli" of the end of the fourth century points in the same direction.[6] In it, Satan tries daily to seduce Job into apostasy, but Job remains constant in his faith and love, expecting his recompense in the World to Come.

Bishop Theodore of Mopsuestia (died 428), disciple of Diodorus of Tarsus and the most influential teacher of the school of Antioch, speaks of an "outstanding and much esteemed story of the saintly Job, retold orally by everybody in a similar form, not only among Israelite people but also by

5. Cf. PT *Sotah* 20d, where Elihu is identified with Balaam.

6. Given in English in Constantin Tischendorf, *Apocalypses Apocryphae* (Leipzig, 1866), pp. 66f.

others."[7] He believed this popular tale of Job the saint to be the true story, adjudging the Biblical Book of Job to be a mere literary product created by an author anxious to display his knowledge and to gain repute. The speeches attributed to Job by the Biblical author, Bishop Theodore considered unbefitting a man "who mastered his life with great wisdom and virtue and piety."

Of interest is also the Moslem version of the folk tale of Job the saint, which is documented by two late manuscripts, one dating from about 1785, the other from about 1840; both, apparently copied in Egypt, are based on a single original.[8] One of the manuscripts refers to Wahb and Kaʿb-el-aḥbar as the authorities for the tale; both were Yemenite Jews, converted to Islam. Wahb died after A.H. 110, Kaʿb in A.H. 32.[9] In this tale, Satan (Iblīs), angered by the lack of veneration accorded him by Job and his wife, receives permission to test Job's faith. This motif for Satan's action is reminiscent of the reason given in the "Testament of Job" and, as we shall note later, by the Zohar.

Job's faith is unshakable. Iblīs finds him in a mosque, praying: "Behold, the misfortune that Thou hast brought upon me only served to increase my gratitude and my patience," an attitude by which he acknowledges the example of the prophets and messengers of God. He calls himself "the servant of his Master and His messenger" and proclaims his readiness to satisfy his hunger by calling upon His name and his thirst by praising Him. As in the "Testament of Job" the hero refuses to be cured by a physician. God Himself, partly through the mediation of Gabriel, cures Job by a fruit from Paradise — a quince — and paradisiac garments.[10]

II

The medieval Bible exegetes, who confronted the Book of Job in its entirety, could not concentrate on the motif of Job the saint, which confines the reader's view to the prose story and the epilogue of the Book. The medieval

7. G. D. Mansi, *Sacrorum conciliorum nova et amplissima collectio* (Venice, 1759–98), IX, 223–225.

8. Naftali Apt, *Die Hiobserzählung in der arabischen Literatur. Erster Teil* (Kirchhain, N. L., 1913). Published dissertation, University of Heidelberg.

9. Duncan B. Macdonald, "Some External Evidence on the Original Form of the Legend of Job," *American Journal of Semitic Languages and Literatures*, 14: 146, n. 6 (1898). Macdonald offers a translation of the Arabic story of Job in Thaʿlabi's "Stories of the Prophets" (early eleventh century), partly based on traditions that originated with Wahb and Kaʿb.

10. The combination of the Job theme with one or another motif of the Biblical Adam story appears too frequently in the Job literature to be dismissed as a coincidence. The nature of the relationship between the two complexes and its relevance to the interpretation of the Book of Job would require a separate study.

commentator had to do justice to those portions of the Book in which Job appears to be challenging God's justice, to regard Him as hostile to man, and as unwilling to give answer to man's insistent queries. In describing Job's character, the commentator had to decide what measure of rebellion to ascribe to Job, or, as was the case in many commentaries, what tradition with regard to Job's rebelliousness to follow, or whether to remove the stigma of rebellion in order to absolve a Biblical hero from offending divinity. Obviously, the point of view assumed by the commentator determined the details of his exegesis.

In the sections that follow some of the main medieval views of Job will be reviewed as they appear in the commentaries.

1. *Job the imperfectly pious man*

The view of Job as imperfectly pious is best represented by Rashi (Rabbi Solomon ben Isaac, 1040-1105), who seems to have composed his Job commentary in the latter part of his active life; the master's hand stopped at 40:20; his commentary was completed by others and the entire work emended by disciples and copyists.[11]

Rashi's Job did not dare to rise in protest against divinity. His fear of God, though imperfect (comment on 1:2), was deep-seated. In his comments on chapter 9, Rashi greatly modified Job's rebellious utterances. Rather than expressing Job's protestation, this chapter, in Rashi's opinion, denotes Job's submission in a spirit of fear of God. Thus, to the text, "God will not withdraw his anger" (9:13), Rashi added the words, "from fear of man"; to the text, "Yet would I not believe that He would hearken unto my voice" (9:16), he added, "because of my fear of Him, and how could I not fear Him"; to the text, "Though I be righteous, mine own mouth shall condemn me" (9:20), he added, "fear [of Him] would silence my voice." On 13:15 Rashi commented: " 'Though he slay me' I shall not separate myself from Him and I shall always trust in Him; therefore, there is no rebellion and transgression in my words." And on the verse that follows he commented: "As I am wholly with Him, so is He salvation to me," referring the word *hu* not to the second part of the verse, but to God.

Yet, Job's piety was imperfect. He said that God "destroyeth the innocent and the wicked" (9:22) and asked God not to let the Divine terror make him afraid (13:21). Worse still, he had talked too much and by his verbosity he had upset God's plan "to have the divine name rest upon him" (comment on 38:2). These imperfections required correction; this was achieved by

11. The problem of the variant readings has been discussed by Isaac Maarsen, "Raschis Kommentar zu Sprüche und Job," *Monatsschrift für Geschichte und Wissenschaft des Judentums*, 83: 442-456 (1939).

Elihu's remark on man's insignificance in the cosmos (comment on 33:12) and by God's reference to Abraham, whose piety was perfect because unquestioning.[12]

Another example of an interpretation of Job as the symbol of an imperfectly pious man is the Job commentary of Joseph Kara, the northern French Bible exegete (eleventh to twelfth century).[13] His Job, though on the whole a just man (comment on 12:4), is helpless before the evil urge and conscious of his sinfulness before God (comments on 7:20 and 9:20). He wonders why the all-knowing God had to test him[14] of whose trust in Him He must have been aware (comment on 13:15). Yet, despite his suffering, he feels certain that God will be his salvation (comment on 13:16). Elihu extols both God's independence from man's actions and His compassion for man (comments on 35:9f. and 36:26). "Your suffering came upon you to save your soul from darkness... He reproves you because He loves you" (comment on 33:24). The speeches of God elaborate on Elihu's statement on Divine independence (comment on 38:4ff.) and His concern with His creation. "I am full of compassion for the beasts and animals that live in deserts and I feed them, and all the more for man created in [My] image and likeness" (comment on 38:26f.). This is a Job who had no reason to rebel, for he never really doubted God's providence. It required but little effort to dispel his confusion and restore his perfect faith. The problem of evil was not an issue in Kara's commentary.

A similar interpretation of Job as imperfectly pious is provided by *Maʿayan Gannim*, a midrash on Job by Samuel ben Nissim Masnut of Aleppo, who is known to have been visited by Judah al-Ḥarizi in the second decade of the thirteenth century.[15] This work[16] is, except for the author's own notes,

12. In Rashi's interpretation of Job 38: 2, Job says: "Had I know your plan I would not have multiplied words!" Whereupon God reminds him of Abraham "who did not know [My plan] yet stood the ten [trials]." Another significant reference to Abraham is Rashi's comment on 1: 6–7, where Satan's accusation of Job is understood as motivated by the Tempter's meritorious desire to protect the memory of Abraham's righteousness (cf. BT *Baba Bathra* 15b).

13. Most of Kara's commentaries on Biblical books were soon forgotten, and they have been published only in the modern period. The commentary to Job was printed from a manuscript containing the major parts of the commentaries, written in Rome at the end of the thirteenth century and acquired in 1853 by the Breslau Jewish Theological Seminary. It appeared in *Monatsschrift für Geschichte und Wissenschaft des Judentums*, volumes 5–7 (1856–1858); unfortunately, the text was carelessly copied and the reading presents unnecessary difficulties.

14. Job's suffering as a test of his piety is the interpretation also of *Sefer Ḥasidim*, 1512.

15. *Taḥkemoni* (ed. Paul de Lagarde, 2nd ed., Hannover, 1924), XLVI, 173.

16. *Majan-Gannim, Commentar zu Job* (Berlin, 1889), edited by Salomon Buber from a manuscript in the Bodleian Library. Leopold Zunz lists the author in his *Literaturgeschichte der synagogalen Poesie* (Berlin, 1867), p. 597, incorrectly quoted by Buber as *Zur Literatur und Geschichte* (introduction to *Maʿayan Gannim*, VI).

largely a compilation from the Targum (in its two versions),[17] Talmud and Midrash, Ibn Ezra, and, to a large measure, Rashi.[18]

Masnut's Job was allowed by God to be tested by Satan, who feared that Job's piety might cause God to forget the piety of Abraham (compare *Baba Bathra* 14b). Throughout his ordeal Job remained a man of faith. His harsh, provocative statements — for example, in chapter 9 Masnut attributes to events of the past, to Pharaoh (verse 4), to Sodom and Gomorrah (verse 5), and the like. Historically localized, the verses bespeak the well-ordered and purposeful Divine power, rather than a blind, terrorizing force. For his description of Job's deep faith, Masnut borrowed extensively from Rashi's commentary.[19] It is a humble, self-effacing Job that he presents. "I do not rely on my prayer and on myself, because I am not worthy that He answer me and hearken unto my voice" (comment on 9:16). "I cannot justify myself in order to accuse Him, because He is high above all glory and praise" (comment on 9:22). Thus the commentary turned Job's assertion of the utter futility of man's argument into a pious person's humble recognition of God's mercy. Job's friends were unable to stand their ground before God (comment on 27:2); their apparent justification of God was, in reality, heresy (comment on 32:4).

It was only his suffering that led Job to believe that God considered him to be His enemy (13:24). According to the Talmudic dictum, a sufferer is not to be held responsible for his outbursts (comment on 28:26). Yet Job's failure to understand God's ways called for rectification. The Lord's address "made him realize that he had no knowledge and that he was unable to fathom the ways of God" (comment on 38:1). Once "he had been made to know what he had not known," Job regretted his doubts that had interfered with his piety and his repentance was complete (comment on 42:2). Addressed by God, he reached "true understanding" (comment on 42:6).[20]

17. The original version of the extant Targum, composed in Palestine probably in the fourth or fifth century, reduced the impact of provocative or obscure passages of the text by referring them to events of the Biblical past or by reading into them meanings suggested by rabbinic thought. This version was revised in the eighth or ninth century by a translator who planned to restore the plain meaning of the text, at least in the case of crucial sentences. His work is evident in forty-six places, where the older version is replaced by the reviser's own, to which, in most instances at least, he appended the original rendition, marking it *targum 'aḥer*. Four verses record a third rendition. Cf. Wilhelm Bacher's discussion of the two versions in "Das Targum zu Hiob," *Monatsschrift für Geschichte und Wissenschaft des Judentums*, 20: 208–223 (1871). Bacher (pp. 283f.) suggested that the author of the revision lived in Italy.

18. In some of his own notes, Masnut draws upon his knowledge of Arabic. His reliance, in the main, on the Talmudic-Midrashic material justifies his calling his book a midrash; indeed, it takes the place of a classical midrash on the Book of Job. Masnut mentions the rabbinic authorities by name, but gives no references to sources.

19. Cf. Rashi on 9: 4, 5, 11, 13, 15, 16, whose terse notes he expands. For Masnut on 9:22, *baʿaverah*, read with Rashi *baʿavurah*.

20. The friends were reprimanded, for they did not undergo a change of heart, but continued their arguments against Job (comment on 42: 7).

Compositions such as Rashi's, Kara's, and Masnut's failed to achieve an internal unity. They describe Job as a completely devout man, then establish, somewhat arbitrarily and inconsistently, his error, in order to justify the obvious correction that is the purpose of the Lord's speeches. One notes that the authors would have preferred to concentrate on the piety of Job. It is the evidence of the text that compelled them to picture this piety as imperfect.

2. *Job the rebel*

The interpretation of Job as a rebel, a doubter of Divine justice in the distribution of good and evil, is most poignantly presented by Abraham ibn Ezra (1092-1167). His commentary on Job, written in Rome about 1140, made abundant use of his predecessors; he followed Saadya Gaon in some one hundred instances (though he quotes him only six times); in his explanations of words he is dependent on Jonah ibn Janāḥ, whom, however, he mentions only once.[21] Profiat Duran complained that Ibn Ezra "composed attractive works," but that "there is not much in them that is new."[22] What is, however, novel in Ibn Ezra's commentary on Job is his remark that much of the difficulty in interpreting the text stems from the fact that our Book is a translation (comment on 2:11).[23] Moreover, it is remarkable that, especially in his lengthy epilogue to the commentary, Ibn Ezra manifested a profound interest in the book as a whole, over and above exegesis, and let himself be guided by its insight, even where this insight was at variance with his own philosophy.

In Ibn Ezra's view Job became a rebel, protesting against the unjust Divine rule, when he, an innocent man, was made to suffer; consequently, he could not but think that God considered man to be His enemy. He was unable to believe that in afflicting a righteous man a just God could have a purpose in mind. It was Elihu who prepared the way for Job's conversion from a rebellious skeptic to a humble man of faith; he accomplished this by making Job aware of the mysterious essence of the acts of God both in nature and in the human world; man must suffer and be silent.

Elihu's argument was perfected in the speeches of the Lord. Whether or not he was fully conscious of the importance of his observation, Ibn Ezra pointed to the key phrase in these speeches: "Knowest thou... ?" — a question addressed to man, who in self-pride has arrogated to himself knowledge. The references in these speeches to the mighty creatures were intended,

21. Julius Galliner, *Abraham ibn Esra's Hiobkommentar auf seine Quellen untersucht* (Berlin, 1901), pp. 18, 30, *et passim*.

22. *Maʿase 'Efod*, p. 44.

23. Ibn Ezra states this in conscious opposition to the Talmudic opinion that attributed the authorship to Moses (BT *Baba Bathra* 14b).

according to Ibn Ezra, to demonstrate man's limited dominion on earth, and, by implication, his impotence in confronting the higher realms.

Ibn Ezra's own view on evil—namely, that it is occasioned by the imperfection of matter and that God is the author of good only—did not enter into his discussion of Job. Rather, he emphasized the limits of human knowledge, which prevent man from comprehending the universe he inhabits. It is the presumption of knowledge, he argued, that posits certain aspects of existence as evil and that results in skepticism.

Job as rebel against God appears also in the work of Naḥmanides (Moses ben Naḥman, 1194-1270?), both in his Job commentary[24] and in his treatise *Shaʿar ha-Gemul*, which is the concluding chapter of his *Torath ha-Adam*.[25]

In the view of Naḥmanides, the afflicted hero (who could not realize that his faith was being tested) assumed that man's fate is not directed by God but determined by the constellations; God considers man too insignificant to merit His attention; He is too great to be concerned with man.[26] Therefore, Job concluded, both the righteous and the wicked are at the mercy of chance (commentary, preface to chapter 3, and comments on 9:2 and 9:22). He admitted the proposition that Divine providence extends only to the species, desiring their preservation, but not to the individual man, who is too lowly in God's eyes.[27] Job "was inclined to heresy"[28] and rebelled against a God who ignored individual man and allowed Job, a righteous man, to meet an undeserved fate.

In his answer to Job, Naḥmanides differed significantly from Ibn Ezra. Whereas the latter pointed to the limits of human knowledge, Naḥmanides, the mystic, referred the rebel to a "world of souls" (*ʿolam ha-neshamoth*) in which the ills of the material world would be resolved. With the mystic's caution he alluded to the transmigration of souls, "a deep mystery" accessible not to a thinker but to the initiate alone.[29] By focusing attention on the soul — over which Satan has no dominion, as our author

24. Published in the rabbinical Bibles (Venice, 1517, and Amsterdam, 1724–27).

25. First published in Constantinople in 1519; *Shaʿar ha-Gemul* appeared in separate editions in Naples in 1490, and Ferrara in 1556.

26. The extensive introduction to the commentary places the Job issue into the context of the general problem of Divine providence. Since the Torah postulates God's providential knowledge and care for the individual, a tenet that is, however, often contradicted by human experience, Scripture was bound to deal with the problem. In Psalm 73 the solution is left in a state of ambiguity, whereas the Book of Job contains the full answer. Following the Talmudic tradition, Naḥmanides considered the Book to be the work of Moses, who wrote it on command from God, just as he wrote the Book of Genesis.

27. *Shaʿar ha-Gemul* (Ferrara, 1556), p. 11.

28. *Ibid.*, p. 15.

29. Cf. Naḥmanides' similarly veiled reference to transmigration in his commentary on Gen. 38: 8.

interprets Job 2:6 — Elihu impelled Job to realize that the thesis of the undeserved suffering of the righteous man could not be maintained (commentary, introduction and comment on 33:30). Man's soul thus having been taken care of, Job apprehended that God "watches over His world and exercises providence over it." Indeed, "all terrestrial beings have been created for the sake of man, because none of them know the Creator but he" (comment on 36:2). Of Job's three friends it was Zophar (in modern opinion, the least profound of the three) who contributed to the solution of the problem created by "the prosperity of the wicked": all existence evidences both "manifest wisdom" and "hidden wisdom" and no man can pass judgment on the affairs of the world; the good fortune of the wicked may be a sign of the Creator's mercy. [30]

While Zophar and Elihu suggested nonrational notions ("the world of the souls" and "hidden wisdom"), the speeches of God offered what must have appeared to Naḥmanides to be logical proof. God's account of the marvels of creation — intended in the Biblical text as a repudiation of man's proud assertion of knowledge and power — was understood by Naḥmanides as giving Job proof of providence and the good order and guidance in the universe at large and as intended to convince Job by inference that, this being the case, there must be still greater design and purpose in the creation of the higher being, man; the details of this order, however, must remain a mystery which human reason cannot penetrate. [31]

Job, according to Naḥmanides, is the symbol of a man whose rebellion resulted from his attempt to explain good and evil by his own reason. Gradually he was made aware of the aspect of the mysterious in the world and he "returned to his Creator," perceiving that everything is under a rule of righteousness and mercy. [32] Accepting as a basis that which he could grasp through reason, he discerned measure and justice in "what is distant and hidden."[33]

30. *Shaʿar ha-Gemul*, pp. 12–14. Among the parallels between this treatise and the Job commentary are the references to Psalm 73; to the fate of Rabbi Akiba; to the influence of constellation on human life; to the essential difference between the issue of "the righteous man who suffers" and "the wicked who prospers," and to the solution proposed by Elihu. One of the major differences is the evaluation of the Lord's speeches.

31. *Shaʿar ha-Gemul*, p. 16.

32. *Ibid.*, pp. 16f.

33. *Ibid.*, p. 17. In his article "Über die Authentie des Commentars Nachmani's zum Buche Job" (*Monatsschrift für Geschichte und Wissenschaft des Judentums*, 17: 449–458 [1868]), Zacharias Frankel noticed some discrepancies between Naḥmanides' Job commentary and his other writings and concluded that this commentary was the work of a later mystic who ingeniously used the master's style and attributed it to him. Frankel thought to have found convincing proof for his assertion in Naḥmanides' failure to formulate Elihu's theory in *Shaʿar ha-Gemul*, whereas the commentary is more explicit on this point. From a remark of Gersonides in the introduction to his Job commentary (to the effect that, except for Maimonides, no interpreter had analyzed the opinions posited in the Book of Job)

Naḥmanides' reading of Job reappeared in *Kad ha-Qemaḥ*, a manual of religious thought by the Spanish Bible commentator Baḥya ben Asher ibn Ḥalāwa (died 1340).[34] The idea of the transmigration of souls, to which Naḥmanides referred with considerable caution and subtility, appeared in Baḥya's argument quite explicitly formulated.[35]

Transmigration, according to Baḥya, implies special providence and establishes man as being superior to other creatures, who were created but for the sake of man. To know this is true wisdom, in the name of which Elihu speaks,[36] while Job, rebellious by denying providence, "multiplieth words without knowledge" (Job 35:16).[37] Elaborating on Naḥmanides' interpretation of the speeches of God, Baḥya understood them as revealing both the Divine attributes of mercy and of justice, the former in chapters 38 and 39, the latter in chapters 40 and 41, which describe the giant creatures, Behemoth and Leviathan. As does transmigration, so too creation, depicted in the speeches of God, implies providence, both universal and individual.[38]

The rebel in Job was converted by the gift of knowledge. After having been confronted by Elihu and the Lord, Job realized that he could not have knowledge of God's wonders "unless He, in His mercy, makes them known to him."[39] The emphasis by Baḥya on the motif of knowledge, clearly intended by the Biblical text, is significant; it was often overlooked in medieval Jewish exegesis.[40]

Rebellion against a God who withholds His providence from individual

Frankel concluded that the author of the pseudo-Naḥmanides, who did offer such an analysis, must have written after Gersonides. But, as already pointed out by Bela Bernstein (*Die Schrifterklärung des Bachja b. Ascher ibn Chalâwa und ihre Quellen* [Berlin, 1891], p. 15, n. 36), Frankel's argument is refuted by the testimony of Baḥya ben Asher, who used Naḥmanides' commentary in his own *Kad ha-Qemaḥ* and, being close to Naḥmanides' period and his doctrines, must have been sure of the identity of the true author. As to Frankel's other charge: the change in the measure of reluctance to reveal what is hidden should not be found astonishing in the writings of a mystic. Naḥmanides' Job commentary is quoted also in *Sefer ha-Emunoth* by Shemtov ibn Shemtov (Ferrara, 1557), VII, 3.

34. *Kad ha-Qemaḥ*, a critical edition by Hayyim Breit, based on manuscripts in Oxford and Parma (Lemberg, 1880).

35. *Kad ha-Qemaḥ* 73b. For Baḥya's reference to Naḥmanides as his source, see 68a. He took over Naḥmanides' introductions to, and interpretative summaries of, the Book's sections, while omitting the exegesis of the text.

36. Elihu, like the friends and Job himself, came from the seed of Abraham, "the root of faith" (*Kad ha-Qemaḥ* 69b, 73a).

37. *Kad ha-Qemaḥ* 74a.

38. *Ibid.*, 74b-76a.

39. *Ibid.*, 76a, commenting on Job 42: 4.

40. Equally significant is the remark that the Book of Job corresponds to the Book of Genesis; both teach the creation of the world and providence; both refer to God predominantly as *'elohim*, thus emphasizing the attribute of Divine justice. Baḥya ben Asher's *Sova' Semaḥot* (Amsterdam, 1768), presented on the title page as a commentary on Job, is only an abridgment of certain sections of *Kad ha-Qemaḥ* and the author's *Shulḥan 'Arba'*, an ethico-religious treatise.

man is the motif also of the Job interpretation of Meir, son of Isaac Arama (1460-1545), in his *Meir 'Iyyov*. This commentary on Job was completed in 1505-1506, some thirteen years after the author and his father, exiles from Spain, found refuge in Naples.[41] According to Arama, who on this point follows an established pattern, Job's affliction impelled him to abandon his original faith[42] and adopt the "despicable belief" (*ha-'emunah ha-megunah*) in an unconcerned God.[43] After Elihu's powerful assertion of providence[44] came the definitive answer from God.[45] In contradistinction to the Greek mode of thinking, says Arama in interpreting chapters 38 and those that follow, Creation testifies to Divine closeness to, and concern for, all creatures, and especially for man.[46] In this exposition Arama, following older traditions, is aided by the rendition of Job 38:36, *batuḥoth* by "reins," and of *sekhvi* by "heart," implying that the very existence of a thinking being is proof of God's nearness to man's intellectual self.[47] In response Job bows to this supreme evidence of providential care inherent in creation and sustaining the universe.[48]

It may be suggested that the author's experience of the expulsion of 1492 determined his choice of the Book of Job as the first of his commentaries, to be followed by interpretations of Psalms, Isaiah, Jeremiah, Canticles, and the (unpublished) commentary on the Pentateuch. Arama was, no doubt, searching for an affirmation of his own faith and of its source, the element of the personal concern of God — and read this faith into the majestically neutral, objective speeches of God. Thus, to him, the Book of Job is "in its beginning, its end, and all of it [dedicated to the] fear of Heaven."[49]

3. *Job the dualist*

Since human suffering cannot be ascribed to God, "who is good and who causes good," the existence of a second god must be assumed, a god who is the

41. The date appears in the concluding note to the book, printed in Salonica in 1517. The references that follow are according to the Venice edition of 1567.

42. Arama interpreted Job 19: 25 as referring to Job's faith during the years of well-being and the rest of the sentence as indicating his current state.

43. *Meir 'Iyyov* 57b f. In Arama's interpretation, Eliphaz considers Job's suffering as either a test of piety or a chastisement for sins, since no man is perfect; the suffering of the pious is, therefore, a providential act and rebellious man is simply in error (*Meir 'Iyyov* 18a f. on Job 4 and 5). Bildad goes a step further by denying that there is ever a case of a righteous man suffering without reason (*Meir 'Iyyov* 23b on Job 8).

44. *Meir 'Iyyov* 93b and 111a.

45. After Elihu's defense of providence no further argument was needed, Arama maintains; God appeared only in response to Job's quest to be addressed by his Creator.

46. *Meir 'Iyyov* 111a f.

47. *Ibid.*, 115a.

48. *Ibid.*, 122a.

49. *Ibid.*, concluding note.

origin of evil and who works destruction, especially if aided by the constellations and not opposed by the good God. In the opinion of Obadiah Sforno (*circa* 1475–1550), Job symbolizes this trend of thinking. In his commentary on Job, *Mishpat Ṣedeq*,[50] Sforno presented a Job who rises in anger against this good God, Who, because of His greatness, disregards the rights of human kind and thus fails to interfere with the evil force.

Again the answer [51] was provided in chapter 38 and those that follow, which Sforno, like others before him, interpreted as testimony not of God's wondrous majesty, but of His concern for individual man. This concern is manifest in the grant of the power of intellect to man (by which he becomes similar to his Creator) — a motif emphasized by Gersonides and Joseph Albo — and in God's exercise of individual providence, which is not bound to the laws of nature. God removed Behemoth and Leviathan to faraway regions, for otherwise man would have been unable to cope with them. The nonmechanical and seemingly unjust adminstration of retribution is a means of safeguarding man's freedom of choice. By such clarification God convinced Job that there is no "evil god who causes all ills." God "delighteth in mercy."[52] However, evil has its rightful place in the universe (comment on 40:5), since everything issues from the one, good God, who comprises both good and evil (comment on 42: 2). The answer to the problem of evil suggested by dualism is refuted by the providential revelation of the one God.

III

The medieval Jewish philosopher who dealt with Job as a theological problem enjoyed greater freedom than the Bible commentator, who, in addition, was responsible for the very text of the Book. However, no clear-cut dividing line can be drawn between the two: Saadya, for example, was both commentator and philosopher. But it can be stated that in such cases the author's philosophical concerns determine his work as exegete; the philosopher's freedom of movement, however circumscribed, is discernible in his commentary. Again, as in the case of the Biblical expositors, so too in the works of the philosophers, Job became a symbol of distinct approaches to the problem of evil and to divine justice.

50. *Mishpat Ṣedeq* (Venice, 1589), printed together with Simeon Duran's *'Ohev Mishpat*.

51. The friends, according to Arama, explained Job's fate as vicarious suffering for the sin of his generation, or as punishment for his lack of loving-kindness toward the poor or chastisement for his presumptuous wish to reason with God, or as occasioned by the sin of Adam or "the instigation of the serpent." Elihu argued that God deviates from the course of nature in order to fulfill the needs of man, who is the purpose of creation; the mighty movements of the spheres are designed to benefit man, transitory though he be (*Mishpat Ṣedeq*, introduction).

52. *Mishpat Ṣedeq*, introduction, 3b–6a.

1. *Job the pious man in search of an answer*

Saadya Gaon (died 942), deeply concerned with the purity of the God concept, could not admit the notion of rebelliousness in his presentation of Job. His translation and interpretation of the Book of Job, which is one of the parts preserved from his *tafsīr*, bears the title *Kitāb al-Taʿdīl* (Book of Theodicy),[53] in which the all-pervading, unlimited grace (*djūd*) of God is to be demonstrated. Neither Job nor his friends doubted the justice of God.[54] Only, as had Moses and Jeremiah before him, Job wanted to be informed of the cause of his affliction. But, like them, he did not receive a direct answer (comment on 37: 24). "God is too lofty and exalted in His power to answer man word for word" (comment on 33: 13-15). God is completely independent of man; neither will man's good deeds profit, nor his iniquity harm Him (comment on 35: 12-15). In His speech, God used the image of Leviathan as indication of His unlimited power. Job was impelled to realize that human knowledge is unable to fathom "the subtle rule of the Wise, exalted be He, and His affairs" (comment on 42: 6). By scrupulously avoiding anthropomorphisms[55] and by using various exegetical devices, Saadya kept his good, just, and gracious God far removed from unseemly contact with the human world.

We note that Saadya did justice to the original meaning of Job 38 and the following chapters, a section which many commentators turned into a document of individual providence. In fact, Saadya tended to interpret the entire Book in the light of its concluding speeches. Job the pious man did not question Divine justice and providence but sought knowledge; the answer, therefore, was but a reference to the source of all knowledge.

Saadya returned to the Job problem in chapter five of his *'Emunoth ve-Deʿoth*.[56] The suffering inflicted on the pious man is to be understood as

53. A critical edition, by Joseph Derenbourg, with notes by W. Bacher, appeared as volume V of the *Œuvres complètes de R. Saadia* (Paris, 1899). For a critical analysis of the translation, see Roman Ecker, *Die arabische Job-Übersetzung des Gaon Saadja ben Josef al-Fajjumi* (Munich, 1962). Cf. also Erwin I. J. Rosenthal, "Saadya's Exegesis of the Book of Job," *Saadya Studies* (Manchester, 1943).

54. The three friends, however, maintain a narrow view of suffering (which, according to Saadya, may befall one for the sake of moral and intellectual instruction, or as an act of purification from sin, or as a test and examination of faith). Only Elihu, who pointed to "test and examination" as the cause of Job's suffering, had the correct concept. Saadya considered the three speeches of Elihu (Job 32–35) to be the answer to three speeches by Job (comment on 35: 16).

55. In circumventing anthropomorphisms, Saadya went far beyond the Targum, which he used and on which he was in a large measure dependent. Cf. the list in Rosenthal, pp. 188–191. However, Abraham ibn Daud (*Ha-'Emunah ha-Ramah* [Frankfurt am Main, 1852], p. 89) found that "the interpreter" was not thorough enough. Jakob Guttmann, *Die Religionsphilosophie des Abraham ibn Daud* (Göttingen, 1879), p. 31, identified "the interpreter" as Saadya.

56. This chapter circulated in the Middle Ages as a separate treatise, known as *Sefer ha-Teshuvah* (The Book of Repentance).

punishment for whatever transgressions he committed, or, as in the case of Job, as a test visited upon a man whom God knows beforehand to have the strength to bear it and remain faithful. Such a trial "enables mankind to realize that God has not chosen a pious man gratuitously."[57] Job passed the test. Unlike the Biblical Job, Saadya's did not rise in protest against a seemingly unjust God; his confidence in God remained unshaken throughout his trials. His only wish was to know the reasons motivating Divine acts.[58] As a man of faith[59] he found no difficulty in realizing the incompatibility between Divine knowledge and human knowledge.[60]

2. *Job the man lacking true knowledge*

Moses Maimonides (1135–1204), who devoted to an analysis of the Book of Job chapters 22 and 23 of the third book of his *Guide to the Perplexed*,[61] observed that the text (1: 1) ascribes to Job uprightness and ethical virtues but not wisdom and intelligence. His denial of a just rule in the universe and the perplexity engendered by his afflictions were consequences of his lack of wisdom. Satan was identified by Maimonides with the evil inclination[62] which is present in man from birth onward.[63] Job's error, instigated by Satan (from the root *satah*, "turning man away from truth and leading him astray in the way of error"), was thus indicative of the stage in life when wisdom is not yet in evidence. Lacking wisdom, knowing God only from tradition, and confused by his misfortune, Job viewed God as contemptuous of man, laughing at the trials of the innocent, and permitting the wicked to prosper.[64] The good inclination, that force by which man may overcome

57. *'Emunoth ve-Deoth* (ed. D. Slucki, Leipzig, 1864), p. 87. Saadya continues by saying that God would not have chosen a man unable to endure the test of suffering; a pious man's status among his fellow men rises once his faith is proved firm against the challenge of seeming injustice.

58. As in the *tafsīr*, so here too Saadya maintains that there is no Divine answer to a quest such as Job 10: 2; only when suffering is meted out as punishment is the definite reason revealed to man or nation, as the case may be.

59. See esp. Saadya's rendition of Job 13: 14, 15, and 19.

60. The Bodleian manuscript (Neubauer 125) which contains Saadya's Job translation and commentary includes, in addition, a second Arabic translation of some 600 of the 1070 verses of Job and an Arabic commentary of some 140 verses from the first half of the Book: remnants of the work of Moses ben Samuel ha-Kohen, called ibn Gikatilla. Wilhelm Bacher published these texts, which previously had been confused with those of Saadya (*Festschrift zur Ehren des Dr. A. Harkavy* [St. Petersburg, 1908], pp. 221-272). Moses ha-Kohen's commentary was used by Abraham ibn Ezra, in a number of passages, in the latter's Job commentary.

61. Maimonides believed he had offered an exhaustive and final elucidation of the idea contained in the account of Job (*Guide*, III, 22, end). For one of his chief observations he claimed prophetic inspiration (*kidemut nevuah*) (*Guide*, III, 22, middle).

62. *Yeṣer ha-raʿ*; BT *Baba Bathra* 16a.

63. *Aboth de-R. Nathan* I, 16.

64. Job's and his friends' opinions on providence correspond, in Maimonides' view, to the theories of the various schools of thought: Job's view parallels the opinion of Aristotle;

"Satan," the evil drive, comes only when the mind is developed. Consequently, "as soon as he [Job] had acquired a true knowledge of God, he avowed that there is undoubtedly true felicity in the knowledge of God," which "no earthly trouble can disturb."

Elihu is depicted by Maimonides as introducing the concept of the angel's intercession on behalf of a person in peril, which he designates as the principal objective (*ha-kavvanah*) of Elihu's speech. [65] One gains the impression that Maimonides considered such an interceding angel to be the counterpart of Satan, the adversary and evil inclination. If this impression is correct, the transformation of Job the wisdomless to the intellectually mature Job ready for the knowledge of God would then be symbolized by the replacement of the angel of error and accusation by the angel of intercession. [66]

In addition, Elihu, in his discourse on the observation of nature as leading to a comprehension of God's rule in the universe, prepared Job for the prophetic revelation (*nevu'ah*) in chapters 38 on. These speeches aimed at communicating the radical difference between God's creation and human production, between God's rule, providence, and intent, and the corresponding human faculties. Intellectual maturity is attained once man has freed himself from "the error of imagining God's knowledge to be similar to ours." True human wisdom leads to a humble acknowledgment of the uniqueness and incomparability of Divine knowledge. It is this recognition that enables man to bear suffering and evil, and that silences his doubts about "whether God knows our affairs or not, whether He provides for us or abandons us."

Like Saadya before him, Maimonides did not attempt to interpret chapters 38 on as inferring individual providence. Rather, in close attention to the text's intent, he tried to remove the issue of providence from the realm of human concern. In this reorientation of human thought he saw the source of what Job, who feared the Lord, was wanting before his conversion: the love of God.

Maimonides' interpretation of Job was made use of by Zeraḥyah ben Isaac ben Shealtiel of Barcelona (thirteenth century), author of a Job commentary, written in Rome in 1290-91. [67] In a fairly extensive introduction he states that he was prompted to write his commentary by the fact that none of his pre-

---

Eliphaz' insistence on strict justice is the view of the Torah; Bildad's defense of the theory of reward and compensation suggests the doctrine of the Mutazilah, and Zophar's recourse to the Divine will as the source of all events coincides with the view of the Ashariya (*Guide*, III, 23).

65. Maimonides opined (*Guide*, III, 23) that in Elihu's speech were intermingled ideas already expressed by the previous speakers, in order "to conceal the opinion peculiar to each speaker" from the sight of the ordinary reader.

66. Maimonides made a point of calling both Satan and the two inclinations "angels" (*Guide*, III, 22, end).

67. Published by Israel Schwarz in his *Tikvat 'Enosh* (Berlin, 1868), pp. 167–293.

decessors went beyond a literal interpretation of the Book. [68] Paradoxically enough, this declaration is followed by a digest of Maimonides' discourse on the various philosophies represented in the Book — a discourse with which our author wholeheartedly agreed. [69] Possibly Zeraḥya's most interesting point, not borrowed from Maimonides, is his perception of the parallel structure of the Book of Job and Genesis.

3. *Job the Aristotelian denier of providence*

In making Job and his friends representatives of various schools of thought on the subject of providence, Maimonides assigned to Job the role of advocating the views of Aristotle,[70] in a strange combination with the notion that Job, before his conversion, was lacking in knowledge.

The parallel between Job and Aristotle, whose God had no knowledge of particular incidents, was more definitely elaborated by Gersonides (Levi ben Gerson, 1288-1344), mathematician, astronomer, and exacting follower of Averroes. To the Book of Job, to which he was particularly attracted, Gersonides devoted an extensive commentary [71] and an analysis in part four of his *Wars of the Lord.* [72]

The Aristotelian view, Gersonides postulated, commends itself because of the human experience of the "faulty management," the "imperfect order of events" (*roʿa ha-seder*): that is, the suffering of the righteous and the prosperity of the wicked; the alternative view would be the attribution of injustice to God. However, in following Aristotle, Job displayed a tendency to heresy and rebellion (commentary on chapter 37, general principles). For, if man is abandoned to the fate that emanates not from God but from the order of the heavenly spheres—that is, from the universal laws of nature—then incapacity and deficient power must be ascribed to God, Who was not

68. *Ibid.*, pp. 170f. The commentary contains critical remarks against Abraham ibn Ezra's and Nahmanides' interpretation of Job.

69. The author tried to understand Maimonides' reluctance to reveal to the ordinary reader the true meaning of Elihu's view beyond proffering a slight hint (*remez raḥoq*); he himself, however, felt inclined to lift the veil somewhat (*Tikvat 'Enosh*, Zeraḥya's comment on 32:3). On the nonesoteric level, Elihu in rejecting Job's denial of providence, affirmed divine concern for human beings, both during their lives and thereafter (comment on 34:21f.).

70. See my Note 64.

71. Written in 1326; published at Ferrara in 1477 and Naples in 1486 and included in the rabbinical Bibles. An English translation, with introduction and notes by Abraham L. Lassen (*The Commentary of Levi ben Gersom* [*Gersonides*] *on the Book of Job*), appeared in New York in 1946. This translation has been used in the present chapter.

72. *Milḥamot 'Adonai*, completed in 1329. Published at Riva di Trenta in 1560. The references in the present chapter are to the Leipzig edition of 1866. Direct quotations from the *Wars* are found in the commentary. In the introduction to the commentary, the author refers to the treatment of the central theme in the *Wars*, and in the *Wars* he refers to his analysis in the commentary (*Wars*, IV, 2, p. 155). In the introduction to the commentary, Gersonides states that the Job interpretations of his predecessors (except that of Maimonides) hindered rather than advanced his understanding of the Book; they failed to "direct the explanation of the words in accordance with the meaning of the contents."

able to create a more perfect order (commentary on chapter 40, preface).[73]

The way out of this dilemma was indicated by Elihu, Gersonides thought. The Divine purpose is indeed the "bestowal of good," but the actual determination and order of good and evil God left to the functioning of the heavenly bodies. However, He endowed man with reason, which effects a measure of union with the Active Intellect; this serves as protection against evil happenings. The stronger man's attachment to reason, the greater is his potential protection. In addition, there are direct acts of Divine providence, independent of the prearranged order of the heavenly bodies — a fact that Elihu failed to consider (commentary on chapter 33, general principles).

After an extensive analysis of Elihu's arguments,[74] Gersonides was comparatively brief in his comments on the speeches of God. He concentrated on the meaning of Behemoth and Leviathan; their exaggerated description, he contended, was intended to demonstrate "that God is not incapable of giving to every creature the highest possible measure of good" (commentary on chapter 41, the discourse as a whole).

All that Job needed was a revision and a qualification of his Aristotelianism, not its abandonment.[75] His sin was light; had he heeded the chastisement and surrendered, he would have realized that God extends providence to "intellectual man" (*ha-'adam ha-maskil*) according to the degree of his intellectual union with God (commentary on chapter 37, general principles). Finally he realized this, without being forced to surrender his correct assumption, namely, that "Divine providence does not pertain to individuals — as far as the majority of men is concerned" (commentary on chapter 42, end).

The Biblical drama of rebellious man who defied his God as being hostile to humanity is here reduced to an account of the conversion of an Aristotelian with a strong Jewish consciousness to a faithful follower of Gersonides.

73. The friends represent current popular opinions, Gersonides thought. Eliphaz affirmed individual providence but admitted that some suffering is caused by man's defective knowledge and some good is due to accident. Bildad believed that everything comes from God, but that men lack adequate understanding of what is really good or evil. Zophar questioned man's ability to judge the character of the righteous and the wicked correctly. Job rejected these affirmations of God's justice as mere assumptions.

74. According to Elihu, the sin of Job consisted in negating the value of man's following in the ways of God—a view that leads to a paralysis of social life and intellectual perfection. The divinely established order in the universe reflects His "justice, equity, goodness and grace." God, mighty and wise in the work of Creation, cannot be considered to be less effective in dealing with the comparatively simpler issue of "bringing good to the good and evil to the evil" (commentary on chap. 34, general principles). Elihu justified Job's affliction as a providential measure, intended to free him "from his tendency toward rebellion" (commentary on chap. 37, general principles).

75. In ascribing chap. 28 to Job, Gersonides has Job acknowledge the ultimate value of wisdom; its essence being known only to God, it is accessible to men in a measure dependent on the degree of their closeness to God. Though both the righteous and the wicked are alike in matters of external success, only the former attain eternal happiness, which is wisdom and understanding; this state is to be reached by the fear of the Lord and by avoiding evil (commentary on chap. 28, the discourse as a whole, and the general principles).

4. *Job as confusing the work of God and the work of Satan*

The above view was presented by Simeon ben Ṣemaḥ Duran (1361-1444) in his commentary on Job, *'Ohev Mishpat*,[76] and in a short account in his religio-philosophical work *Magen 'Avoth*.[77] In his interpretation the sufferings of Job were instigated by Satan; it was not God who planned these sufferings, "for He is good to everybody and will give [man] only what is good."[78] But Job, uninformed about the true cause of his trouble, accused God of injustice and imputed to Him a hostile attitude toward man.[79]

It was Elihu who instructed Job in the difference between God's ways and man's, in the peculiarity of Satan's doings, and in the work of the interceding angel, who is the counterpart of Satan.[80] Elihu's arguments silenced Job and made him repent.[81] Having been granted knowledge of what is eternal, Job "renounced the life of this world — where both material bliss and calamity are matters of no consequence."[82] According to Duran, the Book of Job "hints at the full recompense which is to come in the world to come, with the resurrection of the dead and in the days of Messiah."[83] Assuming the existence of this vastly expanded universe with the accent on the beyond, it was easy to affirm unlimited providence, which, Duran believed, "the Book of Job attempts to prove."[84] Also, in such a universe it was not difficult to distinguish between the circumscribed regimen of evil and the limitless, eternal realm of good, between the work of Satan and the work of God.

5. *Job the determinist*

It has long ago been demonstrated that, as was the case with other aspects of Simeon Duran's philosophy, his discourse on providence[85] was taken over by Joseph Albo (1380?-1445?). In his *Sefer ha-ʿIqqarim*,[86] IV, 7-16, Albo, without mentioning his source, followed not only the details of Duran's argument but also his formulation.[87] However, in his analysis of Job,

76. *'Ohev Mishpat*, written in 1405, was published at Venice in 1589 and in the rabbinical Bible (Amsterdam, 1724–27).

77. Completed in 1425.

78. *'Ohev Mishpat*, introduction, chap. iv, end.

79. *Ibid.*, comment on 9: 24.

80. It can be assumed that in the concept of the Intercessor as the force opposing Satan, Duran followed the suggestion of Maimonides.

81. *Magen Abot* (Leghorn, 1785), 33b.

82. *'Ohev Mishpat*, comment on 42:6.

83. *Ibid.*, 204b.

84. *Ibid.*, introduction, chap. viii.

85. *Ibid.*, introduction, chaps. ii–iv and xiii–xvi. In his edition of *ʿIqqarim* (see Note 86), IV, 49, n. 5, Husik refers erroneously to *Magen Abot;* read *'Ohev Mishpat*.

86. Completed (according to Zacuto) in 1425 and published at Venice in 1485. Isaac Husik published a critical edition and English translation (*Sefer ha-ʿIqqarim, Book of Principles*, by Joseph Albo, 4 vols. [Philadelphia, 1929-30]).

87. Heinrich Jaulus, "R. Simeon ben Zemach Duran. Ein Zeit- und Lebensbild," *Monatsschrift für Geschichte und Wissenschaft des Judentums*, 23 (N.S.,6): 447–463 (1874). Already Jacob ibn Habib and Isaac Abravanel had referred to Albo's borrowings. See Manuel Joel, *Don Chasdai Creskas' religionsphilosophische Lehren* (Breslau, 1866), p. 76f.

contained in the fourth, and concluding, part of *ʿIqqarim*, Albo deviated from his *Vorbild.* Like Naḥmanides and Gersonides before him, Duran turned Job into a symbol of a man who believed that good and evil in life are determined by the heavenly bodies (IV, 5). There is a preordained order of things (IV, 18), he argued, and neither man's righteous conduct nor prayer will counteract the unchanging law that rules the world. Though he affirmed the notion of God's knowledge — a changeless knowledge — Job denied God's providential care for the world, because he was painfully aware of the "imperfect order of events" (*roʿa ha-seder*), a term we encountered in Gersonides' argument.

What convinced the determinist's mind of his error? According to Albo, it was not the veritable manifestation of God, creator of the universe, but the compelling character of logical proofs, "arguments for providence, found in this book [of Job] and elsewhere." Here, the medievalist embarked on a lengthy presentation of "three kinds of proofs": the first, "derived from general things," consisted of two arguments (IV, 8), the second, "derived from special and particular events in human life," consisted of three arguments (IV, 9), and a third, "derived from the intellect," consisted of two arguments, the second of which had two forms (IV, 10). In the course of this detailed analysis, Albo (interpreting Job 38: 28) argued that "the existence of rain cannot be ascribed to nature" but demonstrates special providence (IV, 8). By interpreting (like others before him) the word *sekhvi* in Job 38: 36 as "the intellectual power in man" (*ha-koaḥ ha-sikhli she-ba-'adam*) and *batuḥoth* as an allusion to the *prima intelligibilia*, or axioms, Albo was able to point to the gift of reason as designed by God to elevate man above the animals mentioned in the context: incontestable proof of Divine grace and providence (IV, 10). It would contravene reason to assume that God, who has the power to lead man to perfection, would not come to the aid of man who has the potential of intelligence. Indeed, all is encompassed in providence, even "all evil that comes to the righteous is due to providence" (IV, 10). Divine power is the guarantee of divine providence.

The more deep-seated reason why, according to Albo, Job required the discipline of logical arguments is to be found in the fact that he served God not out of love but for reward; throughout his defiant speeches, Job justified Satan's suspicion, his certainty even, of the true nature of Job's piety (IV, 7).[88] In Albo's view, only the attitude of being the servant of God for love of Him,

88. Had Job been a servant of God out of perfect love and not merely "a God-fearing man," then, Albo thinks, Job would have accepted his suffering "gracefully, for the love of God" and the question of reward and punishment and the underlying issue of providence would not have arisen (IV, 11). He would have understood the happiness of the wicked and the misfortune of the just as being ultimately justified (IV, 14 and 15). Albo lists "four reasons or explanations for the prosperity of the wicked and four for the instances of evil befalling the righteous" (IV, 13).

as Abraham was, can silence the doubts concerning the just rule of the world and the seeming dominance of evil; only this ultimate — unquestioning — trust prepares man for the realization that "all the good that comes from God is due purely to His loving kindness, and is not compensation for one's good deeds" (IV, 16). In contradistinction to Abraham, Job, who feared God, had to be dealt with on the level of rational argumentation. However, once he comprehended the extent of God's knowledge and power, Job found peace (IV, 10), and the former determinist turned into a man of faith.

IV

The Zoharic literature offers a series of Job interpretations which, at several points, show material affinity to the Talmudic-Midrashic observations on the subject,[89] while at the same time retaining their — at times daring— originality. The Zoharic reflections — scattered over the entire work and only loosely related to each other — deal primarily with the Job of the folk story, rather than with the Job of the dialogue. The figure of Satan is greatly in the foreground. Most of the texts attempt to understand Job in the context of the reality of evil, as represented by Satan, the "other side," in order to probe into the deeper reasons for Job's fate, and to determine his place in the cosmic drama of the fall and redemption.

The brief analysis that follows is restricted to the main part of the Zohar; the *Midrash ha-Neʿelam*, *Raʿya Mehemna*, and the *Tiqqune Zohar* were not considered.

1. *Job the man who failed to pacify Satan*

In one of the principal Zoharic compositions on the subject, Job symbolizes the man who failed to be "cognizant of both good and evil." Cognizance of evil is demonstrated by permitting a portion of one's sacrifice to go to Satan, "the other side."[90] Job offered burnt offerings (*ʿoloth*; Job 1: 5), a sacrifice that ascends in its entirety to heaven; this is taken to imply that he tendered no portion to the "other side." Had he satisfied Satan's due, the "unholy side" would have separated itself from the holy, and by so doing have permitted the holy side to rise undisturbed to the highest spheres; the "other side" would then have been unable to prevail against him. Since Job failed to appease Satan, God himself let "justice be executed" on him and suffered Satan to take what was his due. "As Job kept evil separate from good and failed to

89. E.g., the juxtaposition of Job and Abraham, the national origin of Job, his position at the court of Pharaoh, the New Year as the day of the assembly in heaven, one year as the duration of the trial, the play on the words *'Iyyov* and *'oyyev* ("Job" and "enemy"), the exegesis of Job 2: 10. On the Zohar's literary sources, *see* G.G. Scholem, *Major Trends in Jewish Mysticism* (New York, 1954), pp. 172–176.

90. In the Zohar's interpretatipn of Gen. 4: 8, Cain sacrificed mainly to the "other side," rendering his gift unacceptable to God, while Abel brought his offering mainly to God and spared only "the fat thereof" to the "other side" (Zohar, II, 34a).

fuse them, he was judged accordingly: first he experienced good, then what was evil, then again good. For man should be cognizant of both good and evil, and turn evil itself into good. This is a deep tenet of faith." [91]

2. *Job the scapegoat*

Another Zoharic interpretation points to Satan's arraignment of Abraham for having substituted an animal sacrifice for the offering of Isaac, a transaction at variance with the law in Leviticus 27: 10. Recognizing Satan's right, God apportioned to him the heathen branch of Abraham's family, the house of Uz, descendants of Abraham's brother Nahor. Job, hailing from the land of Uz, deserved to be given into the power of Satan. For, as counselor to Pharaoh, he had advised the Egyptian ruler to deprive the Israelites of their possessions and to subject their bodies to heavy toil, without, however, exterminating them. He was judged according to his own scheme: his possessions and his body were given to the power of Satan, who was, however, bidden to "spare his soul" (Job 1: 12). Therefore, Job, the schemer against Israel, serves as a scapegoat to be thrown to Satan, when, on the Day of Judgment, he rises to accuse Israel. Satan's attention is diverted and he leaves Israel in peace. This can be compared "to a shepherd who throws a lamb to a wolf in order to save the rest of the flock." [92]

In a Zoharic discourse on the Day of Atonement, Satan is presented as attempting to hinder God in effecting Israel's crossing of the Red Sea. Satan declares that the period of servitude originally specified had not yet passed and that Israel is unworthy of entering the Holy Land. To placate him, God allows him to occupy himself with Job in order to leave His children unharmed. The simile of the shepherd and the wolf is again quoted. "Thus, while Satan was busy with Job, he left Israel alone and they were not accused." [93]

3. *Job the isolationist*

Still another Zoharic observation situates the story of chapter 1 of Job at a time when the world was judged and its fate depended on but one person to turn the scale in either direction. Satan, eager to denounce the world, was

91. Zohar, II, 34a.

92. *Ibid.*, 33a. Another account speaks of Job as a righteous man among Pharaoh's advisers, one to whom Exod. 9: 22 refers, and who was impelled to suffer together with the Egyptians, because under certain conditions "the righteous are punished for the guilt of the wicked." It was to this fact that Job referred in his speech, 9: 22 (Zohar, II, 52b f.).

At variance with the Biblical characterization of Job's wife (Job 2: 9f.), Zohar, III, 5a, speaks of her as being as God-fearing as her husband; it was because of her that he was called "great" (Job 1: 3).

93. Zohar, III, 101b. A different role is assigned to Job in a brief discourse on Job 1: 6. As in the Targum and elsewhere in the Zohar, "the day" is interpreted as the New Year and Job is understood to have been "smitten to make atonement for the sins of the world" (Zohar, III, 231a).

maneuvered into concentrating on Job. The latter was singled out because he "was known to be apart from his people"; his separation from the community made him a target for accusation "in the upper realm."

Job's reaction to the ensuing trials proved Satan to have been partly right in doubting his victim's piety. "He did not sin with his lips" (Job 2: 10), "but he did sin in his mind, and later also in his speech." However, "he did not go so far as to attach himself to the 'other side,' " and this steadfastness in resisting Satan saved him in the end.[94]

4. *Job's suffering as a sign of Divine love*

The Zohar presents Elihu as a descendant of Abraham and also as a priest and descendant of the prophet Ezekiel; his exemplary behavior earned him the honorable name, "man" (Adam).[95] In a remarkable note on Job 34: 10f. the Zohar has Elihu discourse on Divine justice and mercy in the governing of the world and on the meaning of suffering that befalls a righteous man. Such suffering is declared to come "from the love which God bears for him; He crushes his body in order to give more power to his soul, so that He may draw him nearer in love."[96]

The motif of suffering as a path to the love of God appears also in *Ḥelqat Meḥoqeq*, the Job commentary of Moses ben Ḥayyim Alsheikh (*circa* 1508-1600).[97] In commenting on Job 33: 17, Alsheikh has Elihu extol the merit of suffering, which aids man in overcoming sin, in acquiring humility, and in escaping the punishment of hell.[98] Furthermore, a world in which the wicked would meet with Divine repudiation and the just with approval would make piety a matter of expediency; the dominant motivation for goodness would be "fear of God." Only the apparent imbalance in the relationship between human action and Divine response is the proper background for selfless faith and "worship out of love."[99]

To summarize our review: the central figure in the Book of Job lent itself to a great variety of transformations. Poets, commentators, and philosophers

94. Zohar, II, 33b.

95. *Ibid.*, 166a f.

96. *Ibid.*, I, 180a f.

97. Appeared at Venice in 1603. Alsheikh accepted the traditional notion that Job lived at the time of the exodus from Egypt and was used by God as a scapegoat to pacify Satan (*Ḥelqat Meḥoqeq* 4a, commenting on Job 1: 7).

98. *Ḥelqat Meḥoqeq* 79a. The problem of the suffering of the just and the prosperity of the wicked would be resolved in the World to Come (*ibid.*, 23b, on Job 9: 22).

99. *Ḥelqat Meḥoqeq* 91a, on Job 37: 22. In Alsheikh's view, Job exemplifies such faith. Commenting on Job 13: 15, he has Job express his conviction that the Lord, who sees the heart, is aware of his uprightness (35a). Job's wish that his words be written in a book (19:23) Alsheikh interpreted as referring to the book of the Torah (51a f.). His slight imperfections were corrected by the redemptive experience of suffering (101b, commenting on Job 42: 2).

depicted Job as reflecting their own doubts and beliefs, their quests and hopes. He was seen variously as a symbol of sainthood, of rebellion against the unjust order in life, of confusion about providence, of human imperfection, of a man in error concerning the nature of evil, or as a scapegoat. Very few commentators were guided by the Book itself; among them was Maimonides, who pointed to the theme of knowledge as a central motif of the Book.

Knowledge as the central theme of the Job poem was also recognized by Saadya, ibn Ezra, Naḥmanides, and Baḥya ben Asher. As we have seen, it was Saadya who grasped the original meaning of chapter 38 and the following chapters. A very few (for example, Saadya and Maimonides) escaped the temptation of forcing upon the speeches of God a declaration of individual providence. On the other hand, Saadya was not ready to permit the text to manifest the rebelliousness of Job.

On the point of individual providence the difference between the concept of God as maintained by the author of the Book of Job and that maintained by the commentators becomes especially evident. Like the Talmudic interpreters of Job before them, the latter could not possibly accept the idea of a God whose universal power, as displayed in Creation, would not imply concern for man. He could not remain inaccessible, impenetrable. The God Who, in the text, *asked* questions of Job, was made to *answer* Job's question.

The figure of Elihu deserves special mention. Whereas in the "Testament of Job" he is depicted as inspired by Satan, he figures prominently in most commentaries; it is he who answers Job, preparing the ground for the appearance of God. In the Zoharic tradition he becomes the spokesman for the redemptive quality of suffering.

In general the interpreters who based their Job on the hero of the folk tale or on the haggadic exposition of Job did not feel called upon to account for the hero's conversion following the speeches of Elihu and the Lord.

The interpreters who did not impute rebellion to the Job of chapters 3ff. or who underplayed his rebellion read the speeches of Elihu and of the Lord as providing the necessary minor correction in the hero's views of God.

Those who did recognize the rebellion of Job under trial transformed the converted Job into a symbol of true philosophical enlightenment, of perfect knowledge; they rarely approached the radical position of the text, which presents Job as humbly acknowledging his own inability to know, silent before God, knowing only that He knows.

The Greek Garments on Jewish Heroes in The Dura Synagogue

By ERWIN R. GOODENOUGH

In the first chapter of my *Jewish Symbols* I described how I had been impressed as a graduate student at Oxford by the varieties of clothing and composition in early Christian art. Briefly, I had begun studying the theology of Justin Martyr immediately after several months' intensive reading of Philo, and had found to my surprise that while I could not trace in Justin actual quotations of Philo which would indicate that Justin had "read" Philo, as philologians ask, Justin's expositions of the Old Testament were patently Christian adaptations of a Philonic type of allegory. Both Justin and Philo explained that God had manifested himself to the great Jewish heroes as Light, and especially in the form of Three, the Logos and two Powers, a Three which to the highest mystic became the One. As the mystic was taken into this company he too became a creature of the Light.[1]

In the midst of this study I went to Rome and saw the Old Testament mosaics of Santa Maria Maggiore, which had seemed to others to have been inspired by the Old Testament interpretations of Justin himself. Coming to the mosaics as I did with Philo and Justin freshly in mind, it suddenly occurred to me that in the fourth or fifth century, when Justin played a minor role in Christian literature, it would have been a strange artist indeed whom Justin had so deeply guided in his thinking. As a matter of fact, the mosaics, especially those that depicted the Old Testament heroes, would have served much better to illustrate the allegories of Philo than those of Justin. I suddenly asked myself: could the Christian artist have been drawing on a tradition of Jewish art that originally illustrated a Philonic sort of interpretation of the Old Testament, as Justin was drawing on the literary tradition of such a Judaism? Why had Christian art begun with an adaptation of Dionysiac symbolic art and with allegorized Old Testament scenes instead of with New Testament scenes, and why, I soon asked myself, were the figures in New Testament scenes so patently adaptations of figures from the Old Testament art, as that Christ still wore the dress and carried the rod of Moses? The

1. This is more fully treated in the forthcoming volume IX of my *Jewish Symbols in the Greco-Roman Period*. It has recently been recognized, but inadequately elucidated, by Franz-Norbert Klein, *Die Lichtterminologie bei Philon von Alexandrien und in den hermetischen Schriften* (Leiden, 1962), especially pp. 61–66, 78, 213–215.

Christians had reinterpreted the Dionysiac trees, vines, crops, pressing scenes, cupids, peacocks, and birds to express as art forms and symbols ready at hand their Christian hopes of immortality. Did they not also begin with Old Testament art because the Jews had developed a Jewish art which, like the allegories of Philo, the Christians found available and appropriate?

Not being given to solving historical problems with rhetorical questions, I laid the problem aside for some years while I continued to work on Philo. As the thought of Philo seemed to become clearer to me, and I was ready to write *By Light, Light*, the early Christian art of the Old Testament seemed all the more Jewish in its inspiration, Jewish as we know Judaism through Philo. In that very year the synagogue at Dura was discovered, and its paintings seemed fully to confirm my guesses. Not only had there indisputably been a Jewish Old Testament art, but it was centered in the great heroes of early Israel, who were represented as wearing the light-colored, usually white, Greek garb of chiton and himation. Figures who symbolized divine appearance, like the three men who came to Abraham at Mamre, likewise wore the garb, and there was a tendency to group such figures in significant numbers, especially in threes. All of this seemed to me designed to reflect a mystical allegory of the significance of such figures, and indeed I had originally prophesied the existence of Jewish Old Testament art precisely on the basis of such allegorical implication in the way Jewish heroes were presented.

It quickly became apparent, however, that to scholars who did not know Philo—that is, to the vast majority of scholars—explanations of the paintings in terms of Philo seemed a priori impossible. Since I had to wait twenty-five years for Kraeling to publish the synagogue paintings, I decided to see what other remains of Jewish art had survived, and to devise something approaching a method for interpreting it. The art itself turned out to be almost omnipresent in the ancient Mediterranean world, though except for a scene of the sacrifice of Isaac at Beth Alpha, one of Daniel and the lion at Beth Sheʿarim, and one in which the animals are entering or leaving the Ark of Noah, no more scenes appeared from the Old Testament. But the synagogues and graves of the Greco-Roman period gave an abundance of material indeed, especially Victories, cupids, and the vine, tree, and bird symbols, with which Christianity began the other aspect of its early art. These were symbols of mystic salvation in paganism and Christianity, and seemed to me most probably to have been the same in Judaism. That is, they seemed to be basically in the same Philonic sort of Judaism as I had felt the Old Testament pictures to be. Proof was not possible, either for or against that thesis, but the evidence I finally assembled in the first eight volumes of my *Symbols* seemed to me, and has seemed to almost everyone who has studied it, to establish my interpretation as definitely the major probability. Alternative interpretations have been suggested for details, but none attempted for the evidence as a whole.

I had just finished this when my long wait for the Dura paintings was ended. Like Jacob, I left Laban a richer man for the interval, for I had learned that one does not take paintings or symbolic designs in one hand, and one's favorite texts in the other—the texts of Philo, the Rabbis, the apocalypses, the early Christian theologians, or whatever—and force a given painting or symbol to comply with the text. Art, my new method was telling me, especially symbolic art, while not a verbal language is itself a language and is to be understood first and foremost out of its own elements. Literary suggestions may help our understanding of such representations, but soon confine us. Quite apart from the problems of the meaning of nonrepresentational art, to understand representational art one must begin with what is represented, where it is represented, how it is represented. To recognize that a scene is based upon an incident in the Bible is only the beginning of understanding, for all depiction, like all paraphrase, is interpretation. Similarly, in a synagogue or grave, to recognize that a given figure represents the Greek goddess of Victory, or her crown, or that another is Helios in his chariot within the circle of the zodiac, raises fresh new questions. What did the Biblical scene mean to the artist? Why did the Jews want pagan symbols and figures in such holy Jewish places, and why did they select the ones they did? So I returned to ask the first question again in a new sense: what were the Jews really representing?

The symbols studied in the earlier volumes made me look with entirely new eyes at what the Dura synagogue actually contained: at the many representations of the fertility goddess of the East, at the club of Hercules in the hands of Moses, at Aphrodite and the Nymphs dominating the infancy of Moses, at the Dionysiac details of masks and felines and clusters of grain, fruit, and grapes, at the fact that all the paintings were set in the interstices of a great vine that encompassed the room, and at the vine above the Torah shrine, up which, by the mediation of Orpheus playing to the animals, the tribes of Israel rose to stand round the great King at the top on his throne. Such a list, which is far indeed from being complete, shows how only a long and disciplined interpretation of symbols could possibly prepare one for studying the Biblical paintings which appeared at Dura. Disciplined interpretation means, among other things, that one refuses to pass judgment on isolated phenomena. For modern science has taught us this much, that an isolated phenomenon cannot be evaluated. We must see the place of the single phenomenon in a context of some regularity before we can attempt to study it. A single phenomenon, like the apple that fell on Newton's head, may suggest a train of investigation, but we can approach its significance only when it becomes part of a larger process. I would not commit *hubris* by suggesting that my interpretation of symbols bears any relation to modern science, but even we humanists can be disciplined and learn from science at least some of the basic principles of drawing conclusions from empirical data. For only as we follow a strict methodology can we hope to advance beyond the clever suggestions of "couldn't it be" to the one important problem, that of what it can on the whole be taken most probably to be.

In this spirit I returned to the matter of the dress, the problem which this paper can only summarize. Indeed I can consider only the peculiar Greek dress of chiton and himation, which, in combination, I shall abbreviate as the pallium (though that was properly the Latin term for the Greek outer garment, the himation or mantle). Those who wear it are the *palliati*. Conclusions about the meaning implied by the pallium will by this method be drawn not from its use in a single painting at Dura, for here our circle of reasoning will be small indeed. One's interpretation of any one painting as a whole must depend upon one's interpretation of details, and so the interpretation of the whole hardly certifies the meaning of the details. It does, however, give a working hypothesis for the meaning of the details, a hypothesis which gains probability only as a similar interpretation of the same sort of detail illuminates the meaning of a considerable number of other paintings, in fact of all paintings of its type.

So we begin by seeing what sorts of people wear the pallium at Dura and under what conditions they do so.[2] The two guards at the great throne atop the reredos wear it, as do the guards by the throne of Solomon, but not the similar figures with Ahasuerus and Pharaoh. A king, apparently, could be presented only in the Persian royal dress, but the two pagan kings, Pharaoh and Ahasuerus, do not have *palliati* as throne guards, while Solomon and the great king above the vine do have them. The pallium, apparently, marks only thrones especially sacred in Judaism. Moses wears the pallium in the four portraits that frame the reredos, as he does in the three representations of him leading the tribes out of Egypt. Two groups of twelve figures in this migration scene also wear it, figures which can reasonably be taken to be the twelve heads of tribes, in contrast to people in the Jewish rabble who go out from Egypt but perish in the Red Sea. The great size of Moses in contrast to the other Israelites makes his symbolic importance especially likely, in view of the universal use of relative size to express the contrast between ordinary people and the gods or divine kings of antiquity. Moses also towers above the other Israelites as, *palliatus*, he touches the rock of the wilderness

2. I must presume that the reader of this paper will have access either to E.G. Kraeling's reproduction of the paintings in his *The Synagogue* (New Haven, 1956) (*The Excavations at Dura-Europos, Final Report*, vol. VIII, part 1), or to those in my almost simultaneously forthcoming *Jewish Symbols in the Greco-Roman Period*, vol. IX (New York, 1963).

and makes water flow to the twelve tribes. Elijah wears it as head of a smaller, but similarly dressed, group of six (seven with Samuel) while he anoints David, who seems to be being received by the seven. Jacob wears it as he dreams. Ezekiel does so not as he begins preaching to the bones, but only as they, finally assembled into bodies, get the breath of life and are restored, themselves *palliati*, but he returns to his original Persian dress as he is arrested and beheaded. Elijah, larger than his assistants, who pour water on his sacrifice, wears the pallium but is smaller than three huge *palliati*, whose gestures would indicate that they were bringing down the fire which burns on the altar. This would suggest that divine intervention might be indicated by figures in the pallium, and the same convention seems indicated by the three *palliati* who walk behind the Ark as cattle draw it on a cart from the shattered idols. Four such figures appear as the dramatic center of a Purim scene and, like the four gods blessing the religious procession of the temple of Bel in Palmyra, seem to be blessing, indeed to be managing, the triumph of the Jews over their Persian enemies. Four is the number of justice, eight even more so, and accordingly I see divine intervention also in the eight *palliati* who flank the futile altar of Baal, under which Hiel is being destroyed by a great snake.

We beg the whole question when we identify as divine manifestations the three *palliati* in the scene of the Ark on the cart and in that of the sacrifice of Elijah, or the four or eight *palliati* in the Purim scene and in that of the futile sacrifice to Baal. But we do so equally when we make any other identification of these majestic figures. Elsewhere at Dura we see the pallium only on figures where it seems to designate supreme dignity, and this fact would appear to indicate a slight probability in my favor. But not enough. We must go on to ask whether Jews invented the costume, and whether, if we find it used elsewhere, any such special dignity in a religious sense seems attached to it. So would the probability of my interpretation be strengthened,

At once we recognize that the pallium is a familiar, though by no means common, garb in non-Jewish sources. In the first place, while we have no whole garments from the ancient world, we have a considerable number of cloth fragments. Especially important are the fragments found near the synagogue at Dura in the great embankment. They are fragments marked in an astonishing proportion with the stripes and the sorts of designs common on the corners of himations in the synagogue paintings, marks to which we shall return. That they represent the ordinary dress at Dura seems to me a dangerous assumption, for they may well have been the contents of a box where sacred vestments were kept, or they may have been fetishistic marks, originally on sacred robes, that were preserved after the garments had been outworn. They do tell us vividly that the sort of clothing depicted was actually worn, but not by whom or on what occasions.

We can hope to learn about these matters only from pictorial representations, representations perforce largely from other places than Dura. We see that the combination of chiton and himation occurs rarely in the earlier period, but men and women alike often wear both garments in grave reliefs, as does Dionysus when he leads Hephaestus to Olympus on an ithyphallic ass.[3] In the Hellenistic period the garments were enriched by adding dark vertical stripes on the chiton and the peculiar mark of one or another shape on the corner of the himation. Various people could wear this dress, but most of our examples come from memorial statues or grave reliefs, so that Margarete Bieber[4] sensed that the pallium, which was still depicted long after it seems no longer to have been commonly worn, had become a form of sacred dress. We get the same impression as we see it on Etruscan tomb paintings and carved sarcophagi for the dead, and here it seems for the first time (with the exception of a single vase from the time of Alexander the Great) that the chiton is marked with the stripe. Our evidence is too scattered for consecutive history, but by the beginning of the Christian era the pallium is worn only by a holy person, one going on to deification in the next world, or, at Pompeii and Ostia, one engaged in a religious rite, unless it characterizes a poet or philosopher. But we recall that a "philosopher" in those days was, like a poet, a holy man. I could not examine all Roman representations, so took the publication of sculpture at the Vatican in three volumes by Amelung[5] as a random sample which had been collected with no reference to what I was seeking. In this large body of material I found only twenty-three figures in the chiton and himation, of which fourteen were on funerary monuments, three on enthroned goddesses, one on what is probably a standing goddess, one on Hera, one on Dionysus, and one on a woman who stands at an altar sacrificing beside a man who wears the toga. The last is the portrait statue of a man, who, in view of all the others, may reasonably be supposed to be portrayed in ceremonial garments. That is, the pallium in this random sample leads so inevitably to monuments of ritualistic, mystical, eschatological, or divine associations that it seems a special garment indeed.

Greco-Roman Egypt inherited an age-old tradition of a sacred garment of light (The Pyramid Texts) or of purity (The Book of the Dead), and from Apuleius we learn that putting on such garments marked the climax of the initiation. So in an Isis painting at Herculaneum all the people wear white robes except one in dark, which would seem to suggest that the the person in dark was about to be, or was in the process of being, initiated.[6] Different as is the

3. See my *Symbols*, vol. VI, figs. 187–190, 192.
4. *Entwicklungsgeschichte der griechischen Tracht* (Berlin, 1934), pp. 52f.
5. Walter Amelung, *Die Skulpturen des Vaticanischen Museums* (Berlin, 1903–36).
6. P. Marconi, *Le Pitturi dei Romani* (Rome, 1929), fig. 108.

composition of the Dura scene where Samuel in white pallium anoints the dark-robed David in the company of the six other light-robed figures, the analogy is unforgettable. David too seems to be being initiated. Most of the mummy portraits of Greco-Roman Egypt show only the busts, but, again using one collection as a random sample,[7] we have some basis for generalization. In this collection, out of seventy-six portraits, at least fifty have clothing with a stripe on the undergarment, and nineteen seemed to wear the chiton and himation. The peculiar mark appears with some of these on the himation when that is shown at full length, but several times on the shoulder when the portrait is only bust-length. Since we have no reason to suppose that the himation with chiton was a usual form of dress in Egypt, it is highly likely that many of these people were initiates into Isis or Osiris or both, and, like followers of so many religions, that they are represented on their tombs in the religious regalia which they took on at initiation in the hope of immortality.

The same convention appears for the dead and for "philosophers" (or mystagogues) on the sarcophagi of Syria.[8] The people with pallia usually carry scrolls. In the Antioch mosaics the pallium does not appear often, considering the extent of the mosaics, but, when it is represented, usually a divine or funerary figure wears it.[9] That is, the Antioch mosaics in themselves suggest no special significance for the pallium, but many of the scenes take on new meaning with its religious interpretation, and no instance specifically contradicts such an interpretation. As we go out into the funerary and religious art of the rest of Syria, the pallium again appears more frequently.

On the monuments of Palmyra we meet for the first time a thorough commingling of Greek with Oriental dress.[10] A person lying on the tomb may be in either dress, but if he is in the Greek, it is the Greek chiton and himation. The relation between the Greek and Oriental dress on such monuments has by no means been demonstrated to general satisfaction. The corpse may lie clothed in either way, holding the cup in the fashion of Dionysiac funerary banquets. Seyrig expressed the opinion that, as represented on the tombs, both Persian and Greek costumes are too elaborate to have been ordinarily worn in the city. We have no definite basis for saying that they were the costumes of religious rather than social pomp, but since our representa-

7. C. C. Edgar, *Greco-Egyptian Coffins, Masks, and Portraits* (Cairo, 1905) (*Service des Antiquités de l'Egypte: Catalogue général des antiquités du Musée du Caire*, vol. XXVI).

8. Using as a random sample the rich collection of C. R. Morey, *The Sarcophagus of Claudia Antonia Sabina...* (Princeton, 1924).

9. A few exceptions have been noted and discussed in my *Symbols*, vol. IX, but there is not space for the matter here.

10. The art of Palmyra has not been collected satisfactorily. It can best be reviewed in D. Simonsen, *Sculptures et inscriptions de Palmyre à la glyptothèque de Ny Carlsberg* (Copenhagen, 1889); J. B. Chabot, *Choix d'inscriptions de Palmyre* (Paris, 1922), and in the serial numbers of *Syria* and *Berytus.*

tions are all religious and funerary, that possibility here as elsewhere seems perhaps more likely.

In pagan Dura the pallium appears very rarely. In the Mithraeum it is put upon Ahuramazda represented as Zeus hurling the thunderbolts, but the priests and gods have usually a long Oriental robe or the trousers of the East. Sometimes, as notably on the pallia of the priests sacrificing to Adonis,[11] and on the Oriental robes of those in the "Sacrifice of Conon,"[12] the pronged ornament of the synagogue is vividly marked.

Nothing in all this suggests the rigid convention of the synagogue, in which the Jewish heroes in their glory (not necessarily in lesser moments, as in the earlier and later incidents of the career of Ezekiel) wear the pallium as large superhuman figures with complete regularity, along with figures which seem to me to represent divine intervention. In early Christian art the same convention was continued, and here, at last, we have specific literary comment in Tertullian's *On the Pallium.* He describes how the pallium was used in the mysteries of Demeter, Bellona, Saturn (where the "phylacteries" were unusually broad), and Aesculapius. Now that Christians have adopted it, he continues, it surpasses all the clothing of the gods or priests.[13] Scholars and philosophers also wear it, he says, but he concludes: "I confer on it likewise a fellowship with a divine sect and discipline. Rejoice, mantle, and exalt. A better philosophy has now deigned to honor thee, ever since thou hast begun to be a Christian's vesture."[14]

Here we have one of the very rare direct allusions in writing to the phenomenon of a symbol's being adopted for what I call its "value," while its explanation is changed for the new religion that adopts it.[15] Anyone who knows early Christian art will allow me without further documentation to say that the pallium was the uniform of the saints, never put upon any but the great heroes of the Jewish or Christian Bible (or upon angels). When God manifested himself as the Three to Abraham at Mamre, the three of course wear the pallium. A few figures seem to have had costumes of their own, such as Noah emerging from the Ark and the three boys in the furnace, but the convention of the pallium in general took over almost completely.

The feeling of a special meaning in the Jewish-Christian version of the pallium tradition is intensified by the common use of the marks in the corners of the himation as well as of the stripes on the chiton. To these we have

11. Frank Brown in the *Dura-Europos Preliminary Reports* (New Haven, 1929–52), VII/VIII, 159f., fig. 44, plates XIXf.

12. J. H. Breasted in *Syria*, 3:190 (1922), plate XIX.

13. Tertullian, *On the Pallium*, IV, 10 (ed. Wein in *Corpus scriptorum ecclesiasticorum latinorum* (Vienna, 1901), LXXVI, iv, p. 120).

14. *Ibid.*, VI, 4 (p. 125).

15. On this phenomenon see especially my *Symbols*, IV, 35–37.

several times alluded. I find it hard to believe that even the stripes were "purely ornamental," though I cannot trace their origin or explain their meaning. The ornament on the himation, however, while ultimately just as inexplicable, is too importantly displayed to have had no significance. The form of this ornament in the Dura synagogue may well be the original one, or at least it was early, for it appears on a pagan robe in Palmyra,[16] in two scenes of pagan sacrifice at Dura,[17] and on mummy portraits of Egypt.[18] It is found on nineteen cloth fragments from Dura. This form is of a bar with prongs at

a b c d e

either end (a), though in a painting usually only one end of the form actually appears, with the other half lost in a fold of the garment. It could also appear as an angle (b). The straight form also appears on the robe of Virgil as he is enthroned in the pallium in an early medieval illumination, and occasionally in Christian art. It also appears on pagan religious banners.[19] In both forms it appears on pagan portraits from Greco-Roman Egypt, but there it seems already to have begun to degenerate. The bar could be abbreviated until it became only a straight line, and produced a capital I (c). The whole could become a right angle (d and e), and in several instances, it is a swastika.[20] Apparently from the first of these latter forms (d), it came in Christianity to be called a *gam* or gamma or gammadia. [21] Whatever it originally represented, obviously it had some sort of religious potency, perhaps explained and re-explained as it went from religion to religion, or perhaps just persisting as a symbol in its own right without explanations.

These pallia are invariably of a light color. Literary sources usually refer to *leukos*, "white," garments, but white and black in ancient as in modern Greek can, and often do, mean light and dark, and it would seem that the painter selected colors for the robes in the paintings, light yellow or pink along with what was probably as near white as he could get, in order to

16. See H. Seyrig in *Syria*, 18:25 (1937), fig. 16.

17. See Frank Brown in the *Dura-Europos Prelimimary Reports*, VII/VIII, 159f., fig. 44, plates XIXf., and J. H. Breasted in *Syria*, 3:190 (1922), plate XIX.

18. See Edgar, *Coffins*, plates XXI, nos. 33.154 and 155; XXIX, no. 33.209; XLVII, no. 33.281; and my *Symbols*, vol. VI, figs. 255 and 257.

19. See the Roman-Egyptian cloth in the Golenischev collection, commented upon by M. Rostovtzeff, "Vexillum and Victory," *Journal of Roman Studies*, 32:92-96 (1942); G. Lugli, "La Seda degli araldi publici," *Capitolium*, 9:451 (1933).

20. For a Christian example of this on Moses see A. Ferrua, *Le Pitture della nuova catacomba di Via Latina* (Vatican, 1960), plate CXV.

21. H. Leclercq in F. Cabrol and H. Leclercq, *Dictionnaire d'archéologie chrétienne et de liturgie*, VI (Paris, 1924), 610–614.

give variety to his groups. They were always light, that is, "white." Plutarch says that they dress a corpse in white because they "cannot do so to the soul which they desire to dismiss bright and clean, as one that has now come victorious from a great and complex struggle [*agōn*]. For a dead man is become simple, unmixed, pure, in short freed from the ingrained dye of the body."[22] So, when we have any description of the garments of pagan worship they are usually specified as "white." When Lucius finally put on the robe of Osiris in his initation it would seem to have been *candore puro luminosi*, as he describes the sacred robe in another passage, which seemed to mean it was a robe of light like the final robes of earlier Egypt.[23] The same tradition of the garment of light as indication of deity or deification, or of a heavenly being, continues in the New Testament. Of the transfiguration it was said that Jesus' face shone like the sun, and his garments became white like light.[24] Similarly Mark (16: 5) has a young man "dressed in a white robe" sit beside Jesus' tomb, but he becomes an "angel descended from heaven... his appearance like lightning and raiment white as snow" in Matthew 28:2f.; in Luke 24:4 the one man becomes two in garments "like lightning," while John 20:12 makes these simply two angels in white. As with Plutarch, those in Revelation 3:4f., 18, who have conquered in the great *agōn* will walk in heaven in white garments with Christ.[25] It is no wonder the Christians continued the Jewish custom of clothing the great saints with the garment of light. Jewish artists had themselves taken the convention from paganism.

We finally ask whether the artists were the only Jews thus impressed by the symbolism of the white dress, specifically of the "light" pallium. Here we must turn to the more traditional Jewish sources, where a few excellent studies of the subject have been made.

Krauss[26] tells us that the Jews then paid great attention to their clothing, and dressed as richly as their means allowed.[27] In particular, the religious and political aristocracies of Palestine took care to show their social importance by their clothing. For example, Josephus tells that shortly before the fall of Jerusalem the Levites persuaded King Agrippa to call a sanhedrin, with instructions to its members to reverse the former law and grant permission to Levites to wear linen garments like those of priests.[28] It is

22. Plutarch, *The Roman Questions*, XXVI (trans. H. J. Rose [Oxford, 1924]), 131.
23. Apuleius, *Metamorphoses*, XI, 9f., 23f., 27.
24. This is the gloss of Matt. 17: 2 upon Mark 9: 3.
25. Cf. Rev. 7: 9–14.
26. Samuel Krauss, *Talmudische Archäologie* (Berlin, 1910): "Kleidung und Schmuck," I, 127–207. For this subject see also the rich collection of material in Harald Riesenfeld, *Jésus transfiguré* (Lund, 1947), pp. 115-129 (Acta Seminarii Neotestamentici Upsaliensis, vol. XVI).
27. Krauss, I, 130–136.
28. Josephus, *Antiquities*, XX, 216–218 (ix, 6).

generally presumed that these were white, or at least "light." Jews distinguished between "white" and "colored" garments, with, I suspect, the general meaning of "light" or "dark." White was the garb of joy, of purity, and of social dignity, while colored clothes were left to women and to men of the lower classes.[29] God himself, Daniel had said, is clothed in a garment white as snow,[30] while a Psalm says, "Thou coverest thyself with light as with a garment."[31] God appeared to Moses as a flaming bush, and on Sinai as insupportable light and glory, and the light was so transferred to Moses himself that his face also shone.[32] This idea continued in Jewish tradition. God has a face of fire, and the light of the universe at creation was kindled from God's light, while Enoch, who saw this, was himself given a robe of light.[33] The risen righteous and elect will have garments of glory and light,[34] in which they will be like the angels.[35] Krauss sees the white-robed angels of the New Testament, whom we have just discussed, to be a part of the tradition, continued in the Talmud, that angels wear white.[36] The garment seems the same as the celestial clothing, that "of light," which the Rabbis say Adam originally had, but lost at the Fall, a garment which Gabriel brought to Enoch.[37]

Connected with this, though in what way I cannot say, is the white robe of the rabbi on the Sabbath, for when Rabbi Judah ben Ilaʿi washed himself for the Sabbath and sat in his fringed linen robes he "was like an angel of the Lord of Hosts."[38] Blau said that the Rabbis, like the philosophers, had a distinctive mantle, but that we do not know what it was.[39] I strongly suspect that Rabbi Judah ben Ilaʿi has given us the hint, and that it was a white or light dress much like those we have been discussing, a robe of holiness which the Essenes also took over. For we know that the Essenes gave a white robe to each new member as a mark of his final entry into the order, that is, upon his initiation, and that thereafter he wore white always.[40] Herein the Qumran community probably resembled the Essenes, for members of the community

29. Krauss, I, 144f.

30. Daniel 7:9. Cf. A. Rosenzweig, *Kleidung und Schmuck im biblischen und talmudischen Schriften* (Berlin, 1905), p. 38. God has fringes at the corner of his robe: L. Ginzberg, *The Legends of the Jews* (Philadelphia, 1909–38), II, 362.

31. Ps. 104:2.

32. Exod. 3:2; 19:16–18; 24:17; 33:18–23; 34:29.

33. II Enoch 22–25.

34. I Enoch 62:15; 108:12; cf. 5:6f.; 14:18–21.

35. *Ibid.*, 71:1; 87:2; 90:21f., 31.

36. Krauss, I, 550, n. 212.

37. Ginzberg, *Legends*, I, 79, 135, 139; V, 103, n. 93.

38. BT, *Shabbath*, 25*b*.

39. L. Blau in *HUCA*, 3:210 (1926).

40 Josephus, *Jewish War*, II, 123, 137 (viii, 3 and 7).

called themselves "sons of light," in anticipation of heaven, where, in a life of eternity, they would wear "a crown of glory and a raiment of majesty in everlasting light."[41] That community could also have had no more fitting mark of their dedication and hope than to wear white robes in this life. For their dress we have no such evidence, however, as for the Essenes. But the Jewish tradition that angels wore white is early witnessed by the Testament of Levi,[42] who "saw [in a dream] some men in white raiment saying unto me: Arise, put on the robe of priesthood," et cetera. He was thus invested by seven heavenly figures, a conception that seems to me reflected in the scene of the anointing of David at Dura (Plate I).

The convention of the sanctity of the white-robed figure may have been very old. We most obviously think of it in connection with the High Priest who took off his official garments on the Day of Atonement and went into the Holy of Holies wearing only a white linen ephod,[43] a garment that seems to have been the robe of light, at least in later interpretation.[44] We must also note that Samuel as a boy wore a "linen ephod,"[45] as did David when he danced before the Ark,[46] in both cases probably the same type of garment the high priest wore when he entered the Holy of Holies. Each year Samuel's mother made for him in addition a little *meʿil.*[47] It was in this latter robe that he was still dressed when he appeared from the grave to the witch of Endor.[48] As such he looked to her like God, or a god.[49] Josephus expanded the sentence to say that Samuel appeared to her "distinguished and of divine majesty [*theoprepēs*]," so that she reported that he had a "form like God."[50] The Septuagint reads "gods" and is best expounded in the *Biblical Antiquities* of Pseudo-Philo:[51] " 'What is his form [species]?' And she said: 'Thou inquirest of me concerning the gods. For behold his form is not the form

41. The Manual of Discipline, as published by M. Burrows, *The Dead Sea Scrolls* (New York, 1955), p. 375.

42. Testament of the Twelve Patriarchs: Levi, 8: 2.

43. Exod. 28: 4; Lev. 16: 4.

44. It is to this aspect of the problem that Riesenfeld, pp. 115–129, has made especially rich contribution.

45. I Sam. 2: 18f. See the remarks on the articles of clothing by K. Budde, *Die Bücher Samuel* (Tübingen, 1902), p. 20 (Kurzer Hand-Commentar zum Alten Testament, vol. VIII).

46. II Sam. 6: 14.

47. Cf. Exod. 28: 4.

48. I Sam. 28: 13f.

49. On how "Elohim" is to be understood here commentators disagree: see Budde, p. 181. The A.V. translates "gods"; A.R.V. "a god"; P. Ketter, *Die Samuelbücher* (1940), p. 172, cf. pp. 175f., "gottahnliches Geisteswesen" (*Die Heilige Schrift für das Leben erklärt*, III, i).

50. Josephus, *Antiquities*, VI, 332f. (xiv, 2). Marcus properly translates that Samuel looked to the witch like *ho theos*, which can only mean "God."

51. Pseudo-Philo's *Lieber antiquitatum biblicarum*, LXIV, 6 (ed. G. Kisch, Notre Dame, 1949, p. 269) (Publications in Medieval Studies: The University of Notre Dame, vol. X).

of a man. For he is arrayed in a white robe [*stola*], and has a mantle [*diploïs*] wrapped around it, and two angels lead him.' And Saul recalled the *diploïs*[52] that Samuel had rent when Samuel saw him." Here the Septuagint plural, "gods," is interpreted to mean Samuel accompanied by two angels, and the clothing is distinctly understood to be the "white" chiton and himation. Pseudo-Philo seems to have taken the *stola* to be the long Greek chiton, for on it he says the *diploïs*, which the Septuagint here uses to translate *meʿil*,[53] seems to be an abbreviation of the *tribōn diplous*, a form of the philosopher's *tribōn*.[54]

Whatever the original form and significance of the *meʿil*, therefore, it would appear that by the time the Septuagint translation of I Samuel was made, the garments of Samuel, which made him look like God, or a god, were already associated with the Greek dress of sanctity we are investigating. We may suppose that at least Josephus and Pseudo-Philo envisaged Samuel as wearing this dress. If anyone were to represent the incident in an illumination for the Greek text, he would inevitably have represented Samuel (with or without the two angels) in the Greek robe, and would have done so fully convinced that Samuel actually wore such clothing in life and death. That Samuel should be painted as he is in Dura, accordingly, seems not only natural but inevitable. It may be that this passage was the bridge over which the white wardrobe of the Jewish saints was carried from paganism to Jewish art. If Samuel was thus dressed, it is very possible that other Jewish heroes would be put into these garments, and so shown to be "in the form of God."

The "bridge," however, may have been less the convenient passages about the dress of Samuel [55] than a general adapting of the robe by Jews other than Essenes. For there is some reason to suppose that this dress was commonly seen in Jerusalem as the garb of Scribes and Pharisees. Our evidence for this is late, indeed the fourth century: Epiphanius' comments on Palestinian clothing at the time of Jews, which I have not seen considered in discussions of the subject. He says in commenting upon Matthew 23: 5:[56]

52. I Sam. 15: 27 (LXX).

53. This is true not only here but in I Sam. 2:19; 15:27. It also translates the *meʿil* as the "robe of Saul" in I Sam. 24:5, 12. But *meʿil* has other translations: I Sam. 18: 4; Job 1: 20; 2: 12.

54. In their studies of the *tribōn* both Brilliant and Schuppe recall that the *tribōn*, the commonest term for the himation of the philosophers, was often worn "doubled over." The Cynics especially wore the *tribōn*, and Diogenes, a Cynic, is the only pagan I can find who wore the *diploïs: Greek Anthology*, VII, 65 (Loeb Classical Library, New York-London, 1916–18, II, pp. 39f.).

55. The special power of the mantle of the prophet has no such tradition of color and form in the Bible, but that the "virtue" of the prophet was in his mantle appears in Elijah's leaving his for Elisha: II Kings 2: 8–14.

56. *Panarion*, XV, i, 3–7 (ed. K. Holl, I, 209) *Die griechischen christlichen Schriftsteller*, vol. XXV).

They [the Scribes] had certain "borders" [*kraspeda*][57] as tokens of their citizenship [*politeia*], alike to show their pride and to win the commendation of those who saw them. And they put "phylacteries"[58] upon their himations, that is broad purple stripes [or marks, *sēmata*]. Now one must not think, because in the Gospel they are given this name, that the reference is to amulets [*periapta*: literally, amulets of the type bound around] since some people are used to understanding "phylacteries" [in the Gospel] as amulets of this kind. The account has no reference to this sort of thing. But since these people dressed in outer garments of the type of *ampechonai*[59] and dalmatics of the type of colobia, adorned with broad stripes [*platusēma*, the word most used in Greek for the *latus clavus*] of purple made of purple cloth, those who were most accurate were accustomed to call the stripes of purple "phylacteries," and for this reason the Lord called them "phylacteries" as worn by these men. What follows makes clear the meaning of the words, "and the borders of their cloaks." For he [the Lord] said "borders" [*kraspeda*] in the definite sense of fringes [*krossoi*], and "phylacteries" in the sense of the stripes of purple, when he said "Ye make broad your phylacteries and deep the fringes on your cloaks." And each of them wore certain tassels at the four corners of the cloak [*tribōn*],[60] attached to the cloak by being extensions of the warp itself,[61] during the time when they were fasting or living as virgins. For as each man appointed for himself a time of holiness or discipline, so these were their tokens to be seen of men by which they made it known that no one should touch them while they were sanctifying themselves.

In the next section Epiphanius says of the dress of the Pharisees: "They outdid the scribes in the above described dress [*schēma*], that is in the *ampechonē* and other articles of dress and in their effeminate himations, going beyond them in their broad high boots [*en plateiais tais krēpisin*] and in the lacing of their boots [*hupodēmata*]."

Epiphanius seems to have had amazingly detailed information about the dress of the religious aristocracy of Judaism at the time of Jesus. His account tallies so perfectly with the Dura paintings that if he had had them before him he could not have given a more accurate description of the costume. Perhaps the most striking feature of this passage is Epiphanius' description of the shoes, for the type he mentions, the laced *krēpis* or *hupodēma*, was called by the Romans the *calceus*, and such boots distinguished the Roman patrician or senator, though occasionally they are found in the provinces upon representations of Roman officials of lesser dignity. In the Dura paintings men clothed

57. Cf. Matt. 9: 20, where the woman touches the "border" of Jesus' garment.

58. Epiphanius, *Panarion*, XV, i, 3–7.

59. *Ampechonē* is a variant of *ampechonon*, which A. Mau, in A. Pauly and G. Wissowa, *Real-Encyclopädie...*, I (Stuttgart, 1894), describes as a cloak (*periblōma*) of great size: "In the temple inventory of Diana Brauronia it is distinguished from the himation, but the distinction between the two is not known."

60. The confusion of the *ampechonē* with the *tribōn* is noteworthy. Sharp distinctions in terms cannot be made.

61. Such tassels, made in exactly this way, are shown in the Dura paintings.

Plate I
Samuel Anoints David (Gute's copy)

Plate II
Moses at the Burning Bush (Gute's copy)

in the white robe wear sandals, but the boots are twice shown beside Moses as he stands barefoot before the Lord. All the details—*ampechonē*, *colobium*, himation, stripes, tassels, fringes, and boots, as Epiphanius describes them—correspond perfectly to the dress of the chief figures in the Dura paintings (Plate II). Epiphanius characterizes the garb as effeminate because the effeminacy of the *ampechonē* was proverbial, and an *ampechonē* with fringes and tassels would all the more merit the scorn of both Greeks and Romans. When he distinguishes the "phylacteries," as stripes or marks of purple cloth appliqué, from the *periapta* with which many were associating the word, it is quite likely that the original meaning of "phylacteries" was already being forgotten, and that the tradition had begun of identifying the "phylacteries" with the tephillin, the little box with scriptural quotations bound to the forehead, worn by Jews in prayer, a tradition still reproduced in all commentaries with the confidence of repetition. Epiphanius obviously had definite information, but from what source and how reliable was it?

Unfortunately we have no way of answering the question. Epiphanius as a historian does not have the standing of Eusebius or Hippolytus, and he not only used poor sources uncritically, but seems not to have been averse to filling in gaps from his imagination.[62] His explanation of the phylacteries as stripes rather than tephillin, however, makes sense, since there is a definite limit to the size of tephillin — the limit of the breadth of one's forehead — and that the reference should be to stripes is inherently quite plausible. Still Epiphanius may have been drawing not upon an ancient and reliable source but upon illustrations in some one of the now lost, and so to us still hypothetical, illustrated texts from Hellenized Jews. His description of the costumes, even to the shoes, makes it highly unlikely that he was here improvising as he wrote. I should myself guess that he was right, and that Jews took over the sacred white costume with its stripes, not only for Biblical illustration, as Dura shows, and not only for actual dress in the Dead Sea communities, but also, by Scribes and Pharisees, for a mark of their piety.

Such a conclusion must, of course, be subject to evidence on dress in rabbinic writings. This was fortunately collected by Krauss, and we find that, as with other evidence, much of it supports our conclusion, and nothing that I can find discredits it, although nothing definitely "proves" it. We have

62. The best discussions of the sources of Epiphanius are still: R. Lipsius, *Zur Quellenkritik des Epiphanius* (Vienna, 1865); *idem*, in *A Dictionary of Christian Biography* (London, 1880), II, 149–156. Lipsius here, pp. 152f., calls him "an honest but credulous and narrow-minded zealot," and speaks of his collecting "a large but ill-arranged store of historical information." He adds, "His communications concerning the various Jewish sects are for the most part worthless," but they seem to me to be like his records of Jewish-Christian and Gnostic sects, in "exhibiting a marvellous mixture of valuable traditions with misunderstandings and fancies of his own." See also A. Hilgenfeld, *Judenthum und Judenchristenthum* (Leipzig, 1886), who discusses the passages on the dress of the Scribes and Pharisees on p. 72.

already mentioned the angelic resplendence of Rabbi Judah in his white garments. Rabbinical Hebrew and Aramaic had many words for different sorts of clothing, but the influence of Greek civilization was such that the Tannaim themselves borrowed and transliterated the Greek word *colobium*, explaining it as a sort of dalmatic, a word they also transliterated.[63] To these words, which seem to have been used for the undergarment we here ordinarily call the chiton, corresponded an outer garment, called, among other names, the pallium—a word likewise transliterated. This mantle, more usually called the *tallith*, carried the tassels of piety.[64] The Aramaic word for "ornament on clothing" came to have as a variant a transliteration of the Greek word for "purple stripes," or for a garment trimmed with such stripes, *periporphuros*,[65] and Krauss tells us that the rabbis were careful so to arrange their clothing that its ornament would be visible,[66] another detail which recalls the carefully shown ornament on the garments of the Dura synagogue. It then becomes significant that the word for such ornament was also transliterated by the rabbis, and became *gam* in Aramaic, used several times for ornament in clothing. The great Babylonian scholar of the eleventh century, Hai Gaon, explained the *gam* as the Greek gamma, and described it as "a piece of fine stuff, like purple cloth, sewed on a seam."[67]

Only one hypothesis seems to me to account for all these facts: the Jews, not only the Essenes and Qumran sects, but the learned and distinguished rabbinic Jews, borrowed this robe, borrowed it in such a way that it kept its pagan value as the dress of piety, even of divinity, but, by adding fringes and tassels, made it the dress of Jewish piety. Indeed Blaufuss suggested, on the basis of a statment in the Tosefta to the *ʿAbodah Zarah*, that the Jewish white robe of the time not only was the robe of Isis but often still had on it for Jews the moon and stars of Isis symbolism.[68] Without any evidence but his profound knowledge of antiquity, Lidzbarski suggested that the white robe still worn by the head of an orthodox Jewish household on especially festal occasions is a survival of the ancient usage, pagan as well as Jewish, of such garments. A pious Jew will be clothed in that robe when he is buried, "so that he may appear white before God."[69]

63. S. Schemel, "Die Kleidung der Juden im Zeitalter der Mischnah" (diss., Berlin, University, 1912), p. 28, n. 4. The meaning of these words seems to have changed with different times and places.

64. *Ibid.*, p. 36, n. 2; cf. Krauss, I, 167; Rosenzweig, p. 64.

65. Krauss, I, 163f.

66. *Ibid.*, I, 589, n. 439.

67. *Ibid.*, I, 596, n. 499.

68. H. Blaufuss, *Götter, Bilder und Symbole nach den Traktaten über fremden Dienst (Aboda Zara) in Mischna, Tosefta, jerusalemer und babylonischem Talmud*, (1910), pp. 30, 44. (*Jahresbericht des K. Neuen Gymnasiums in Nürnberg für das Schuljahr* 1909/10, Suppl.).

69. M. Lidzbarski, *Auf rauhem Wege* (Giessen, 1927), p. 43.

In short, the Greek robe seems to have been treated like all the other borrowed symbols. Originally the robe of philosophic mystical piety, then the robe of Osiris, it was borrowed by Jews, but could no more be the robe of Osiris for them than it was for Christians when they put it on their saints. In Christianity, the pallium, like the halo, marked divine, or supernal, holiness in heaven or on earth. For Jews it seems to have meant much the same in terms of Jewish holiness. When used in the synagogue as the garb of the great heroes, it suggests that the heroes—Moses, Jacob, Elijah, Samuel, to name only a few—by their having this robe are marked as people of a distinctively holy character in contrast to those beside them. When others whom we cannot so easily identify are put into the same dress, we must be careful before concluding that they are merely bystanders, let alone the accursed prophets of Baal. Their "light" pallia still seem to mark them as holy men or angels.

INDEX OF SCRIPTURAL QUOTATIONS

INDEX OF SUBJECTS

INDEX OF AUTHORS